CHARLES
KING OF ENGLAND
1600-1637

Uniform with this volume

King Charles and King Pym
King Charles the Martyr

CHARLES, A BOY OF THIRTEEN—*from a mezzo-tint engraving by Charles Turner after Delaram in the British Museum*

CHARLES
KING OF ENGLAND
1600-1637

by

Esmé Wingfield-Stratford, D.Sc.

*"For God! for the Cause! for the Church! for the Laws!
For Charles King of England!"*

MACAULAY

*"He who fixes his course by
a star changes not."*

LEONARDO

GREENWOOD PRESS, PUBLISHERS
WESTPORT, CONNECTICUT

Library of Congress Cataloging in Publication Data

Wingfield-Stratford, Esmé Cecil, 1882–
    Charles, King of England, 1600–1637.

    Reprint of the 1949 ed. published by Hollis &
Carter, London.
    Bibliography: p.
    Includes index.
    1. Charles I, King of Great Britain, 1600–1649.
DA396.A2W48 1975   941.06'2'0924 [B] 74-31871
ISBN 0-8371-7949-1

To

ERNEST SHORT

amicitiæ causa

Originally published in 1949 by Hollis & Carter, London

Reprinted with the permission of B. Wingfield-Stratford

Reprinted in 1975 by Greenwood Press,
a division of Williamhouse-Regency Inc.

Library of Congress Catalog Card Number 74-31871

ISBN 0-8371-7949-1

Printed in the United States of America

Introduction

I WISH that it were possible for me to adopt the style of the Icelandic scald, and begin with the plain sentence, "Charles Stuart was the name of a man," in the confidence that this would be his first introduction to my audience, and that they would be prepared to take story and man on their merits.

This is just what nobody, who is enough interested in King Charles to want to read about him, is capable nowadays of doing. It is perhaps a tribute to his greatness, that in the mind's eye of posterity he became, almost from the fall of the axe, a symbolic figure. One might say that every generation has fashioned his image after its own mind, and with as much resemblance to the original as the Old Guy on a barrow to that gallant, if mistaken, soldier, Guido Fawkes. It would be a fascinating venture to write a biography not of the real, but of the imaginary Charles, reincarnating by turns the whole list of his predecessors, from holy Henry to villainous John, with all their possible permutations and combinations.

The worst of it is, that it has become no longer a matter of opinion, but of faith. However much people may differ in other respects, they are all united upon the motto, *Nolumus Carolum nostrum mutari*. If my own experience is anything to go by, the first thing that the average educated person does, when he hears of a new life of Charles I, is to test its soundness by the measure of its agreement with the Charles of his own dogma. And if the agreement be not sufficiently exact, perceptible feeling is aroused. To a true devotee of the Royal Martyr, the least imputation of any human fault or flaw in his idol is as the sin of blasphemy ; while to austere upholders of the still powerful Whig tradition, the mere suggestion that the men who brought down the Throne may have been no simple patriots, but a well-organized group of intriguing politicians, is too monstrously perverse to be worth refuting. "Let that man alone," as Frederick the Great once said ; "he is biting granite."

I suppose that there is hardly anyone, in English history,

whose life has had such influence, for good or ill, on its development, as that of Charles I, and yet there is scarcely any personality
that makes so faint an impression on the average mind. Even during
his life, there was something about him aloof and enigmatic ; he
had not that faculty, so indispensable to kings, of making instinctive contact with his human environment. The legend of the dark
cloak cast over him in his cradle, only too plainly adumbrates the
life-long inability of a partially tongue-tied man to make himself
understood. That inability has persisted beyond the grave.

Perhaps, however, we do him wrong in putting the blame on
his nature. For until we get to the plain cut and thrust work of
the Civil War, the other leading figures of the time seem scarcely
easier to appreciate. In the world of Mr Pepys and the Merry
Monarch we may feel at home ; the great Elizabethans, Drake
with his bowls, Sidney with his cup of water, have been our
friends from the nursery ; even Bluff Hal has proved all too easy
to humanize. But to how many of us are Pym or Eliot, Laud or
Strafford, familiar personalities, apart from the principles they
are supposed to represent? Even the amazing career of Buckingham seems somehow to have missed the human appeal that
makes us interested in every scrap of information about Raleigh,
or Elizabeth's Essex.

There is one exception, of the exceptional kind that may
really be said to prove the rule. For did not the age produce its
representative Englishman in Hampden, John Hampden, whose
bare surname seems as incomplete as that of Bull? With that
honest patriot, that simple, lovable squire and apostle of liberty,
may we not at least claim some sort of affectionate familiarity?
Unfortunately, when we come to enquire into the actual facts
about him—and those that have survived are tantalizingly few—
we shall find no more historical foundation for this idol of popular
imagination, than for John Bull himself, though there was a very
different sort of person, remarkable enough in his way, bearing
the name of Hampden.

In spite of all the labours of all the historians, this time of
Charles I has never ceased to be legendary. The whole story is
overlaid with so much dogma and over-belief, that it has proved
almost impossible for the best informed and most conscientious
narrator—even Gardiner is a case in point—to avoid speaking to
a brief. Nor is this to be wondered at, when we consider that the
differences between King and Parliament, between Rome and

Canterbury and Geneva, are still capable of appealing to invincible passions and prejudices.

In this book, and the two succeeding volumes, I shall try to follow the life of King Charles, from the cradle to the grave, as it is revealed in the earliest sources, and as far as humanly possible, without more than an occasional passing reference to the successive versions of it that have been put into circulation in the course of three centuries. It is the first duty of the historian, though I should never be presumptuous enough to claim its fulfilment, to cultivate that singleness of vision which is enjoined in the Gospel : "If thine eye be single, thy whole body shall be full of light." The pious devotee of Clio could hardly do better than to hang this text in some conspicuous place in his study.

He has always before him the example of Carlyle, who brought back to us the living Cromwell, out of that same phantom world in which the ghost of King Charles has never ceased to wander. He did this by letting his hero speak for himself, standing by all the time in the role of announcer or commentator. We may—many of us do—strongly react against Carlyle's conclusions ; we may altogether fail to participate in his worship. But to those of us who are not incurably prejudiced, the man Oliver will for evermore appear in his habit as he lived, intensely interesting because intensely human.

Not to ordinary mortals is it given to bend the bow of Odysseus, and it is an even more difficult task than that accomplished by Carlyle, to make the reserved figure of Charles step forth from the canvas and—as the nursery rhyme has it—walk and talk after his head was cut off. But, if the feat should ever be accomplished, we should, I believe, become acquainted with a personality as human as that of Cromwell, and certainly not less lovable.

One hesitates to say greater. But it would be possible to make out a case even for that. For Charles was, or developed into, a man of principles, for which he stood fast, in despite of expediency, and which he sealed with his death. Cromwell, by his own admission, was never more than a splendid opportunist, with the opportunist's faith that a man never rises so high as when he does not know where he is going. That—it may be argued—was the essential difference between the two men, and explains why the dead King proved stronger than the living Protector.

But that is to anticipate. In the present volume the figure of Cromwell has hardly made its appearance. The adversaries with whom Charles is confronted are of very different calibre, men whose natures and motives have been more absurdly misconceived than those of Charles himself. The idea of the Parliamentary chiefs as simple-minded enthusiasts, political *ingénus* who laid bare their hearts in their speeches, and whose actions had no other springs than the devotion to liberty, their country, and even the person of their Sovereign, that it suited them to profess, one might have thought rather much for the credulity even of Macaulay's schoolboy, let alone Macaulay himself. The idea of them as austere or fanatical enthusiasts, fired by single-souled Puritan or any other sort of religious zeal, is, in the light of their proceedings, no less preposterous.

It is only by the fact of history having been so generously adapted for juvenile consumption, that we can account for the tendency to treat its most sophisticated characters as if they were a sort of mental children, and to simplify their motives in the way that nursery tradition has done for the Children of Israel. The application of this method to such accomplished wirepullers as Pym and Hampden has had the effect of turning the whole story upside down, and converting it into an incredible melodrama of the good patriots, who saved the people from the naughty tyrant. The possibility that almost, if not quite, from the beginning of his reign, Charles may have been faced by a revolutionary conspiracy, pursued with an entire lack of scruple, and with a ruthless determination to employ all the resources of propaganda and mass suggestion, is simply ignored.

I do not for the moment suggest that we should go to the other extreme of converting Charles himself into a plaster saint, with no responsibility for the fate that overtook him. If ever man undermined his own throne before he ascended it, it was he. During the period of his hypnotization by Buckingham—surely the most disastrous counsellor that monarch ever had—he omitted to do few of the things that he should have left undone, if he would have preserved the place of the Crown in the Constitution. He was playing all the time, with the most perverse accuracy, into the hands of his enemies—and they were not the men to give him a chance to recover.

I wish that I could bring out by proof rather than suggestion, the decisive nature of the spiritual crisis through which I feel that King Charles must have passed, when, on receiving the shock of his friend's murder, he signed for morning service to proceed, and remained on his knees : with what thoughts passing through his mind and—dare one add ?—with what unseen sources of strength opened to him! It is from that hour that he would seem to have founded the sovereignty of his kingdom upon that of his own soul. But by no process of conversion can a man save his fortunes as well as his soul from the nemesis of accomplished errors.

And yet how magnificently, during the eleven years of his personal rule, did he labour to retrieve a situation whose ultimate hopelessness he himself had ensured ! And how nearly did he come to success ! But to govern by law and without military force, in the abeyance of Parliament, was at best a temporary and precarious expedient. The first mistake was bound to ruin it, and the first mistake did ruin it. But in that ruin the nation suffered hardly less than the monarchy. Not for generations was England to know such peaceful prosperity, or a government so mild in its incidence and—in the best sense—national in its aims.

This is not to say that in the longest run it would have been good for England and mankind if, by some inconceivable chance, that system of government had been perpetuated. My own belief, as far as it is worth mentioning, is that the continuity of development that has evolved a commonwealth of free nations from seeds of the old Common law, was worth preserving at all costs, and perhaps—God only knows—by any men or means. But that belief, if anyone chooses to share it, need not affect our judgment of the protagonists in the drama, who could not be expected to see three centuries ahead. And after all, it was not King Charles, but King Pym and his associates, who turned traitor to representative government, and paved the way for the nearest approach England has ever made to the Totalitarian tyranny.

CONTENTS

Introduction

I *The Younger Brother*

II *The Basic Conflict*

III *Prince of Wales*

IV *The Duke*

V *King Charles*

ILLUSTRATIONS

I

The Younger Brother

I

THE DARK CLOAK

JUST an hour before midnight, in the palace at Dunfermline, on the 19th of November, in the year 1600, Anne, Princess of Denmark, the Queen of Scotland, was delivered of her third child, a boy. The birth had been difficult ; Her Majesty had been undergoing a good deal of worry since the shocking and mysterious tragedy in the preceding August, when the young Earl of Gowrie and his brother, the Master of Ruthven, had been stabbed to death by the retinue of her husband, James VI, whom, it was said, the two had conspired to murder. That was the official version ; but there was—there still is—another, in which the King himself figures as both conspirator and murderer. The finger of scandal had even pointed at the Queen : jealousy was suggested as the motive, jealousy of the handsome Master. And she, who was almost certainly innocent of anything worse than an amiable silliness, and whose favourite maid of honour had been sister to the slain noblemen, had allowed her tongue to wag in a way that must have been disconcerting to her husband. Relations had been strained, that Autumn, between the royal pair.

James had not been present when his child was born. He had been on the other side of the Firth of Forth, in Edinburgh, absorbed in business congenial to the morbid streak in his nature. For the now rotting carcases of the brothers, condemned in due form by a Scots Parliament, had been carved up, that day, by the executioner, for public exhibition. The noisome operation had sealed the King's triumph over an anarchic nobility. But the news from Dunfermline brought him post haste, by horse and ferry, to his consort's bedside. If there had been any bitterness lingering in his mind, it was forgotten in the excitement of this new event.

It was an excitement the reverse of pleasant. Not only did the mother's condition give cause for anxiety, but the infant turned out to be so weak and sickly that it appeared to be only a question of getting him baptized quickly enough to avert the dire and eternal penalties with which his other Father, in Heaven, was certain to visit the omission *post mortem*. Accordingly the little creature was hurriedly initiated into the Scottish Episcopalian form of Christianity, under his father's first name of Charles. As, however, he cheated expectation by surviving, this precautionary rite was followed by another, two days before Christmas, at Holyrood, in which, with all due pomp and ceremony, he was not only readmitted to the fold, but invested with the Dukedom of Albany and a string of other titles.

We know little about his infancy. Such information as we have is fragmentary, and not all of that reliable. The omens and portents of which his life and death are prolific, begin with his cradle. The good people of Dunfermline had a story, started heaven knows how or when, and handed down the generations, in several different versions, about an old man appearing from nowhere in particular and casting a dark cloak over the sleeping child—perhaps some avenging spirit of the House of Ruthven. Such happenings were by no means remarkable in a country whence, only a few years before, no less than two hundred witches, each in her private sieve, and chanting lustily to a reel tune, had put to sea, according to the evidence of one of them, to bedevil the Queen's voyage to Scotland.

What is more credible to modern ears is a story, which though it rests on the authority of an astrologer called Lilly, concerns the old Scottish lady, his nurse, who appears to have been convinced of the poor bairn's evil disposition, even in the cradle, and who, in that case, is not likely to have been too well disposed towards him herself. We note, in this connection, that the court physician, Sir Thomas Mayerne, ascribed the beginning of King James's innumerable bodily troubles to the milk of a drunken wet-nurse, though it is more likely, as a modern doctor* suggests, that it was a case of unconscious infantile disgust. The bodily and mental havoc wrought by the nurses of a still more than half barbarous Scotland in their charges, may well have put into the shade the most lurid horrors ever alleged against witches.

What we do know for certain is that the infant Charles was abnormally weak and backward. It seemed as if he would never learn to walk, and although Lord Fife, who had charge of him at Dunfermline, tried to make out that his mind and tongue were

* *Mere Mortals*, by Dr C. Marlaurin, p. 128.

more forward than his body and feet, he remained still practically inarticulate well on into his fifth year.

It was during these years, when he lay under the black cloak of silence, that the seeds of eventual tragedy were sown.

2

DEFECT OF SPEECH

It was on a March night of 1603 that a gentleman, in the last stage of exhaustion, with travel-stained garments and blood on his face, where his horse had kicked it, was shown up to King James's bedchamber at Holyrood. He was a certain Sir Robert Carey, whose grandmother had been Queen Elizabeth's aunt, Mary Boleyn, and who was remarkable, even about Court, for the skill with which he habitually contrived to feather his own nest. On this occasion he had performed a feat worthy of the slickest modern newspaper reporter. He had not only tipped a porter to let him into the palace on the first report of his royal cousin's death, but he had contrived to elude the vigilance of the Council by getting out again, with one of the Queen's rings on him as a token, and had broken all records by a three days' ride up north, to curry what favour he could by being the first to communicate to James VI of Scotland the glad tidings that he was now, in addition, James I of England.

James lost no time in proceeding south to secure his new inheritance ; and in the summer Queen Anne followed with her two eldest children, after an undignified row with Lady Mar about the custody of Prince Henry. Poor little Charles, who would probably not have survived the journey, had to be left behind for another year at Dunfermline.

Hither presently repaired the indefatigable Sir Robert. "God put it into my mind," he tells us, "to go to Dunfermline." Virtue had, in fact, been inadequately rewarded ; for the bedchamber appointment that he had solicited, and obtained, after the London to Edinburgh ride, had almost immediately fallen through in a general redistribution of Court posts, and the lucrative Wardenship of the Middle Marches, which he had held under Elizabeth, had come to an end, because, with the Union of

Crowns, the Marches, as such, had ceased to exist. But your true pusher is nothing if not persistent, and Sir Robert Carey was beginning to view the little Prince in the light of a speculative investment. He found him "a very weak child," and was off, south with this information for the Queen, who, motherly soul became all the more impatient to have her Benjamin under her eye. And when at last—after some weeks' delay in consequence of a fever—the cavalcade was reported to have arrived at Newcastle, Carey was sent up the familiar road to meet it, and provide all things necessary for the remainder of the journey.

And now it became necessary to find some English lady to take over from Lady Fife—or Dunfermline as she now was—a matron's responsibility for the establishment of His Royal Highness. The great ladies of the court were at first tumbling over each other with eagerness to secure the post, but, as Sir Robert tells us, "when they did see how weak a child he was, and not likely to live, their hearts were down, and none of them were desirous to take charge of him."

This was Sir Robert's opportunity. What he had seen of the child must have convinced him that its survival was a chance worth backing, and he knew that if anybody could make a success of the task, it was the Cornish widow whom, braving the wrath and objurgations of a Virgin Queen, he had married eleven years before. This lady, in the true Carey spirit, had already contrived, by paying sedulous court to Queen Anne, to get sworn of her privy chamber, and established, with a lodging in Court, as mistress of her sweet coffers. From this point of vantage, it was comparatively easy for a masterful woman, who knew exactly what she wanted, to advance to the main objective of the Duke's care and keeping.

There were few to envy her a success so perilous. "Those who wished me no good were glad of it," says her husband, "thinking that if the Duke should die in our charge (his weakness being such as gave them great cause to suspect it) then it would not be thought fit that we should remain in court after."

But God, of whose devotion to the Carey interest Sir Robert was never in doubt, did not forsake him now. "Out of weakness He showed His strength, and beyond all men's expectations so blessed the Duke with health and strength under my wife's charge, as he grew better and better every day. The King and Queen rejoiced much to see him prosper as he did, and my wife for the care she had of him, and her diligence (which indeed was great) was well esteemed of them both, as did well appear. For by her procurement she got me a suit of the King that was worth to me afterwards four or five thousand pounds. I had the charge given me of the Duke's household, and none allowed to his service but such as I gave way to, by which means I preferred to hire a number of my own servants. ... My daughter was brought up with the King's daughter, and served her, and had the happiness to be allowed to wait on her in her privy lodgings. My wife and self, by waiting still in the privy lodgings of the Duke, got better esteem of the King and Queen."

Providence had, in fact, done extremely well for the Careys, but we need not grudge them the fruits of their speculation. Never was more excellent value given for favours received. From the moment Lady Carey took him in hand, little Charles began to make up for his bodily and mental arrears. He grew stronger every day. His father, in despair of his ever being able to walk or talk, had wanted to put the child's feet into iron boots, and have the string under his tongue cut. But Lady Carey was having none of this nonsense. She may have been a pusher, but she was no crawler, and she was not going to have her work, and nature's, ruined by amateur interference. She withstood the Monarch to his face, not once, but in many a battle royal, and he, like the sensible man he was, gave way. For seven years she continued in charge, and at the end of that time all that remained to bear witness of the boy's bad start in life was a certain tendency to stammer.

This, however, was serious enough, in a Prince, for it caused him to speak with self-conscious deliberation, and formed a bar to that spontaneous touch with his fellow-men that is the first essential of popularity. There was always something aloof about Charles ; he never seemed capable of realizing intuitively the motives and characters of those with whom he was brought in contact ; his mind's eye saw men as it were trees walking.

Moreover, it is well known to modern psychologists that such a defect as stammering acts like a subtle poison on its victim's mind. Perhaps without consciously realizing it, he feels himself handicapped, humiliated, in contact with normal people, and in consequence adopts a habitually defensive attitude. He either retires into his own shell, or else—and especially if he happens to be royal—seeks compensation in a cold and cultivated dignity.

It is only too easy to over-simplify so complex a story as that of a human soul, and to ascribe to one cause the effect of many. What we do know is that Charles, when at last he began to walk about and take an interest in things, gave the impression of being a very reserved and even a sullen little boy. To what an extent his defect of speech may have accounted for this, or how far it may have been due to repressions implanted by that old Tartar of a nurse—which themselves may not inconceivably have implanted the stammering habit—or what twist of mind he may have inherited from his walking hospital of a father, are things about which we are free to speculate, but of which we can never have anything like exact knowledge.

Be the causes what they may, the effects were lifelong and cumulative.

3

"SWEET, SWEET BROTHER"

THE world that first opens itself to the consciousness even of little princes is fragmentary and personal. When, not long after his fifth birthday, the Dukedom of York was conferred on Charles as the King's second son, the circumstance that probably most impressed him about the accompanying festivities was that of his mother having blacked her face, to go with her Moorish costume. That was in the January of 1605. It is just possible that in the autumn of that same year he may have been struck with the appearance about his lodgings of a new and rather frightening grown up person, the sort of person one *would* notice, for he had a fiery countenance, a very broad beard, a tall stooping form, and legs too short for him ; he was nosing about in a vaguely un-pleasant sort of way, asking questions ... but it was not till later that Charles was to realize how this gentleman had hired a cellar, and how he and his friends had filled it with gunpowder, to blow up Daddy and Big Brother like Grandfather Darnley ; and how they had planned to kidnap him and Sister Elizabeth, to make one or other the puppet Sovereign of an England reconciled to the True Church.

It is more probable, however, that he never saw, or at any

rate noticed, Mr Thomas Percy, and that the original Fifth of
November signified less to him than it does to many little boys of
the same age nowadays. Backward and reserved as he was, he
must have lived, to an even greater extent than the average child,
in a world of his own imagination. Outside that world, there
would have been plenty of things to attract him, for his was a
colourful and changing environment. Horses and dogs certainly
figured prominently in it, and there were games, of which his
mother was childishly fond, for she would always be making her
maids-of-honour find out new, or remember old ones, and she
would certainly have passed them on to her boy. There was
"Rise, pig, and go" ; there was "Fire" ; there was "I pray, my
lord, give me a course in your park." And to satisfy desires
fulfilled in a later age by the circus and pantomime, the court
provided an endless succession of pageantry.

His loneliness must have been increased by the lack of other
children's society ; and that would have made him all the more
dependent on the companionship of his elder brother and sister,
though owing to their separate establishments, even this was by
no means constantly available. His reserved nature was slow to
conceive affection, but for that very reason, once he gave his
heart, it was without stint. And on whom would affection fasten
so naturally as on his brother Henry, six years older than himself,
and so enviably his opposite !

For this brother, even at what to-day would be a private
school age, was the very model of what a popular young prince
should be. He was not the last Prince of Wales to be fonder of
living than of learning. He was an open air boy, devoted to horses,
a keen player of tennis and of another game, already Royal and
Ancient in his native Scotland—"very like Mall," the French
Ambassador described it. We are told how on one occasion, when
he was addressing his ball, someone warned him that he was
about to drive into his tutor. "Had I done so," he said feelingly,
"I should have paid my debts." However, the gentleman in
question, in spite of his proud vaunt, "I am meet for the whipping
of boys," does not appear, even in that age of intensive scholarship, to have succeeded in keeping His Royal Highness to his
books for more than a beggarly two hours a day, the rest of the
time being strenuously devoted, not only to sports and games, but
to every sort of athletic and martial exercise.

Unlike Charles, who shrank instinctively from contact with

the outer world, Henry was never happy except when he was up and doing ; his knowledge of life was direct and intuitive. Having no inner world to distract his attention, he was the more free to develop tact and magnetism in dealing with other people ; he had a way with him that enabled him to counter even his tutor's direst fulminations with cheeky repartee—and apparently to get away with it. He must have had a singularly sweet nature, if we are to judge by the delicacy of his mediation, at the age of sixteen, in a tiff between his parents, caused by Anne's failure to take notice of poor James's gout.

Even in his teens, not only had he begun to take himself extremely seriously, but to get himself taken with equal serious-ness by people in the highest positions. It was not only in a spirit of courtly flattery that Ben Jonson likened the future Henry the Ninth to

> that other thunderbolt of war
> Harry the Fifth, to whom in face you are
> So like.

for it was on the lines of that great ancestor that the Prince gave every sign of developing. He wanted to see England assert herself, as the champion of the Reformation, against the supreme effort, that was obviously coming, to win back the Continent for Rome. He affected the Puritan devoutness that was not only a popular, but a genteel fashion, at the beginning of the seventeenth century. The young zealot actually placed collecting boxes in his different houses, to which all swearers had to contribute at so much an oath, the proceeds being distributed to the poor ! King James's policy of resolute pacifism and friendship with Catholic powers, was worse than dishonourable—it was godless. Henry became more and more obviously the rising hope of a potential war party : it was characteristic of him that he should have taken the part of that imprisoned firebrand, Sir Walter Raleigh—only his father, he said, would have kept such a bird in such a cage ; character-istic, too, that he should have taken up the cudgels for Sir Phineas Pett, the royal ship-designer, in his efforts to create an efficient navy.

Even in his early teens, the popular young Prince was becom-ing a power in the land. The great Earl of Salisbury, the all-powerful chief minister, was said to be disturbed about him ; his Court at St James's was becoming more frequented than that

of the King himself. The father was beginning to enquire queru-
lously, whether this self-willed son of his was going to bury him
alive.

In the dawning consciousness of a lame, tongue-tied, boy, the
figure of his big brother, whom everybody admired, and who did
everything so well, must have been magnified to heroic dimensions. What were the feelings of little Charles for Henry are plain
from the earliest of his letters, written for him, evidently, by some
older person, but signed by him in great copybook script,

"Sweet, sweet brother," it runs, "I thank yow for your letter.
I will keep it better than all my graith : and I will send my
pistolles by Maister Newton. I will give anie thing I have to
yow ; both my horss, and my books, and my pieces, and my
cross bowes, or anie thing that yow would haive. Good brother
loove me, and I shall ever loove and serve yow.
"Your looving brother to be commanded,
"YORK."

That the scribe, whoever he or she was, was correctly trans-
cribing the Prince's sentiments, must be evident, if we reflect
that the only grown-up person with enough insight into the child
mind to have been capable of composing such a letter for himself,
was an actor fellow from Stratford, who had other employment
for his pen.

But behind this love and admiration, there must have been
latent, in Charles's mind, a certain jealousy ; that, if we may
trust contemporary gossip, did blaze to the surface on at least
one occasion. The story is that the grim old Calvinist Archbishop
of Canterbury, Abbot, was having an audience with the King,
and had imprudently left his black, square cap, within range of
young Henry, who not only put it on his own head, but improved
the occasion by a little only too brotherly chaff, to the effect that
if Charles was a good boy, and stuck to his books—a sore point,
because their father had been recently holding up Charles's
studious example for imitation—Henry would some day make
him into an Archbishop, with a long gown to hide his rickety legs.
This was too much for Charles, who relieved his feelings by tearing
the cap off his brother's head and furiously trampling on it—the
only occasion of his life on which he is reported to have lost
control of himself. About His Grace's subsequent comments, if
any, even gossip preserves a discreet silence.

It was only to be expected, under these circumstances, that
Charles, as he found his legs beginning to get strong under him,
should have striven with all his might to establish his self-respect,
by becoming as like as possible to his brilliant brother. As far as
bodily prowess was concerned, he was wonderfully successful.
So far from growing up weak-legged, like his father, he became,
like his eldest son after him, so fast a walker that, according to
Lilly, "he rather trotted than paced." Where he did take after
his father was in his bold and skilful horsemanship. Among those
early letters of his to his brother, we find him saying, "I do visit
sometimes your stable and do ride your great horses," and,
again, "I do keep your horses in breath and I have very good
sport."

It is hard to realize how much of a King's or Prince's life, in
former times, was passed, not in affairs of state, but in that most
primitive of all human occupations, hunting the beast. It afforded
a perpetual outlet for the crude animal energy needed by one who
had to be a leader of men, in the most literal sense ; the finest
animal of the human herd. It is true that this conception of
princely functions was already passing out of date ; the new type
of ruler required to be as much fox as lion, and could sometimes
afford to dispense with the lion altogether. But royalty is a
conservative institution, and James I was as great a lover of the
tall stag as William the Conqueror. Under what ideal conditions,
from the hunter's point of view, sport was carried on, may be
judged from a note addressed in October, 1617, to the constables
of certain Hertfordshire townships, conveying the King's express
command to occupants of arable land not to plough in narrow
ridges, or suffer swine to go unringed and root holes to the
endangering of His Majesty and the Prince of Wales hawking and
hunting ; also to take down the bounds between lands that
hinder His Majesty's ready passage.

Charles was not only a first-class horseman, but was reputed,
like Henry VIII before him, and George V after him, to be
among the best shots in the country. They still used the cross-bow
then, for sporting purposes, and how desirable it was to be
proficient is shown by the fact that not only did the Queen, on
one occasion, succeed in bagging her husband's favourite dog,
but Archbishop Abbot brought himself into dire trouble by
transfixing a keeper. In the tilting yard, Charles was as distinguished a performer as in the hunting field—on more than one

occasion he carried off the palm in the difficult accomplishment of riding at the ring. He took up tennis, having a course of special instruction in quite the modern way, and golf, which he continued to play even in his final captivity.

In short, a decade or so sufficed to turn a hopeless little cripple into an upstanding athletic young fellow, "a fine youth of sweet disposition," as the Spanish Ambassador reported of him shortly before his thirteenth birthday. But though the trouble with his feet was conquered, that with his tongue persisted—it was not so much that he could not conquer the tendency to stammer, as that he was forced to do so by deliberate effort, every time he opened his mouth. It is probable that all his life he never knew what it was to have a good talk with anyone ; never experienced the joy of letting his thought overflow freely into speech.

And thus, in spite of his success in making up his physical leeway, it was never possible for him to become the popular and sympathetic figure that his brother was. He remained a shy, studious, enigmatic boy—about whom few stories were told, and whose sayings were never, like those of young Henry, passed from mouth to mouth. This, in one way, was all to the good, for while the elder boy was a radiant centre of vital energy, perpetually diffusing itself through its surrounding world, the younger, with less to give, was the more able to receive and share the substance of a rich inner life.

And that, it might have been thought, was an ideal apportionment of gifts between the two brothers. For the future Henry IX it would be all-important to impress his personality on his subjects. If there is any class of persons of whom it can be said that what they seem is almost as important as what they are, it is the order of Kings. Whatever value they may have can never be realized unless it can be expressed in terms of popular symbolism. Henry would be just the king to fire the popular imagination. He might easily have become an English Gustavus Adolphus, crossing swords with Wallenstein and Tilly on the plains of Germany, or perhaps—for he was already a naval enthusiast—organizing the capture of the Plate Fleet. He might have wasted the country's resources in ruinous adventure ; he might have come as near as an English king could to establishing himself as a popular despot on the Continental model—one thing that he would never under any circumstances have done, would have been to walk out to the scaffold through the windows of his own palace.

And Charles ? Perhaps Henry would have been as good as his youthful word, and found the ideal employment for his brother as Prince Archbishop, guiding the destinies of the Church he loved so well. Had not his father, no mean judge, said of him that he could manage a point in a theological controversy with the best studied divine of them all ? We can well believe that his purity of life, his dignity of a Christian gentleman, his cultured and well-stocked mind, and his single-hearted devotion, combined with the immense prestige that his rank would have conferred, might have enabled him to steer the ship of the Church through those rocks on which, with a Laud at the helm, she was destined to crash.

But no Henry IX was to sit on an English throne. In the autumn of 1612, something that the Prince of Wales ate or drank contained the germs of typhoid fever—no very unusual occurrence, one would have imagined, in those insanitary times. When he was beginning to sicken he characteristically exerted himself so violently at tennis, that he got a chill on the top of it. He took to his bed now, only too evidently in mortal danger. It was in vain that Sir Walter Raleigh, in the Tower, tried to pay his debt of gratitude by giving the prescription of some secret and potent remedy : the drug stimulated, but it did not cure. In a few days it was all over, and the country was plunged into unfeigned grief and consternation. There was even talk of poison—though we have the records of an admirably scientific post-mortem to disprove it.

So it was to be the throne of Edward the Confessor, and not that of Saint Augustine, for the bereaved younger brother. He was just on twelve.

4

BOYHOOD

OUR information about Charles's boyhood is so fragmentary, that we are left to conjecture the effect upon him of thus losing the brother, whose personality must have constituted the most important factor of his environment. We know that he was chief mourner at the funeral, and the shock of his bereavement may be at least partly accountable for the fact that he himself was soon afterwards down with an alarming bout of illness. But he had recovered in time to act as bridesman at the wedding of his sister, Elizabeth, four years older than himself, to the Elector Palatine— one of the fateful marriages of history, for it was destined, in the fullness of time, to endow England with a line of German Sovereigns.

The loss of his sister, by marriage, following so hard on that of his brother, by death, must still further have increased the boy's loneliness—for it was on her that his bereaved affections naturally tended to fasten. She was, indeed, a female version of his brother, a radiant creature, some of whose charm comes to us even now, with a lingering fragrance, like that of crushed roses.

"The eclipse and glory of mankind,"

as she is described in the one immortal poem of the innumerable written in her honour.

Her brilliance—and perhaps the same is true of her elder brother—had little depth beneath its surface. She proved, through the course of a long and chequered career, to have inherited her mother's extravagant and frivolous disposition, though she added to it an infectious charm which in royalties is more than half the battle. To her small brother the charm must have counted for all in all ; Elizabeth was the ideal sister. There is no doubt that she was one of the three or four people during his life to whom Charles vouchsafed his unreserved affection. That affection was to be fraught with serious political consequences.

Lady Carey had already ceased to have charge of him, after he had turned eleven, for it was considered beneath his princely dignity to keep him under petticoat government. As, however, her salary of four hundred a year was continued as a pension, and she also continued to hold her office in the Queen's household, she did not come out of it so badly. As for Sir Robert, he had already established himself as the chief personage in the Prince's household, and he was not the man to be easily shifted, not even when Prince Henry himself had come forward with a new candidate of his own for the post. "My God," says Carey, "who never forsook me," put up the Lord Chamberlain Suffolk to do a little backstairs work for him with the King. Prince Henry had had to fall back on diplomatic persuasion—would not Sir Robert like to exchange his mastership of the robes for the surveyorship of the lands ? Sir Robert was all thanks and apology—"If I should accept, I should wrong my master and discredit myself ; and if I had skill in anything, I thought I could tell how to make good clothes ; and therefore I desired humbly I might continue in the place that I had," which indeed he did, doubling it with that of Chief Gentleman of the Bedchamber.

This was not the last of Carey's anxieties, for Charles had often talked of appointing him his Chamberlain, when he became Prince of Wales, in lieu of his appointment in the Bedchamber, to which that faithful servant "did always answer, that I would not be put out of his bedchamber for any office that could be given me ; but I did see no reason why I could not hold them both." There were others, however, who did, and this time they succeeded in getting the King's definite decision to appoint the Earl of Roxburghe to the new post. But Sir Robert was equal even to this occasion. Off he went to the Queen, to inform her how Roxburghe had been going behind her back with her husband, to wangle himself a post in her son's household—how dare he ? How indeed ! Her Majesty boiled over ; her wrong was greater than Sir Robert's ; the Earl certainly, and presumably the King, were given to understand what she thought of them both—exit Roxburghe in disgrace to Scotland—enter Carey into the sweets of the new office without forfeiting those of the old. "Thus," comments that devout pluralist, "did God raise up the Queen to take my part."

It was not, however, until four years after Prince Henry's death, that this happened. That canny Scot, James I—we think of him as old, but he was only forty-six when his elder son died,— had had more than enough experience of a Prince of Wales's powers of self-assertion. So for four years he kept the title in abeyance, no doubt until he had satisfied himself that Charles was not likely to kick over parental traces, in the way only too characteristic of heirs to a throne.

But not even his ingrained suspiciousness can have discovered much cause for anxiety in Charles's conduct. From James's point of view, nothing can have been more unexceptionable than the quiet way in which he stuck to his studies with his tutor, Archibald Murray, and in which he continued to perfect himself in the various accomplishments, physical and mental, proper to his station. "He had," says the astrologer Lilly, "many singular parts in nature ; he was an excellent horseman, would shoot well at a mark, had singular skill in limning and pictures, a good mathematician, not unskilful in history, well read in divinity, and no less in the laws and statutes of this nation, would write his mind singularly well and in good language and style, only he loved long parenthesis.''

He was a boy who seemed destined to give a minimum of trouble ; he played his part in state pageantry with that dignity which was never to forsake him, and had begun to earn golden opinions from all sorts of people, without courting that rather unfilial sort of popularity that had begun to invest Prince Henry at the time of his death.

In his early years he had been rather his mother's boy, as is the way of the youngest and weakest. James does not seem to have thought him worth the trouble he lavished on the brilliant Henry, for whose guidance he had unlocked the treasures of his experience in the manual of princely instruction that he had called *Basilikon Doron*. But the wisdom of Solomon himself would have been thrown away on a son determined, from the first, to follow his own line regardless of instruction—and Henry had been of that type. Whereas Charles——

Besides, the loss of his firstborn had left an empty place in James's heart. He was very human—perhaps too human for a King—and he had a craving for affection not easily satisfied in Kings, to whom all affection is necessarily suspect. It is a curious, and rather touching circumstance, that it is not the child, but the young man, of whom his father, now prematurely aged, came to talk and think as "Baby Charles.''

II

The Basic Conflict

THE SCOTTISH KING AND THE ENGLISH
CONSTITUTION

IF ever there was a sovereign with a right to complain of his
treatment at the bar of history, it is James I. At best, he
receives a patronizing tolerance ; more often he is presented
as a mere figure of fun or object of contempt ; the only person to
do him anything like justice being that other wanderer in the
paths of curious learning, who was the father of Benjamin Disraeli.

And yet there is one sense in which James may be said to have
brought it on himself. Whether or not it is true that an Englishman loves a lord, there can be no doubt whatever that he loves a
King, and that he has extremely definite notions of what a King
ought to be. As always, the ideal he aims at is a compromise, or
golden mean, between two opposite extremes ; his King has got
to be popular and kingly at the same time ; he has, like Shakespeare's Henry V, to be capable of going about the camp and hob-
nobbing with the soldiers, and yet of instantly annihilating the
least attempt at a liberty, even from a Falstaff. All the popular
English Kings, from Edward IV's time to our own, have been like
that.

Now it is a significant paradox that the very one of all the
English Sovereigns who had the most exalted notions of the
dignity attaching to his office, was the one who had the least of it
attaching to his person. Not even James's warmest defender
could describe his deportment as in the remotest sense kingly.
He had a positive genius for surrounding his most solemn acts and
pronouncements with an atmosphere of low comedy. At one
moment he would be flaunting his divine omnipotence in the face
of his Parliament, at another he would be warning them of the
fate of the cow who cut off her own tail—the tail being his divine
self. To the style of a God he added on one occasion that of a
Christ, with his latest favourite in the part of St John. When asked
to grace a court wedding with his presence, he had been known to

enter so far into the spirit of the thing as to get into bed with the bride ; when he had condescended to enter into controversy with some unfortunate Arian, nothing would serve him but to reinforce the argument of his tongue with that of his toe. Where he did not create ridiculous situations, he attracted them. No one but James, after having gone about for months in fear of his life from the treasonable pursuit of one of his Scottish Earls, would have been caught at last emerging from the privy, in a state of indescribable *déshabillé*.

Add to this that the innumerable gross and petty ailments, with which he was afflicted, were the source of an extreme unpleasantness in his personal habits. He shambled, he slobbered, he belched, he did other things that rendered him anything but refined company. His dreadful youth, in which he was never safe from kidnapping or actual murder, had left him with a crop of nervous disorders. Though, in a critical situation, he could display both courage and resource, he had an obsessive phobia of the sight of naked steel, and a tendency to panic and cry treason on any sudden alarm, as, for instance, when the students of Gray's Inn started firing off the Tower guns by way of a Twelfth Night rag.

If it is the first duty of a King to be kingly, then indeed we must allow James to have been one of the most unrelieved failures on record. But it is at least arguable that England has thriven best under the least romantic of her rulers. The job of governing her was never done better than by that skinflint usurper, Henry VII, unless it was when the first two Georges committed it into the hands of that enormous realist, Sir Robert Walpole. It is the modern discovery that the gift of kingliness is best developed in a caste of hereditary specialists, who have ceased, except on the rarest occasions, to exercise power.

In the often unkingly mystery of what he himself called kingcraft, James, when he was called from the throne of the smaller to that of the larger kingdom, had shown himself something more than an expert. Had he died at the same time as Elizabeth, he must have gone down to history, with the doubtful exception of Robert Bruce, as the greatest of all the Kings of Scotland. Five Kings of his name and line, all of them men of outstanding abilities, had wrestled with the task of governing the ungovernable —all of them had come to bad ends before their heirs were grown up to succeed them ; Mary, our James's mother, as if the feudal chaos were not enough, had been faced by the aggressive disloyalty of the all-powerful Kirk, and she had crashed more ruinously than any of her fathers. James, a helpless infant, kidnapped—not for the last time—in the nursery, and treated like dirt by the ministers of the Kirk, had to face both these problems in their most aggravated form. Before he could be fairly described as middle-aged, he had solved them both. The Gowrie affair, whatever view we may take of it, put the seal on the long struggle between the Stuarts and their nobility, so far, at any rate, as James's life was concerned. And on the top of that, he accomplished the even more surprising feat of bringing the Kirk to heel. At long last, the King of Scotland was master of his realm.

Nor was this all, for he had played, all this time, and with consummate finesse, the difficult and doubtful game of securing for himself the English succession, a game whose rigour compelled him to sacrifice whatever chance there may have been of saving his own mother's life, or avenging her death. But he made no mistake, and he had himself to thank that at Elizabeth's death his succession turned out to be so much a matter of course that no one dreamed of disputing it.

But we need not only judge him by results. He was no opportunist, but a philosopher, a poet, and a man of letters, who made a profounder study of his profession of kingship than any contemporary, and most subsequent Kings. For this he has been dubbed a pedant by critics who proceed on the good old English assumption that no one who bothers about the theory of his subject is competent to practise it, and this in spite of the fact that James had practised with triumphant success before ever he started to formulate his theory.

Such was the monarch who, in the prime of his powers, was transferred from his now completed task of bringing order out of chaos in Scotland, to that of guiding the ordered State and loyal Church of England along the way of prosperity on which she had been put by Elizabeth and her ministers, the two great Cecils, father and son. Having succeeded in the first, it might well have seemed almost unbelievable that he should fail in the second.

Just why, and how far he failed, is a matter of vital importance for us to grasp, because the same difficulties that faced him were bequeathed, in an aggravated form, to his son Charles, to whom failure would mean death.

Let us first disabuse ourselves of the easy explanation that James failed because he was a pedant or a fool—even "the wisest

fool in Christendom." No sort of a fool, wise or otherwise, would
have achieved his record in Scotland, nor is such a work as his
Basilikon Doron the product of a fool's brain. We would go farther,
and suggest that if James had been called to rule any country of
Christian Europe, with the exception of England, there would
never have been the least question of his folly or pedantry, but
that on the contrary he would have been acclaimed on all hands
as a master of statesmanship.

The trouble lay in the fact that the evolution of England had
already begun to branch off on a line of its own ; that between
the Channel and the Tweed a different political species had
begun to take shape from that of the Continental and Scottish
monarchies, and that the conditions confronting an English King
were subtly, but fundamentally, different from those of his good,
Christian brothers.

2

ENGLAND'S UNIQUE CONSTITUTIONAL PROBLEM

It has often been remarked that Parliament was in no sense an
English invention. There was a time, in the Middle Ages, when
representative assemblies were springing up like mushrooms all
over Western Europe. But with the coming of the modern age,
those on the Continent began to wilt, and Europe came to
resemble a patchwork of virtually absolute sovereignties. But it
was just at this very time, under the House of Tudor in the
sixteenth century, that the Parliamentary way of government
became more essentially a part of English national life than ever
before. England differed from her Continental neighbours
precisely in the fact that with her, in the dawn of the modern age,
the representative principle was on the up and not the down
grade, and Parliamentary government not a decaying, but a
living and growing thing.

If we seek to comprehend how and why this difference had
come about, we shall need to go back not only to the dawn of
history, but far beyond, to the event that has determined the
whole subsequent course of British, and Greater British development : the breaking of the chalk bridge that joined England to

Europe and left her separate from, and yet in sight of, the continental land mass. The full effects of this were only brought into
being by two subsequent events that thus form the decisive
landmarks in British history. One was when, at the Norman
Conquest, England gained a command of her sea approaches
that enabled her to secure her own immunity from invasion,
except by her own consent, for at least nine centuries to come.
The other took place at her so-called Reformation, when, after a
long process of weaning, she asserted, and proved capable of,
maintaining her formal and spiritual independence of the civilization of the Continent.

But for this unique situation of England, and the way it was
turned to account, there could by no possibility have been anything like the English way of constitutional development. Nor
could there have been any such conflict of forces as that which
proved fatal to King Charles. For what was it that enabled the
Sovereigns, great and petty, of the Continent to shed their Parliaments, and to do so with the acquiescence, at least, of their
peoples ? The first and great reason, which in itself would have
sufficed, was that these Sovereigns came to acquire professional
armies capable of crushing opposition to their will within their
own frontiers. With open land frontiers, and no supernational
power, temporal or spiritual, capable of imposing its peace,
nobody but a madman or a traitor could have gone about to deny
such power to the Head of the State. But he who has the power of
the sword can snap his fingers at that of the talking shop. Iron
necessity, therefore, constrained the peoples of Continental
Europe to sacrifice whatever they had acquired of free constitutions, in order to concentrate all power in the hands of a
Sovereign.

Now this need did not constrain England to anything like the
same extent as her Continental neighbours. When Shakespeare
put into the mouth of John of Gaunt his immortal panegyric of
England as a

> Fortress built by nature for herself
> Against infection and the hand of war

he had stated the essential truth about her ; but it would have
been out of character with John of Gaunt, not to speak of
Shakespeare himself, had he gone on to draw the moral, that the

effect of her insulation was to enable England so far to ignore military necessity as to leave her Sovereign practically without an army, and thus utterly dependent on the goodwill of his people.

That is the master key to our understanding, not only of the tragedy of King Charles, but of the great unfolding drama of Anglo-Saxon world civilization. Tyranny implies military force ; without an army there can be no question of a tyrant. England was indeed destined to experience the tyranny of an army, but not of a royal army.

And paradoxically enough, her last experience of military conquest had proved another powerful factor in making her safe for liberty. For her strong Norman and early Plantagenet Kings had built up a central power, with an administrative machinery without a Continental counterpart, over the compact and manageable area defined by the English coastline. They had held England in a grip that squeezed her into unity. Consequently Parliament, when it came, was forced to become the nearest possible approach that the time would allow to a national assembly, instead of a loose federation of independent estates, united by no other bond save of that formal allegiance to the Sovereign. For in England, no single estate was capable of standing on its own feet. If Parliament were to bargain effectively, it must do so in at least the formal capacity of the representative *body* of the nation confronting the representative *man* of the nation.

But since the main purpose of Parliament was after all to hold the nation's purse strings, the danger was that it might in effect come to represent only the part of the nation that paid, and therefore, which *had* the money. And when wealth became fluid and divorced from its roots in the soil, that danger might take a very acute form—and the representative man of the nation be left to represent it alone against a body representing but a small and privileged part of it.

Such was the English Constitution as it emerged from the Middle Ages, and as it was accepted and developed by the great Sovereigns of the House of Tudor, during the supremely critical century of transition that practically everywhere on the Continent saw the scrapping of representative institutions and the principle of absolute sovereignty triumphant. And as such, that Constitution was bequeathed by them to their successors of the House of Stuart.

It was neither a law nor a code ; nobody to this day has

succeeded in formulating it explicitly. Perhaps we should best describe it as, in the most comprehensive sense, a *Way*—the way that Englishmen discovered for themselves of managing their own affairs ; a way indicated on no map, but found and cleared foot by foot, through a virgin wilderness, by guess and by God, and by sheer native sense of direction.

It was thus never like one of those Roman roads on the Continent, that are driven ruthlessly ahead in a straight line towards a predetermined point, and whose course any traveller can plot for himself. The English way has to this day defied all attempts to survey it accurately, so as to determine in what direction it was tending, or what was in the minds of those who were making and using it, at any given time. All attempts to rationalize it, and explain it on the analogy of developments abroad, or to bring it into harmony with abstract principles of political science, are merely calculated to befog the issue.

And yet unless we have some sufficient working notion of what this English way actually was, and *why* it was, we can never hope to get a less distorted notion—and more would be inconceivable— of the tragedy of King Charles, or the still unfolding drama of which it is but one episode, than may be derived from text-books and current biographies. For, to use an appropriately English expression, the whole case for or against the King turns on whether he or his opponents, or both, or neither, did, in fact, play the constitutional game. By the answer to that will be determined whether he was the cunning tyrant that *they* depicted him, or the martyr for the people that he, with his dying breath claimed to be.

3

DIVISION OF SOVEREIGNTY

Now let us look at the matter from the point of view of what is still solemnly characterized as the Tudor despotism—the whole point about the Tudors being that, with a constitutional tact and insight amounting to genius, they elected to differ from their fellow Sovereigns of the Continent in going, as you might say, with the grain of the nation, and following the Parliamentary and not the despotic way.

It was the first of the Tudors, that consummately astute though far from attractive usurper, Henry VII, who grasped the root of the matter : namely that a King of England who knew his own business would make it his first and unalterable object to carry on that of the country out of the frugal but sufficient income that accrued to him from his own royal estate and lawful perquisites. The King, to adopt the medieval way of putting it, must live of his own. And he could do this on one sole condition : that except for the policing of the seas, he should refrain from war or even the preparation for war. "Be ye wise as serpents and harmless as doves" might have been Henry Tudor's recipe for successful Kingcraft.

So long as a King of England could contrive to walk according to this rule, he and his subjects could be happy together. And it was a rule that he alone, among all the Sovereigns of Europe, could afford to honour, because he could sit quiet behind his moat and his wooden walls, with no army to speak of, and neither quake nor quiver. As for his people, they desired nothing better. They had had their bellyful of wars, domestic and foreign, and were well content to cultivate their soil and push their trade, and leave His Majesty to keep the peace and operate the adminis-trative machine. Provided only that he did not expect them to contribute out of their own pockets to the running expenses, they themselves would strengthen his hands to deal ruthlessly with any conceivable opposition—or, as they would have called it, treason. In the Sovereign's power was the subject's peace.

Under such circumstances a wise King would not deny himself the luxury of an occasional Parliament. So long as he did not come to them with a request to supplement his income, Parlia-ments were useful, if humble allies, upon whose support he could count. He stood for the people quite as much as they did. The very word King is derived from the same root as kinsman ; the King was the universally representative head of the national family, and unlike Parliament, he was continuously representative. So long as he could carry on without it, he was under no consti-tutional obligation to summon Parliament at all. It was a family council summoned by its head for some special emergency, that all things might, in the words of the Prayer Book, be ordered and *settled* by their endeavours, on the best and surest foundations. After which that particular Parliament would be dissolved, and the King, as acting representative of the nation, would continue to carry on its business until some new emergency called for the summoning of another family council.

It was only when the King had to come to his Parliament with a request for a special contribution, or subsidy, over and above his normal income, that his troubles began. Even so it is an entire mistake to imagine that he did so out of a scrupulous regard for constitutional propriety. He knew that without the assistance of Parliament he was at least as likely to raise a rebellion as a tax. He had no standing army, and the ordinary Englishman had an insuperable objection to being touched for money, unless he could see the reason for it very plainly indeed. The members, who no more coveted their function than jurymen today, had to choose between facing the wrath of the King and that of their constituents.

But the King's necessity was Parliament's opportunity. Once he approached them with his hat in his hand, the members would have been less than human not to ask what he was bringing in the other. There are two sides to every bargain ; and it is not in the English nature to part with hard cash for nothing. If the King proposed to touch Parliament, Parliament might be disposed to squeeze the King. It might even get to the point of blackmailing him. All the privileges to which, during the Middle Ages, Parliament had rather precariously staked out claims, had been extorted from Sovereigns who were fain to mortgage power for cash down. Even so, at the time the Tudors came to the throne, it was more than doubtful to what extent Parliament would be able to foreclose on these mortgages of the Kingly prerogative.

A strong King might easily have elected to take the way of his Continental brethren, and find means of arming himself with a professional nucleus of troops capable, in its turn, of extracting its own pay from civilian pockets. Whether England would have stood for this (and the fate of Richard II, who did try something of the sort, is reason for doubting it) was never put to the test, for the strong and able Tudors did, from the first, elect to secure their thrones, and get what they wanted, in the constitutional way. But to tread that way involved the acceptance of inexorable limitations which the Tudor genius intuitively grasped.

So much for the chatter about Tudor despotism. But that legend has no very deep roots. Except among propagandists of the old faith, who have their own understandable score to settle with the first Defender of the Faith and his second daughter, the name of Tudor awakens no hostile reactions.

The glory of the age and the glamour of its protagonists are such that the man in the street or even the cinema house is agreeably thrilled to discover that the Tudors were not quite so despotic as they were painted. But when you come to the Stuarts the case is altered. Here public opinion and academic orthodoxy are no more to be moved from a pre-conceived verdict, than was the tribunal presided over by Lord President Bradshaw.

In fact anything conceded in favour of the Tudors is capable of being used, by contrast, to strengthen the indictment against their successors. The less despots the Tudors, the more tyrants the Stuarts ! For what could be more melodramatically appropriate than the passing of a beloved Queen from a merry and contented England, to make way for a slobbering pedant, obsessed with his divine right to ride his will roughshod over the Constitution, and too great a fool to ride it anywhere except to ruin ? The farcical, would-be tyrant setting the stage for the entrance of the sinister actual tyrant !

An ideally simple plot, if it were not a shade too simple to cover the facts. James Stuart, Sixth of Scotland and First of England, was no tyrant, and whatever folly he may have evinced was mostly on the surface, and due to the fact of his being a life-long invalid, while underneath was a wisdom that went deeper than that of most monarchs.

Yet it was during the first decade of his reign, before his personal foibles had begun to obtrude themselves and while the country throve in peace and prosperity under a government as enlightened and beneficent as any of Tudor times, that relations between Crown and Parliament began to define themselves as those of irreconcilable conflict, veiled by a lip service of loyalty that had no reference to matters of business.

It may be that, with our human weakness for dramatization, we tend to give too much weight to the personal factor in such conflicts. It is impossible to say for certain that some ideal super-king, combining the constitutional flair of the Tudors with the subtlety of Charles II, the sheer drive of Edward Longshanks with the personal magnetism of Edward VII, might not, if he could also have succeeded in reigning as long as Queen Victoria, have contrived to establish some way of fruitful partnership between Crown and Parliament, on the basis of the existing

Constitution. The notion is not so fantastic as it might appear, since the feat was eventually performed, not by any English king, but by the founders of the American Constitution. For that constitution embodies the principle for which the Tudors stood, and Charles I and Strafford laid down their lives ; that which George III, in his ideal capacity of Patriot King, strove to re-establish in England : of a Head of the State who should choose his own ministers and frame his own policy as the direct represent-ative of his people, subject to the limitations and checks imposed by a representative assembly charged with the business of framing legislation, and regulating the supply of the money power that is the driving force of the administrative machine. The American President is merely the Tudor "Despot", the Stuart "Tyrant", and the Hanoverian "Patriot King", who holds his power not by hereditary succession, but direct popular mandate renewable every four years, and stands in essentially the same relationship to Congress as that of the Tudor kings to their parliaments.

Thus it may be said that George Washington drew the sword, in order that the constitutional ideal for which his royal namesake had fought a losing battle in the Old World should not perish from the New.

But this unharmonized duality of representative powers would have been suicidal in nations with open land frontiers like those of the European Continent, or indeed in any nation that is not in the happy position that the United States believed itself to enjoy up to the day of Pearl Harbour, of being so secure from invasion that it could afford to let considerations of military efficiency go by the board. That, given control of the seas—a most essential proviso, and one by no means to be taken for granted—may be said to have been the position of seventeenth-century England, except for the fact that, thanks to the success of the rich men in the Commons in safeguarding their own profits by putting their veto on a real union, England still retained a narrow though open frontier in the North, with a Scotland rooted in a tradition of hostility that the Union of Crowns had merely the effect of driving below the surface.

The question to be decided under the House of Stuart thus resolved itself into a choice between three possible solutions of the constitutional problem :

First there was that which we may call European, since it was in fact adopted by the overwhelming majority of Continental states, and endorsed by all the leading contemporary authorities on political philosophy : which was to concentrate all power in the hands of the Sovereign, including a military power capable of making his will irresistible. Under such a state of things this one man becomes sole representative of the nation—"The State am I"—and the Parliamentary principle is practically, if not formally, eliminated.

The opposite solution is that which was ultimately arrived at in Britain : which is to retain the Monarch, if at all, as a crowned symbol or figurehead, transferring all power to a more or less representative assembly, and leaving that assembly's nominee, as Prime Minister, to discharge all but the ceremonial functions of kingship.* This, whether glorious or not, is rightly spoken of as a revolution ; though at the decisive date, 1689, it was still far from being consummated.

The third or middle way, of an apportionment of sovereignty between a representative man and a representative body, may be described as the Tudor or American solution. It was that which, without a voice of open dissent, was accepted for that of the British Constitution at the time when King James came to the throne. The wonder is not that, nurtured as he was in clear cut Continental notions of sovereignty, he should have found it hard to adapt his logical Scottish mind to this ill-defined compromise, but that he should have done so at all.

4

SKIRTING BANKRUPTCY

THUS the conflict between King and Parliament which had been gathering to a head even under the adored Elizabeth, was determined by causes deeper than personal. It was the almost inevitable result of having two separate and rival Sovereign Powers in the State, without a fixed constitution, as in the United States, to stabilize their relative positions. However benevolent the intentions of the one and however loyal the disposition of the other, it is not in human nature to confine

* Except in certain very special and rare circumstances that do not affect the main issue.

itself within bounds, and say to its own urge for self-expansion, "thus far shalt thou go and no further". Least of all is this possible with corporate bodies, that in course of time acquire a personality of their own with the appertaining ambitions. For not only was Parliament beginning to develop its own team spirit and technique, largely by the use of committees ; but the King's government likewise had its own technique and team spirit, which could hardly be sympathetic with what it was only natural for its hard working experts to regard as a collection of amateur busybodies, incapable of governing, and possessed of no other desire than that of starving and paralysing the increasingly intricate machinery by which the day-to-day business of the community was carried on.

For what has contributed most of all to the dream picture of this time that passes for history, is the habit of regarding kings from the standpoint of the nursery. King Charles and King James are thought of as individuals who ruled the country according to their arbitrary caprice, presumably by giving a few orders now and then ; and who wanted all they could get of their subjects' money in order to live the life of luxury and splendour that kings in fairy stories are supposed to live, and that the readers of fairy stories like to day-dream of themselves as living.

Taxes are thought of as contributions to the King's personal expenses that good Kings will refrain from demanding from their subjects, and that Parliament will only allow them to receive in the form of carefully rationed occasional free gifts.

Anyone who desires to disillusion himself of this pleasing fancy has only to spend a few afternoons in the British Museum or London Library, browsing about among the state papers that modern research has placed at his disposal, and he will realize that the Sovereign was about the most hard-worked drudge in his realm, slaving away for hour upon hour, day in and day out, at the routine of the vast and intricate business for the smooth running of which he was responsible, and in which at any moment his decision might be required on matters ranging from the highest statesmanship to the most niggling points of local government or sectarian controversy.

Not that the Sovereign himself, if he were wise, would try to run all the departments and details of the business himself, his success being largely dependent on his capacity for getting efficient team work out of a staff of ministers for whose choice he was responsible, and with even the ablest of whom it was imperative for him to maintain his relationship of master to servant. He might, and indeed commonly did, have a chief minister ; but for such a one to aspire to the status of Prime Minister in the modern sense, would have been treason in the highest degree.

It will be seen that to make a success of his task, a monarch needed to combine in his own person an almost superhuman variety of talents : knowledge, judgment, firmness, tact, courage, organizing ability, mastery of detail, and sheer slogging capacity for work. An English Sovereign needed to be a man of far more than average ability to carry on at all. For centuries previously to the House of Tudor, a bare moiety of strongest and ablest had kept their thrones, or even their lives. It had been the rough and ready way of our ancestors to provide against the chances of heredity by killing off all but the hardiest royal specimens. That the weeding process was not applied to any Tudor is not due to any greater security in the position of the monarch, who without military power was in no better position than that of a Plantagenet, but to the fact that chance or providence provided a succession of rulers who without exception (leaving out of account the consumptive minor Edward VI) were of ability far beyond the average of hereditary expectation. Heredity, we may say, instead of throwing alternate heads and tails, had thrown a run of heads.

We are, then, to think of the Sovereign as having to make good in the most exacting of all the many callings in his realm, and the one with the highest vocational mortality. But that is not the whole, or even the worst of the case, as it affects the Stuarts. For at the time of their advent it is at least arguable that the scales were being tilted so increasingly against monarchy, that short of a complete revolution, such as did eventually take place, involving his reduction from a ruler to a figurehead, the position of the Sovereign, from being precarious, was fast on the way to becoming impossible.

It is an obvious lead to blame the resumption of the old, pre-Tudor alternation of Kings who died in their palace beds with those who were deposed or murdered, on some fatal defect incidental to the Stuart blood. Obvious perhaps at a glance, but on a closer view, rather less so. For of the five Sovereigns (not counting Mary of Orange) of that House, it might be said that the only thing each of them had in common with the rest was his or her conspicuous difference from the other four : the high tragedy of Charles I was as different as possible from the brilliant comedy of Charles II and the laurelled hen-wifery of Anne. And it may be said of the four Kings that they were all, in their contrasting ways, men of an ability not less ostensibly remarkable than that of the greatest of the Tudors.*

We must look deeper if we want to find the real clue to the tragedy of their House. I do not say that they never made mistakes. They were bound to, being human—though it would not be too easy to specify those of Charles II. But the first two of them, who are all that now concern us, certainly *did*—a thing that might equally be said of even the most successful of rulers, from Caesar to Churchill. But the position of the early Stuarts was like that of a man on the face of a precipice. Even a single false step was more likely than not to be irrecoverable. Fate had cut down their margin of error to vanishing point.

Now this was due to a variety of causes, but chiefly to the most prosaic of all, that of finance. For the King, as I have tried to show, was in the position of having to manage an extremely complicated business, on an income no more than just sufficient to keep it, with the strictest economy on a peace-time basis, from collapsing in bankruptcy.

That the business of governing the nation then, as now, had got to be adequately financed, nobody but a madman would have denied, in the abstract. But the managing director was not in a position then, as he is now, to budget on the assumption that ways and means will somehow be found to meet the estimated expenses. It was rather as if the nation's business had been farmed out to the richest individual in it, who was expected to find the wherewithal out of the resources and perquisites of an estate that he held on this explicit understanding. If he should find himself under the abhorred necessity of asking for more, he must call a Parliament, and instead of framing a budget in the businesslike way, proceed to haggle with it for one or more doles of an anti-quated and leakily exiguous land and property tax called a subsidy. But to apply for even a single subsidy was to ask, not in vain, for trouble. To become dependent on subsidies was to set

---

* Even James II who, whatever his faults on the throne, has a record as an admiral afloat and ashore that gives *Duke of York* as authentic a claim to figure on our battle-ship strength as *Anson* or *St Vincent*.

foot on the inclined plane to revolution. It was to prove literally a life and death matter for the King to make do somehow with what he had got ; to carry on his own government on his own income.

Now in the palmiest Tudor times, to balance income and expenditure had been barely possible, and had led to such questionable expedients as those by which Henry VII had contrived to sweat individual plutocrats, or as Henry VIII's loot of the monasteries and his inflation (then called debasing) of the currency. Even so the niggardly support that Elizabeth had been compelled to give to her war with Spain had come near to causing the whole system to collapse on her throne, as it would have certainly done on that of James, unless he had promptly and firmly achieved peace and made it the corner-stone of his policy.

Nor was it even as if the Stuarts had been called upon to solve the same problem with the same resources as the Tudors. Their position was in almost every way worse, and tending to get worse still. For the mainstay of their income had consisted of the customary profits of lands and all sorts of miscellaneous and mostly petty feudal dues that were expensive to collect and a perpetual source of irritation. Now these represented, like debentures and preference stocks nowadays, a fixed income reckoned in the nominal value of money. But the real value had slumped, thanks to the enormous influx of the precious metals year by year in the Spanish treasure fleets, to not much more than two-fifths of what it had been when Henry VII had come to the throne. And this at a time when the real, and how much more the nominal, expenses of government were progressively increasing !

It may be asked how, under these circumstances, the firm of Stuart did not go into liquidation in a matter of a few years or even months. Any one acquainted with business will deduce that even partially to compensate for these diminishing fixed assets of theirs, they must have had one that was in the nature of an equity, and whose value might increase instead of diminishing with the process of time. And such a last resort, a veritable financial life-line, was available for these hard-pressed Sovereigns in the shape of the ancient right of the Kings of England to levy customs duties at the ports. This was more than a right ; it was an essential function of royalty, since such duties operated not only as a source of revenue, but as part of a very elaborate system for the protection of native trade and industry of which Parliament itself was so much enamoured that it preferred to keep the island divided, rather than enlarge the protected circle to include the Northern Kingdom.

The main source of this revenue was the fixed percentage on imports called Tonnage and Poundage, which had been levied without a break from far back in the Middle Ages, and which thus constituted, in a double sense, one of the ancient customs of the realm. It had indeed been the custom of Parliament, at the beginning of each reign, to make a loyal show of granting these customs for life to the King ; but the idea that this was anything more than a loyal gesture had long ceased to be entertained, and there was no more serious question of it being refused, than there would be to-day of the King exercising his right to veto legislation—if only for the reason that to throw the fiscal system thus out of gear would have violently dislocated the economic life of the country and plunged its administration into chaotic bankruptcy.

Now it was obvious that the expanding prosperity, that it was the duty of the Crown to foster, would be reflected by a proportionate increase in the yield from customs, and that this might to some degree enable the Government to fill the vast gap in its resources that had resulted from the shrinkage of what we might call its estate revenue. It was also obvious that if this last support were to be taken away from the King, he might as well abdicate, for any chance that he might have of carrying on his Government at all. The revolution would have arrived.

James I's first Parliament had not come together with the idea of deliberately upsetting the Constitution in this way. It voted him the usual life grant of the customs as loyally as its predecessors. But within three years of its assembly a merchant called Bate had challenged in the courts the hitherto undisputed right of the Crown to vary, from time to time, the incidence of protective tariffs. Bate lost his case, and for the moment the matter dropped ; but before the eight years' life of this Parliament was out it had become evident that the Crown's right to its customs revenue, on which depended its last hope of solvency, was not to pass unchallenged ; and that Parliament was beginning to switch over the main weight of its offensive to this deadly line.

5

DIVINE CAESAR *versus* JOHN DOE

IT would provide a pregnant field of research for some historian, if he were to try to determine at what time, or in what quarter, we can fix the beginning of a conscious intention to deprive the Crown of all power within the Constitution, and thus to render its position impossible just as in our own time there is a certain school of social revolutionaries that aims at exacerbating every industrial dispute in order to make the position of the employers impossible. It may have been that the unresolved duality of Sovereign power was such that Crown and Parliament were like two young cuckoos in the same nest, who are bound to go on shoving and barging till one has fallen out. But my own belief, for what it is worth, is that our ancestors of the late Renaissance were not quite so simple and childish as we are pleased to imagine, and that among the hard-headed plutocrats who packed the benches at Westminster were some who knew very well what they wanted ; who had conned their Machiavelli, and marked to some purpose the proceedings of the burgher oligarchs who came to rule the roost in Holland.

Whether the conscious intention was there or not, the effect was precisely as if it had been. Parliament, for all its fervent and even fulsome protestations of loyalty, was beginning to shape its course more and more unmistakably in the direction of a direct and ultimately mortal conflict with the Crown. I do not say that there was no fault on the royal side, even in the great days of Salisbury's administration. James was far from applying Eliza-beth's thrifty housekeeping methods to the expenses of his court. But the most rigid economy would not have sufficed to render his position tolerable on the only terms Parliament was disposed to concede.

Let it be granted, however, that if any Sovereign had been capable of coming to a *modus vivendi* with this rival sovereignty in his realm, it would not have been James. All his native wisdom and shrewdness could not make up for the handicap of his being a foreigner called on to wrestle with forces as much outside the scope of his experience as those of any other foreign monarch—forces that even Elizabeth, with her almost miraculous understanding of the temper of her people and Parliament, had barely succeeded in neutralizing. Small wonder that James should have failed to master or even understand them.

"The House of Commons," he once protested, in a mood of aggrieved reasonableness, "is a body without a head. The members give their opinions in a disorderly manner. In their meetings nothing is heard but cries, shouts and confusion. I am surprised that my ancestors should ever have permitted such an institution to come into existence. I am a stranger, and found it here when I arrived, so that I am obliged to put up with what I cannot get rid of."*

That James should have had the sense to make a virtue of what must have seemed to him this crazy necessity of working with and through Parliaments, and have done his best to keep within the constitutional limits he found imposed on him, is surely as much as could fairly have been expected of him—and more than might have been expected from almost any other monarch brought up in the Continental tradition.

For the Scottish monarchy, like every other Christian sovereignty outside England, honoured the principles and thought in terms of the Roman Law—that vast, scientific system of ordered human relationships, in which the whole of society is centred in the person of a Divine Caesar or Sovereign, and may be likened to a vast, intricate machine with the main control under the hand of a single operator and with all the friction of centrifugal forces, and of individual rights against the State Almighty, eliminated. Under such a law, representative institutions could no more thrive than they had in imperial Rome ; sooner or later all states were bound to conform to what came to be the eighteenth century model of administrative despotism.

In all except England, because there the native law, the English Common Law, had been tough enough to preserve its independence of Rome, and to impart a unique and original trend to English history. It was this ugly and unpleasant duckling that had confronted James when he entered upon his new inheritance, and it had given no promise of developing into anything swanlike. It was illogical, chaotic, selfish, often oppressive and cruel ; it notoriously favoured the long purse against the short ; it was to all appearance a vast, fortuitous jungle of rights and liberties—a very different thing from liberty—that had

* Gardiner, *History of England*, ii, p. 251.

no other reason for their existence except that, according to the lawyers, they happened to be the law, and that anybody who could fee counsel to establish in the courts his claim to one of them could have the law, to that extent, on all other persons, and even on the State itself. What the Divine Caesar had been to Rome, these imaginary plain but litigious citizens, John Doe and Richard Roe, were to England.

For while Rome sacrificed everything to the efficient working of the State, England sacrificed logic, system and efficiency itself to the rights and privileges, as by law established, of individual men and bodies of men. It was this uncoded and uncodifiable law of which the unwritten contribution was the political aspect, embodying as it did the spirit that had already begun to distinguish England from the nations of the Continent, that was destined in fullness of time to give birth to a free Commonwealth of Nations.

But James, whether or not he was a Solomon, was no Merlin to have forevision of these things, and he had not, like the Tudors, been born with the English tradition in his soul.

III

Prince of Wales

I

KING JAMES THE PEACEMAKER

IT will be seen that James, whose mind had been formed in the Roman or Continental tradition, had started on his adventure of governing England under a handicap that was all the more crippling because he himself was incapable of appreciating it. Even the experience that he had gained in his brilliantly successful rule of Scotland was more calculated to mislead than to guide him aright.

And yet it would be less than half the truth to talk as if on crossing the Border, the ablest of all the Scottish Stuarts had undergone some metamorphosis that transformed him into a mere muddler and maunderer, who could do nothing right on the throne of England. On the contrary, he quickly gave proof of the same cunning in kingcraft, the same insight into the realities of statesmanship, that had served him so well from his adolescence upwards. He at least, and instantly, grasped the essential truth that the one thing to be avoided, at all costs, by an English monarch, was war, or any policy calculated to lead to war. James had come into the heritage of an Anglo-Dutch war against Spain that was already sixteen years old, and showed every sign of becoming chronic. That war, in spite of the desperate parsimony with which Elizabeth had waged it, had already strained the royal resources almost to breaking point, and in fact, it had only been Elizabeth's extraordinary tact and prestige that had prevented the ever-growing aggressiveness of her Parliaments from exploding into open mutiny.

James lost as little time as possible in liquidating this now pointless and profitless war, which he contrived to do on extremely reasonable terms—certainly as good as he could ever have hoped to attain by fighting. And henceforth, until, at the end of his reign, his hand was forced, he set himself, with unwavering determination, not only to secure peace for his own country, but actively to promote it abroad.

In this he had the loyal co-operation of Robert Cecil, Earl of Salisbury, that last upholder of the high Elizabethan tradition, to whom, until his death in 1612, James was wise enough to confide what we should now call the Premiership of his administration. Salisbury was not the last Premier of his name to make a perfectly unsentimental commonsense the guiding principle of his policy ; he was well content if the King's government should be carried on from day to day with quiet efficiency, and he had a temperamental aversion from grandiose schemes of policy. Such a mind was the ideal corrective and supplement to that of a philosophic Stuart.

Never was there a time, with the exception of our own, when England's interests so plainly committed her to seek peace and ensue it. For dire trouble was brewing on the Continent ; in the debatable land of Germany the forces of Reformation and Counter-Reformation were organizing for the supreme struggle that was to make a blood bath of Central Europe. England, now for the first time without a land frontier, with her trade expanding and her shores secure from any serious threat of invasion, had no concern in a European war but to keep out of it, unless it was to prevent it from breaking out at all.

This exactly expresses James's state of mind, and explains his persistent efforts not only to keep the peace himself, but to act the part of peacemaker. He believed that it would be possible, now that he had got peace with Spain, to revert to the time-honoured English policy of friendly collaboration with her ; and to secure the King of Spain's daughter as a bride for his son, first Henry, and after him, Charles. With his own daughter married to a Protestant German Prince, this would have put James in the best possible position for acting as mediator between the rival faiths.

The Spanish Court gave him every reason to believe that an Infanta might be had—on conditions. That was just the rub, for the conditions comprised at the very least the toleration of the Catholics in England. Nor did they even stop short there, for it is not the way of Rome to compromise with heretic bridegrooms, and it was stipulated, at the outset, that the young Prince must be sent to Spain to be educated as a Catholic, though in subsequent negotiations it was the prospective children's education that was stipulated for. What Rome wanted was a Catholic King on the throne of England, actively determined to bring back the country into the true fold ; and in the end—though not through a Spanish marriage—Rome was to get her way, for three years.

Neither James nor Cecil were bigots, and they would have been only too pleased to turn Catholic recusants into loyal subjects by giving them a fair deal. But they were contending with emotional forces whose strength James, at least, was incapable of gauging, and it was not long before these forces received such an increment of strength as to put them out of all possible control. If James could only have got the Pope to meet him half-way by confirming the allegiance of his Catholic subjects, a start might have been made, but His Holiness was nervously afraid of going too far with heretics, and James, touched on his most sensitive point, fell back on the enforcement of what amounted to martial law against potential rebels. These reprisals —and it must be remembered that they did not stop short at martyrdom—provoked some Catholic extremists to the great attempted counter-reprisal of the Gunpowder Plot. The effect on popular opinion was to harden prejudice into obsession. To the ordinary John Bull, Rome now signified these three things ; the fires of Smithfield, the Spanish Armada, and Gunpowder Treason. James himself, who after all had most reason to complain of the activities of Guy Fawkes, was sensible enough to distinguish between a handful of desperado conspirators and the whole body of his Catholic subjects ; but with obsession you cannot argue, and the very idea of concession to Catholics was enough to start a panic. And of all Catholics, those of Spain were singled out for special detestation. Spain, with her Inquisition and her Armada, her measureless wealth, and her unconquered armies, was viewed in the light of a natural enemy, and not only that, but an enemy with treasures to be plundered and pirated ; one who, in fact, could be profitably assailed in the Lord's name.

If James had been an absolute monarch, able to play his pieces at will on the diplomatic board, and had an Anglo-Spanish Entente, with toleration for Catholics, been capable of realization, it might have been the means of assuring, for a long time to come, that peace without which there was no chance for monarchy in England. But, as things were, not only was the project chimerical, but its pursuit constituted a dangerous defiance of public opinion. Prince Henry, with his instinctive sense of such tendencies, hit it off by saying that two religions could not lie in one bed.

All the same, it could be pleaded for James that even if no

marriage were ever to eventuate, the long, fitful negotiations for it had the effect of keeping the wire with Madrid, as Bismarck would have put it, uncut, and thus of preserving the peace. So long as nothing in particular continued to happen, nothing could better have suited England's book. It was only a forward policy, and not one of marking time, that she had to dread. Any diplomacy that kept the peace was more enlightened than a popular prejudice that lusted for war.

It was only after Prince Henry's death, that Charles, as heir to the throne, became the prospective bridegroom for what his father persisted in believing to be a not impossible Infanta, though at first James had toyed with the idea of a French princess for him. But eleven years were to pass before the affair came to a crisis, and meanwhile troubles had begun to thicken round the path of monarchy.

It is only too easy to explain James's failure to make the success of his English that he had of his Scottish rule, on one of two grounds—either that he was incompetent, or that his task was impossible. The latter certainly comes nearer to being the truth, but whether or not there was a way of working the dual sovereignty of a King who governed, and a Parliament that controlled, it can hardly be argued that it was the way in which James chose to walk.

And yet his failure, such as it was, was most often that of an enlightened policy to prevail over the opposition of selfish or narrow minds. So far as we can talk of a right or wrong in history, James was right in his passionate constancy to the cause of peace ; he was obviously right in seeking to effect a complete union of his two kingdoms—a project that was wrecked on the greedy nationalism of the English mercantile interest. His attempt to find a religious *via media* between Catholic and Calvinist intransigence is one that will commend itself to most modern minds ; and there are some, at least, who will hold that any failure of his to conciliate the rival extremists is more than balanced by his success in promoting that Authorized Translation of the Bible, with which his name is not unworthily associated.

But yet, though he succeeded in carrying on without any serious disaster, and though under the peace that he kept, the country throve and prospered as much, probably, as it had done under any of his predecessors, he failed to do more than to preserve, outwardly intact, the edifice of kingly power, while its foundations were being undermined. It was something that he even succeeded in doing as much, seeing that his relations with his Parliaments were those of ominous and ever-increasing friction ; but so long as he steered clear of war, they had not the chance of getting a strangle grip upon his throat.

Nevertheless, after six years of haggling and bickering with the first of them, he and Salisbury did come forward with a bold and constructive proposal for an arrangement that would have provided the Crown with a small, but fixed income, in return for the abandonment of a number of vexatious feudal dues, and a compromise over the customs revenues. The bargain was to all intents and purposes concluded, and its final ratification left over to an Autumn Session, but by that time the Commons had changed their mind and decided to go back on their own decision, rather than come to any settlement whose effect would be to prolong the *status quo*. It was only too evident from this time forward, that nothing short of a constitutional revolution would bring lasting satisfaction to His Majesty's Faithful Commons.

So ended, in open rupture, the King's first and longest Parliament.

2

UNSTABLE EQUILIBRIUM

SALISBURY's death in 1612 marks the real close of the Elizabethan and of the Tudor age, the retirement of Shakespeare and the issue of the Authorized Version of the Bible having taken place in the previous year. The great Cecil administration, the longest and most successful that England has ever enjoyed, had at last come to an end. And even that administration had signally failed to solve the constitutional problem. The Scottish King, who could hardly speak the language, and who had already been forced, in despair, to get rid of the first and longest of his Parliaments, was left to carry on his government with such men as he could find, and to adjust his relations, within the framework of the existing Constitution, with this rival sovereign power in the state, that was plainly resolved not to co-operate with him on any terms whatever.

What could he do but play, as he did play, for time ? For ten years, that oddly enough have never been stigmatized by the term "Tyranny", he contrived to carry on the business of the nation with such an administrative team as he had to hand, without resort to arms, to taxation, or to Parliaments, except for one that was so plainly bent on mischief that it had to be sent home within a few weeks of its coming together. The country remained quiet and, presumably, satisfied, since there was as yet no propagandist machinery capable of working up discontent to a revolutionary head. So long as the King continued to live quietly of his own, the common Englishman, in normal times, desired nothing better, and so long as his own pockets were not touched, harboured no grievance against his Sovereign for now and then raising the wind by such anticipations of modern practice as providing snobs, for cash down, with handles to their names. Nor does he even appear to have made very heavy weather about a court life that gossip alleged to be neither edifying nor dignified. So long as His Majesty continued to pay the piper, he was welcome to call what tune he liked behind his own doors.

If any one had a grievance, it was not the common man, but those territorial magnates whose estates were charged with various petty but immemorial contributions to the royal income, and financiers who found the activities of the customs officers irksome —the plutocratic upper crust that, almost exclusively, was represented in Parliament. But so long as the King could contrive to make both ends meet without resource to the tax collector, there was nothing much that these malcontents could do about it, except grumble and bide their time for the opportunity that was bound to come sooner or later.

For nobody can have realized better than the canny old monarch himself that his policy of spinning out time was one of desperation. But what else could the King of England do ? He was like a man clinging to some foothold on a cliff face, who can continue to survive so long as he keeps perfectly still, but who, unless he can climb up or climb down to comparatively safe ground, is bound, sooner or later, to topple headlong. To climb up—after the example of practically all his fellow Sovereigns on the Continent—would have meant a standing army, and of this, even if such a thing had been possible, the ultra-pacific James, of all people, would never have dreamed. But to climb down—and that was the inescapable truth that the experience of every Parliament rubbed in with more and more brutal emphasis— meant nothing less than abdication of all but the style and trappings of royal sovereignty : abdication not to the people, but to a wealthy minority of what we should now know as "the best people". Never from first to last, was there the faintest hint that any compromise short of this would have satisfied the Parliamentary leaders, who as such, though they might be different persons in each successive House of Commons, pursued one unswerving line that in process of time became more and more consciously set towards revolution.

King James had admittedly no better solution to offer than to scrape along somehow, from hand to mouth, without Parliamentary assistance, trusting in the one great resource that the Crown possessed in the shape of a customs revenue that continued to expand with the prosperity of the country, and in such barely lawful expedients as that of touting—and through the judges of all people !—for voluntary assistance : how voluntary will be realized from the fate of one obstinate non-subscriber whom James, an incurable humorist, caused to foot-slog in his train, through August dust, all the way from Carlisle to London. He also contrived to raise a certain amount by the sale of honours and titles, which, though a commonplace of modern politics, was not, in those days, calculated to enhance the credit of royalty in any but a financial sense.

But with all this, it proved impossible to make income balance expenditure. Debt began to accumulate, and to approach what was then the formidable figure of three quarters of a million, which James had neither the means of paying, nor of handing on to posterity in the fashion of a later age. It was necessary to seek ways and means of economizing even on a peace time basis, and to put some stop to the waste and peculation that were rampant in high places. James had the happy and novel idea of entrusting the new broom to the hands of a self-made business man, Lionel Cranfield, who used it to clean up one department after another of his administration. The results were astonishing. The deficit was changed to a surplus, and the King was able to last out the second decade of the century without bankruptcy or resource to Parliament. The corner had apparently been turned, and there seemed no reason why the normal expenses of government should not continue to be met out of its normal income. But not even a Cranfield could conceivably go beyond this, or balance accounts on any but a normal, which is the same thing as a peace time basis.

Even so, the whole state of affairs was thoroughly unsatisfactory.

Co-operation between King and Parliament had completely broken down ; and the monarchy was now driven to the sad resource of living like an invalid, on a starvation diet, and unable to get up or take the least extra exertion, for fear of precipitating a collapse. That this was an equally bad thing, or a bad thing at all, for the country, it would be hard to prove. Quietness is the mother of prosperity, especially in an island state without frontiers.

It would have been well for James if he could have kept himself as well as his realm quiet, instead of going out of his way to affront the prejudices of his English subjects by the logical consistency with which he would keep deducing the consequences of his admitted status as the Lord's Anointed. It is merely inept to talk as if this were some special fad or obsession of James himself ; there was probably not a sovereign in Europe, or out of it, for that matter, to whom the idea of Divine Right was not both familiar and fundamental. It was as old as Rome, the keystone of whose arch of Empire had been her Divine Caesar. It was no new thing even in England ; Elizabeth had gone about everywhere expecting and receiving the worship of a goddess— England's Gloriana. But Elizabeth, being an Englishwoman, regarded words as you might bridges, which can take the strain of a passing pageant, but would certainly break down under that of a logical edifice. James knew of no such limitations ; he kept rubbing in the consequences of his Divine Kingship to his Parliament, in a way that these English gentlemen, who had not got to the point of denying it in the abstract, felt, in their English way, was not playing the game. And as with a husband and wife, so with a King and his subjects, the fiercest quarrel is not to be dreaded so much as the habit of daily and mutual irritation.

Both in the figurative and the literal sense, King and subjects talked a different language. Every time James opened his mouth, his broad Scots accent proclaimed him a foreigner in his own realm. It was only human that, like his great-grandson William of Orange, he should wish to have compatriots of his own about him, and that he should like to have posts in his administration filled by men he could understand and work with. But whether or not kings are divine, it is the burden of their office that they cannot always afford to be human. The spectacle of these alien immigrants diverting the golden stream of royal favour into their own pockets was calculated to bring into play a love of country the opposite to that of King.

And when every allowance is made for the almost hopeless nature of James's task, and his handicaps of nationality and up-bringing, we are forced to acknowledge that his wisdom and statesmanship were marred, more and more as the years went on, by a certain twist or kink in his nature, which probably dated from his infancy, or even from before his birth, but which became far more pronounced in the latter, or English, phase of his career ; like some obscure malady that, having lain dormant for a long time, gradually begins to infect the entire system. The simile is the more apposite, when we remember that physically, James, in the declining years of his life, was a very sick man. During his successful rule in Scotland, his strength had been reasonably adequate, but it was perhaps the luxury that he was able to command in England, and his own self-indulgence, that caused his physical system to break up under the complication of maladies that we have already described. Such physical degeneration might be expected to bring to the surface any mental or moral defects that had hitherto been incubating beneath it.

His native shrewdness and wisdom remained unimpaired to the last, but he more and more lacked the will power, the guts, as we might say, to implement them. He grew flabby. Knowing, as he must have done, that his most vital need of all was to reduce expenditure, he was weakly and good-naturedly extravagant, and before the coming of Cranfield, he completely failed to check the leakage and extravagance that deducted several shillings from the net value of every pound that came into his treasury. It is true that such wastage was nothing to be compared with that of the cheapest war, but at a time of chronic deficits and mounting debt, it was serious enough.

There was another weakness that was even more serious than the extravagance for which it partly accounted. For James, though a kind and indulgent husband, had an incurable pro-pensity for passionate friendship with members of his own sex. It would be as unwarranted as it would be prurient to assume that there was anything more criminal in these relationships than in that of Shakespeare to Mr W. H. of the Sonnets. For anyone like a king, to whom all professions of attachment must be necessarily suspect, the desire to break out through the encircling loneliness and to give and receive affection must be pathetically strong. And with James there appears to have been something else, that we can best describe as a craving for vitality. It was as if he had a need for recharging like an exhausted battery, by contact with some superior source of energy. The more his bodily infirmities accumulated upon him, the greater became his compensating delight in the loveliness and lustiness of youth, as if it were possible for him to possess in another what he most lacked in himself.

The craving was therefore one that grew upon him with advancing years. In his Scottish days, it had been no more than a comparatively innocuous private foible, which he had had sufficiently under control. It was only in England that it developed into a public nuisance gross enough to endanger both the solvency and prestige of the Crown.

At the time of James's accession, the chief, though not the sole, object of these affections was a certain James Hay, whom he had brought with him from Scotland, and who eventually rose, step by step, to the Earldom of Carlisle. He was a thoroughly amiable young fellow, with such a gift of making himself popular that even the English prejudice against Scots was relaxed in his favour. He had, however, one besetting weakness, which he had certainly not picked up at home, but which he may have acquired during his apprenticeship as a courtier in Paris. He was the most magnificent of dandies, and after the fashion of dandies, magnificently extravagant. It not only demanded a princely fortune to keep him in clothes, but also in food. On one occasion he went so far as to invite a large company of friends to sit down to a board, groaning under innumerable dishes of the most exquisite and costly cold confections ; but before they had had time to feast more than their eyes, an army of servants swept down, like harpies, and whisked all away, substituting at the same time for every dish, its exact replica, only hot.

It may well be asked where this almost penniless young gentleman, who had come to seek his fortune at court, could find the means to raise this tremendous wind. The answer is supplied by Clarendon, who credits him with "having spent, in a very jovial life, above four hundred thousand pounds, which, upon a strict computation he received from the Crown." Four hundred thousand ! Considerably more than half the long accumulated debt, that, but for Cranfield's economies, would have broken the back of the royal finances !

That was bad enough, but worse was to follow. Hay, though a ruinously expensive luxury, was a good-hearted fellow, who developed into a reasonably competent diplomatic servant, and continued to bask in the sunshine of royal favour even after his place as favourite-in-chief had been taken by another young Scottish gentleman, who had also received his finishing at Paris, and who, as a page at court, had had the good luck to fall off his mount and break his arm in the King's presence. This Robert Carr, who rose in six brief years to be Earl of Somerset and the most powerful person in the realm, was of an altogether lower type from that of his predecessor. Beneath his veneer of courtly polish, he was a greedy, uncultured adventurer, who talked the broadest Scots, and had to be taught Latin by James in person.

Carr was incapable of running straight, even in prosperity, and his career closed in one of the most monstrous scandals of all time. He had already shocked public opinion by wooing and winning the girl wife of the young Earl of Essex, after the cynical farce of a nullity suit, and thus securing an alliance with the great Catholic House of Howard. It was only later that it came out how the bride had followed up this success by the cold-blooded poisoning of Carr's familiar friend, Sir Thomas Overbury, who had been honest enough to warn him against such a union. How far the Earl was privy, before or after the fact, to his wife's proceedings, is to this day doubtful ; but he, like her, was convicted of murder, and sentenced to the fate that had already overtaken the small fry of the conspiracy. The man whom the King had delighted to honour—it made no difference that the sentence was commuted to imprisonment—stood branded in the public eye as the most odious criminal in his realm. The effect of the trial in damaging the prestige of Royalty can only be compared to that of the Diamond Necklace case before the French Revolution.

This was in 1616, and James had still nine years to live. It remained to be seen whether he would find it possible to make a choice even more disastrous than that of his previous two favourites.

3

THE AMATEUR HERO

During the time of Somerset's ascendancy we hear very little of the reserved, tongue-tied boy who was now heir to the throne. What effect on him had that court life, whose meaty exuberance

reminds us so vividly of the sort of thing described by Rabelais ?
How did he react to his father's grotesque personality ? And what
effect on him had the spectacle of the upstart Somerset lording it
at court as if he were greater than the King ?

Direct evidence fails us ; for Charles had already learnt the
secret, that he never forgot, of keeping his own counsel. But his
character itself reveals what he never put into words, in its
fastidious refinement, its abhorrence, as Clarendon puts it, of
"all deboshry," everything, that is to say, gross and Rabelaisian.
His own court, when he came to have the running of it, became
the exact opposite of his father's, as if he wished to tear that very
memory out of his mind. Such a fast set as that of Frances Essex
would have been no more tolerated by him than it would by
Queen Victoria ; it was more than any man dared to fire off a
spicy joke in his presence, and as for drunkenness, the very idea
of it disgusted him. His deportment, too, was as aloof in its dignity
as that of James had been incontinent in its familiarity. If we
consider how different is this more than feminine delicacy from
the common form of kingship at that, or in previous times, we can
hardly fail to deduce a subconscious aversion from his youthful
environment, so deeply planted as to have become lifelong.

But the environment of both father and son was about to be
transformed by the intrusion of a new and compelling influence.
The last and greatest of the favourites had already come into
view, when the star of Somerset was still not perceptibly beyond
its zenith. This one was at last English, but he conformed to
precedent in being the needy scion of a good family, the Villiers
of Leicestershire, and in having been polished up in the inevitable
Paris, before coming to court to seek his fortune. One story has
it that when the King first picked him up, on a race-course in
Cambridgeshire, he was literally out at elbows. We know, at any
rate, that however it started, his progress was rapid and continuous.

There was more in George Villiers than a mere courtier on the
make. He was the sort of youth who would have been bound to
come to the fore in any active walk of life. To translate him into
modern terms, he would have been if not the head boy, at least
the athletic champion of his school, and the unchallenged leader
of university society. Extremely tall and, by all portraits and
accounts, a beautiful creature, both of face and form, he overflowed with a vitality that, while he was still unspoilt, was

invincibly good-humoured. He became a veritable playboy of the court, delighting to join with the gentlemen-in-waiting after supper in leaping and all kinds of horseplay. His charm seems to have taken almost every one by storm : the great Earl of Pembroke, the worthy nephew of Sir Philip Sidney, took him under his wing ; the literary Countess of Bedford honoured him with her patronage ; even Archbishop Abbot talked of "my George" as his son, and gave him fatherly advice. The Queen, who had at first very sensibly warned her husband against the dangers of turning the young man's head, was soon carrying on an elderly flirtation with her "kind dog," as she now called him.

There was only one person who remained impervious ; and that, it need hardly be said, was Somerset. It was not the fault of Villiers, who, so far from trying to oust the reigning favourite, very humbly waited upon him with an offer of faithful service. All the thanks that he got was :

"I will have none of your service, and you shall have none of my favour. I will, if I can, break your neck, and of that be confident."

Even so, Villiers seems to have been too good-natured to join in a neck-breaking competition, and when, shortly afterwards, Somerset fell, it was with no assistance of his ; he even, with notable magnanimity, refused to accept one of his forfeited estates, which had been forfeited before by Sir Walter Raleigh, on the ground that he would not found his fortunes in the ruin of another.

Such was the splendid young man in whom James, declining towards a premature old age, thought that he had at last discovered the ideal friend and confidential assistant he had failed to make of Somerset. With the curious streak of the pedagogue there was in him, he believed he could educate mind and character, so as to form the perfect instrument of his own wisdom. And always there was that pathetic desire of his to love and to be loved : "I am neither a god nor an angel," he once said, "but a man like any other, and confess that I love those dear to me more than other men. You may be sure that I love the Earl of Buckingham (as Villiers then was) more than anyone else." He called him Steenie, because of Stephen in the Bible, whose countenance had resembled that of an angel.

In an extraordinarily short time, he had exalted his new favourite to dizzier heights than any of his predecessors. Within little more than three years from the time that plain George Villiers had worn his battered black coat at Newmarket, he was a Marquis, with a string of other titles. Five years more sufficed to make him a Duke, fabulously rich, and the most powerful subject in the country since the fall of Wolsey—all this, not on account of any educational or statesmanlike qualifications, but in sole virtue of his good looks and captivating personality.

There was still, besides that of the King and Queen, one conquest for him to make of much greater difficulty. For the mere fact of his success with the father might have seemed a decisive bar against any chance he might have had with the son. A favourite—and such a favourite !—was hardly likely to be viewed with favourable eyes by the heir to the throne ; even if the Prince had not already been inclined to react adversely against anything associated with his father's way of life. But the death of his elder brother had left a void in Charles's heart such as adolescent nature abhors. There was no big brother now to take the overflow of his repressed affections, and his reserved disposition did not easily make contacts. But here, in this new companion, was an even more attractive version of what Henry had been ; what the successful, popular elder boy has always been to the diffident junior, be he prince, be he urchin, whom he takes under his wing. There is something in his relation to Charles that reminds us of that of Steerforth to David Copperfield—even though Villiers was now past twenty.

But it was not an easy or an instant conquest ; in fact it would seem as if, at first, Charles was inclined to react violently against the influence of his father's new favourite. There were quarrels, trivial in themselves, like those of schoolboys, but none the less significant. We hear of a valuable ring, which the Prince somehow managed to transfer from one of Villiers's big fingers to his own smaller one, and which he consequently soon managed to lose. Poor George's usually serene spirits were enough damped by the loss for the King to notice it, and the result was such a wigging as reduced Charles to tears. However the invaluable Sir Robert Carey was as equal to this as he was to every other occasion, and a search through His Highness's pockets soon put the matter to rights.

And then we have the only instance in which Charles is known to have indulged in a practical joke, or indeed, a joke of any kind. There was, in the garden of Greenwich Palace, a fountain statue of Bacchus, made to spout by pressing a spring, which the Prince did with such timely accuracy as to direct the current full in the favourite's face. This time James was sufficiently roused to give his son two hearty boxes on the ear.

At another time it was Villiers's turn to be taught that there were limits beyond which even friendship could not go. The two young fellows had been ragging together for the possession of some weapon, and Villiers, losing his temper, had not only sworn at the Prince, but even raised his hand in a threatening manner. But Charles, in a very quiet voice, had merely said, "What, my Lord, I think you intend to strike me"—which had been enough to deflate the assurance even of such a companion.

Such incidents, which can have lost nothing in the telling, were enough to convince the Court gossips that all chance of friendship between Prince and favourite was now ruled out; but they were wrong. These petty quarrels were almost necessary incidents in the building up of a friendship between natures so diverse. They left no wounds. And even to Charles, Villiers could be very useful, as we gather from an undated letter in which his aid is solicited in the probably not too difficult task of getting James to overlook some offence he had taken at his son's conduct.

It was not long before the friction of temperaments was finally eliminated, and the possibly unique spectacle witnessed of a Sovereign and his heir linked in bonds of affection equally strong with the selfsame privileged favourite. Charles did not express his love with the undignified effusiveness of James, but once given, it was given without reserve. From George Villiers, or Buckingham, to give him his more familiar title, it was never withdrawn, and with it went a boundless trust. The brilliant creature, in his friend's eyes, could do no wrong; he was fit to be entrusted with the destinies of a kingdom. Which was a tragic belief, since, if ever a man was fitted to play the part of evil genius to his Sovereign and country, that man was Buckingham.

This is not to say that he was a worse man than those other favourites who had already done so much to undermine the prestige of the Crown. On the contrary, he stood head and shoulders above the best of them, in moral even more conspicuously than in physical stature. Somerset, and even Carlisle, were from first to last pushers and climbers, whose highest ambition consisted in the successful exploitation of the royal bounty. Buckingham, indeed, did this more successfully than either of them, but the wealth and power he acquired were like Cecil Rhodes's millions, not the goal but the gate of the quest, the necessary means to the realization of great public ends.

"The young hero" was what anyone, who had come under his influence, might have called Buckingham. For there was a magnificence about him, a careless generosity, a laughing courage, that bore the heroic stamp. His brain was prolific of vast projects. As a statesman, as a soldier, even as an Admiral—though he had no more practical experience of seamanship than Gilbert's Ruler of the Queen's Navee—he had a wider vision than ordinary men, a *flair* for brilliant combinations, and an infectious self-confidence that is one secret of leadership. He who had risen, in so few years, from nothing to the utmost summit of greatness ; who had in his keeping the heart not only of his present but of his coming Sovereign ; who enjoyed still the plentitude of his youthful vigour—what might he not, with such boundless opportunities, have been expected to achieve ?

But about this kind of greatness there is one fatal defect, in the very easiness of its achievement. Buckingham's good looks and vitality had been a talisman, that had turned everything he had touched to gold. In his conquest of James's facile affections, in his rise at court, he had encountered no serious resistance, nothing calculated in any sufficient degree to test his grit or concentration. Was it not inevitable that a young man, with such an experience of life, should have unconsciously come to generalize from it, and to imagine that all walls would fall flat at the mere sound of his trumpet ; that he should in consequence, when he framed those brilliant schemes of his, have habitually underestimated the difficulties they would have to encounter, and, when such difficulties presented themselves, have lacked the qualifications for overcoming them ?

Writers of fiction, and even of fact, are apt to give a dangerously misleading account of heroism. They leave out the whole element of its spadework ; they convey the impression of a Hop-o'-my-Thumb, with seven-league boots, striding along the mountains from summit to summit, instead of an expert climber, descending into the valleys, and then, with pain and sweat, winning his way, foot by foot, back to the heights. It is not the writers who are to blame, so much as average human nature, that demands an easy hero. For most men achieve heroism in their dreams ; most men are secretly convinced that they have it in them to be great, and that only the luck of circumstances has prevented them from realizing it. They love to see the great captain, calm on the battlefield, ordering the decisive manœuvre ; to see the statesman bringing off some dazzling coup of policy— they can so easily imagine themselves in either situation. But to follow the sordid and technical detail of the daily grind that alone made success possible, would be too discouraging. The ordinary man cannot visualize himself as that kind of hero, perhaps would not even want to achieve heroism on terms so unromantically hard.

Now the sort of greatness after which Buckingham aspired was that of the ordinary man's dream world. He had no idea of shunning delights and living laborious days in its pursuit ; he was one of those spoilt children of life who believe that life will go on spoiling them forever. It is the tragic destiny of such men to fail in their most splendidly conceived projects. Something always goes wrong in the working, that makes the difference between triumph and disaster. And yet it is so easy to show, in theory, that nothing but sheer ill luck robbed them of success. Their lives are the happy hunting grounds of apologists.

The defects incidental to such a temperament, and such a rise, as Buckingham's, were not long in making themselves apparent. To use one of the most expressive of undergraduate phrases, he got above himself. He believed that everything had got to give way to his will, and even to his whim. In spite of his laughing good-nature, he could not bear to be crossed in the least matter. He would go to all lengths to crush or annihilate anyone, great or small, who dared to offer him direct opposition, though he could be the soul of generosity to a properly humbled enemy. Nor, in the first blush of his splendour, was there anything that could possibly disillusion him. Throughout the length and breadth of the land, his will appeared to be law. The greatest, the most intractable magnates, crawled for his favours. The Chancellor Bacon employed his consummate literary talents in wheedling his good graces ; the ex-Chief Justice Coke, who had braved the King himself, was ready to force his own daughter into a hated marriage in order to ally himself with Buckingham. The whole of the royal patronage was, in fact, at the disposal of this irresponsible young man. He set up one and put down another at his sovereign caprice.

At the court of James it followed, as a matter of course, that

Buckingham should exploit his advantage, so as to supplement an already princely income. He was not venal, according to the standards of the time ; he was genuinely anxious to get the right men into the right posts, and he could be magnificently disinterested on occasion ; but he expected to have his favours made worth his while. He thus became the focus of a vast system of corruption, in which a number of courtiers made a handsome profit by acting as middlemen between the great man and his suitors. Nor was this the worst, for a man may part with his money without losing his soul ; but with Buckingham money was never the main object, and he could not endure that any man should have a conscience or a will independent of his dictatorship. To this every other consideration had to give way : a man might be of never so great value to the State, but the wages of independence were political extinction.

It might not have been so bad if Buckingham, like his great contemporary, Cardinal Richelieu, had been able to identify his own fortunes absolutely with those of the State. But unfortunately he was hardly less loyal a member of the Villiers family than he was a patriot, and he never forgot what he owed to the very capable and pushing mother who had launched him on his court career. All his brothers and relations were expected to share in his good fortune, and all other considerations had to yield to that of their advancement.

What sort of a tyranny this implied may be judged from the treatment of the invaluable Cranfield, the man whose economies had, in the nick of time, staved off financial collapse. Cranfield, like Dick Whittington, had been the poor but well spoken apprentice who had married his employer's daughter, and so thriven that he had risen to the affluence and dignity of a great London merchant. But now his first wife was dead, and the widower, on the full tide of worldly success, was planning a less romantic union with the mature, but important widow of Lord Howard of Effingham. This, however, did not happen to suit the book of Buckingham's mother, who had a pretty but penniless cousin to settle in life as Lady Cranfield. The merchant statesman was at first inclined to jib at this second compulsory romance, and to carry on with his courtship of the widow. It was the unforgivable sin. Things began to go wrong with Cranfield : he was due to be a Privy Councillor, but no summons came to the Board. In a few months' time he had learned his lesson, and, with a no doubt aching heart, consented to throw over wealth and the Howard alliance for the simple charm of Anne Brett. For a second time in his life he discovered how romance can be the foundation of prosperity, for it was not long before Anne found herself Countess of Middlesex.

Thus had King James and his heir added to the English monarchy a super-king, with royal family complete.

4

"SEDITIOUS FELLOWS"

IT was in 1621, the year that Charles came of age—Buckingham being then twenty-nine—that James, who had, save for those few barren weeks in 1614, carried on without Parliamentary assistance, took the momentous step of summoning the third Parliament of his reign.

It was a move that could no longer be postponed, for now the clouds, that had so long been gathering over Central Europe, had burst ; the great Catholic counter-offensive had been launched, and the Reformation was fighting for its life against odds that might well prove overwhelming. No wonder that sentiment in Protestant England was inflamed to the height of war fever.

For James and his son, not only the national interest, but family honour was at stake. It will be remembered how the King's only other surviving child, the charming Elizabeth, had been married to a German Prince, Frederick, Elector Palatine, who stood for the left, or Calvinist wing, of the German Protestant interest. This young man had committed one of those acts of light-hearted folly, of which history affords more than one instance, and which let loose hell upon earth. In that old, religious storm-centre of Europe, the Slav country of Bohemia, the obvious intention of its Hapsburg overlords to win back all for Rome had excited first unrest, and then open mutiny. By an excited mob of nobles, two ministers of the Emperor Matthias had been pushed out through one of the lofty windows in the Hradcany at Prague, to fall on to a muck heap in the moat, and escape, miraculously, with no more than a few minor contusions. As if this were not

enough, these nobles proceeded, on the accession of the new
Emperor Ferdinand II a year later, to declare the Bohemian
crown elective, and then to elect Frederick, who, not without
the enthusiastic approval of his young wife, proceeded to accept
the fatal gift, and thus to fling down the most outrageous defiance
that could be imagined to the great, Spanish-Austrian Hapsburg
family entente. Not for the last time it became a question of
whether the control of Prague should go to an Axis or an International. Only this time the Axis was constituted by the Austrian-
Spanish-Catholic alliance under the imperial House of Hapsburg ; and the International was the Protestant Islam whose
prophet founder had been Jean Calvin, and whose Mecca was
his holy city by the Lake of Geneva. It was a gamble against a
certainty, for even with the forces of Bohemia added to those of
the Rhineland, Frederick had not the least chance of withstanding the leagued armies of the Counter Reformation. Even
while he was lording it uneasily in his new kingdom, his Rhineland principality was being invaded by Spanish troops from the
west, and Bavarians from the south-east. The Catholics had
spoken of him as the Winter King, but it was not until the Autumn
of 1620, just over a year after he had embarked on his insane
venture, that the Imperial army, of seasoned, professional
soldiers, arrived outside Prague, and easily dispersed the armed
mob that was all Frederick could bring out to oppose them. The
new King and Queen were lucky to get away, not to their own
Palatinate, from which they were cut off, but to a homeless exile.
And the long-expected contest of faiths, in Germany, had opened
with a shattering blow at the Protestant cause.

That frightful and futile struggle, known as the Thirty Years'
War, whose result was to put back the clock of German civilization for at least a century, and to make clear the ultimate path
for Prussian militarism, was now fairly launched. As State after
State got sucked into the maelstrom, it became less and less a
conflict of principle, religious or otherwise, and more and more
an abominable competition in murder, rape and devastation,
for the most sordid ends of policy.

Looking back on it now, we can see that, for England, there
was but one sane or safe policy, which was to stay peacefully at
home behind her encircling sea, and refuse, on any consideration
whatever, to sacrifice an English life or a pound sterling in a
contest in which her prospective gains were nil, and losses un-

limited. The man in all England who most clearly realized this truth, was King James.

Thus was raised the question that was by far the most momentous of all those presented to the first two Stuarts and their subjects—was England to be dragged into armed intervention in what was to lengthen itself out into the Thirty Years' War ? But the real issue at stake was more fundamental—was England to be regarded as a power and personality sufficient unto herself, or as a mere unit in a wider entity ? Had she ceased to be a province (or formally two provinces) in the Empire of a spiritual Caesar, merely to assume membership in an as yet informal federation of leagued Protestant sovereignties ? Was patriotism enough ? Or was ideology more ?

The Stuarts may have had little English blood in them. King Charles was half Scot and half Dane ; his father was a quarter French, and may not inconceivably have been half Italian.* Royalty was the most cosmopolitan of all human breeds. But it was the *métier* of the Sovereign, irrespective of his blood, to be the representative man of whatever people fate had called him to rule over. And in intent and practice, these first two Stuarts were as uncompromisingly national as the Tudors themselves. Their policy was an out-and-out English policy. Their Church— which is as good as to say their ideology—was neither that of Rome nor Geneva. They were, in fact, a great deal too national for those of their subjects who were (or found it convenient to pose as being) good Protestants or Catholics before they were good patriots. King James started his reign by being nearly blown up by the extremists of one ideology ; King Charles ended his by being publicly butchered by those of the other.

Now King James, though as staunch a Protestant, according to his lights, as the most fanatical of his subjects, had not the faintest desire to enlist himself in the service of a Calvinist Jehovah by persecution at home, and still less by war overseas. In practical policy he was ideologically neutral. He desired at all costs to keep himself and his country out of trouble. If England could thrive by peaceful trade while her rivals were immolating themselves and each other in an all-in combat of all against all, so much the

---

* "Solomon, thou son of David" was the taunt that some of his Scottish subjects had flung at King James. His reputed father, Lord Darnley, would not, I fancy, have considered it misplaced. The surname of this David had been Rizzio.

better for England, and for the English monarchy to which war on any serious scale would be certainly fatal.

Poor James has had a terrible time at the hands of the historians, for the many shifts and indecisions of his European policy at this time. They are all agreed that he ought to have acted in some very firm and decisive way, instead of talking and negotiating endlessly to no very great apparent effect. Unfortunately it is no good being firm and decisive, unless your words have force in reserve to make them good, and unless your force has money in reserve to make that good. James had neither. He had no army, and hardly enough money—if that—to foot his peace time expenses. For any more that he might want he must find means of loosening the close fist of his Parliament, which meant exposing himself to ruthless blackmail for the most exiguous returns.

Talk and negotiation, even if they only mark time, are at least cheap and bloodless, and merely to have kept on talking was to have gained—or perhaps we should say to have avoided—the whole battle. Besides, the issues, as they must have presented themselves to so subtle an intelligence as that of James, were far from simple. For in this year, 1621, in addition to the German War, the Dutch Republic had resumed its struggle with a Spain for which it was now something more than a match. And the Dutch were not only incomparably more formidable seamen than the Spaniards, but they were becoming a more serious menace to English trade. The situation in Elizabeth's time on the Spanish Main was now reproduced in the Indian Ocean. Two Companies, English and Dutch, were competing for the trade of the coveted East Indies, and the Dutch Company, many times more highly capitalized, succeeded in driving out its rivals—not without bloodshed and massacre—forcing them to gather what crumbs of trade they could from the potentates of the Indian Peninsula, and thus to plant the seeds of the British Indian Empire. Even in home waters, the Dutch were beginning to encroach more and more menacingly on the English fishing preserves. Sooner or later the answer to these disputed questions would have to be spoken through the cannon's mouth.

But to the people of England, and above all to their representatives in Parliament, the European crisis was one of melodramatic simplicity. God was at issue with the Devil; the crusading spirit was abroad. To James, his son-in-law may have been a thorough nuisance, who, in the teeth of his father-in-law's advice, had brought his troubles upon his own head ; but Protestant sentiment in England had made a Christian hero of him, and the woes of his beautiful English wife were matters of universal concern. And yet it was at least doubtful how deep the average Englishman was prepared to put his hand into his pocket in such a cause. He had his own notions of a war for Christ and His Gospel, a war of plunder on the good old Elizabethan model, against the arch-enemy, Spain. Such was his fixed hatred of the Spaniard, that he was ready to wink at the most flagrant aggression and outrage committed by the Dutch, as if the fact of these hard-bitten realists being Protestant and anti-Spanish were excuse for everything they had ever done or ever could do to English shipping and seamen.

James had quite different notions. He clung more than ever to his idea of an Anglo-Spanish entente. He knew that the Spanish monarchy, with its diminishing resources, was in no condition to embark on a holy war for the extirpation of heresy, and that its desire for peace was perfectly sincere. By working on this common need of the two countries, it might be possible for him to use his friendship with the Hapsburgs of Madrid, in order to exert a restraining influence on those of Vienna, and thus to secure tolerable terms for his beaten son-in-law. And the pivot of this policy was the perennial negotiation for a marriage between his son and the Spanish Infanta, a different son and a different Infanta from those of the original programme.

This scheme had powerful support. Count Gondomar, the Spanish Ambassador, was a diplomatic genius of the first order, who thoroughly understood James, and had been working patiently to smooth the path for the desired union, on the most favourable terms to his country and religion. What was even more important, the weathercock of Buckingham's mind was pointing towards the Spanish quarter.

For Buckingham's phases of statesmanship a personal cause is usually to be discovered, and this was no exception. What was more natural than that he should seek to crown his splendid career by a proportionately splendid marriage ? Old Lady Buckingham—for his mother had also taken that handle to her name—could be trusted to see to that. The young lady selected for the honour was the daughter and heiress of the Earl of Rutland, who being one of the heads of the proud, unbending, old Catholic nobility, turned anything but a favourable eye on the whirlwind wooing of the magnificent parvenu, already his superior in the peerage. He could not easily stomach the idea of his daughter marrying a heretic, and perhaps even less easily the colossal dowry for which old Lady Buckingham was careful to stipulate. James himself was horrified to think of his favourite being married to a Catholic. However, one of his chaplains was a certain Dr Williams, who was as determined a climber as Buckingham himself, and whose rectory happened to be in the neighbourhood of Belvoir Castle, the Rutland seat. Here was the very chance for which Williams had been looking. With his persuasive Welsh tongue, he managed to talk round the old Earl, and to persuade Lady Katharine, who was very anxious to be persuaded, in what precise way she might reconcile her conscience to conformity with a ritual in which she did not believe. And then one day Katharine left the Castle, in company with Lady Bucking-ham, and did not return that night, nor would her father allow her to return next day. According to Lady Buckingham, Kathar-ine had been taken ill and passed the night under her chaperonage —the Earl thought otherwise, and in a pretty stiff letter as good as told the Marquis to make an honest woman of her. It is said that only the intervention of Prince Charles prevented an open brawl. However, after Buckingham had countered by threatening to call the match off, the couple were quietly married, in the presence of the King and the bride's father, by the obliging Dr Williams, who, for his part in the business, got the Deanery of Westminster. It was something more than a coincidence that Buckingham should have swung round after this to the side of the Spanish entente, and a Catholic bride for his friend Charles.

But this business of the Elector Palatine, who happened to have got into Buckingham's bad books by forgetting to write to him, was after all a matter of family honour for James, and of acute personal concern for Charles, who, when he heard, at Royston, of the frightful disaster that had fallen on his sister, very characteristically shut himself up with his own grief for two days. James was more philosophic ; he had fully expected this, and what he most wanted was to keep the peace and save his face. A handful of English gentlemen were allowed to volunteer for service in the Palatinate. An endeavour was made to finance this venture by a more or less voluntary national subscription or benevolence, which produced, in spite of the furiously bellicose sentiment abroad, surprisingly little cash and a great number of excellent excuses for not giving it. After this, there was nothing for it but to see if sentiment could not be turned to account, by summoning a Parliament.

In one sense, there was never such a propitious moment. The country was seething from end to end with patriotic and Protestant fervour ; the man in the street was more concerned than the King himself about the King's daughter and son-in-law. The Commons, when they came together, were worked up to such a pitch of war fever, that they forgot to pick up the threads of their former quarrels with the King. Even that matter of the customs was allowed to sleep. The Faithful Commons were brimming over with loyalty and goodwill—only let the King give them a lead against the enemy of his House and faith ! They were even—most wonderful of all—ready to dole him out a little money without demanding, in return, some essential part of his royal prerogative.

Unfortunately King and Parliament were, from the first, fundamentally at cross purposes. James had opened the session with an address in which he reminded them that he had reigned eighteen years, during all of which time they had had peace, and in which he had received less in the way of supply than any of his predecessors. Parliament was not thinking in terms of peace, and had hardly begun to think seriously in terms of finance. It was, even more than most public assemblies, swayed by its emotions, and these soon began to be tinged with hysterical vindictiveness and even cruelty.

It was easy enough to talk about helping the Elector Palatine to enjoy his own again, but how to do this effectively was another matter. The enemy commander on the Rhineland front was the great Marquis of Spinola, at the head of his invincible Spanish infantry. To put an English army into the field that would have the least chance of making head against him, would cost, according to a commission of military experts appointed to consider the question, a quarter of a million down and an annual £900,000 ; about a dozen of those subsidies, one or two of which were the utmost that were ever likely to be dragged out of Parliament. James himself did not dare to inflict on it the full shock of these figures, but put it at a matter of at least half a million.

The effect of a firm policy, backed by arms, would, as the shrewd old King perfectly well realised, be negligible as far as the German struggle was concerned but sheer ruin and bankruptcy

for the English monarchy, and he was too old a hand to walk
blindly into the trap thus set for him.

Parliament was, indeed, prepared to do everything for the
Palatine and the Protestant cause, except the only thing it could
do, which was to foot the bill. Meanwhile, in default of annoying
the Emperor or Spinola, it could at least dig its claws into the
unfortunate, and now quite harmless, Catholics at home. One of
its first steps was to demand the utmost vigour of great and petty
persecution that the law allowed.

How utterly beyond reason was the spirit of both Houses, is
shown by a shocking incident that occurred three months after
Parliament had opened. There was a venerable Catholic barrister,
called Floyd, or Lloyd, who was lying in the Fleet Prison under
sentence of the Council. It turned out that this poor old man had
been imprudent enough, when the fall of Prague was reported
among the prisoners, to have let fall some rather indiscreet words
about Goodman and Goodwife Palsgrave having taken to their
heels. This bit of jail tittle tattle, being repeated in the lobbies,
sent the Commons into a sadistic frenzy. Member after member
jumped up, each trying to think of a more ferocious torture than
the last. Let the old man be put into the dungeon Little Ease, to
endure as much pain as he could without loss of life ; let him be
whipped ; let him be whipped and pilloried ; let him be whipped
twice and pilloried twice ; let hot bacon be dropped on him
between every six lashes ; let him have his beads hung round his
neck and have as many lashes as he had beads ; bore a hole
through his tongue ; slit his tongue ; cut off his ears and nose ;
and—this the contribution of a gentleman named Angell—whip
him with a "gag in his mouth, that he may not cry to have any
man pity him." At last, when it had simmered down a little, the
House consented to reduce the sentence to three pilloryings, a
bareback ride, face to tail, in a paper cap, between each, and a
fine of a thousand pounds. A member for a West country constituency, a large, grave man, hitherto undistinguished, but with a
singularly impressive delivery, added the characteristically
thoughtful suggestion that in the event of Floyd not having the
wherewithal to pay the fine, he should be provided with a
whipping. The member's name was John Pym.*

But next day, instead of the spectacle of Floyd in the pillory,
Honourable Members received a gentle reminder from His

* Commons' Debates 1621, by Notestein, Relf & Simpson, III, p. 127.

Majesty, not only that they had condemned the man without any sworn evidence, but that the House of Commons was committing a flagrant breach of law in assuming the functions of a court of justice. This, the House was forced sullenly to admit, was more or less so. It had taken too much upon itself. The next time that the Faithful Commons were destined to snatch the sword from the hands of Justice the victim would be no obscure subject, but the King himself.

Floyd did not gain much from being turned over, as he was, to the Lords to try. The Peers were determined to show themselves greater savages even than the Commoners. They multiplied the fine by five ; they passed a sentence of imprisonment for life ; they substituted for the pillory branding with a hot iron and whipping at the cart's tail all the way from London Bridge to Westminster. But now Floyd found pity in what must have been an unexpected quarter. Prince Charles, in spite of the fact that it had been his beloved sister who was said to have been insulted, gave evidence of that "tenderness and compassion of nature, which," says Clarendon, "restrained him from ever doing a hard-hearted thing." He used his influence both with his father and the Peers—used it successfully—to get at least the whipping remitted. It was his first public act of any importance.

But the Commons had bigger game in view and more effective methods of bringing it down.

Even in the comparatively short time they had sat, they had brought into play an even deadlier weapon against the Crown than that of the financial stranglehold. The King, like an American President to-day, was, by a hitherto undisputed convention, responsible for the shaping of his own policy through ministers of his own choice. But what chance could the ablest King or President have of steering to anything but disaster, if it were open to a permanent opposition to pick out any minister whose outstanding ability seemed likely to strengthen the Crown, and strike him down, if not literally with an axe (though it would come to that), at least with a sentence, after a framed-up political trial, that would effect his personal ruin and political extinction ?

This was done by reviving the medieval weapon of impeachment, or prosecution by the Commons before the Lords. The method was applied, in the first instance, with astute plausibility, to one or two real sharks, who had grown fat on abuses of the patent laws. But this was only a preliminary to switching over the attack to incomparably the ablest statesman in England, and probably in Europe * the Lord Chancellor Bacon ; on the hypocritical plea of his having conformed to the practically universal custom of accepting presents from suitors. King James, determined to appease his Parliament at all costs, had stood aside and allowed his minister to be broken. It was a fatal precedent, for during subsequent Parliaments the same weapon was employed without fail against every minister of outstanding personality. How, with government thus automatically de-brained, any monarch could have carried it on with success, is not easy to see.

The effect of this deadly expedient was never more fatal than in this first application. For the removal of Bacon set Buckingham's erratic genius free from the one influence that might conceivably have harnessed it to fruitful work. Henceforth he was free to launch forth on his dazzling projects without restraint, for poor James was now physically incapable of asserting his own will against his minister's hypnotic domination.

Here again, we find Prince Charles doing all in his power to mitigate the severity of the treatment meted out to the philosopher statesman, whose worst fault was that he had conformed to the almost universal practice of his day. Charles did his best, as a member of the House of Lords, to get them to accept Bacon's submission without passing sentence, and failing that, to get the sentence mitigated. And it is pleasant to record that, when sentence was passed, the solitary dissentient vote was that of Buckingham, who, with all his faults, was not the man to throw over a friend in adversity.

All had so far gone forward without any ostensible breach between King and Parliament. The Commons actually voted two subsidies, and the King complimented them on their excellent spirit. But as the year wore on, the incompatibility of aims became more and more evident. The King was pursuing a peace policy, based on an understanding with Spain ; the Commons wanted to rush him into a war, preferably with Spain. The King continued to spin out time by negotiation—Lord Digby went to Vienna to intercede with the Emperor for Frederick, and was overwhelmed with politeness and diplomatic evasion. The Houses were adjourned, much against the will of the Commons, at the beginning of June, and did not meet again till November.

* Richelieu had not yet come into power.

By this time the situation in the Palatinate had gone from bad to worse, and the English volunteers, unprovided with food or pay, were beginning to live in German fashion, by eating up the country they were supposed to be defending.

In the short winter session, matters came to a head. There was no longer any concealment about figures—if the Palatinate was to be saved, money was urgently required to keep things going until the next campaigning season, when a proper army would have to be equipped at an estimated cost of £900,000. The Commons contented themselves with granting one beggarly subsidy—a sum ridiculously inadequate to tide over even the immediate necessity —and then proceeded to debate themselves into a fine frenzy of demand for a policy of war abroad and persecution at home. Ex-Chief Justice Coke, the great Common Lawyer, carried the house with him in a speech that rose above even his high water mark of vituperation, in which he denounced Spain as the fount and origin of everything evil he could think of, including the scab in sheep and the pox in men. On the persecution issue, the debate gave John Pym an opportunity to display the most essential gift of the born politician, that of affording a rational justification for the irrational passions of his audience, and, as Gardiner puts it, of placing "the duty of persecution on a firm and intelligible basis".

The upshot of it all was a petition, in which, besides enforcing the Anti-Catholic Laws with the most drastic severity, His Majesty was urged "speedily and effectually to take your reward into your hand"—the enemy, or first enemy, indicated being Spain. He was also to marry his son to a Princess of his own religion.

The petition was anticipated in a message from James, in which the Commons were told, in so many words, to mind their own business, instead of meddling with decisions of high policy for which the King alone was responsible. Here was a complete *impasse*. It was hardly to be expected that the captain of the ship of State should tolerate interference with the navigation by a mob of amateurs. To James, with his principles of Roman Law, such an idea was as preposterous as it would have seemed to any other contemporary sovereign. Even in England, precedent was against it. Neither Elizabeth nor her father would have stood this sort of thing for a moment.

On the other hand, the Commons cared much less about the

efficiency of government, than about that sacred and peculiarly English thing called privilege. They were going to have their rights, even if they had to invent them first, and the dispute culminated in a protestation of their "ancient and undoubted birthright and inheritance" to speak freely on any subject whatever.

But James was by this time thoroughly roused. There was less than no help to be expected from this Parliament, in spite of all its loyal professions. The Commons were determined to wreck the policy of peace that he had pursued successfully for eighteen years, and that had brought prosperity to England ; to rush him into a costly and unnecessary war for which he could not, and they certainly would not, provide the financial backing. He dissolved Parliament, having first torn their protestation with his own hands out of their journals ; he sent Coke and one or two more of the most fiery warmongers to cool their heels in the Tower ; as for Pym, he was told to put himself under arrest in his own house.

We have two letters from the Prince of Wales, during this Session, to his friend Buckingham, which plainly show what answer his mind was beginning to frame to this overshadowing question of King versus Parliament. He notes in the first that the House has been "a little unruly," and reveals that he has been trying to stiffen up the resolution of the King and Council to make an example of one or two "seditious fellows." But a little later, when the one subsidy has been granted, and the Commons are petitioning his father to have the Session wound up before Christmas, we find him in a more indulgent mood : "I would not wholly discontent them," he says, "... but withal I should have him command them not to speak any more of Spain, whether it be of that war, or of my marriage."

That is the language of one whose conscience is clear. Charles was sure of his ground, as only a young and very impressionable man can be. Subjects who set themselves deliberately to oppose and thwart their sovereign, even if it be in the Chapel at Westminster, are "seditious fellows," with whom it behoves the sovereign to take order. A kingdom divided against itself, or against its King, cannot stand. That philosophy was lucid and obvious enough to hold good in any other monarchy except that of England. But it was not English—and on that hidden rock Charles Stuart, with Buckingham at the helm, might come to grief.

For the effect on the diffident young Prince of his friend's
magnetic self-assurance had been to induce that most dangerous
of all states of mind, of a man who knows and can prove himself
in the right, and whose mind is closed to any other, and perhaps
deeper sense, in which his opponent may also have right on his
side. For life is not a melodrama of right against wrong, but an
heroic, or tragic, conflict of souls, each of which has some part
of the right on its side, and mistakes that human fraction for the
divine whole.

Charles was thus able to see his own side of the case with
extraordinary lucidity, but to see no other—not even to suspect
that any other existed. The defect in his speech had driven him
back on himself; had forced him to close his own world in a
shell of icy dignity through which he could see, as through clear
glass, but through which no voice could penetrate, except where
love had opened a channel of access for that of some extraordinary
friend—not more than two or three in the course of his lifetime.

With all his rare gifts of intellect and character, he was fated
to be the most misunderstood, because the most misunderstanding,
of mortals.

5

CASTLE IN SPAIN

THE Parliament of 1621 met for the last time on the 19th of
December, though it was only formally dissolved on the 6th of
the following January. During that next year, 1622, King James
managed to carry on, as he had before, with that policy of
calculated procrastination which is seldom characterized by any
more complimentary epithet than "foolish" or "futile." It was, as
a matter of fact, entirely successful in its essential purpose of
maintaining unbroken the peace which he had established when
he came to the throne, and maintained ever since. His shade, if
it could speak, might retort on his critics in words like those
of Walpole on a very similar occasion :

"There are fifty-thousand men slain this year in Europe, and
not one Englishman."

But such ignoble services as that of keeping their blood unshed and their pockets full, are seldom received with thanks by those on whom they are conferred. James was finding the path of peace one of ever-accumulating unpopularity. Public opinion had been solid behind Parliament in its insistent bellicosity, and there were few who did not blame the breakdown of co-operation on to the King.

During the year, the situation on the Rhineland went from bad to worse. James did his best, by negotiation, to get his son-in-law out of the mess into which he had got himself; but Frederick was one of those hopeless people who defy all efforts to help them. The least gleam of success started him reasserting his most arrogant claims in a way calculated to convince not only the Emperor, but all Europe, that there would be no peace for Germany until he was turned, bag and baggage, out of his dominions. His cause was maintained by gangs of the worst scoundrels who ever disgraced the profession of arms, who roamed about the country, looking not for the enemy, but for fresh districts to loot. The Catholic armies, no less cruel, but guided by a definite strategic purpose, could not fail to wear down such opposition. Early in September Count Tilly, who had taken over from Spinola, captured Heidelberg, Frederick's capital. Sir Horace Vere, with a contingent of English volunteers which had acquitted itself very creditably, was shut up in the fortress of Mannheim, from which he was allowed to march out with the honours of war.

The Palatinate lay at the feet of the Emperor, who, though he held out some prospect of allowing Frederick to come back if, and when, he made proper submission, took the decisive step of transferring his electoral vote to a Catholic Prince, Maximilian of Bavaria, thus tilting the formal balance of power in Germany hopelessly against the Protestants. To the patriot Protestants of England, it might well seem that the cup of bitterness was full. The foundations were cast down, and what could the righteous do?

There was little, as it happened, for any far-sighted Englishman to bother about. The Emperor had succeeded a shade too well. Religion or no religion, Europe was never going to allow the Hapsburg or any other family to rule the roost. Not only the Lutheran Princes of Germany, who had hitherto held aloof, but Catholic France, not to speak of Protestant Sweden and Denmark, could be trusted, sooner or later, to take a hand in redressing the balance. England had only to sit still and await events behind her wooden walls, which, for greater precaution, it behoved her to strengthen. And this was just what, largely thanks to Buckingham, she had actually been doing. For it is the thing that stands most to Buckingham's credit, that with all his faults, he did grasp the importance to England of building up an efficient navy ; and although he himself had neither the application nor singleness of aim to rank him among great naval administrators, he had the faculty of imparting drive to the work of other men, and the sense —for the time being—to make use of Cranfield's *flair* for cleaning up this, as he had other less vital departments, of the King's service.

But Buckingham was not the man to play a delaying game. As changeable as a weathercock, he was only constant to the hope of bringing off some sensational coup. In the Autumn, in spite of his having been foremost in promoting the entente with Spain, he was seized with a sudden access of war fever ; he was thundering on the Council for an army of thirty or forty thousand to be thrown into the Palatinate under Prince Charles, Parliament to be summoned to go through the formality of voting the trifle of a million or so necessary for its support. Of course he carried Charles with him. But the mood passed as quickly as it had come. A new idea was beginning to form in his mind, and to light up with the prospect of chivalrous adventure. This Spanish marriage business that had dragged on so interminably—what could be simpler than to end it once and for all by taking Charles to Madrid, and inspiring him to woo and win the lady on the spot ?

The idea had not originated with him, but in the subtle intelligence of Count Gondomar, who bespoke its reception by oiling Buckingham's palm. I have spoken of Gondomar as a diplomatic genius, but I should hesitate to describe him as a profound statesman. He seems to have imagined that it would be quite simple to make Charles turn Catholic, once he was on Spanish soil, and to get James to jettison the Anti-Catholic legislation of successive Parliaments by his Royal fiat. Whereas, the forcing of matters to a decision was the surest way to wreck a project that was most useful to both parties while it remained in suspense.

There was one man, however, who did realize this, and that was James himself, whose at any rate passive acquiescence even Buckingham would have to secure before starting on the ride to Madrid. But James was no longer the man he had been when he had reduced Scotland to order, and brought to England the blessing of peace. Although only in his fifty-seventh year, he was already beginning to break up, not only physically, but also morally. His mind was as shrewd as ever, but his will had grown flabby. No longer did he retain that faculty, that he had had in common with Elizabeth, of keeping his favourites from dominating his political action. He had got to that stage when he could refuse nothing to sufficient pressure from Steenie, especially when backed by Baby Charles—and Steenie knew it.

After all, what had the poor invalid, with his pathetic craving for affection, to fall back upon ? Except for those two, he was worse than alone. His Queen was dead ; Carr, if he was not dead, was as damned as any living soul can be. James had never been more than tolerated by his English subjects ; and now the obstinacy with which he clung to his rôle of peacemaker had made him furiously disliked. Some time during the year an unknown pamphleteer, calling himself Tom Tell-Troath, had put into circulation a farrago of treasonable invective, in which the King was branded with every sort of iniquity, from sacrificing the national honour to keeping a male harem. That such stuff could be hawked about with impunity, shows how thin and worn the traditional respect for the throne. If his son and favourite were to turn against him, what would be left for James but to fall crushed under a burden beneath which he already staggered ?

The two young men having decided between themselves on the adventure, were careful to catch James in a good mood before springing the project upon him. Having got him alone, down went Charles upon his knees, while Buckingham stood by, ready to chime in at the appropriate moment. James appears to have been so utterly surprised, as to have allowed himself to be rushed into some expression of assent. But as soon as he had time to recover himself, and think the matter over, his instinct for king-craft told him what an insane blunder his son proposed to perpetrate. Even if he were to get safely through France, his appearance at Madrid would have the effect of delivering him as a hostage into the hands of the Spaniards. James knew enough of the megalomania of the Spanish court to realize that control of his son's person would induce the dons to raise their terms for the Infanta's hand to a height that would render all negotiation hopeless. And if these terms were refused—was it certain that Charles would find it so easy to leave Madrid as it had been to get there ? While as for Buckingham, if the expedition should end in disaster, such a fury of indignation would be bound to be kindled against the favourite, for having counselled it, that even his King would be powerless to protect him.

Such arguments did poor James urge, with sighs and tears, entreating Charles and Steenie to be advised by him and think better of their resolution. But their minds were made up, and they did not condescend to argue. Charles, in respectful language, as good as told his father that he would be a liar if he went back on his promise : Buckingham did not trouble to wrap up his meaning, but openly bullied his unprotesting Sovereign, telling him that nobody would ever be able to believe anything he said ; that it was quite evident that some rascal had been inducing him to break his word ; that he, Buckingham, would make it his business to find out who that rascal was ; and lastly, that Baby Charles would never forgive his Dad for this conduct.

James could only protest, with many oaths, that he was quite guiltless of having betrayed the secret to anyone ; but though cowed, he was still not quite at the end of his resources. One of those who had been selected to accompany the party to Madrid was the Prince's secretary, Sir Francis Cottington, an ardent pro-Spaniard and, at heart, a Catholic. To Cottington, therefore, who knew his Madrid, having been brought up there, James resolved, as a last resource, to appeal. While they were waiting for him to appear, Buckingham managed to whisper that he knew Cottington would be against the journey, and Charles to answer that he dared not. Men knew what it meant to get the wrong side of Buckingham.

"Cottington," said His Majesty, "here is Baby Charles and Steenie who have a great mind to go into Spain to fetch home the Infanta, and will have two more in their company and have chosen you for one. What think you of the journey ?"

It was a dreadful moment for Cottington, who—as he often used to confess afterwards—fell into such a trembling that he could hardly speak. But with a moral courage which must have been rare indeed in that venal atmosphere, he replied that he could not think well of it, since it would have the effect of wrecking the whole marriage negotiations. Upon which James, finding his worst fears confirmed, flung himself on his bed, in a fresh paroxysm of weeping, crying out that he was going to lose Baby Charles.

Promptly Buckingham turned on the unfortunate secretary a

perfect volley of abuse, telling him with insolent rudeness that the King had only asked for his opinion on the best route, and not for his advice on a matter of State ; moreover, that he should repent of this as long as he lived ; whereupon James, who saw only too clearly what was in store for his faithful servant, bleated hopelessly :

"Nay, by God, Steenie, you are very much to blame to use him so. He answered directly to the question I asked him and very honestly and wisely ; and yet you know he said no more than I told you before he was called in."

After which, it need hardly be said, the King surrendered at discretion. There was nothing for it but to make the best of a bad business, and trust to youth and the chapter of accidents for the event. Since there was no more question of preventing it, it was no doubt wise to enter into the spirit of the adventure, and sink the statesman in the indulgent father. King James was a tired old man, and life was too hard for him.

6

EN ROUTE

BUCKINGHAM had one of his many mansions at Newhall in Essex, and it was from this that the two friends started in the dusk of a February morning on their great adventure. Buckingham, true to his part of hero in melodrama, had resolved to invest their progress with the most theatrical secrecy. Having made themselves as conspicuous as possible with hoods, pistols, and unplausible false beards, and having assumed the conspicuously ordinary names of Tom and John Smith, they contrived to shed, on various cunning excuses, all of their retinue, except a certain Sir Richard Graham, before they arrived at the Greenwich ferry. Here one of the party occasioned some surprise by dropping his beard, and another—almost certainly Buckingham—by tossing a gold coin to the ferryman. The grateful fellow, who promptly concluded that these must be gentlemen bound overseas to end each other's lives in a duel, rushed off to the local magistrates, who, like John Gilpin's wife, promptly dispatched a post-boy in pursuit. But they got through Rochester ahead of him, and were just climbing the

slope beyond, when they fell in with the cavalcade of the Flemish
Archduchess Regent's ambassador, escorted by the Lieutenant of
Dover, Sir Henry Mainwaring, who thought that these highly
suspicious strangers must be sons of the executed Dutch patriot,
Oldenbarneveldt, on their way to avenge his death by assassin-
ating the Prince of Orange. However, they escaped detention by
galloping off over fields and hedges at a speed that defied pursuit.

At Sittingbourne the post-boy came up, and was presumably
squared, but at Canterbury they found themselves in the clutches
of the Mayor, who had received warning from Mainwaring to
intercept them. It must have been a great moment when the
tallest of the party pulled off his beard and disclosed the Lord
Admiral of England, going, as he said, to inspect the Channel
Fleet. Since it was evidently Buckingham, his Worship passed
them through, keeping to himself whatever thoughts he may have
had about the Admiral's novel get-up. They seem to have been
spotted at least once again—by a luggage boy this time—before,
at six o'clock in the evening, their tired horses brought them into
Dover.

Here a ship had been chartered by Cottington, with whom
Buckingham had patched up some pretence of a reconciliation,
and a fifth member of the party, Endymion Porter. They put
out from the harbour at five in the morning, and, as Buckingham
put it in one of the startlingly familiar letters he sent in his own,
and Charles's name, to their "dear Dad and gossip" on the throne
—"we wish to say, the first that fell sick was your son, and he that
continued it longest was myself." However, in the early afternoon, they were safe ashore at Boulogne, and lost no time in
getting on the road. Before dark they had covered the twenty-
three miles to Montreuil ; two more days sufficed to bring them
to Paris.

It was a glorious, care free adventure ; Charles, in spite of his
twenty-two years, was as excited as a schoolboy on holiday.
Buckingham came no less than four croppers on roads that were
no doubt slippery with frost, but Charles, though, as his friend
put it, his horses "stumble as fast as any man's ... he holds them
up by main strength of mastery, and cries still on ! on ! on !"

They had one clear day to amuse themselves in Paris—the Paris
of Athos, Porthos and Aramis. The Prince had never been abroad
before, and it must have been a thrilling experience for him to be
shown the sights of what was even then pre-eminently the Gay

City, by so seasoned a Parisian as Buckingham. What naturally interested them most of all was the Court, and to this there was no difficulty in obtaining admission, since the French Royal Family passed its whole time in the democratic publicity that it maintained up to the time of the Revolution. It is something more than probable that the only mystery about their presence was that with which they chose, and were tactfully allowed, to invest themselves. Even on the road to Paris, they had been recognized again by a couple of German travellers, who had been outfaced—at least so they flattered themselves—by Graham, and we know that the French Embassy in London had had almost immediate news of their departure. They had added to their stage properties an outfit of false perukes, which probably made them more conspicuous than ever. But whatever the French authorities may have known, they had every reason for playing their visitors' game.

The main, if not the sole, attraction of the Louvre, for Charles, was the sister of his intended bride, that very Infanta Anne who had been wooed on behalf of his brother Henry, and was now Queen of France. He had the best opportunity for studying her, since that evening she was performing in a masque with the other ladies of her suite. His mind was so full of his Spanish love that he does not appear to have taken much conscious notice of a fairy-like little creature, with flashing dark eyes, who was also taking part—and with exquisite grace—in the ballet. This was the more remarkable, since it was this very Princess who had, but a few years previously, been the subject of some tentative feelers put out on his behalf for a marriage alliance. She was thirteen—Juliet's age—and her mother, like Juliet, was an Italian. Her father was the great Henri quatre, and at the first glance you could see she had inherited that infectious, high-hearted gaiety, that has left him, to this day, a warm place in the heart of every Frenchman. She was called, after him, Henriette, and after her mother, Marie.

Her first remark, when she learnt who had been in the audience at that night's performance, revealed a chip of the old block :

"The Prince of Wales needn't have gone all the way to Madrid to find a wife."

The party could not have had much sleep after their entertainment, for at five o'clock next morning, with nearly two hours to ride in the dark, they were off on the road to their next halting place, Orleans. Charles's spirits had been still further raised at the sight of the beautiful Spanish Queen, and he was beginning to work himself up into quite a frenzy of romantic infatuation for her sister, very different from his cynical mood at home, when he had been heard to remark, after looking at the Infanta's portrait, that but for the sin, it would have been a good thing, if Princes could have had two wives, one for reason of State, and one to please themselves. But there is no infatuation to equal that of a shy and model young man to whom girls are like some unknown species of animal, of which all things are possible and about which any dream may pass for true. And there was Buckingham at his side to keep him up to the mark ; to make him see himself in the light of a Prince Charming come to carry off the Princess from her enchanted castle, a lover fully capable of holding his own even in the land of Don Juan.

As the journey through France continued, the only difficulty seems to have been that of keeping up the farce of their not being recognized. At Bordeaux, the governor, the Duc d'Épernon, wanted to entertain the royal tourist in proper style, but the desperate excuses of the party soon made him grasp the situation and do the tactful thing. Their principal trouble consisted in the fact that, it being Lent, and the country devoutly Catholic, it was hard to come by anything better than a vegetarian diet. Near Bayonne, however, they fell in with a herd of goats, one of which Graham offered to "snap," but Charles slyly remarking, "Why, Richard, do you think you may practise here your old tricks again upon the Border ?" gave a fat tip to the goatherd, after which they proceeded to stage a regular kid hunt, which the Prince ended by a clean pistol shot through the head.

And it is said that after they had crossed the Spanish frontier, the unique spectacle was witnessed of Prince Charles literally dancing with glee.

7

PRINCE CHARMING AT MADRID

For the embassy at Madrid, King James had, since 1611, chosen the pick of his diplomatic team, the newly created Earl of Bristol, who, as Lord Digby, had been employed to intercede for the Elector Palatine at Vienna. This had only been an interlude in the Ambassador's normal business, which for nine years past had been that of negotiating, on the spot, the conditions of the elusive marriage contract between the Spanish Infanta and the heir to the English throne.

It was not a task that Bristol would ever have chosen for himself. He had been against the principle of a Catholic marriage from the start, and had said so to the King ; but having put his opinion on record, he set himself, like the good and faithful servant he was, to make what success he could of the policy imposed upon him. Long experience had made him a specialist in its complexities. Nothing could exceed the patient finesse with which he bargained to improve conditions that never got to the stage of being binding. Above all, he had got the exact and leisurely tempo of Spanish negotiation ; he knew that the dark-browed grandees with whom he had to deal had their own diplomatic gait, out of which it was worse than useless to try to hurry them.

Nevertheless he had, of recent months, though with much tactful circumlocution, been trying to impress them with the need for bringing the affair to some sort of a conclusion. So far as it was possible, under the circumstances, he was becoming optimistic. He had a new King now to deal with, the Infanta's brother, Philip IV, with whose weak but not unamiable features Velasquez has made all succeeding generations familiar. Philip was a boy of sixteen, already wrapped up in what was to be his undeviating purpose, throughout a long and disastrous reign, of keeping himself amused ; and he was content to leave the dull work of governing Spain in the hands of his favourite, the Count-Duke of Olivares, in whose sombre lineaments stand revealed all the pride and tragic futility of declining Spain.

Both monarch and statesman were prolific of assurances about their eagerness to meet James more than half way in getting the contract concluded. It is true that Bristol had reason to know what Spanish assurances were good for in practice, but he must also have realized, if any man could, how much the need of Spain for a peaceful understanding exceeded that of England herself. For Spain, in spite of her world-wide empire and invincible armies, in spite of the fact that she was almost as unquestionably the arbitress of European culture as France was to become under Louis XIV, was already an exhausted, if not a moribund, Power. Her deliberate policy of glutting herself with gold and silver from the Indies had killed her industry ; her all-powerful Church was

CHARLES, PRINCE OF WALES—*from a portrait by Paul van Somer in the National Portrait Gallery previously catalogued as Prince Henry and recently confirmed as being one of Prince Charles. Paul van Somer (1576–1621) was the favourite painter of James I's Court*

PRINCE CHARLES *in the Robes of the Garter with*
THE INFANTA MARIA—*from a contemporary engraving
in the British Museum*

a monstrously bloated parasite draining her vitality ; idleness
was the vice of all classes, clerical and lay ; her services were
rotten with corruption ; her population was declining ; ferocious
taxation did not suffice to relieve the bankruptcy of the royal
finances. With her resources so near to collapse, the one thing
that could conceivably save Spain was peace, and a long period
for recuperation. To increase her military liabilities, on any
pretence, was suicide.

An enlightened selfishness would therefore have impelled the
Spanish government to embrace any opportunity of an entente
with a Power that it could not afford the luxury of fighting. There
was more union than conflict of national interests in getting the
young couple married. But enlightenment was hardly the strong
suit of Spanish statesmanship ; and when all was said and done,
its sole impelling motive was not selfishness. If any country had
ever been in earnest about its religion, that country was Catholic
Spain, where the memory of Ignatius Loyola, of St Theresa and
St John of the Cross, was still green, and to whose soul fanatical
self-sacrifice was as native as cruelty. Along with these, went an
indurated pride. No Spaniard could base a calculation, however
selfish, on humiliating data ; he would spend what he had not
got, and stand out for conditions that he had no chance of
imposing, rather than lower his dignity in his own eyes.

To negotiate successfully with such people would have required
the patience of a Job added to the wisdom of a Solomon. For the
Spaniards peace was not nearly enough ; nothing less would
satisfy them than to accomplish by finesse what the Armada had
failed to do by force ; to undo the work of the Reformation in
England, and reduce her, as in the days of Philip and Mary, to
being a satellite Power of the Hapsburg interest. The Infanta
would go forth as terrible as an army with banners ; she would
capture what to the Spanish mind constituted the key of the whole
situation, the conscience of the ruling House ; she would constitute her suite, at Whitehall, a Catholic army of occupation ;
certainly in the next generation, and preferably in this, the King
would arise who would, like Henry VIII and Elizabeth, bring
about a change of religion by his royal will, only in a reverse
direction from theirs. All of which was to be made safe in the
contract ! While to add to Bristol's difficulties, his own master was
stipulating that the King of Spain should do something to help
the wretched Elector Palatine to get back into his electorate,

a thing that Spain had not the power, and still less the inclination, to effect in teeth of the Hapsburg Family alliance.

But the devoted ambassador kept pegging away, in the hope
that the manifest interest of both parties concerned would
eventually lead to some compromise, which would result on one
side in tolerable conditions for the English Catholics, and on the
other in saving the face of English policy in Germany. His mind
was fully occupied with this when, on a night in early March,
two solitary travellers, one of them carrying a portmanteau,
knocked at the door of the embassy and were shown up to his
bedroom. Long experience had taught Bristol to conceal his
feelings, but he must have needed all his self-control when he
realized who his visitors were, and what their arrival portended.
Here was the whole patient edifice of his diplomacy toppled in
ruins ! Here was the Prince of Wales delivering himself up as a
hostage for terms that would never be fulfilled, and that his
arrival would assuredly have the effect of stiffening beyond hope
of compromise ! And here—which was almost as bad—was
Buckingham, who would certainly insist on taking charge, and
who, as the Ambassador must have realized, would handle the
gossamer threads of negotiation with all the delicacy of a bull in
a china shop.

However, there was nothing for it but to make the best of the
new situation, and confide, in Don Quixote's country, to his faith
that chivalrous romance will work any miracle. Certainly nothing
could have seemed more propitious than the warmth of the
reception accorded to the new arrivals at Madrid. Never was the
courtesy of old Spain more magnificently lavished. Count
Gondomar, the original proposer of the expedition, and now
living in retirement at Madrid, was the first to arrive—flinging
himself on his face with a cry of *Nunc Dimittis !* Next the great
Olivares fell on his knees before the Prince, kissing his hand and
hugging his thighs—at a later interview he was to surpass himself
by assuring Charles that if by any chance he failed to get the
Infanta for his wife, he should certainly have her for his mistress.
An elaborately accidental encounter was arranged, by special
request, with the royal party in the Prado, the Infanta, in the boot
of the Queen's coach, being distinguished by a blue ribbon about
one of her arms ; at the sight of him she flushed hotly, which
Charles, in his simplicity, took to be a sign of affection. All this
was incognito ; another meeting of formal recognition had to be

arranged with the boy King, and a strenuous competition took place in civilities. In a few days' time Charles had been persuaded to leave the embassy for a magnificent suite of apartments that was placed at his disposal in the Palace ; there was the exchange of costly presents ; there was a series of splendid festivities in his honour. All Madrid caught up the spirit of the romance, and took the handsome young lover to its heart ; all Madrid was singing the lines of its greatest poet, Lope de Vega, translated, it is said, by Charles himself :

> Charles Stuart I am,
> Love guides me afar,
> To the heavens of Spain
> For Maria my star.

The joy overflowed when His Majesty decided to celebrate the occasion by letting loose all but the very worst prisoners and galley slaves.

No welcome could have been more propitious, nor is there any reason to characterize it as insincere. The Spanish King and his people were no doubt genuinely delighted to see the English Prince among them. But the countrymen of Cervantes, with all their hot passions, were no sentimentalists. Their delight was based on a perfectly rational assumption. After all these years of ineffective bargaining, it must surely have been plain to Charles that it would be sheer madness to come to Madrid unless he were able to make some decisive advance on all previous offers. That advance could only be of one nature. The great stumbling block of his heresy was about to be removed. Surely, surely, he had come either converted to the true faith, or prepared to be converted. Granted that, all the rest would be easy ; failing that, he might as well never have come to Madrid at all.

It is hard to blame the Spaniards for thinking thus, when we find that the English Ambassador was himself more than half inclined to credit the rumour. Almost the first thing that Bristol asked of the Prince was for him to declare quite frankly his religious intentions—otherwise how would it be possible to serve him effectually ? Charles was first evasive and then indignant at the very idea that he could be base enough to change his religion for a wife. Bristol, more puzzled than ever, could only advise him to make this clear, from the outset, to the Spaniards. It had unfortunately not become Charles's way to make unpleasant facts clear, even to himself.

Compliments and courtesies signified as little as they cost. Business was business, even in Madrid, and if Charles were not come prepared to do business he might just as well have stopped at home, for all the chance there would ever be of his returning with a bride, even if he were allowed to return at all.

It would not have been easy for Philip and Olivares, even if they had had the will, to have obliged him, in face of the horror with which the Infanta herself regarded the prospect of union with one who, as her confessor had not failed to point out, was quite certainly damned. For Maria Althea was no puppet, but a young woman of high principles and decided character, much addicted to the practice of such good works as preparing lint for hospitals, and taking her religion with all the concentrated seriousness of the true Spaniard. If she went to England, she expected nothing better than the grim satisfaction of martyrdom, and consequently, so far from being inclined to reciprocate the passion of her heretic wooer, the very idea of his advances filled her with repulsion.

There have been lovers capable, by sheer audacity, and a sort of hypnotic fascination, of facing and overcoming even such a prejudice, but Charles was not one of them, nor had Spain, or Buckingham, communicated to him the secret of Don Juan. That tendency of his to stammer was responsible for a reserved diffidence of approach, that is the way of all others least calculated to take by storm the heart of any normal girl. The interview that with great difficulty he succeeded in obtaining with his "star" was a ghastly fiasco. The King with all the grandees of the Court accompanied him in solemn state to the Queen's apartments, where he found the Infanta sitting, very prim and impassive, beside Her Majesty. Charles, after saying his piece to the Queen, was ill advised enough to start pouring out his lovesick soul to her companion. But he had not got very far before he began to realize that the performance was anything but a success—the Queen was plainly scandalized ; the courtiers were whispering ; as for Maria, she was a colder icicle than ever. The unfortunate youth faltered to a dead stop ; whereupon the Infanta, who did not so much as condescend to appear annoyed, recited the few formal words that she had learnt in advance for the occasion.

To anyone as far gone in infatuation as Charles, repulse has the effect of stimulus. The desire of the moth for the star, of the Knight of the Mournful Countenance for his Dulcinea, is unquenchable, because it has no relation to the brute facts of life. The human Maria did not, she never had existed for Charles, and even if he were capable of being disillusioned, the freezing etiquette of the Spanish Court denied him the least opportunity of making human contact with her. He could only feast his eyes and imagination at state functions, where, as Olivares put it, he watched her as a cat watches a mouse. And the more he looked, the more determined he became that nothing should prevent his quest from ending in the approved fashion of all fairy tales.

Which did not smooth his path to a diplomatic bargain with the' cynical and calculating men of the world, whose only desire was to exploit his visit and his passion for whatever they could be made to fetch. There was not only the interest of the Spanish Court to be reckoned with, but also—which by no means amounted to the same thing—that of Rome ; for before the marriage could be lawfully effected, a dispensation had to be obtained from the Pope, and on conditions acceptable to the super-subtle ecclesiastics, who, in spite of all changes on the Papal throne, maintained the continuity of the Vatican policy.

It would be waste of time to chart out all the cross-currents of negotiation that occupied the next few months. The great, dominating fact was that, so long as Charles remained—as he was—a faithful son of the Church of England, the position was one of deadlock that there was no hope of resolving. At a very early stage of the proceedings it had become apparent to Olivares that the best he could do, under the circumstances, would be to ride for the inevitable fall, and if possible to avoid trouble with England by shifting the blame for it on to somebody else's shoulders. Thus, when, all smiles and compliments, he was pretending that all he wanted was to get that vital dispensation from the Pope, he was actually dispatching a special envoy to the Vatican to beg that the dispensation should on no account be granted. But the Vatican was too cunning to be used as a catspaw of even the Catholic King. Before the messenger had arrived, the dispensation had been forwarded to Madrid, though it was only to be granted on condition that Philip himself would undertake the entire responsibility, by force of arms if necessary, of holding down England to the fulfilment of the treaty conditions. Diamond had cut diamond very neatly.

All would have been well, from the Spanish point of view, if Charles could only have been prevailed upon to see reason and enter the fold of his own accord. There were no theologians more expert than those of Spain at applying persuasion to those heretics to whom it was inexpedient to apply fire. The young lover was presumably in a yielding mood—was not an Infanta worth a Mass ? Not for the last time in his life, those who had to do with Charles misconceived the dogged constancy to principle that underlay an appearance of pliability. In theology, he was on familiar and congenial ground, and his training with Dr Murray had rendered him capable of standing up to the doughtiest theologian. Buckingham, however, who had no taste for such interchanges, or patience with Charles for engaging in them, lost his temper, and became extremely rude—jumping, eventually, on his own hat. After such provocation, it is no wonder that the punctiliously urbane fathers saw little use in prolonging the discussions.

Buckingham's headlong methods, that had carried everything before them in England, were only calculated to irritate and scandalize the ceremonious aristocracy of Spain. A man incapable of controlling his temper from one moment to another, and who, when crossed, blazed out into some furious indiscretion, was the Englishman abroad in his worst traditional aspect. He had not the least idea of accommodating himself to the formal circumlocutions and procrastinating ways of his hosts ; he would ride roughshod over their ridiculous susceptibilities, as any honest Englishman ought to do. Nor was the suite behindhand in following his example. In spite of the magnificent hospitality lavished upon them, some of them were boorish enough to jeer, in true English fashion, at the Spanish fare provided.

It is not surprising that the two favourites were soon at loggerheads. It began to dawn on Buckingham that the elaborate civilities of Olivares were merely a device for spinning out time, and that so far from desiring to come to any reasonable arrangement, he was actually in process of raising his terms to a more intolerable height than any that had been under discussion before the visit. Before long there was an open rupture. Olivares protesting that Buckingham had given him the lie, and Buckingham expressing his willingness "to maintain the contrary to his affirmative, in any sort whatever." Such incidents may be smoothed over, but they are seldom forgiven.

All through the spring and into the scorching Spanish summer the negotiation dragged its weary length, and never, during that time, did the hospitality of his prospective brother-in-law to Charles Stuart show any decline in the magnificence of its cordiality. Pageants, bull-fights, hunts, were the order of the day—nothing was spared that could do honour to the Prince or add to his pleasure. And indeed, whatever may have been thought of Buckingham, Charles himself, with his grave demeanour and ceremonious courtesy, was just the Prince to endear himself to Spanish hearts.

He was royally equipped, since James had hastened to send out everything calculated to sustain the dignity of his position, not excepting Archie, the Court fool. Sir Robert Carey, now sixty-three and promoted to the peerage, arrived in charge of a bevy of fresh attendants, though Charles considerately refused to allow him to stop on, once it had begun to heat up. So Carey fades out of the story, with an acknowledgment of God's having so blessed him during the visit that "I had such a stomach to my meat as in my younger days I never had the like." He was to end his days, by a crowning dispensation of Providence, as Earl of Monmouth—the one life, of which we have to tell in these pages, that goes happily forward to a happy ending.

It was soon after Carey's departure that Charles made a supreme attempt to capture the heart of his ladylove in the true romantic style. The idea was certainly Buckingham's, and the Prince must have taken a terrible lot of persuading before, in the cool of a summer dawn, he allowed Buckingham, or perhaps Porter, to hoist him up to the top of a high wall, behind which, as he knew, the Infanta would be taking the air. At the risk of his ankles, he jumped down, and made eagerly towards her. The Infanta was the first of her party to catch sight of him, and with one shriek, she took to her heels. This was the more significant, as Maria Althea was so far from being liable to panic, that not so long ago she had been the one person to keep her head when the stand, on which she had been watching some public spectacle, had caught fire. On this occasion, it may be presumed, her scream was more of indignation than of fright. Nor was there any question of pursuit, for His Highness found his path barred by an aged and kneeling chaperon of a Marquis, who conjured him, in a way that brooked no denial, to retire. Retire he did, feeling, no doubt, particularly foolish, through a door that was unbolted for his convenience in that selfsame wall over which he had just climbed. It says much for the strength of his infatuation, that he should have persisted with his suit even after this rebuff.

But Charles, if he resembled the typical Englishman in no other respect, was almost incapable of knowing when he was beaten. No doubt he felt that to slink out of the Infanta's country, as he had out of her presence, would be too humiliating, now, to be thought of. Better consider anything—promise anything, rather than that ! And when every courtesy continued to be showered on him ; when the Infanta was styled officially Princess of England ; when the English fleet was standing by for orders to escort the Prince and his bride home ; when St James's Palace was being got ready for their reception ; was it the time for the devout lover to abandon hope of his beloved, or to boggle over a condition, more or less, in the contract ?

Olivares, manœuvring for a breakdown, found his game almost defeated by the willingness of this impossible young man to pledge himself, and his country, to any conditions, however preposterous. It might have seemed enough, in all conscience, when Charles agreed to, and got James to confirm, articles that allowed the Infanta to maintain in England an enormous ståff of Catholic ecclesiastics, amenable to no jurisdiction save that of their own bishop, and with a church of their own to which all Englishmen might resort ; that provided for the education of the royal children, till the age of ten, in the Catholic faith ; and that pledged the English Soveriegn to make perpetual dead letters of all laws against Catholics, and never allow any new ones to be enacted.

And yet this programme, which could hardly have been forced upon Protestant England without a revolution, proved to be only a first instalment of the price that Spain intended to exact for her Infanta's hand. In July a fresh set of secret articles was presented, in which "I Charles, Prince of Wales" engage to lengthen the Catholic education of our children by another couple of years ; to be accessible at all times, laying aside all excuse, to the solicitations of our Consort's divines ; to pledge our royal honour to carry out the complete programme of Catholic toleration within three years ; to extend it to Scotland and Ireland. Charles asked leave to refer these articles to his father, who was expected to be bound by them too—this was refused, upon which he meekly toed the line. Olivares was perfectly dumbfounded, and could only gasp out that he would as soon have expected his death.

But that crooked grandee was not at the end of his resources or his demands. It now turned out that King Philip was not going to part with his sister on the mere faith of Charles's word. He would first see the programme put into effect in England, and meanwhile, as a supreme concession, the marriage might take place in Spain and the couple remain there till the following spring, by which time, as the wily Olivares no doubt foresaw, the lady would hardly be in a condition to undertake the journey. The effect of this modest proposal would thus have been to make hostages not only of the heir to the English throne, but of his heir in the next generation. And yet it appeared, that rather than go without his Maria, Charles would be willing to submit even to this ! And having beaten him down thus far, Philip and Olivares were not only ready, but eager, to make a match of it.

But there were limits to the amount of blackmail that Charles was prepared to stand. All through his life it was his fate to be misunderstood, no less than to misunderstand others. Olivares was the last person to be capable of realizing that whatever else he might pledge away, there were certain fundamental loyalties that Charles would die rather than betray. One of these was to his sister, Elizabeth, of the Palatine. And it had been stipulated all along, in these marriage negotiations, that King Philip should join with King James in getting her and her husband back to their Rhineland principality. Olivares, in his usual flowery way, had professed his master's willingness to put his signature to a blank sheet on which Charles might write his own conditions about the restitution. As a matter of fact, there was not the least chance or intention of a Spanish finger being lifted on behalf of so peculiarly obnoxious a Calvinist as Frederick. And Olivares, who had no doubt by this time come to believe that Charles would stand anything, was at last imprudent enough to let him into the truth. Asked whether Spain would join with England in putting pressure on the Emperor, he blurted out that one Hapsburg would never under any circumstances employ his forces against the other—in other words, that Frederick might whistle for his electorate so far as Spain was concerned.

This time Charles, if we may trust Buckingham's account of the matter, flashed out in honest indignation :

"Look to it, sir, if you hold yourself to that, there is an end of all ; for without this you may not rely upon either marriage or friendship."

The end of all was plainly approaching—this dance would no further go. In the heat of the Spanish summer, nerves and tempers were becoming unendurably frayed. Buckingham alone would have been enough to have infected his environment with Anglophobia ; the patronizing familiarity with which he treated his Prince—he was supposed to have sat in his presence without breeches—was particularly shocking to Spanish notions of decorum, and his swaggering conceit must certainly have earned him any equivalent there may have been in Madrid, of the word "bounder." We may dismiss as too good to be true, the story current in England about Buckingham having tried to seduce the Condessa d'Olivares, and having been fobbed off, in the dark, with a diseased strumpet ; but there is no reason to doubt that one of King Philip's ministers told him plainly they would sooner throw the Infanta down a well than entrust her to his keeping.

The Protestant gentlemen in Charles's suite were getting more and more alarmed at the spectacle of their master like wax in the hands of the Papists. It is scarcely to be wondered at that their conduct began to grow more and more outrageous, as they felt the toils of Rome closing round their Prince ; and that they should have relieved their feelings by deriding the Catholic ceremonies, the Spanish garb, and the country generally ; that some of them should even have gone so far as to commit acts of irreverence in the Royal Chapel. Their worst fears of Jesuit proselytizing seemed to be confirmed when Cottington, believing himself at death's door, allowed himself to be received into the Church, though as soon as he began to convalesce he went Protestant again. And then a lad called Washington, who really was at death's door, sent for an English Jesuit to grant him the last consolations of orthodoxy. The good father, when he arrived to do his office, found his way to the sick room barred by a bevy of excited Protestants, one of whom, young Sir Edmund Verney, so far forgot his own chivalrous nature as to hit him in the face. This, in a country where an ecclesiastic was almost as sacrosanct as a Brahmin in India, was the direst provocation that could have been imagined ; it is impossible to say to what lengths the Madrid mob might not have proceeded, had not the Alcalde arrived with Gondomar to quiet them down. We can scarcely blame King Philip that, after some angry interchanges, he intimated to Charles that if he wanted to stop in Spain for the winter, he must get rid of every Protestant in his suite.

That even Charles could not be expected to stomach. He must

go now and go single. He was fortunate in being able to go at all. But apart from his Favourite's political manœuvres, Philip's personal conduct was throughout that of the honourable, though ineffective, gentleman who appears on the canvas of Velasquez. He even went so far, when, subsequently, the rupture became open, as to return the costly presents, including Prince Henry's jewelled sword, that Charles had given in his capacity of the Infanta's lover. But so far, there was no open rupture—the marriage was now decided upon, and Charles had left a proxy for it to be celebrated in Madrid as soon as a new dispensation had arrived from the Pope who had just been elected. And his bride would follow him home in the spring.

Never was the cordiality of his hosts more overwhelming than at this time of parting. It was all that Charles could do to prevent his prospective brother-in-law from accompanying him the whole way to the coast. The entertainments rose to a climax of magnificence ; presents were showered on the Prince, and on Buckingham, of fabulous value. At the spot where Charles and Philip parted, a pillar was set up in token of their perpetual amity.

Buckingham, however, could not resist a parting shot at Olivares. He would be eternally obliged, he told him, to the King, Queen and Infanta, but as for himself, he need never consider him as a friend, but must expect from him every possible opposition and enmity. To which the Count-Duke replied with what must have been maddening blandness, that Olivares very willingly accepted what was offered him.

On the 18th of September, Charles set sail, with the fleet, for England, and looked upon Spain for the last time. If anything could have been calculated to add to the bitterness of his cup, it must surely have been the sight of the magnificent State room that had been fitted up, on the flagship, to accommodate his bride.

What were the feelings of Maria Althea on his departure ? One might imagine them to have been those of profound relief and thankfulness, especially in view of the fact that even Charles had become acutely apprehensive that after betrothal, or even marriage, she might seek to escape him by shutting herself up in a nunnery. But this is by no means so certain. She was now recognized as Princess of England ; had been taking lessons in English ; had had time to become accustomed to the thought of the handsome and courtly young Prince as her destined husband. The heart of few girls would fail to have been touched, to some slight extent, by so romantic a devotion as that which had inspired the journey to Madrid—perhaps even the jump from the wall may, when she had stopped screaming and had time to think it over, have been judged an error on the right side. At any rate, it was confidently asserted that she had been extremely indignant when it transpired that Charles had actually decided to go home without waiting any longer for her ; and that afterwards she had not only repudiated with scorn the nunnery suggestion, but had called her father's ministers blockheads for refusing to let her present Charles with a parting token, on the ground that this would disqualify her from any future engagement. As if she were the sort of girl who would allow herself to be wooed twice !

The main source of this evidence is the Countess of Olivares, and truth was hardly a speciality of the Olivares family. But, on the other hand, it was accepted and endorsed by Bristol, whose honesty is above suspicion, and than whom there was no man whose judgment one would be more inclined to respect. It is at least consistent with what we know of human nature, that the Infanta should have begun to fall in love, just when the Prince was beginning to fall out of it.

It was, at any rate, a merciful dispensation that kept her from becoming in fact, as well as name, a Princess of England. The lot of a Spanish Infanta in that Protestant and Hispanophobiac atmosphere would have been wretched, at the best, and it is only too probable that she would sooner or later have found the martyrdom that she had, at one time, anticipated. It is satisfactory to record that in due course she was happily married to the Austrian Prince who became Emperor Ferdinand III. She was only forty when she died, in child-bed.

8

HOMECOMING

A DISILLUSIONED lover crossing the Bay of Biscay in a sailing ship, may be expected to undergo some revulsion of sentiment, especially if he has, before setting sail, shown signs of hedging. The depth of Charles's romantic infatuation for Maria is, in fact, hardly more remarkable than the precipitancy of his haste, once the engagement had become definite, to throw the poor girl over and repudiate the bargain that her brother had succeeded in driving with him.

Even while he was on his way to the coast, Charles had sent back one of his suite, bearing instructions for Bristol to hold up the proxy for the marriage until he had obtained a definite guarantee that the bride would, under no circumstances, escape him by getting herself received into a nunnery. This message was not to be delivered to the Ambassador till the arrival of the Pope's dispensation, the object being to hold up the marriage ceremony until the required guarantee could be sent to England for the approval of the bridegroom. Bristol, who got the message, owing to a false alarm of the dispensation having arrived, while Charles was still in Spain, was urgently concerned to hush up all suspicion of this piece of insulting sharp practice lest the Prince should never be allowed to leave the country at all.

If anything could have been wanted to complete the revulsion that Charles was obviously beginning to feel against the whole idea of the Spanish alliance and marriage, it would have been the reception he got on his arrival. Though he had never been disliked, he had never, till now, known what it was to ride on the full tide of popular applause. When, on the 5th of October, he landed at Portsmouth and proceeded to Buckingham's house in London, he found himself the nation's darling, and Buckingham its hero. All London went as mad to greet him as if he had been another Black Prince returning from another Crécy. The crowd outside Buckingham's house was so thick that it seemed as if the coach were being carried on its shoulders, and they were begging the Prince at least to stop long enough to allow them to gaze their fill on him. Tables of provisions were spread out in the streets ; hogsheads of wine were broached ; all the bells of the city mingled in one wild carillon with the boom of the Tower guns ; a cartload of condemned felons, whom the Prince met on the way to Tyburn, were reprieved ; at St Paul's was sung that Psalm of thanksgiving, "When Israel came out of Egypt and the House of Jacob from among a strange people." As soon as it grew dark the sky reflected the blaze of no less than 108 bonfires ; if a cart of wood was met, the mob would take out the horses, and burn it, cart and all. Not since the days of the Armada had there been such unrestrained jubilation.

What precisely was it all about ? It is the habit of mobs to symbolize their emotions by some human embodiment, and Charles had become a hero, not on account of anything that he himself was, or had done, but because for months past the heir to the English throne had been visualized as in the physical and spiritual clutches of the unspeakable Spaniards—at the best, doomed to the darkest dungeon of the Inquisition ; at the worst, saddled, and through him, England, with another Bloody Mary, who would never rest until she had brought England, body and soul, into slavery. The Spanish marriage had been a fiendish nightmare, that now was beginning to dissolve into what most honest Englishman hoped would be the rosy dawn of a Spanish war.

It would have required a deeper insight into human nature than had been vouchsafed to Charles, not to have taken these demonstrations at their face value. As for Buckingham, with his instinct for setting his sails to the most propitious wind, the opportunity was golden. He was already the favourite of the King ; he would add to that something greater still, in becoming the favourite of the people. It mattered little that he had thrown himself heart and soul into the Spanish *entente*. Hatred of Spain, war with Spain, was obviously a winner, and on this Buckingham was now prepared to put his shirt. Besides he, even more than Charles, had a personal grudge to work off on his late hosts. He had conspicuously failed to carry all before him, in his accustomed manner, at Madrid. He had even been snubbed. Olivares accepted what was offered him, did he ? He should accept something more than he had bargained for, if all hell had to stir for it.

It was all the more necessary for Buckingham to seize this opportunity of putting himself on the popular side, as during his absence there had been signs of such a gale of indignation rising against him, as King James had foreboded. Not only had the great nobles, who had crawled to him while he was present, begun to pluck up enough courage, during his absence, to hint at their real sentiments, but as the author of the Prince's ill-starred journey into Spain, he had been the subject, according to his biographer, Wotton, of "millions of maledictions." To put himself at the head of the crusade, so long desired, against Spain— that would be a stroke of genius indeed ! With his Prince's heart, his Sovereign's will, and the support of a peace-weary nation at his command, to what heights of power and glory might he not expect to climb ! And how mean-spirited would it be, to be niggardly of hazarding a few thousand lives, more or less, for such a stake !

The two returned heroes—heroes because they had succeeded in returning without the terrible young lady they had set out to seek—only stopped in London for a short breathing space, before getting on to the North Road to seek out their "dear Dad and gossip" in his hunting box at Royston. Poor old James—and when we call him old, we must remember that he was still two years short of sixty—was now beginning to show more plainly than ever signs of breaking up under his complication of maladies. His whole system was infected with gout, and he was becoming terribly drowsy—he played cards to keep himself from dropping to sleep. The absence of his "Dog Steenie" and "Baby Charles" had been a terrible trial to him, though he had done all he could to make the best of it, and to enter into the spirit of their adventure, speaking of them as "two dear adventurous knights in a new romanso"—though this had been far from expressing what he really felt about an enterprise undertaken in the teeth of his better judgment, and from which he foreboded dire peril.

His affection for both of them grew greater with their absence, and expressed itself in a paternal solicitude for Buckingham's young wife, and for her little daughter, "pretty sweet Moll," to whom he constituted himself a sort of adoptive grandfather. He, according to the disapproving testimony of a Puritan chronicler, "that never much cared for women, had his court swarming with the Marquis's kindred, so that little ones would dance up and down the privy lodgings like fairies."

By this time, what with his failing will-power and increasing affection, he had rached that stage at which it was no longer possible for him to deny or resent anything where Steenie was concerned. The Duke—for that supreme title had been conferred on him while he was in Spain—had taken liberties in his correspondence in which few real sons, even to-day, would dream of indulging with their fathers. There is one joint letter from Madrid for fresh supplies of jewellery, which ends with a postscript in Buckingham's own name, in which His Majesty is informed, "If you do not send your Baby jewels enough, I'll stop all other presents [they had sent home an assortment of animals including an elephant]. Therefore look to it."

But James was incapable of any other emotion but longing for their safe return—"I apprehend," he had written, "I shall never see you, for my extreme longing will kill me"—and here at last were his "sweet boys" home again, safe and sound. It must have been with an unwonted alacrity that he shambled downstairs to greet them, and as they knelt before him, fell, like the father in the parable, on their necks and kissed them. All three were in tears. Then they retired to an inner room, and there remained for four hours on end ; the courtiers outside the door could only hear their voices, sometimes low and sometimes loud, mingled with bursts of laughter. It would appear that Charles was telling his father what he thought of the Spaniards and all their works, asserting that he was quite ready, if permitted, to undertake the conquest of the country. When at last they emerged, to partake of a late supper, the King seemed perfectly satisfied with the negative outcome of the journey, since, as he expressed it, he liked not to marry his son with a portion of his daughter's tears.

But indeed it mattered little now what he liked, or disliked. Even if he had been as vigorous and resourceful as in his Scottish youth, instead of a tired and moribund invalid, he would have found it hard to withstand the combined pressure of his son and Favourite, backed as they were, by the Protestant and patriotic sentiment of a peace-weary nation.

One thing that must have given him unalloyed pleasure was the difference that these six months in Spain had made in his now fully grown-up "Baby." Charles had come back, no longer with the oval, boyish countenance with which he had set out, but with the beginnings of the pointed beard that, more than any other feature of his, has impressed itself on the imagination of posterity. It was symbolic of the mental and spiritual development that these difficult months had speeded. He was beginning to enter, with an assured confidence, upon the responsibilities of a public career. His grave, and yet gracious, deportment, that had so favourably impressed the Spanish Court, was all the more noticeable in contrast with the incurable unkingliness of his father. In an England more and more tending to Puritanism, it was especially important that not the least sexual peccadillo should have been alleged against him. At this stage of his career all things seemed to be working together in his favour—even the collapse of his Spanish adventure had had the effect of a triumph. He was still something of an enigma, but there were few who can have doubted that the heart of its mystery was golden.

Buckingham, whose will was now supreme as that of few

THE BETROTHAL OF CHARLES AND HENRIETTA
MARIA SOLEMNIZED BY CARDINAL RICHELIEU IN
NOTRE DAME, PARIS, 1625—*from a contemporary print in the
collection of Mrs E. Wingfield-Stratford*

The right Honorable John Digby Earle of Bristol
Baron of Shirborne, Vice Chamberlaine to his Ma.tie
and one of the Lords of his Maiesties most Honorable
privy Counsell; and Embassador extraordinary to the
high and Mightie Philip the fourth king of Spaine
Are to be Sould by William Peake

LORD DIGBY, FIRST EARL OF BRISTOL—*from
a print in the British Museum*

English Sovereigns have been, and who had Charles to all intents and purposes hypnotized, did not intend to let the grass grow under his feet. Already, before they had reached Royston, the Prince had taken the opportunity to snub the Spanish Ambassador, who had demanded an audience. The break with his perpetual friend, Philip, and his almost betrothed, Maria, could not now be made too soon or too brutally.

There was no doubt every reason for crying off this contract of a Spanish marriage, but unpleasant as the business of its repudiation must necessarily have been, there was not the least reason why it should have involved the transition from friendship to war. The last thing that Olivares or Philip were likely to want, was to make Charles's breach of promise the excuse for plunging into a conflict that their country neither desired nor could afford. There was no reason, in fact, why the peace that had lasted now, for nearly twenty years, should not have been maintained for at least another twenty.

But this would never have suited Buckingham. It was his habit to do everything by extremes. If his masterpiece of diplomacy, his attempt to dominate the European situation by means of an Anglo-Spanish *entente*, had failed, he would step forth in shining armour as the young war-god, the leader of a nation in arms, reviving, on sea, the triumphs of the Elizabethan age, and on land, providing the spear-head of an anti-Hapsburg coalition, and eclipsing the glories of Agincourt upon the plains of Germany. As for Charles, his motives were more narrowly personal. He loved and pitied his sister ; he loved and idolized his friend ; he had loved "Maria his star"—and that love had been scorned. He had drained the cup of humiliation to the dregs, and now he was tasting for the first time the intoxicating draught of popularity. The lover scorned had become the people's hero. He, even more than Buckingham, was breathing fire and slaughter against his late hosts.

The poor old King—what could his opposition count now ! "What !" he had cried to his son, in a voice broken with tears, "would you engage me in a war in my old days, and make me quarrel with Spain !" Such feeble protests could easily be brushed aside. Steenie and Baby Charles knew well enough how to overrule their Dad and gossip for his own good. King James, though his mind's eye was undimmed and his tongue as voluble as ever, had ceased to guide the Car of State. The reins—and the whip—

were in the strong hands of the real King, George Buckingham, whose five years' reign—one of the most momentous in the nation's history—dates from his return from Madrid.

9

YOUTH AT THE PROW

THE Infanta's business was soon settled. The Pope's dispensation arrived in due course. Wedding by proxy was fixed for the Prince's birthday ; the streets of Madrid were decorated with the gayest colours in anticipation of the event. But now a very different language began to be heard from that of the bland acquiescence and willingness to concede everything to which the Spaniards had grown accustomed. The astonished Philip found himself presented with a virtual ultimatum. He was bidden to grant the full English demands in that matter of the Palatinate ; he was to join in restoring Frederick, if it meant driving out his cousin, the Emperor, by force of arms. Even so he kept his temper ; promised to use his best offices, but pointed out—what Charles had known perfectly well when he had left his proxy—that a war of Hapsburg against Hapsburg was not practical politics. That being tantamount to a refusal, the whole business of the marriage was held up indefinitely, and the Princess of England found herself thrown over, practically at the church door.

Neither Buckingham nor Charles was minded to let off Spain with a mere snub. Nothing but blood and plunder would satisfy them now, and they were determined to get their war started as soon and effectively as possible. But war is not to be waged without its sinews, and James's peace time finances, even after Cranfield's reforms, were not capable of bearing the least additional strain. There was only one thing to do, and that was to bring Parliament back to Westminster. It is true that the record of King James's three previous Parliaments had not been encouraging ; but that was doubtless because James had never understood the art of capturing their imaginations with a popular policy. That art Buckingham was confident that he possessed. He would give them their war, and he made no doubt that they would furnish him with the money to wage it.

What sort of spirit was abroad in the country had been shown only too plainly by a shocking tragedy towards the end of October, when a number of Catholics had gathered together to worship God in an upper room of a building adjoining the French embassy. Owing to the collapse of a beam, not only that floor, but the one below, fell through. No less than ninety-five men and women, including the officiating priest, were found crushed to death amid the debris. The event was hailed with jubilation by the good Protestants of the London mob, who far from making any effort to help those who were still alive, taunted and jeered at their sufferings. One poor girl, who was carried away, half dead, from the ruins, was reported to have been set on by certain of the elect, who were hardly restrained from finishing her off. The thing was quite obviously a judgment of God on the Papists —some ingenious person discovered that the day had been the equivalent, in the Roman calendar, of the Fifth of November ! The Bishop of London showed himself worthy of his flock, by refusing Christian burial within his diocese to any of the victims, and when at last they were shoved into pits dug in the embassy grounds, the Council thoughtfully ordered the pulling down of the black crosses that had been put to mark them. Who could doubt, under these circumstances, the popularity of an anti-Catholic crusade !

It was on the 14th of January, just before the elections to the new Parliament, that Buckingham put before the committee of the Council, whose business it was to deal with Spanish affairs, a proposal for making the refusal of co-operation in the Palatinate a *casus belli*. This was a little too much for these responsible statesmen who, though they were unanimous in wishing to cancel the marriage treaty, yet, by a majority of nine to three, voted down the war proposal, driving Buckingham into one of those towering rages of his, and eliciting from him torrents of abuse. One of the Councillors had even been bold enough to ask Charles, who was present, the more than awkward question whether, when he himself had sworn to the marriage treaty, he had stipulated for the restoration of the Palatinate. The Prince could only, after a long silence, stammer out something unplausible about his will being his father's.

However, a mere expression of opinion was not likely to check Buckingham in his warlike career. The support of Parliament was what he most needed now, and Parliament could be trusted to meet in a properly bellicose mood. The opening speech from the King, a pathetic and almost humble appeal for help and counsel, still ingeminating "that general peace of Christendom, wherein I have always constantly laboured," was a mere formality, and the real business of the session began by Lords and Commons being summoned into Buckingham's presence, in the hall of the royal palace, to hear from his own lips what he chose them to know, and believe, about this affair of the Spanish journey. At his side was the Prince, to nod or interject such corroboration as Buckingham might deem necessary.

Such assumption of royal power by a subject, not even of the blood royal, was a thing unprecedented since the days of Simon de Montfort. And yet Buckingham's speech, for all its haughty eloquence, was no more than a splendidly disingenuous attempt to explain away his own more than questionable part in a notorious fiasco, and to do this in the meanest of all ways, by putting the blame on to an innocent scapegoat. This was the unfortunate Earl of Bristol, who was still conveniently out of the country, though already under orders of recall, in disgrace, from his post at Madrid ; the impression conveyed being that the Ambassador, in almost treasonable collusion with the Spaniards, had sought to inveigle his Prince into the toils of a humiliating treaty, if not into the bottomless pit of the Catholic faith.

Buckingham and Charles were so much the heroes of the hour, hatred of Spain and Catholicism had become so overmastering an obsession, that Parliament was in a mood to swallow even this. The Spanish Ambassadors were obliging enough to play into Buckingham's hands, by an indignant complaint in which they suggested to James that Philip, in his place, would have had the Favourite's head. Immediately this got known, the Duke became more of a popular hero than ever. The most turbulent members of the Commons were the foremost in belauding him. One of them prayed that he might keep his head on his shoulders, in order to see thousands of Spanish heads off theirs. Even the saturnine Coke waxed almost benevolent : "And shall he lose his head ? Never hath any man deserved better of his King and country."

The great experiment, of co-operation with Parliament on a patriotic basis against a national enemy, had thus been started by Buckingham and the Prince under the fairest auspices. And indeed, Charles showed every sign of blossoming out into a great Parliament man. He was constantly in attendance in his seat in the

House of Lords, and had begun to take frequent part in its debates, his somewhat hesitating delivery and the dignified seriousness of his pronouncements being exactly suited to the style even then favoured by the Upper House.

It is true that the ominous issue of privilege had been raised again in the Commons, in a speech of arresting eloquence, by Sir John Eliot, who, though still a young man—he was not yet thirty-two—was already a person of some notoriety. Scion of a rich, Cornish family, he had all the impulsive, emotional temperament of the true Celt. When still a boy, he had, in a fit of ungovernable temper, stabbed a certain Mr Moyle, who had complained to his father about his extravagance ; he had afterwards apologized with such warm-hearted frankness as to make a friend of the victim. He had had the luck, while finishing his education in Paris, to strike up a friendship with young George Villiers, who, as Duke of Buckingham, took charge of Eliot's career, and got him appointed to the lucrative Vice-Admiralty of Devon. In this capacity he had distinguished himself by the capture of a famous pirate, Captain Nutt, whom he had lured into his clutches by what seems to have been a piece of decidedly sharp practice, though fair play is hardly what a pirate has a right to expect. This one, however, had made to himself friends of the mammon of King James's court, and Buckingham being in Spain, not only did Nutt get himself restored to the freedom of the High Seas, but the Vice-Admiral found himself in the Marshalsea Prison, from which Buckingham, on his return, quickly secured his release.

With such an experience fresh in his mind, it was perhaps natural that Eliot should have rounded on the Court, by resurrecting that claim to unqualified freedom in criticizing the royal policy, which had caused the breach between the King and his last Parliament. But though this speech established him in the first rank as a Parliamentary orator, the House was not ready, as yet, to be diverted from its crusade against the Papists, to its chronic struggle of privilege against prerogative.

On one thing everybody—except possibly the King, who had almost ceased to count—was agreed, and that was on the complete and formal repudiation of the treaties with Spain, and with them, all idea of a Spanish *entente* or a Spanish marriage. But after this no one was quite clear what was to happen. Parliament wanted the King to provide them with a good war, but with the unspoken proviso that it was to be a good cheap war—if such a thing could conceivably exist—the war indicated being one of glorified piracy against Spain. James, who had no quarrel, and did not want to pick one with Spain, could only conceive of drawing the sword on behalf of his exiled daughter, and that only as a last necessity. Buckingham's towering imagination already included both these objects in the plan that he was beginning to form for dominating the whole European situation. He had got his chance, at last, for the display of those heroic and statesman-like qualities to which the whole of his amazing career, hitherto, had been designed to afford scope.

The Duke's megalomania infected the mind of his princely second. They saw the world spread before them like a promised land, into which they would march conquering and to conquer, confident that all walls would collapse at the first blast of their trumpets. They scorned to enter into nice calculations about the sufficiency of means to ends, still less to split moral hairs about the rightness of the means they employed to smash down opposition.

That Buckingham should behave like a beggar on horseback was no new thing, but it is certainly remarkable that Charles, who had already given proof of the sweet courtesy and kindliness that he was to retain, even to the bitter end, should have committed the key of his manners to such keeping, in this, the last year of his Princedom. There are some incidents which, if they were all we had to judge him by, would leave us with the impression of a boorishly unpleasant young man. His manner of breaking off his engagement, and his calculated rudeness to the host who had entertained him so nobly, and to whom he had so recently vowed undying friendship, is hardly the sort of conduct one would have expected from a Prince and a gentleman. While Philip was punctiliously returning Charles's presents, on the termination of his engagement, Charles was giving Philip's choicest gifts to his lackeys, and when two cartloads of hams, raisins, figs, capers, and other Spanish delicacies, arrived as a gift to him from the Condessa d'Olivares, he was caddish enough not only to refuse them without thanks, but contemptuously to hand them over to his suite, to divide up among themselves in any way they chose.

But there was worse to follow, conduct that we can only under-stand, or explain, by the complete ascendancy that Buckingham appears to have established over Charles at this time. That the Prince should have condescended to unprincely rudeness to

Spaniards, who had fooled him to the top of his bent, was at least human, but that he should have deliberately set himself to ruin the two most tried and faithful servants that the Crown possessed, that he should have lent a willing hand in striking from beneath the throne its strongest props, this one can only describe as criminal lunacy.

The first victim to be marked down was Cranfield, who had now been promoted to the Earldom of Middlesex, and who, at the Treasury, continued to maintain the new standard of business-like efficiency that was probably as valuable to the Crown as the yearly grant of one or two Parliamentary subsidies would have been. But all this went for nothing when Middlesex was found guilty of the unforgivable sin, treason to Buckingham. The old merchant was far too shrewd to be deceived about the possibility of a cheap war ; he realized only too well the effect that the breaking of the peace must have on his struggle against odds to make income balance expenditure. More than anyone else in the country—more even than the King—he was capable of realizing how, and why, the path of war was, for the English Crown, that of inevitable ruin.

He had been in the opposition, of which he was probably the backbone, on the Council to Buckingham's war policy ; he had even had the courage to tell the Prince that, having pledged his troth to the Infanta, he supposed he "ought to submit his private distaste therein to the general good and honour of the Kingdom." To which Charles had retorted, with that overbearing rudeness he had borrowed from Buckingham, reminding the Minister of his humble origin, and bidding him judge of merchandise, since he was no arbiter on points of honour.

If elementary decency could not have restrained Buckingham and the Prince from prosecuting their vendetta, an even more elementary prudence might have made them careful about their choice of means. If there was one thing the Crown had more reason to dread than another, it was that medieval process of impeachment, by which the last Parliament had already deprived the Crown of the services of Bacon, and by which it would be possible, in case of a serious conflict, to strike down all its loyal servants one after the other. It is extraordinary that Buckingham should not have realized how this practice of flicking off the heads of the tallest poppies would be bound to affect the tallest of all. But neither he nor Charles appears to have been capable of looking further ahead than the accomplishment of their desire on anyone who dared to stand in their path.

It was easy for a man who pulled as many wires as Buckingham, to get an impeachment started ; once started, there was no question of its failing. There was not a statesman of that time in whose record, if it were closely enough examined, some irregularities could not have been discovered, just as in the days of the old twenty mile speed limit, there was not a motorist on the road who did not render himself liable to prosecution. A minister who practises rigid economy, and makes a point of getting his master twenty shillings in the pound, is raising up against himself an army of enemies. And a minister who is even suspected of being lukewarm towards a popular war policy, is politically, and was in those days often personally, a doomed man.

So it proved with Middlesex. Any stick was good enough to beat a suspected Pro-Spaniard. His defence, that was courageous and substantially convincing, went for nothing with his fellow peers. Nor did it even avail him when Buckingham, owing to a bout of malaria—the legacy of some Spanish mosquito—had to retire from the proceedings ; for Prince Charles was there to take his place, driving home every point against the devoted Treasurer, as if he had been an aspiring junior suddenly called to take his leader's place as prosecuting counsel.

Poor old James was not unnaturally appalled. He had begged Charles and the Duke to refrain from a course that, he foresaw, would inflict an injury on the Crown not easily healed. To all his solicitations, arguments, commands, they had turned a deaf ear. At last, losing his temper completely, he had retorted upon Buckingham with words of prophetic insight :

"By God, Steenie, you are a fool, and will shortly repent this folly, and will find that, in this fit of popularity, you are making a rod with which you will be scourged yourself."

Then, turning to his son, he warned him that he would live to have his bellyful of Parliaments, and that he would have cause to remember, some day, how much he had contributed to the weakening of the Crown by this precedent he was so fond of—by which, if we may trust Clarendon, the King was referring not only to the precedent of impeachment, but also to that of war.

He might as well have spoken to stones, for all the attention he was likely to get from his audience. They knew that he would do nothing, so what heed need they pay to his maunderings ?

James did indeed make one pitiful effort to save his Treasurer, or at least to soften his fall. He summoned the Peers to his presence at Whitehall, and told them that he had come to sing a psalm of justice and mercy. And when, on his putting forward some plea in Middlesex's favour, he had been contradicted by his son, he had given him the lie in front of them all. Nobody cared—they were used to the old man's tantrums.

So Middlesex fell. He was sentenced to a swingeing fine, to lose all his offices, to be banished from Court, and to lie in the Tower during the King's pleasure—who of course had him released after a few days. But the Crown had been deprived for good of its ablest administrator ; had surrendered its power to keep, or to save, its chosen servants. Neither Pym nor Eliot nor any of the Parliamentary extremists could have planned, or struck, a deadlier blow at the Throne than this, which had come from the wanton fist of its heir.

By this time, it had become only too painfully evident that, for all its professions of loyalty, the Parliament of 1624 was destined to be only a degree less troublesome to the Crown than its predecessors. It did indeed authorize the levy of a sum amounting to about £300,000, but this was to be conditional on the breaking off of the Spanish treaties, entirely earmarked for war and preparation for war, and, to prevent the King getting a penny for his own needs, placed under the trusteeship of Commissioners that Parliament itself appointed.

Meanwhile, as James the Peacemaker still made every possible shift to play out time and to postpone the outbreak of a war that he could now hardly hope to avert, Parliament could at least speed up the good work against the Catholics on the home front. They put forward what the King truly described as a stinging petition, for the enforcement of persecution up to the utmost legal limit, to which the King, who, as he himself put it, was resolved not to be "coney-catched," or made party to a religious war, returned a soothing answer. But when Parliament tried to make the sting effective, by framing a Bill on these lines, the King refused to pass it.

At the end of May, the Houses were prorogued, ostensibly till the Autumn. His Majesty may well have felt, like Cromwell of a later Parliament, that they had been there too long for any good they had been doing lately. His peace policy was on its last legs ; his administration fatally weakened ; his finances in no way

relieved ; and the eternal process of whittling down his prerogative had started again with a Bill, restricting the Crown rights—
which had no doubt been gravely abused—in the matter of
patents, or, as they were called, monopolies. His Parliament's notions of statesmanship had proved to be limited to
the pursuit of war abroad and persecution at home—and to
these he was expected to conform. Worn out as he was, he
could at best act as no more than a feeble brake upon them,—
hardly felt now that his son and Buckingham had gone over to
their side.

But Buckingham, who had staked everything on the support of
Parliament, was incapable of holding this, or any, course, for
longer than it took for a new idea to penetrate his brain. He,
backed of course by Charles, having achieved popularity by
exploiting the popular aversion to a Catholic marriage, was now
minded to crown that achievement by a master stroke of diplomacy, in the shape of—another Catholic marriage !

For this sort of work, Parliamentary support was out of the
question. And so James, though his failing strength was enough
to carry him on through that Autumn and into the following
spring, had looked his last on Parliaments. Even Charles was
never again to encounter a Parliament with which his relations
were not those of active hostility, or, until armed men had put a
barrier of steel between him and his people, to taste the sweets—
the bitter sweets—of popularity.

10

LOYALTY REWARDED

THERE was one other piece of work that Buckingham and Charles
had to do, before developing their new policy. They had deprived
the Crown of its ablest administrator, in Cranfield ; it only
remained to strike down the ablest, as well as the most loyal, of
its diplomatic servants.

The Earl of Bristol, left behind in his thankless post at Madrid,
had marked, with a heavy heart, how matters were drifting
towards a needless war, and strove, against increasing odds, to
preserve those friendly relations that the Duke and Prince were

determined to sever. In December he had written to Buckingham appealing to him, in language that might have touched the conscience of anyone capable of putting country before self, to overlook any errors or misunderstandings, "since the present state of the King's affairs requireth the concurrency of all his servants, and the co-operation of all his ministers."

It was in vain ; it was not as a colleague but as a scapegoat that Buckingham wanted to use Bristol, and at the end of the next month he was recalled to England. By this time he had so impoverished himself in his master's service that he had to sell his plate to pay for his passage home. Philip and Olivares, who had acquired during their long association with him an affection-ate respect for the English Ambassador, and who perhaps realized what fate was in store for him, were anxious to heap on him whatever rewards and titles he cared to accept, "only," as Philip said, "to give encouragement to honest and faithful proceedings."

But this he declined, on the ground that Spain was in no way beholden to him, since all that he had done was for his master's service and his own honour. He served a master, he said, from whom he was assured both of justice and a due reward. Whatever his danger, even though it should cost him his head, he would sooner cast himself, like a dutiful subject, on that master's mercy, than be a Duke or Infantado of Spain.

When he was leaving, they approached him again with the offer of ten thousand crowns to put in his depleted purse, and they assured him—one can almost see the smile and gesture of Olivares in saying it—that no one should ever know about it.

"Yes," was the reply, "one would know it, who, I am assured, would reveal it to His Majesty, and that is the Earl of Bristol himself ; and it would not make him so clear in his own heart as he now is."

Such was the servant whom Charles was in conspiracy with Buckingham to drive from his father's and his own service, as if he were an enemy, or a traitor. It might have been different if the Earl had come home wise in his generation, and prepared to take the blame of everything that had happened on his own shoulders. A subtle traitor would have been easier to deal with than an honest man, convinced of his own innocence, and one, moreover, with a tale to tell in its vindication that would have reflected anything but credit on the real authors of the Spanish fiasco.

Bristol had meant exactly what he said when he had expressed his confidence in his master's justice. He desired nothing better than for the most searching light to be thrown on his proceedings ; undeterred by the fate of Middlesex, he was only anxious to be brought to a fair trial. Failing that, there was at any rate his master, who would surely be prepared to judge his case on its merits.

That this confidence was not unreasonable is shown by the line that Charles and Buckingham adopted. For the best of reasons, they desired darkness rather than light on their trans- actions at Madrid. Bristol must be prevented from making his defence public ; he must even be stopped from approaching his King, to pour Spanish poison into the old man's ears, and perhaps strengthen his resolution for peace. What is extraordinary is that James himself should have put up with this treatment, and that he should have allowed the Earl to be forbidden his presence, at least until a Commission should have enquired into his conduct. The Commission did enquire, and Bristol proved to have a conclusive answer to every question that could be put to him.

What was to be done with him now ? Buckingham was ready to let him retire unharmed, under a cloud, into private life, if he would only consent to go quietly. But Bristol was not the man, where his honour and loyalty were concerned, to give way an inch—and now at last James was expressing his willingness to receive him. That must at all costs be prevented. There was at first the idea of putting Bristol into the Tower, but even Bucking- ham was forced to recognize that this would not do. And so, with more than doubtful legality, the Earl was put under a sort of open arrest in his own house at Sherborne. He was thus effectively put to silence, and his proud spirit had to stomach the disgrace, with the appertaining injustice and ingratitude, as best it might. He was not even to be allowed the privilege of access to his Sovereign, nor was his Sovereign to be allowed to grant it. It was no wonder that a state of affairs in which the liberties of subject and Sovereign alike could be so cynically violated, should have been extremely unpalatable to a country wedded to the tradition of Magna Charta and the Common Law. And when such things were done, not even by divine right of kingship, but by the fiat of a mere upstart, it ought to have been evident that the cup of George, Duke of Buckingham, was full to overflowing, and that any regime that depended on him for support was in danger of sharing in the fall that is the sequel of pride, and the destruction that awaits those whom the gods make mad. For the egomania, fostered by success in the brain of the once kindly and generous George Villiers, had brought him perilously close to the borderline of sanity.

But Charles, even now, had not done with Bristol. He seems to have conceived against him the same kind of resentment that he harboured against the Infanta. It was characteristic of his reserved nature that he should have been liable to this sort of brooding resentment. A stammering little boy, such as Charles had been, lacks the outlet for his feelings afforded by a good, honest tantrum. He gets into the habit of swallowing his rages, and thus allowing their poison to infect his system ; and of all resentments the bitterest are those that touch pride. I should be inclined to suspect that what most annoyed both Charles and Buckingham, in their different ways, about Bristol, was the man's sheer impeccability. The uncomplaining service he continued to render in conditions that their folly had made desperate, must have been in the last degree irritating to their pride. He put them most hopelessly of all, by his very refusal to put himself, in the wrong. It is unfortunately less hard to forgive the wrong done to us, than the wrong into which we have been put, by our fellow men.

Accordingly we find Charles's hatred of Bristol expressing itself in the pettiest and meanest persecution. One of his first acts on coming to the Throne was to strike his name from the roll of Privy Councillors. When Bristol asked to be present at the coronation, Charles, not content with refusing, countered with a brazen accusation, which he did not dare to bring to the test of a trial, of the Ambassador's having attempted to pervert his faith. And then, by perhaps the most arbitrary of all extensions of his authority, he tried to prevent him from taking his seat in the Lords.

As we shall see, one of the principal causes of Charles's eventual downfall is to be sought in the disloyalty of his nobility. But we must not forget that when—in the days of his hypnotism by Buckingham—he had encountered loyalty, he had had an odd way of rewarding it.

It only remains to say that the loyalty of Bristol remained proof against the extreme of ingratitude. He lived to receive the honour of inclusion, during the Civil War, in the Parliamentary black list of unpardonable royalists. Of such loyalty as his, it can be said, without qualification, that it is

> Still the same
> Whether it win or lose the game.

I I

COURTING TRAGEDY

WHILE Bristol was on his way home from Spain, a diplomatist of a very different calibre had set forth on a confidential mission to the Court of Louis XIII at Paris. This was Lord Kensington or, as he was shortly to become, Earl of Holland, a younger brother of the Earl of Warwick, and a descendant of the most unredeemed knave in all the gang who had risen to nobility and affluence by doing Henry VIII's perhaps beneficent, but certainly dirty, work. He was an amiable young gentleman, who had done a little soldiering, but found himself better suited to the profession of courtier, as he possessed the art of making himself agreeable to everybody, and particularly to people like Buckingham, whose favour was so much more important than merit to aspiring pushers. As his subsequent career showed, his amiability embraced a willingness to take any side or adopt any principles. If he had any guiding principle, it is summed up by Clarendon, "He did think poverty the most insupportable evil that could befall any man in this world."

He had gone to Paris to sound the authorities, tactfully and unofficially, on the possibility of arranging a marriage between the Prince of Wales and the little, dark-eyed Princess who had already danced before him when he was on his way to Madrid, and who, to judge by the remark she had let fall on that occasion, was quite prepared to fall in love with him.

But the marriages of royalty are dictated by other considerations than those of romance. It is important that we should understand what was in the mind of Buckingham, its prime mover, in forwarding this proposal, which, it may be remembered, was not altogether new, some tentative approaches having been made

towards it before Charles had become committed to the affair with
the Infanta.

Buckingham and Charles had committed themselves very
light-heartedly to a policy of war, and since Charles at least made
the recovery of the Palatinate a *sine qua non*, war on a scale to
which England's resources were absurdly inadequate. She had no
army to speak of, and a very modest navy ; and though twenty
years of peaceful prosperity had rendered her a comparatively
wealthy nation, only so much of her wealth was at the disposal of
the Crown as the clutching fist of Parliament could be induced to
let go. How, under such circumstances, could there be any
question of her making head against the mighty armies, now
flushed with victory, that were at the disposal of the Spanish-
Austrian alliance ?

There could be only one answer—she must take the field in
conjunction with allies powerful enough to supplement her own
deficiencies. She must constitute herself the nucleus of a great
anti-Hapsburg coalition. But where was she to look for such allies ?
The Dutch had their hands full defending their own territory ;
the Protestant princes of Germany were manifestly incapable—
even if they could be brought into line—of making head against
such veteran armies as that of Tilly ; while the King of Sweden,
while willing to come in as generalissimo of a Protestant coalition,
demanded a price for his services payable in advance, that put
him out of the question for needy James. But there was one first-
class Power that was the traditional enemy of the House of
Hapsburg, and all of whose interests were opposed to that House's
domination of Europe. That Power, quiescent hitherto, was France.

A glance at a political map of Europe at that time, will show to
what an extent France was enringed and cramped in by Spanish
territory. In the north-east was the Spanish Netherlands, which
came as close to Paris as Arras ; to the east was the bulge in her
frontier made by the Province of Franche Comté ; to the south-
east, beyond the buffer State of Savoy, lay the Spanish Milanese ;
in the south-west were the provinces of Cerdagne and Roussillon,
inviting the Spanish armies to debouch on the French side of the
Pyrenees.

Moreover, it was a prime object of Spanish policy to keep
France from achieving unity under the strong hand of her Kings.
Any conspiracy of the feudal anarchs against the central govern-
ment, from the time of the Catholic League to that of the Fronde,

was pretty certain to have Spanish backing. The Spanish attitude
to France, at the time of the Counter Reformation, was, in fact,
curiously similar to that which the France of the Third Empire
was destined to adopt towards Bismarck's attempt to unite
Germany. A strong Power does not readily forgo the luxury of a
weak neighbour.

A less acute intelligence than that of Buckingham could have
grasped that a strengthening of the Spanish circle, by an occupation of the Upper Rhineland, was likely to be extremely distasteful
to France ; and that a triumph of the Hapsburg interest in
Germany, reviving the menace of Charles V, and enclosing her
as in the grip of gigantic pincers that might at any moment
tighten on her vitals, was a consummation that she was bound to
resist. Thus what was mainly of sentimental interest to England,
was to France a matter of life or death.

Henri IV, when he had been struck down by the hand of an
ultra-Catholic fanatic, had been about to launch his French
armies in a grand attempt to settle accounts with the Hapsburgs.
Sooner or later, after the confusion of a royal minority, it would
seem that some monarch or statesman was bound to resume his
work. And this year, 1624, after a succession of shadowy adventurers had kept France impotent, the reins of government were to
be once again grasped by a strong hand, that of Cardinal
Richelieu, incomparably the ablest statesman of his time. The
great and growing energies of France, a Power as much on the
rise as Spain was on the decline, were once again to be applied
effectively, and perhaps decisively, to the European conflict. It
was in her obvious and traditional interest that they should be
thrown into the scale against the Hapsburgs ; and for Buckingham, who was committed to employing the wholly insufficient
forces of England to the same end, a French alliance offered the
only apparent chance of success.

But there was one other factor to be taken into account. The
supreme trial of strength between the old, united faith of Western
Christendom, and the great revolt that threatened to end that
unity forever, was now at its height, and England was frankly
inspired by the spirit of an anti-Catholic crusade. But France
was a Catholic country, and Richelieu himself a Prince of the
Church, one who had enjoyed the Pope's special protection, and
who had, like Henry VIII, employed his pen in the defence of
the faith. Was he to betray that Church and deliberately to

shatter her unity just when it seemed on the point of being recovered?

That is exactly what Richelieu did eventually set himself to accomplish. He had a clear choice between serving his faith and his country, and with true French lucidity he chose the latter, even if it meant being the Judas of a supreme betrayal. As a Frenchman, in the tradition of French statesmanship, he could not do otherwise. France had had her phase of Christian idealism, when she had constituted herself the spearhead of the crusades. After St Louis had closed his eyes in Africa, far from Jerusalem, there was to be one policy for the French monarchy—of cold, calculated, nationalist egotism. In spite of his title of Most Christian King, that pattern of French chivalry, Francis I, had not hesitated to call to his aid against the Holy Roman Emperor, the arch-enemy of Christendom, the infidel Turk. It was a card that was to be played again by Louis XIV.

What followed from this? It was a safe calculation that, in the long run, France, once she was in strong enough hands to take a decided line, would take that best calculated to advance her own interests; and that England, if, and so long as, she could make her own line coincide, might reckon on a union of forces. But particular attention is needed to that qualification, "in the long run." It was in February that Buckingham had first started putting out feelers for a French alliance; it was not until August that Richelieu was firmly in power, and even so he had to feel his way cautiously. In these opening phases it was his interest, and perhaps his inclination, to show himself a Catholic as well as a Cardinal.

There was a point that does not seem to have occurred to Charles or Buckingham at the time, and which—as far as I am aware—has never been raised since. Granted that a French alliance was indicated—as it certainly was if England must needs be committed to a war policy—what conceivable object was to be gained by a royal marriage? If there was one thing certain about French policy in general, and Richelieu's in particular, it was its entire freedom from any sentimental bias. The fact that a Spanish Infanta was Queen of France, and a French princess on the throne of Spain, was of purely domestic interest, that did not in the least tend to mitigate the deadly rivalry of Bourbon and Hapsburg. A Bourbon princess on the throne of England would not affect the employment of a single French soldier; but it would affect, very disastrously, the fortunes of the English monarchy, and perhaps of England herself.

The sole reason for the sudden popularity that had blazed on Charles and Buckingham, had been popular relief at the escape from a Catholic marriage, with Catholic toleration by treaty as one of its conditions, a concession that was regarded, by the average English Protestant, as the thin end of the wedge of Catholic conquest. Parliament had, in fact, displayed an almost frantic eagerness to impress on the Crown that the one thing it was prepared under no circumstances to stand, was the least concession to the so-called recusants, or relaxation of the persecuting code. Not only that, but King James had given the most explicit assurance that he would allow no such conditions to be attached to any future marriage treaty, and Charles himself had solemnly sworn that in the event of his marrying a Catholic, "she should have no further liberty but for her own family, and no advantage to the recusants at home"*—and this was in April, when Kensington's mission was already some weeks old. It was no doubt a correct statement of his intentions at the time.

That, after the lesson they had just received, he and Buckingham could be mad enough to be drawn into another Treaty similar to the abortive one with Spain, might well have seemed beyond the limits of credibility. A blunder may be worse than a crime, but *felo-de-se*, being both, is worse still.

Nor did there appear to be any prospect of such a necessity in this opening phase of the negotiation. Handsome Lord Kensington, all gaiety and compliments, was soon a thoroughly popular figure at the Louvre, and he understood exactly how to get round that all important personage, the Queen Mother, Marie de Medici, the massive, heavy-featured woman, whose reputation for beauty it is so hard to deduce from her portraits. The regular ambassador, Sir Edward Herbert, understood the French nature well enough to be extremely sceptical of the prospects of obtaining the Princess's hand on any but the most ruinous terms ; but Kensington was quite sure that everything would be all right, and every one perfectly delightful.

With all the tact of an expert matchmaker, he kept each of the prospective lovers primed with the most favourable impressions of the other. Of little Henriette he wrote to Charles that she was "the sweetest creature in France and the loveliest thing in nature" ;

* Gardiner, v, p. 222.

that her singing voice was the loveliest not only in France but in Europe—"beyond all imagination and that is all I will say of it" ; that she danced as well as he had ever seen anyone ; and —what would probably 'have surprised Henriette—that her wisdom was "infinitely" beyond her years. If anything could have added a spice to these perfections, it was the information that the young Comte de Soissons, who had been desperately in love with her, had, by his own account, been prevented from cutting Kensington's throat only by the fact of his being ambassador to so great a Prince.

With Henriette herself, Kensington went to work with a miniature of the Prince which hung in a gold case from his neck. The ladies of the Court displayed the most flattering eagerness to inspect this, and poor Henriette was terribly annoyed that she alone was prevented by a cruel etiquette from admiring it, except at a distance. However, Kensington knew how to circumvent this, by getting the lady at whose house he was staying to smuggle it into the hands of the Princess, who retired with it to her cabinet, where, after opening it with passionate haste, she remained gazing at it for an hour on end. This, Kensington said, was in strictest confidence : "I would rather die a thousand deaths than it should be published, since I am by the young Princess trusted, who is in beauty and goodness an angel."

He did eventually apply to her mother for a personal interview, on Charles's behalf, with Henriette. Queen Marie, thoroughly enjoying herself, talked it all over with the charming envoy, trying to pump him as to what exactly he meant to say. He eventually let it be dragged out of him that he intended to present the Prince's service "not by way of compliment any longer, but out of passion and affection ... with some little other such-like amorous language."

"*Allez, allez,*" the Queen Mother had purred, her large features lighting up with a smile, "*il n'y a point de danger en tout cela. Je me fie en vous ! Je me fie en vous !*"

Nor, he told Charles, was her trust abused, except that he laid it on even thicker to the daughter, than he had to the mother. Henriette, he reported, had "drunk it down with joy," and made the prettiest little speech in acknowledgment.

This was extremely delightful, but the serious business of diplomacy was yet to come. Not that Kensington anticipated any special difficulties—the French seemed to be in the most accommodating mood. It was true that King Louis did not think it consistent with his dignity to bind himself in set terms to a military alliance—all that would come right if he were only give time. So in May, in order to put the marriage negotiations on an official footing, Kensington was joined by a new envoy extraordinary, in the shape of James's old favourite, the esurient and extravagant Hay, now Earl of Carlisle, and married to a lady whose fascination had made her a theme for the most renowned poets of the day—she was Carew's Lucinda, Cartwright's Lucy ; Herrick, D'Avenant, Waller, Suckling, had paid her lyric homage. She was a daughter of the Earl of Northumberland, who, though at the time of Hay's courtship he had been undergoing a prolonged detention in the Tower, had lost none of his pride, as head of the Percys, and remarking that he was not fond of Scotch jigs, had kept his daughter with him. But Lucy was not the girl to be denied her own way, and was out of the Tower long before her father. She was as fond of intrigue as her husband of food, and specialized in it for its own sake—a faculty that was to have momentous consequences.

But Carlisle, in spite of the Gargantuan attention he paid to his belly, was far from being a mere yes-man like his fellow envoy. They were soon hard at work trying to arrange matters with the French ministers, of whom Richelieu was one, though not yet the chief, this being a certain La Vieuville. It was the object of each side to avoid tying itself down more than it could help. James was determined to keep at least the letter of his pledge to Parliament, and Charles was reported to be even more emphatic in his determination not to be drawn into a French edition of the ill-fated Spanish treaty. It was not believed that the French were disposed to raise serious difficulties about the Catholic question in England. La Vieuville, who protested that he only wanted to do something to placate Henriette's godfather, the Pope, was ready to be satisfied with a secret letter from James, declaring his willingness to show favour to the Catholics. But in this, La Vieuville proved to have gone too far in the way of concession. The conscience of young Louis was aroused ; the chief minister was dismissed, and his place taken by Richelieu, who was to keep it till death.

The new chief, with the lucid deliberation that was characteristic of him, at once began to put the screw on the English negotiators. It was no question of vague assurances ; the price of

Henriette was to be no less than had been demanded for Maria Althea, a formal and binding contract of Catholic emancipation, as stringent in its provisions as the one that Parliament had anathematized, and that both James and Charles had pledged themselves up to the hilt never to renew. To concede this would be to sacrifice the honour of the English Crown, and perhaps, in the long run, the Crown itself. The King who, no less than his son, had made it clear that anything of the sort was out of the question, did the honest and obvious thing in authorizing a dispatch to the effect that if France was going to take this line, there was an end to the negotiations. This was the easier to accomplish, as Buckingham, who was still suffering from the effects of his malaria, was away, taking a cure at Wellingborough. At the Court, it was generally assumed that the match was off.

But the Duke was not to be circumvented so easily. He had wind of what was happening in time to intercept the dispatch, and he had not the least hesitation in breaking the royal seal or in giving His Majesty to understand that quite two thirds of it had got to come out. He had, in fact, come to the decision—no doubt foreseen by the Cardinal—that no matter on what terms, the marriage had got to go through.

Buckingham was, in fact, in the position of one of those modern captains of finance who, finding that his schemes are likely to involve him in a colossal smash, gambles recklessly and fraudulently on the chance of tiding over the evil hour. He had committed himself too deeply to draw back now. He had staked his whole reputation on the success of a war policy that, without a French alliance, had no chance of success. England might as well, if left to her own resources, have tried to conquer the moon, as to relax the Hapsburg grip upon the Palatinate.

Even supposing that no breakdown were to occur in the marriage negotiations, this gamble on French support was speculative to the last degree. Richelieu had very significantly, while he insisted on England binding herself, by contract, to relieve her Catholics, refused to commit France to more than a vague, gentleman's agreement to co-operate against the Hapsburgs. He was not specially interested, for the moment, in the Rhineland, as the first move he had planned for France was to cut the military communications between Spain and the Emperor, by occupying the Valtelline, the passage way between the Spanish possessions in Northern Italy, and the Austrian Tyrol. This, from the French standpoint, displayed sound strategical insight, but was of little interest to England, or her protégé, the Elector Palatine.

Buckingham's idea was as crude as this was subtle. There had turned up in London, during the spring, a certain Count Mansfeld, who had already earned himself a reputation of being the most unredeemed ruffian among all the military adventurers who were making Germany, province by province, into a Hell on earth. He had happened, so far, to find employment on the Protestant side, and was even ready to fight for it on occasion, but his real business was that of quartering his armies, or glorified gangs of robbers, upon any friendly or hostile territory that remained unlooted. Such methods did not tend to efficient soldiering, and Mansfeld was now reduced to touting for anyone appreciative enough of his services to recruit and capitalize a fresh army for him. This Christian hero had been accorded an enthusiastic welcome, and from his obscure lodgings had been taken to the palace, and installed in the very apartments that had been destined for the Infanta. It was proposed to let him loose again on the Palatinate, with an army recruited in England, and to secure the co-operation of France in the venture. And Richelieu was ready to give an informal, if not exactly a binding assurance, that Mansfeld might pass through French territory on his way to the front.

It came to this : the King and his son were to break their pledged word ; advantage was to be taken of its absence from Westminster to double-cross Parliament ; whatever popularity had accrued from the avoidance of the Spanish marriage was to be changed to its opposite by the conclusion of an equally objectionable French marriage—all this had Buckingham staked on the success of his gamble. When Spain had been forced to disgorge the wealth of the Indies ; when English regiments had planted their standards on the battlements of Heidelberg ; when the Anglo-French-Protestant alliance had shattered forever the power of the Hapsburgs and the hopes of the Counter Reformation— then indeed the great Duke would be able to confront Parliament and the nation in all the pride of victory, and they would be content to feed out of his hand.

Why should he dream of failure ? He had succeeded so amazingly, so consistently hitherto ; his belief in himself had been so triumphantly vindicated : let him but clearly visualize the end, and the means would—as they always had—furnish themselves.

Which faith, if a man keep whole and undefiled, he has without doubt ceased to be sane.

Unfortunately, it is a faith that is only too easily communicated to less exuberantly vital natures. The influence of Buckingham was hypnotic to an even greater extent upon Charles than upon his father, for James, though he allowed his will to be overborne, never sacrificed his clarity of judgment. But Charles seems to have committed both his mind and conscience to his friend's keeping. Only thus can we explain the partial eclipse, about this time, of that scrupulous and gentle nature of which we have such unvarying evidence in both his earlier and his later years.

But we must make allowance for another reason that was impelling Charles to make the false step from which he was never to recover. He was a very shy and sensitive young man who had been humiliated in love. His very bitterness against the Infanta shows how deeply his self-respect had been wounded. Had he been as easy-going in his morals as almost any other Prince of his time, he might perhaps have found consolation without a bride ; but whether by reason of coldness or principle, this was not for him. It must be marriage or nothing. And here he was, suing for the hand of another Princess, lovelier than the Infanta, and of no less importance. That this wooing should likewise fail ignominiously—was it to be thought of?

Buckingham and Charles, with their vanities and emotions— what chance had they, pitted against the icy intelligence of the Cardinal, who, as far as was humanly possible, had eliminated all personal bias from his determination to serve France, and yet had not ceased to be typically French in his instinct for driving a hard and close bargain ? He had—and he knew it—something to offer, in that little white hand of the Princess, for which the other party to the transaction was prepared to sign a blank cheque. Whether the cheque would be honoured was another matter.

For it is possible for Shylock to be too successful in a bargain, especially when Antonio happens to be his own judge of the extent to which he shall eventually fulfil what is nominated in the bond. It may be that if he had been what he was to become, a few years later, the practically unquestioned dictator of French policy, Richelieu would not have sought a merely formal victory that did, in the event, lead not to an English alliance, but to an English war. But Richelieu knew—what Buckingham never knew—how to adjust his aims to means at his disposal. His predecessor had been dismissed for letting off England too lightly ; if he had followed suit, he would have ended his career forthwith, and all his plans for France would have died stillborn. A success of Shylock might not be wise, but it was certainly necessary.

Accordingly he set himself, politely, remorselessly, to raise the French terms, and insist on an arrangement by which the English monarchy should pledge itself, in the most formal and explicit way, to conditions to all intents and purposes equivalent to those of the ill-fated treaty that had been forced on it a year previously by Spain, and that an outraged public opinion had insisted on tearing to shreds. No doubt the policy that the Crown wished, and was binding itself to pursue, towards its Catholic subjects, was more enlightened and humane than the permanently panic-stricken persecution that found favour with the mob in the London streets, or in the Palace at Westminster. We must not forget that one of the effects of King James's agreement to suspend the operation of the law, was to save from an agonizing martyrdom such priests as were lying under sentence for the crime of minis-tering, by stealth, to their flocks.

But even this is hardly an excuse for the cynical trickery practised on Parliament and the nation, in the conclusion of a contract that both James and Charles had pledged themselves with the utmost explicitness not to conclude, and which, in spite of their pledged word to France, they had not the power, even if they had the will, to honour for very long—except for one part, and that the most vital of all. For though Catholic attendants might be sent packing, a Catholic Queen was presumably a permanency, and a Catholic Queen in one generation might mean a Catholic King in the next. It did, as a matter of fact, mean two Catholic Kings and a Protestant revolution. In this, at least, the popular instinct was justified.

On how crooked a road Charles and Buckingham had set their feet, is shown by the fact that Parliament, which had been pro-rogued to the Autumn, was, on the thinnest of excuses, prorogued again. With this contract of the French marriage on hand, there could be no question of facing it. There was no way now but to prevent it from meeting until it could be presented with the accomplished fact of the marriage, and bidden, in effect, to like it or lump it. But by that time, if Buckingham's gamble came off, there would be victories on land and sea to afford overwhelming justification of all that had been done or left undone. If——

The Court was at Cambridge when, a fortnight before Christmas, the French ambassadors arrived for the signature of the contract. James was by this time almost on his last legs. He passed most of his time in bed in his lodgings at Trinity, though he did succeed in getting down for a magnificent feast in Hall, followed by a philosophy act, which, we are told, he "slept out very patiently." His hands were so swollen with gout that he could not hold a pen, and he had to sign his name with a stamp. To make all sure, a separate document was presented, in which, "I, Charles, Prince of Wales," am made to promise, on the faith and honour of a Prince, to fulfil all stipulated conditions in favour of the King's Catholic subjects. In a more comprehensive sense than when he set up his standard at Nottingham, he had declared war on his Parliament.

12

VENI DOMINE JESU !

WHILE these things were going on at Cambridge, scenes of a different kind were being enacted at Dover, where Count Mansfeld was beginning to assemble the Protestant army with which Buckingham proposed to make the first move in his great war game. A fine army it was, on paper, many of the most distinguished family names in England being found on its roll of officers—one that occurs twice being that of Cromwell.

It was on the 7th of November that the Count had received his commission from James. There was one consolation about this expedition, in that it did not cause the King formally to break that peace which it had been his life's work to conserve. By the easy conventions of the time, it was possible to furnish troops to combatants without becoming a combatant oneself.* His instructions to Mansfeld were strict, to the effect that his forces were, on pain of the stoppage of all support, to be used solely for the purpose of restoring the Elector Palatine, and not to be employed against any of the Spanish King's territories.

Buckingham, as Lord High Admiral, was to arrange for the transport of this force of twelve infantry regiments, as soon as it

* A practice that has been revived in Spain.

was complete, to Calais, where, it was expected, the cavalry arm, supplied by France, would be awaiting it, and then they would march to the Rhine, to try conclusions with the great Tilly and his unconquered veterans.

England had no military organization to speak of, nor any standing army to provide an expeditionary force. The deputy lieutenants of the various counties were each required to press a fixed quota of men into the service, and probably showed little more appreciation of military quality than Falstaff himself. In one official despatch we read of the heavy countenances and the sad farewells of these poor fellows, who were forced from their native villages, to trudge miserably over the almost impassable roads of that late season to the rendezvous at Dover. When they arrived, they found little or nothing provided for them. That was not Mansfeld's way—he expected his troops to provide for themselves. There was soon a reign of terror at Dover. The recruits were short of pay and would have starved if they had not pillaged. They broke into houses, and seized every scrap of provision that was brought into the town ; they swarmed over the countryside for ten or twelve miles around, slaughtering the sheep and stealing everything they could lay their hands on. Some were killed by the inhabitants in defence of their property, but there were few civilians who dared open their doors or venture into the streets. The men were out of control of their officers, and thought nothing of beating them ; if a soldier did get arrested, his comrades would break open the jail ; they even threatened to hang the Mayor and burn down the town. Some couple of thousand—and they were the lucky ones—contrived to desert. Their commander does not seem to have done anything in particular to remedy matters —happenings of this sort were all in the day's work with such as Mansfeld.

The army, or rabble, was doomed from the start ; and ever to have brought it together, under the circumstances, was sheer manslaughter. James, whose resources hardly sufficed for his peace time requirements, was incapable of providing for their pay or keep after the new year, and though Charles put his hand into his own pocket to the extent of £20,000, this sum was soon swallowed up. There was no question now of applying to Parliament, or indeed of facing Parliament. The only thing to do was to get the men shipped out of the country, on board the 195 miscellaneous craft that had been got together to receive them, but not to ferry them over to Calais, since in spite of all assurances and gentleman's agreements, the French Government now flatly refused to admit this swarm of human locusts to any part of French territory. So the flotilla trailed miserably past the Flemish coast, to drop anchor off Flushing, where the twelve regiments remained packed on their transports. Only after they had consumed the last of their rations and starved for forty-eight hours, were they taken further up the coast and allowed to land, amid the full rigours of a Dutch winter. Abandoned, as it seemed, by God and man, what was there for them to do but die, which they did with appalling rapidity ! Privation and indiscipline soon brought disease in their train. In a very short time, a bare quarter of the original force was left capable of bearing arms. Only through the charity of the Dutch, did even that remnant survive. They never saw the Palatinate ; not many of them saw England again.

Such were the first fruits of Buckingham's splendid policy. If we do not rank Mansfeld's expedition with that to Walcheren as among the major disasters of British military history, it is because these lads, dragged from their peaceful employment at home, are hardly entitled to the name of soldier. But to the least of them life was as dear as it was to Buckingham himself, and far dearer than it would one day become to Charles.

King James, if he had not the means to make reasonable provision for these unhappy subjects of his, did at least put forth his best endeavours to localize the mischief, and to keep the expedition to its original purpose of rescuing the Palatinate, instead of being diverted to the support of the Dutch against the still friendly monarchy of Spain. With the last strength of his failing will he clung to that peace ... there were rumours of his old friend, Count Gondomar, coming back to his post in London, to strengthen his hands against those who were determined to imbrue them with unnecessary bloodshed.

But the long day's work was drawing to a close, and the burden that James Stuart had no longer the strength to bear, was about to be transferred to younger shoulders. To his other complaints had been added, early in the year, a touch of that tertian, or malaria, fever, that was so terribly common in those days. He appeared to rally, but by the middle of March it had become plain that the body, worn out and rotten with every sort of malady, would not longer house the soul.

As the King began to sink, that incurable busybody, Bucking-

ham's mother, with the assistance of her son, and to the wrath of
the royal physicians, put him through a course of amateur
doctoring which was only successful in starting a rumour that
Buckingham—and there were some who even hinted at a more
august confederate—had been guilty of poisoning his Sovereign.
This charge was monstrous ; but the time was at hand when men
would believe anything that could be alleged against the Duke.
There was enough poison already in James's system to do its
work without human aid. It was on the morning of the 27th of
March, that Prince Charles was summoned hastily from his bed
to his father's room. The dying man was just able to recognize
him, and to murmur, "*Veni Domine Jesu !*"—"*Come Lord Jesus !*"
And so, in faith of a more merciful judgment than any he was
destined to obtain on earth, he sank into unconsciousness, and
presently Bishop Williams, who for days had scarcely left the bedside closed his eyes.

Poor James ! Whatever his shifts and shortcomings, he had,
after the great work that he had done for Scotland, kept his
second kingdom at peace—alone among European nations—for
nearly a generation, a peace crowned with unexampled prosperity.
May not we, to whom the assurance of such a boon would be
beyond hope, and almost beyond dream, concede to his memory
this much :

> A good man, through obscurest aspiration,
> Has still an inkling of the one true way.

IV

The Duke

I

CONFIDENT MORNING

KING James's funeral was celebrated with much solemn ceremonial, and his virtues were duly enlarged upon by obsequious divines, but the nation had little attention to spare for mourning him. All eyes were fixed upon the young Sovereign, with his pale countenance and reserved manner, who was still, to the ordinary man, something of an enigma.

There was, at any rate, no reason to doubt of a favourable solution. Nothing was, as yet, known to his disadvantage, and he had none of the ordinary princely blemishes ; he was neither a waster nor a libertine. How fatally he had undermined his popularity by his surrender to Rome in the marriage contract was not yet realized—if he must have a Catholic bride, the daughter of a Protestant hero was the least objectionable choice he could have made. The announcement of his engagement had even been the occasion of rejoicing, with the inevitable bonfire accompaniment, in London.

One thing was soon evident ; the free and easy court life of the last reign was a thing of the past. Unlike his father, Charles was every inch a king, and hedged about with a dignity that he never suffered to be relaxed. There had been no difficulty in approaching James, but access to Charles was a privilege only to be obtained with appropriate formality through official channels.

His own strictness of life was extended to his environment. Behaviour in the palace was henceforth to be no less decorous than in church ; drunkenness and swearing were taboo ; the King was so particular about religious ceremonial that he informed a certain Irish lord, who had not been in the habit of coming to prayers, that he must either do so in future, or get out of his house.

The first indications, to those behind the scenes, of the tendency of the new reign, went to show that Buckingham, who on the first night was allowed to sleep in the King's bedchamber, was likely to be even more unquestioned as the power behind the throne, and that whatever brake James had been able to apply to the new war policy, was taken off. The veto on the employment of Mansfeld's force—or what little desertion and disease had left of it—in the Dutch service against Spain, was promptly withdrawn. One of Charles's first instructions was for writs to be issued for the election of a new Parliament, the last being automatically dissolved by the late King's decease. The Lord Keeper, the slippery Williams, had urged delay, to give time for as many elections as possible to be rigged in the interests of the Crown. But His Majesty would have none of it.

"It is high time," he said, "to have subsidies granted for the maintaining of a war with the King of Spain, and the fleet must go forth for that purpose in the summer."

Williams, "who had little dreamt," says his biographer, "that the almanac of a new year, and a new reign, was so soon calculated for the longitude of a war, or the latitude of such vast sums of money to pay the service," was too good a courtier to oppose even the most disastrous of royal projects, and consented with a few embarrassed words that plainly showed his lack of enthusiasm. Charles was so put out at even this sign of an independent judgment, that he turned his back on the Bishop and caused him to leave the presence. Under the new regime it was evidently not enough for a counsellor to be a yes-man, if the affirmative was not pronounced with sufficiently convincing heartiness.

But the new policy was already getting itself tied up in difficulties. It was only too evident that the French alliance, on which everything hinged, was not coming up to expectations, and that Richelieu was not minded to give the least *quid pro quo* for the concessions he had forced out of England. And even if France had been willing to co-operate frankly against the Hapsburgs, her hands were not free, now that the Protestant stronghold of La Rochelle, on the Bay of Biscay, had broken out into rebellion. Before there could be any question of effective action beyond her frontiers, France must be united within them.

The effect of this was to introduce an awkward new factor into the problem of English statesmanship. It was one thing to make common cause with a Catholic Power against another, but when that Power was mustering all its resources to stamp out a small and heroic Protestant community, was Protestant England likely to tolerate its monarch in the rôle of aider and abettor ? And yet it would not be easy for her to escape from it, since among the other engagements into which Richelieu had succeeded in luring her, was one of providing for the loan of one British warship and seven armed merchantmen, for the ostensible purpose of a diversion against Genoa. Now that a Huguenot—or French Protestant—admiral had almost wiped out what there was of a royal navy in France, these English ships were more urgently in demand than ever, and it would be hard indeed to find an excuse for refusing them. For Charles had none of the lucid unscrupulousness of Richelieu, which sought no excuse for evading an inconvenient obligation.

The Entente Cordiale, of which the royal marriage was to be the seal, had thus done no more than involve England in heavy liabilities, without adding one jot to her assets. Buckingham's scheme for controlling the European situation had not even started to work.

That, however, was no discouragement to so invincible an optimist. The Duke had no doubt whatever that he had only to appear at Paris in person, in order to control the situation, and Richelieu into the bargain. He had an excellent pretext, in the ostensible purpose of escorting Charles's bride to the sea coast ; for, King James's funeral notwithstanding, there was every reason for getting the knot safely tied before the assembly of Parliament. That knot Buckingham would convert into a double one, of a national as well as a personal union. He would carry everything before him ; he would dazzle the French Court by the brilliance of his personality, the unexampled magnificence of his attire and retinue ; he would go on to dazzle the imagination of King and Cardinal by the magnificence of the plan he intended to submit to them—the new English navy thrown into the scale, the French frontier expanded in its critical north-west section, the Huguenots pardoned and quiescent, the Hapsburg dominance broken. That would surely have the effect of bringing France into line and making the alliance a going concern ! It would be a diplomatic coup worthy of its author's genius.

Charles had come to see things so habitually through Buckingham's eyes, that it is improbable that he envisaged the possibility of failure. Otherwise he might have had some disquieting reflections when, a week after his father's death, he walked, on a spring morning, from St James's Palace, across the Park, to take up his residence at Whitehall. For even thus early, his prospects were so fatally compromised that it needed a miracle to save him from disaster. He had, by his marriage policy, forfeited in advance the goodwill of his Parliament ; he was on the way, by his war policy, to put himself at their mercy. No man was ever less addicted to revealing what he thought, but it is to the last degree improbable that any forebodings of this sort marred his enjoyment of what must have been a lovely scene, for beyond the ribbon of buildings lining the Thames from Charing Cross to Westminster, it was practically open country ; the first green must have been in the hawthorn, and the willows just sprouting by the ponds that were, in the next reign, to be joined into one sheet of artificial water. Perhaps, as is the way with quick walkers, he had no energy for reflection.

It was—to the best of our knowledge—the first walk of his reign. It is certainly by this way that he was to pass again on his last walk of all—not with the song of April thrushes in his ears, but with the continuous throbbing of drums drowning every other sound.

The train of events was already in motion that was to set those drums beating.

2

TRAGIC COMEDIAN

EVEN with the signing of the marriage contract at Cambridge, the path had not been quite clear, since His Holiness at Rome had been inclined to stand out for still higher terms before granting the dispensation. But Richelieu, who knew when he had reached the limit of the obtainable, was not going to throw away the fruits of a hard bargain by seeking to make it even harder. He was as capable, at a pinch, of standing up to the Vicar of Christ as to a heretic King, and he made it clear that the marriage was going through even if no dispensation arrived at all.

This had the desired effect, and on the First of May the marriage was celebrated, by proxy, and with great pomp, at the Cathedral of Notre Dame. Charles was represented by the Duke de Chevreuse, a distant relation of his, through the Guise family, and so thoroughly as to withdraw, in his capacity of temporary Anglican, during the service.

A fortnight later arrived Buckingham, for the ostensible purpose of escorting the new Queen to her English kingdom, but really in order to arrange for effective co-operation between the two countries against the common enemy. But the idea that it would be possible, by sheer force of personality, to quicken the diplomatic gait of Richelieu, was a fallacy, and Richelieu would never have dreamed of arousing his young King's latent obstinacy by trying to rush him into any policy for which his mind had not been prepared. The diplomacy of the bull in the china shop was, in fact, no more successful in Paris than it had been in Madrid ; and Buckingham was forced to realize the impossibility of obtaining those quick and striking results from his mission that alone could have enabled him to save his face before the impending Parliament.

The invariable effect of repulse in Buckingham was to make him lose his temper, and on this occasion his reaction was so extravagant that one can hardly describe it as sane. He would have his tit for tat with Louis by capturing the affections of his Spanish Queen, to whom, after a miscarriage, Louis had ceased to be husband in anything but name. No doubt the handsome Duke promised himself an easy conquest, and one that would not lie too heavy on his conscience. The criminal recklessness of the all-powerful English minister inflicting such an insult on the head of a friendly state, does not appear to have struck him.

The whole Court of France, including those of the Queen, the Queen Mother, and the Queen of England, set forth on a progress to the coast, where the English fleet was waiting to convoy Henriette to England. It was like a moving Field of the Cloth of Gold, as it proceeded to an accompaniment of the most extravagant pomp and pageantry. But Louis was taken sick and had to go back to Paris, and then the Queen Mother also went down, which occasioned a fortnight's delay at Amiens—the suspicious Puritans in England would not believe that the excuse was genuine, and talked of a fortnight's penance imposed by the Pope on a heretic's bride.

This left the coast clear for Buckingham. There seems little doubt that Anne was flattered by his attentions, and ready enough for a discreet flirtation, but Buckingham had not the least idea of where to stop. Thanks to a too tactful equerry, he contrived to get her alone round the turn of a garden walk—we cannot be quite certain what actually occurred, but it was enough to convince Anne of the expediency of calling out, in order to get rid of him. Even that might have been hushed up, if Buckingham had been capable of taking a snub. But nothing would satisfy him, even after he had accompanied Henriette's cavalcade on to Boulogne, but to hang up the expedition still further by rushing back on some frivolous excuse to Amiens, where the other two Queens still were.

Here he hastened up to where Anne sat in bed, with her ladies in attendance, and flinging himself on his knees, kissed the sheet in a transport of devotion, and started to say all the passionate things he could think of. It was in vain that the Comtesse de Lannoy, a "wise, virtuous and elderly" dame, told him to get up, as this sort of thing was not done in France. The Duke, nothing abashed, nor apparently incommoded by his posture, started to argue with her, saying that since he was not a Frenchman, he was not bound to observe the laws of the State—and so he went on, until the Queen, who had had more than enough of this highly compromising foolery, ordered him out of the room. The matter was, of course, reported to Louis, who was furious, and dismissed several of the Queen's attendants.

The least result of the Duke's visit was that he had made a monumental fool of himself in public. As long as he remained chief minister, the prospects of friendly co-operation with France were fatally prejudiced. Anyone who knew his temperament might have foreboded that he would never stomach this humiliation, and that he would vent it in enmity to the country in which it was now impossible for him to set foot, except by force of arms. It was something more than probable that to the other fruits of the Buckingham regime would sooner or later be added war with France.

3

FOR BETTER OR——

But for little Henriette, round whom all this magnificence centred, there were no forebodings. Even now she was only fifteen, and thoroughly excited at the prospect of meeting her handsome lover. We catch a glimpse of her on the beach of

Boulogne, "in good health and very merry," getting her feet wet above her ankles and retiring "with great pleasure." After all, she was still no more than a child, enjoying the most stupendous treat that child ever had provided for her.

There were more serious things, if she had had time to think about them. Her mother had, during her illness, produced one of those letters of good advice, by which so many mothers flatter themselves that they perpetuate at least the ghost of an authority over their offspring. It would raise Marie of Medici considerably in our opinion, were it not for the more than suspicion of the real author having been Henriette's confessor, Father—soon to be Cardinal—Bérulle, friend of Descartes, and one of the greatest of French mystics. It was an impressive and eloquent composition, in which the young Queen is exhorted to remember her descent from St Louis, who had died true to his faith among the infidels, and of whom his mother, Queen Blanche, had often said that she would rather see him die than live so as to offend God. The effect of it was, that the girl was going to England in the capacity not only of Queen, but of missionary, charged on the peril of her soul and honour to bear high the torch of faith in a heretic land. This may not have been calculated to produce much effect in the excitement of the moment, but later on it might sink deep into her subconsciousness.

It was not until the 11th of June that Henriette was able to embark on the *Prince*, the flagship of the squadron that was transporting her enormous suite, some 4.000 souls, across to Dover. It was blowing what sailors will never admit to be more than half a gale up the Channel, and even the sumptuous accommodation and band of musicians provided for her, did not prevent her from succumbing to the rigours of her first voyage. It took twenty-four hours until, about eight o'clock on a Sunday evening, the *Prince* drew up alongside the landing-stage in Dover harbour that Charles had had especially constructed for the occasion. The wind, which had dropped a little towards sunset, got up again during the night, and this was taken to show that even the elements had had the little lady's interests at heart.

Charles had not been there to greet her on her arrival. With a rare considerateness, he had stopped at Canterbury, in order to give her a chance to recover from the voyage, and to be looking her best after a good night's sleep. But with a lover's eagerness, he rode over first thing next morning, arriving unexpectedly at the

Castle while she was still at breakfast. Disregarding with an equal
eagerness his courteous message that she should finish her meal,
she ran down the stairs, and fell on her knees that she might kiss
his hand. He caught her up in his arms, covering her face with
kisses. She began to stammer out the words of formal politeness
she had got up for the occasion, but she broke down, and began to
cry in the middle of the first sentence, which gave him a delicious
opportunity to soothe and comfort her, assuring her of every
kindness in her new home. His task was not difficult, and she was
soon the less shy of the two. As he relaxed his clasp, she saw that
he was looking down at her feet, very probably with a return of
that tongue-tied embarrassment of his, and jumped to the
conclusion that it was to see whether she was employing artificial
means to enhance her tiny stature. Displaying a very neat
shoe and ankle, she looked up at him, saying, in her native
French,

"I stand on my own feet, sire. I am just so tall—neither more
nor less."

That same morning, the long procession set out on the road to
Canterbury. On Barham Downs a pavilion had been prepared,
where they sat down to what was almost a picnic meal, at which
Charles, in the true knightly spirit, waited upon his bride. Good
Father Bérulle was hovering about, reminding her that it was
St John the Baptist's eve, when all good Catholics ought to be
fasting ; but Henriette, after her interrupted breakfast, was not
going to spoil this great day even at his behest, and partook freely
of the pheasant and venison that her husband carved for her.

That was no doubt satisfactory, but there had been already signs
of trouble brewing with the enormous French suite that had been
provided for in the treaty. Henriette's governess, whose name was
Madame de St Georges, but whose nature more resembled that
of a dragon, had expected to ride with her charge in the royal
coach, and was furiously angry at finding the old Countess of
Buckingham and two other ladies of the English nobility accorded
the honour on grounds of precedence. The whole suite was
already chattering with indignation at this insult to France.

The young couple were, however, in no mood just then to
bother about anybody's affairs but their own. The marriage
ceremony was performed that evening after the Anglican rite in
St Augustine's Hall at Canterbury, and the courtiers were looking
forward to the immemorial horseplay of the bedding ritual—

tearing off the bride's garters, and so forth—but Charles, who had seen quite enough of this sort of thing in his father's Court, had determined that Henriette should be spared such an ordeal, and the moment he entered the bedchamber, went round bolting all the seven doors. Next morning he was chaffing his lords about the way in which he had circumvented them.

From Canterbury they came by Watling Street to Gravesend. Here the royal barge was waiting to take them up the Thames to Whitehall. There was good reason for choosing this route, since London was in the grip of the bubonic plague, a visitation only less severe than that final one in the reign of Charles II. However, the perpetual rumble of funerals could not quench the enthusiasm of London citizens for a royal wedding—the river was crowded with every sort of craft, and enough ammunition must have been shot away by the fleet, and the Tower batteries, to have sustained a lively battle. A heavy shower came on as they passed the City, but the windows of the barge were open, the new Queen waved her little hand, and all the folk were shouting at the top of their voices. Only once again was Charles to attract such crowds ; but then there would be no shouting—only a horror-struck silence.

4

THREE WEEKS

It was only two days after the arrival at Whitehall of Charles and his bride, that Parliament was opened with a King's Speech whose dignified reserve contrasted with the long, intimate harangues to which the Houses had become accustomed in the last reign. Here was a Sovereign who might compel more respect, but who might also provoke more hostility. For James's way of pouring out his soul in public had at least made it difficult to quarrel with him seriously ; he had been too human to be opposed à outrance.

It is, at any rate, significant that from the first there is an intransigence about the differences of Charles with his Parliaments that we do not find in their liveliest disputes with his father. In a surprisingly short time, not more than a couple of weeks, there develops a state of chronic deadlock, that can only be resolved by the indefinite suspension of Parliamentary government, or the transfer from the Crown to Parliament of Sovereign power. For the remainder of the reign the issue is brutally simple, and is not decided even by the axe at its close.

And yet it would be the greatest mistake to think of the prosperous and respectable gentlemen who, in the midsummer of this year, 1625, came together at Westminster, as if they had started with conscious revolutionary intention. There were probably few, if any of them, who would not have been horrified at the thought ; who did not sincerely esteem themselves loyal subjects. Whether one or two long-headed plotters were not, even now, exercising their minds with revolutionary possibilities is a matter on which, in the light of subsequent events, we can only speculate, for direct evidence we have none. We can be certain, however, that but for these one or two problematical exceptions, the House was eager to make the best of its young King, and that even against Buckingham there was no decided hostility. No one could have told—themselves least of all—what common purpose would result from this concourse of disconnected wills.

It was, above all, a time for leadership. If the King could have stepped forward, before the assembly had had time to form a mind of its own, with a policy calculated to capture its imagination ; if he had been able to take it completely into his confidence about the end in view, and the sacrifice demanded, he would at least have made the best bid possible for its generosity. It would only have been a continuance of the line that he and Buckingham had taken with the previous Parliament ; a development of the popular Prince into the popular King. How is it that we do not find him attempting to do anything of the sort, and that in these critical opening days he does not grasp the helm, but allows the ship to drift at the mercy of wind and current ?

The truth is that he and Buckingham had brought themselves to such a pass that candour had ceased to be practical politics. Buckingham's brilliant foreign policy had only succeeded in tying up the Crown in a network of obligations. How was it possible to explain to Parliament the fact that Charles had pledged his royal honour to set aside the code of persecuting laws, that he had plainly given the previous Parliament to understand he would be foremost in maintaining ? How was it possible to make a clean breast of that engagement to provide English ships that might—and would be—used against the French Protestants, and out of which the Government was now trying to wriggle by engineering a mutiny among its own seamen ?

And then there was the vital, but assuredly not the little, matter of the Bill that Parliament was to be asked to foot. You cannot have the luxury of a European war for nothing ; and Buckingham was determined to provide this—as he did his other luxuries—regardless of expense. To keep alive that ineffective and half-starved rabble of Mansfeld's—reduced during the summer to a tenth of its original fighting strength—alone demanded £20,000 a month, and as if this were not enough, Charles must needs pledge himself, out of his empty coffers, to become paymaster to his uncle, the King of Denmark, whose army, it was fondly hoped, might become the spearhead of a Protestant coalition. This item amounted to another monthly £30,000—a combined total of £600,000 per annum, bespoken in the name of the British tax-payer for these two more than doubtful side-shows alone. That was without counting the war into which England was about to plunge against Spain, and for which a grand combined military and naval expedition was even now being prepared. To put the minimum cost of the new war policy at a million a year would have been ridiculously modest. We have the authority of Gardiner, that to fulfil his engagements the King would want a gross sum of at least seven or eight millions.* We need not dispute the exact figure—if we were to halve or even quarter it, it would still represent a sum beyond the wildest limits of practicability.

It was easy enough to want, but another thing to ask. Even Buckingham's measureless assurance might have boggled at requesting a cool million, especially when all there was to show as firstfruits of his policy was the Mansfeld fiasco.

And so, apart from some vague generalizations about the necessity of giving an adequate supply, the Commons were left without guidance from either the King or his ministers, to work out their own and the country's salvation. It was the most hopeless line the Crown could have taken.

Hopeless, because in such an assembly, left to itself, there is a tendency like gravitation, to sink (or rise, according to the point of view) into opposition to the Crown. Such a tendency may be counteracted by great effort : King Sisyphus may hold his stone steady, and even push it higher, but if he stands aside it will

* Vol. v, p. 404.

inevitably start downhill and gather momentum, until there is no stopping it.

This is what happened to the 1625 Parliament. Left to itself, it poised uncertainly, and then began to move. To judge from the language of its members, one might have imagined that they were one and all inspired by the most devoted loyalty, which they desired nothing better than the opportunity to prove. They no doubt thought so themselves.

But sooner deeper instincts had begun to assert themselves. There was, at the outset, a proposal to make the plague an excuse for adjourning the session—and therewith the voting of subsidies —till Autumn. This was unsuccessful, though it had among its backers a Member from Yorkshire, Sir Thomas Wentworth, who was fast winning recognition as among the most forceful personalities in the House. Next, it became apparent that the Commons meant to keep the King strictly up to the Protestant mark, and were not prepared to admit the thinnest end of the toleration wedge. A drastic petition to this effect was prepared under the auspices—it need hardly be said—of Mr Pym. This was of course excessively awkward for the husband of Henriette.

Then the House—the Crown having omitted to do so—got down to the brass tacks of finance. And it proceeded to dole out, as the utmost limit of its generosity, a couple of subsidies—no more than £140,000, a ludicrous fraction of the minimum war requirements.

Here then was the situation. Parliament had goaded the King into war, and now that he was committed, proposed to leave him without the means of waging it. It is true that the King and Parliament had been at cross purposes about what sort of a war it was going to be, and that the Commons still clung to the delusion of one with Spain that would finance itself out of loot and, in some unexplained way, make the Emperor relax his grip upon the Rhineland. But even a war with Spain had to be got going somehow, and the combined military and naval operations that were even now being prepared would cost a great deal more money than Parliament was proposing to give, even if that money had been available for the purpose, and not more than swallowed up by the requirements of Mansfeld's devoted following. Parliament had, in fact, called checkmate to the King as far as war was concerned, unless he could find some unauthorized means of providing himself with its sinews.

But it went on to do more than this, and to take steps to render it impossible for him to carry on, by the most rigid economy, even in time of peace. The one thing that, in an epoch of quadrupled prices, had kept the Crown from bankruptcy, was the expanding customs revenue. The fixed dues at the ports, the tonnage and poundage as they were called, were the result of a bargain struck as early as Edward I's time, and their confirmation, by Parliament, for the life of each successive King, had been a mere matter of form for the past couple of centuries. James, as we have seen, had gone further, and successfully established, in his own courts, his right to vary the duties

Now Parliament came forward with the revolutionary claim to deny the King's right to levy any customs duties whatever, except by its permission. Instead of the usual form of granting tonnage and poundage for life, a Bill was introduced conceding it for a year only—and even this got held up in the Lords, and failed to pass. This could only mean one of two things—either the Crown must resign itself to feeding out of Parliament's hand and abdicating every vestige of its sovereignty, or else it must go on, in spite of Parliament, collecting those dues that had been part of its unquestioned prerogative from time immemorial. Naturally it decided on the latter course, and the customs officers went on with their immemorial routine, instead of bringing the whole fiscal machinery of the country to a dead stop. That the King should have lent his authority to such hitherto normal proceedings, has been represented by historians, whose pronouncements even in living memory passed for gospel, as the extreme of tyranny.

It was on the 11th of July, little over three weeks from its meeting, that Parliament was adjourned for the remainder of the month. But that time had been enough to bring about a revolutionary change in its relations with the King. Hitherto, in spite of much friction and bickering, the constitutional balance had not been seriously upset.

Now, however, that Parliament claimed to take away from the King his lawful means of subsistence, other means would have to be found, if the King was to remain a king in any, then intelligible, sense of the word. Thus, early in the reign, the two Sovereign powers in the Constitution had arrived at a state of absolute deadlock, that short of revolution or civil war, there was no possibility of resolving.

5

PRIVILEGE OF PERSECUTION

BEYOND the vista of financial troubles that this brief session had
opened before the King, might have been discerned the beginnings of a religious conflict that bade fair to divide the nation
against itself and the Sovereign against his subjects.

It was not only that a ministerial pledge had been extracted
for the strict execution of the anti-Catholic laws, which the Crown
was pledged, with equal explicitness to France, not to execute—
for this was only what might have been expected, but that this
Parliament was determined to widen the scope of persecution to
include not only Catholics, but High Church Anglicans.

A heresy hunt was already up after an Essex rector called
Montague, who, so far from sympathizing with Rome, had
actually, about a year ago, written an anti-Catholic polemic
under the delightful title of *A New Gag for an Old Goose*, to dispose
of the Jesuit emissaries who, as he believed, were tampering with
his parishioners. But Montague had gone about this business of
goose-gagging in too Christian a spirit. He had dared to insinuate
that the successor of Peter might be a goose without being actually
Anti-Christ ; that the Catholic Church, to which England had
belonged for all but the last century of her Christian existence,
might, though honeycombed with corruption and false doctrine,
still form part of the Church of Christ.

This was dreadful. What would Calvin have said about it ?
What would Theodore Beza have thought, or Perkins, or Whitaker, or any of the sound, Pope-damning Reformation fathers ?
What English Protestant could sleep quiet in his bed, when there
were rectors at large who, instead of hewing Peter to pieces before
his Lord, could actually see some possibilities of good in the
fellow ? This was rank moderation ; it was—to employ the new
Dutch term by which Menshevism was distinguished from
Bolshevism in Protestant circles—nothing less than Arminianism.

But Montague had gone further and done worse. Instead of
allowing himself to be quietly suppressed, or to take a hint from
a properly shocked Calvinist Primate, he had gone off to the
acknowledged Supreme Governor of his Church, King James,
who, moderate theologian as he was, had remarked that if

Montague were a papist he was one himself. The result had been another book, *Appello Caesarem*, which had just come out, duly licensed, with a dedication to King Charles, in which the reverend controversialist had not only reaffirmed his position, but had said some very trenchant things about Puritans. This was enough to arouse, in the Commons, a milder outbreak of the hysterical fury that had, four years previously, been directed against the unhappy Floyd. The affair was actually twisted into Breach of Privilege, because the last Parliament had asked the Archbishop to enquire into the matter of the *New Gag*. The House was even brazen enough to arraign Montague for having in some way dishonoured King James, who had notoriously approved of him.

Things were made worse still by the fact that Charles had sought to protect Montague, by making him one of his chaplains. This was calculated still further to exasperate the Commons, who were firmly convinced of their right to strike down any one of his Majesty's servants without reference to His Majesty's wishes—and had been encouraged in this belief by no one more than His Majesty himself, when Prince of Wales. Montague was accordingly committed to the custody of the Serjeant-at-Arms, though he was allowed to return to his rectory during the recess, under his own recognizances of £2,000 to present himself for judgment at its close, which he avoided doing, on a plea of sickness.

This affair, however ridiculous in itself, was one of the utmost importance in what it implied. For now the Commons, not content with rendering impossible the King's position in the State, were determined to undermine it also in the Church. They would possess themselves of the crozier as well as the sceptre. They would assume the functions of an inquisition, and force their own brand of Calvinism on the divines of the national Church, in complete disregard of its Supreme Governor. On one thing, as appeared in their debates, they were enthusiastically agreed, and that was on the iron necessity of every one being compelled, if not to think, at least to speak and write to the same effect on matters of faith.

Now the Protestant Sovereigns of England, ever since the Reformation, had stood for what was essentially a compromise between the old and the new orthodoxies of Rome and Geneva. That compromise, under Elizabeth, had been less a matter of faith than of political convenience, with the object of founding the national unity on as broad a basis as possible. But the coming of a new century, and of a King who was as deeply versed in theology as he was in statesmanship, had seen a new soul breathed into the dry bones of the State Church. Far from being merely formal or obstructive, the Anglican communion was inspired by a spiritual fervour in no degree inferior to that of the extremists who sought to capture or supersede it. It had produced Lancelot Andrewes, Bishop of Winchester, one whose holiness of life and scholarly persuasiveness had made him as much the pattern of bishops, as his younger contemporary, George Herbert, was to become that of parish priests. And the Church of England had this advantage over the disciple of Geneva ; it was a characteristically national product, in the very fact that it offered a *via media* between logical extremes.

To talk as if it were inspired by a belief in toleration would be to anticipate the ideas of a later age. It had hardly dawned on any Christian sect that such a thing was possible, let alone desirable. But of all Christian communities, the Anglican allowed widest scope for differences of opinion ; what it may have lacked in the militant ardour of Calvinism, it made up for in a sweetness that was peculiarly its own, and whose fragrance we can still savour in such writings as those of Donne, Herbert, Joseph Hall, Jeremy Taylor, Fuller, and countless others who adorned this, the most fruitful period of its existence.

The overmastering religious question, in the England of Charles I, was whether the Church should push the Reformation to its logical extreme, or whether it should evolve along the middle way it had chosen for itself, preserving as much of the Roman system and splendour as was compatible with the new privilege that every Protestant claimed of direct approach to his Maker and his Maker's Word.

There was no doubt of the King's attitude. Like those other two fated Sovereigns of modern history, Louis XVI and Tsar Nicholas II, he may fairly claim to have been the most religious of his line.* His brother, Henry, had been right in his estimate of him as a potential Archbishop. Unlike his father, who had been troubled over many things, Charles was single-hearted in his devotion to his faith and his Church. It was a faith that would have satisfied the strictest requirements of St James, for it bore fruit abundantly in works. Few Sovereigns have, in their private lives, honoured so consistently the letter and spirit of the commandments ; even the strictest Puritans were unable to convict

* Counting Louis XVI as a Bourbon only and thus ruling out Saint Louis.

him of any graver personal delinquency than a love of Shakespeare.

It was only natural that he should love this Church of which he was the head. The ordered beauty of its ceremonial appealed to the deepest instincts of his nature, and the unquestioning obedience he received from its hierarchy, in recognition of his divine office, cannot have failed to impress him by its contrast to the chronic opposition of his Parliament. Loyalty breeds loyalty, even in Kings.

But this loyalty of Charles to his Church had in it the seeds of tragedy. For it was one of those rare attachments of his retired nature, to which he would cling with a concentrated earnestness stronger than death. His friend, his wife, his Church—to these three, for good or evil, he gave a love that knew neither limit nor change. But for the Church he was to afford that supreme proof of love that justifies the addition "greater hath no man."

It was a tragic love, since it could not fail to bring upon his person and office all the hostility that was gathering to a head against the Church. The conflict had only been delayed, because the attitude of the Church itself was for a long time in suspense. Archbishop Abbot was what we should now call an extreme Low Churchman, and as much of a Puritan as it was possible for anyone in his office to be ; and there were bishops, like Miles Smith, of Gloucester, who differed little from out and out Calvinists. Up to the end of James's reign, there seemed at least a chance of the Church being captured by its own left wing, in which case the *via media* would have been forsaken for the direct road to Geneva.

But when Charles came to the throne, Calvinism was already a spent force in the Church. Abbot had been under a cloud, ever since he had been unfortunate enough to bag a beater with his crossbow. The lead was passing more and more into the hands of such High Church Anglicans as Montague and of a much more important person than Montague, the recently appointed Bishop of St David's, William Laud, who, in every office that he had filled, had given proof of the pugnacious energy that so often goes along with the diminutive stature, and who, if he opposed the intransigence of Calvinism, would be sure to do so with a proportionate intransigence of his own.

But if, in religion, the heads of the Church, backed by the King, were tending towards the Right, the tendency of Parliament was

equally decidedly towards the Left. Puritanism was especially
rife among the growing capitalist class in the towns ; while
among the great landowners so many of whose fortunes had been
built up on the spoils of the Church, it is not surprising that
Reformation principles, in their most uncompromising form,
should have found favour. But the most powerful influence of all
was that combined fear and hatred of Rome which, as we have
seen, had become a sort of patriotic hysteria. To show the least
slackness in damning or persecuting Catholics, to be convicted of
agreeing with them on any point whatever, was to incur the
suspicion of something not far short of treason. The sight of an
altar at the East end of a cathedral was almost enough to start
devout Protestants looking for gunpowder in the crypt, and the
courtesy of bowing at the name of Jesus constituted a positive
threat to His religion.

It is the way with extremists to lump together all those who
fail to go the whole way with them, in one common hostility.
He that is not with us is against us ; Saul is tarred with the same
brush as Agag. The Montague episode showed that the time was
at hand when the spirit of the penal laws would cease to discrimin-
ate between Roman and Anglican ; when the word Bishop would
be hissed with no less fury than the word Jesuit : and from this it
would not be long before the Prayer-book would be proscribed
like the Mass, and the Primate of England sentenced to be choked
and disembowelled like any seminary priest.

Now will be apparent the measureless blunder involved in the
King's Catholic marriage, and its accompanying conditions. He
had compromised himself fatally by his alliance with the arch-
enemy ; he had plotted on the same side as Guy Fawkes against
the will of Parliament and the law of the land ; in his French
Queen, Protestant alarmists saw the Scarlet Woman established
in their midst, hatching endless devilry. Was it to be wondered
at that His Majesty's notorious patronage of the Anglican
compromise should have rendered not only him, but his Church
and Bishops, suspect of collusion with Rome ? A patient with
persecution mania will see confirmation of his fears in every word
and action ; ideological fanatics will notoriously cry Quisling at
those suspect of the slightest collaboration with their selected
bogey, and something like this was surely the condition of
those who could detect Popery even in a philippic against Popery.
The King, loyal Anglican though he was, had laid himself more

open to suspicion even than Montague, and could hardly expect more merciful treatment.

His temperament had fated him to be misjudged, but in no way more ruinously than in' this suspicion—which would have been perfectly justified about his son and successor—of his being at heart a Catholic. Monstrous as it was, he had brought it upon himself. His two wooings had sowed the wind ; the leaves were already beginning to quiver with the first breath of the rising whirlwind.

6

DEADLOCK

THE immediate necessity for the King was to induce the Commons to go at least far enough beyond their dole of two subsidies, to enable him to put up some show of a fight against the national enemy, and, in particular, to finance the expedition that even now was being got ready to sail against Spain. The straits of the Crown were already desperate. The King had depleted his privy purse to the extent of £50,000, and Buckingham, who, with all his faults, was both generous and—according to his lights— patriotic, had freely adventured his vast wealth in the cause.

But these contributions were swallowed up almost as soon as they were made. Among the State Papers we find a letter from one Thomas Locke to the ambassador at the Hague, dated the 9th of July, and reporting the want of money to have been so great as the like had never been known—no servant of the King had been paid since Midsummer, and ambassadors could not be dispatched for lack of salary. Towards the end of the month things got even worse, for we find one of the Secretaries of State reporting to the Lord Treasurer that the everyday expenses of the royal household can no longer be met ; "it seems things are brought to such extreme necessity"—purveyors being inclined to insist on cash before granting further credit—"as it will be hard to avoid an accident of great dishonour to his Majesty both in his own and in the Queen's household."*

Under these circumstances, it is not surprising that desperate

* Secretary Conway to Lord Treasurer Ley, the 27th of July, 1625.

requests for money were coming in from Plymouth, where the expeditionary force was beginning to assemble. The men were without food, without pay, and even without clothes. His Majesty's Commissioners write to say that "they cannot satisfy with words the hungry bellies of the soldiers nor the empty purses of their hosts ; nor can they secure the country from damage."* An equal difficulty was being experienced in providing for the everyday necessities of those unhappy Englishmen who survived of the Mansfeld army.

It is easy enough to say that the King and Buckingham ought to have been tactful enough to accept with thanks what Parliament had vouchsafed, and refrain from pressing for more ; but with reports like this coming in what was to be done ? No doubt, if Charles had been such a cynical realist as his eldest son was to prove, he might, in effect, have shrugged his shoulders and allowed the men to starve and ships to rot. Another Spanish Armada might even have anticipated, at Plymouth, the performance of the Dutch in the Medway. But Charles was young and conscientiously in earnest—it was not in him to face reality at the expense of his kingly obligations. And as for Buckingham, he was as incapable of admitting bankruptcy as defeat. Somehow or other the supplies must be got—Parliament must be persuaded.

But Parliament had hardened its heart, and was not to be moved by the direst plea of State necessity. Three days before the adjournment, an interview had taken place that was pregnant with momentous consequences. One of the King's Privy Councillors who, as a Member of the Lower House, realized only too well its ungiving temper, had conceived the idea of putting up the most acceptable person he could think of to undertake the task of convincing Buckingham that the cupboard was bare. The person in question was the same Sir John Eliot who had been Buckingham's old companion in Paris, and who, in spite of his having already distinguished himself as the most uncompromising champion of Parliamentary claims, was still on terms of ostensible and even subservient friendship with the Duke.

There had, however, lately been signs of a certain cooling off in cordiality between the Admiral of England and his subordinate of Devon. Buckingham had not seen eye to eye with Eliot about certain perquisites of the vice-admiralty, and Eliot had been stopped from joining his suite on his last visit to France. But there

* Commissioners at Plymouth to the Council, the 30th of July, 1625.

is no need to seek for personal causes to account for an antagonism
that was almost bound to develop on grounds of principle. Eliot
had already come forward as an almost fanatical champion of
Parliament ; in his eyes, it was hardly possible for it to do wrong.
And the time was at hand when it would be no longer possible to
serve Parliament and Buckingham.

However, he appears to have entered on his informal embassy
in no spirit of hostility. He no doubt imagined he was performing
the best possible service to his old friend and patron, by dissuading
him from persisting with what even the King's ministers were
beginning to see was a hopeless endeavour to force a closed door.
When he arrived at York House, His Grace was still in bed, but
he made no difficulty about receiving his visitor, and the Duchess
obligingly got up and went into another room.

We have only Eliot's account of the interview, but even so, the
arguments he puts forward to dissuade Buckingham from pressing
for further supply seem singularly disingenuous. The King has
thankfully accepted the two subsidies already given—no admission, replies Buckingham, that these are the limit of his requirements ; Eliot next tries to make out that it would be taking a
mean advantage to press for money in a House, three quarters of
whose members have already gone home—he might have added,
for fear of the plague. Their absence, rejoins the Duke, is their
own fault, and must not be allowed to prejudice the State.

This rebuff has the effect of heightening Eliot's tone to one of
thinly veiled menace. The King's honour is at stake ; Buckingham's own safety will be imperilled ; on his head will fall the
resentment aroused by any further demands. The King's honour !
That, intimates Buckingham, is bound up not with what honourable members choose to think, but with the success of the great
expedition that is even now being got ready to leave our shores,
and which cannot set forth without money. As for himself, he
proudly adds, where his master's honour is concerned, his own
safety does not enter into the reckoning.

It is difficult to see what exactly "Eliot, Sir John, patriot"—
as he is described in *The Dictionary of National Biography*—could
have replied to this. Perhaps wisely, he appears to have dropped
the subject of honour, and blurted out what was, at any rate, the
brutal truth, that it was no good asking for the money, because
nothing would induce the House to stump up another penny.
This time it was Buckingham's turn to lose his temper, and he

appears to have flashed out something to the effect that even so, the request must be made, if only to be denied. In other words, if Parliament was determined to leave its Sovereign in the lurch, let it do so in the sight of the nation, and let the nation judge.

A great deal more was, and in fact, must have been said, in the course of a two hours' interview, but we may accept this as the gist of it. It is not true to say that its immediate effect was to drive Eliot into active and open hostility to Buckingham, but it did certainly plant the seeds of a great hate. An intensely proud and sensitive nature can forgive anything rather than the humiliation of having been put in the wrong. Even by his visitor's own account, Buckingham appears to have scored all the argumentative and moral honours of the debate, and Eliot's was a large enough nature to have realized it. Most galling of all must have been the reflection that the winning argument was one that, even if it had occurred to him at the time, would not have been very easy to advance. Who would vote for yet more of the nation's money to be poured out into the wildcat schemes of a gambler like Buckingham?

The fact is that the King and Parliament might each from their own standpoint, have an invincible case, since the King could neither govern nor defend the nation without money, and Parliament would not be justified in advancing the nation's money without reasonable security that the King—and the King meant Buckingham—could be trusted to spend it. It was inevitable, then, that sooner or later the demand for subsidies should be countered with the demand that Buckingham must go. To nobody, after that famous interview, would this logic be calculated to appeal more forcibly than to Eliot himself.

It need hardly be said that a final, despairing attempt of the King's ministers to extract money from what was left of the Commons, broke down hopelessly on the eve of the adjournment.

7

BREAKDOWN

THE question now was when Parliament should reassemble. The King and Buckingham, in their dire need for at least enough money to equip the Spanish expedition, had determined to resume the sitting, in three weeks' time, at Oxford, instead of in plague-stricken Westminster. There was only one on the Royal Council bold enough to oppose this course—that Bishop Worldly Wiseman, the Lord Keeper Williams. Like Eliot, he saw that the game was up, and that the only safe course was to continue the adjournment till Christmas, and then for the Crown to try its luck in a new session. It was all very well to say this, but Charles was not the man to sacrifice his duty and his soldiers for prudential considerations. As for Buckingham, prudential considerations had never affected him : he listened, it is recorded, "grinning" with fury and, becoming personal as usual, burst out that public necessity ought to sway more than one man's jealousy. In vain did Williams contrive to breathe into the King's private ear some intimation of the storm that he knew to be gathering round the Duke's head—he had only made certain his own fall.

So by the 1st of August, the Members had left their homes and converged upon Oxford in the worst of tempers. The plight of a few thousand unpaid and starving recruits might be borne with equanimity, but it was a different matter when the nation's representatives were expected to pig it in whatever lodgings they could get at such short notice, and positively to endanger their lives ; for the plague was now all over the country and was among the new arrivals at Oxford. To make things worse, it had come out that the King had been palpably hedging on his promise to maintain persecution in full force. Instances were to hand of priests having been pardoned, and, worst of all, of the martyr's crown having been denied to a Jesuit.

The Commons had no sooner met, than they were off again in full cry after the religious hare ; the Montague case was of course brought up again ; one member characterized Arminianism, or moderate Protestantism, as more dangerous than Popery ; the great Sir Edward Coke demanded a censorship of inquisitorial thoroughness on all religious writings.

In this atmosphere it was a forlorn hope indeed for the King and his ministers to appeal for further supply, even to so modest an extent as £40,000 for the immediate expenses of the expedition. They were stirring up a hornets' nest ; and the debates began to take a more and more ominous tone, the royal policy, and whoever was responsible for it, becoming more and more openly the object of attack.

By the end of the first week, it was evident that unless something very striking could be done to change the situation, things were destined to go from bad to worse. It was time for Buckingham to intervene with one of those strokes of dramatic inspiration which, in spite of the ill success that had generally attended them, he still believed to be his peculiar forte. He had once before summoned Parliament to his presence, to hear his policy from his own lips. He would do that again ; and he confronted them, as superbly confident as ever, from the dais of the Hall at Christchurch. Buckingham could plead a cause as eloquently as any man of his time, and the address that he now delivered was an exposition of policy as lucid as it was masterly. It was—it must needs be—spoken to his brief as Counsel for the Crown, and where the case was hopelessly weak, as in the matter of the Marriage Contract and the ships delivered to France, deliberately evasive ; but on the main issue of supply, where the case was over-whelming, it is hard to see how Buckingham's pleading can have failed to carry conviction. One by one the doubts and objections that had been agitating the House were stated and answered. By what counsels had this Spanish enterprise been undertaken ? By those of Parliament itself. £40,000 was the price of equipping it ; the King had anticipated his revenue, pawned his lands, would have sold his plate if he could have got a buyer, was on the verge of utter misery ; he and Buckingham had each advanced more than the sum now demanded from the whole nation ; the urgency of the occasion was surely great enough to justify any inconvenience to which Parliament may have been put.

"Make the fleet ready to go ; my master gave me command to bid you name the enemy yourselves. Put the sword into his hands, and he will maintain the war. Make an entrance and afterwards it may be defrayed with profit. ...

"Lastly, my master commanded me to pray you to have regard of your own health and of the season ; if you lose time money cannot purchase it.

"If in this report my weakness hath injured the business, the King, the State, the affairs of Christendom, I crave your pardon, my intentions are good."

To say of this speech that Buckingham had surpassed himself would be putting it too modestly ; it is perhaps the one specimen of seventeenth century eloquence to go as straight to the heart of a modern reader as if it had been spoken over the radio in refer-ence to some contemporary crisis. There are none of those frills

and circumlocutions, those involved paragraphs, classical allu-
sions, and that parade of erudition, that keep even the most
moving orations of the time in unfreezably cold storage. It is a
burning, reasoned appeal to that most elementary of all emotions,
patriotism. When we visualize the setting, in Wolsey's Hall ;
when we think of the Duke's towering form, his superb presence,
his flashing eye, his voice reverberating through the vast spacious-
ness—we find it difficult to imagine how that appeal could have
failed to carry conviction even to so sullen and suspicious an
audience. Perhaps it might have succeeded had it been made only
six weeks previously at Westminster ; perhaps it actually did,
before the Members had dispersed to their uncomfortable
quarters to think it over. But by this time the sentiment of the
House had hardened too much for any mere oratory to make a
lasting impression. Perhaps the overwhelming cogency of Buckingham's plea produced the same hostile reaction in these men
who did not want to be convinced that it had in Eliot.

The effect of that reaction was at least not unworthy of its
cause. If Buckingham's speech forms a landmark in English
oratory, the debate, which was its sequel, must be accounted
equally memorable in the annals of the House of Commons.
Backward and forward it swayed ; the King's ministers and such
supporters as Buckingham could command pressing hard for
supply ; the opposition hardening and strengthening as champion
after champion rose in his place to swell the chorus of negation.
The decisive voice was that of Sir Robert Phelips, who was
indisputably the dominant figure in this Parliament.

It may be interesting to glance at this man's character and
antecedents. His father had been Master of the Rolls, and
Speaker of James's first Parliament ; and had displayed his zeal
in his capacity of judge, by condemning to death some unfortunate
householder for merely having given shelter to a Jesuit. Robert,
who had been elected to the 1621 Parliament (having previously
sat in the abortive "Addled" Parliament of 1614), soon found
occasion to show himself a chip of the old block. He it was who
led the torture competition against Floyd by the suggestion of his
being made to endure, in Little Ease, as much pain as he could
without loss of life. He had made himself so conspicuous by his
invective against Spain and the Catholics, that James had put
him into the Tower on the dissolution, and tried to prevent him
being returned for the 1624 Parliament. Returned, however, he

had been, and had made his lusty contribution to the clamour for war with Spain. He was now, in the following year, the life and soul—or perhaps we should say the lungs—of the movement for starving that selfsame war. He it was who had tried to get Parliament adjourned without granting any subsidies at all ; he who, when the beggarly two had been vouchsafed, had successfully opposed the concession of a penny more.

He was now at the climax of his career, and he must have felt that he had the House like wax to his moulding. It would not, he maintained, be for the King's honour to relieve his necessity. Necessity was, of course, a pressing argument, "but if His Majesty's honour be in question and he in such necessity, they who have brought him to this strait have dishonoured the King." As far as one can extract the gist of this curious argument, it implied that if the King was dishonoured it was someone else's fault (and we can guess as easily as anyone then present who "someone" was), and that therefore it would not be for his honour for his honour to be redeemed.

Having made this point, or described this circle, Phelips began to rake up every historical precedent he could think of for refusing supply. During the minority of Henry III, before Parliament had even come into existence, a supply had apparently been refused ; the same in Richard II's time ; the same—and here came the deadly thrust—when Henry VI's Duke of Suffolk had "wholly possessed the Government." Having exhausted his English instances, Phelips proceeded to draw upon French and Spanish history, and came out with the really memorable reminder that "we are the last monarchy in Christendom that retain our original rights and constitutions."

If the King, Phelips went on to argue, could not equip the fleet from his own resources, it ought not to go at all, especially as it would lead to yet further expense, since—this from the most persistent advocate of a Spanish war !—unless this first blow were followed up, it would merely provoke the Spaniards to invade England.

Phelips's speech may not strike us as very lucid in its reasoning, nor particularly ingenuous in its conclusions, but he had already established his ascendency in the House, and he was telling it exactly what it wanted to hear. The effect of Buckingham's pleading, whatever it may have been at the time, was finally dissipated, and the subsequent course of the long debate merely afforded an opportunity for opposition speakers to inflame the passions of their audience not only against supply, but also against Buckingham. Another doughty opponent of the Crown, Sir Francis Seymour—that one of the would-be torturers of Floyd, who had fathered the lashes and beads suggestion—after making the sale of honours a reason for denying the King money from any other source, added that his principal reason against giving was that "a member of the Upper House, under a colour of a message, should press the Commons with arguments for a subsidy." It was out now ! The hue and cry was after Buckingham.

Next day, the 11th, the debate continued, and now there was no doubt of the way things were tending. Seymour openly named the Duke—"Let us lay the fault where it is," he cried ; and Phelips, following him, declared, no doubt amid the applause of an excited assembly, that "it is not fit to repose the safety of the kingdom in those who have no parts answerable to their places."

By this time it had become evident, even to Charles, who was so seldom capable of facing up to unwelcome reality, that now it was not a question of whether or not he would get supply—the negative to that was irrevocable—but of whether he would be able to save his chief minister and best friend from the fate that was only too plainly in store for him, if Parliament were to continue in the course along which its leaders had begun to stampede it. In all these men there would soon be one mind, and it would be against the Duke. No one had better reason than Charles to know what that would imply. He and Buckingham had themselves invited Parliament to taste blood ; had applauded it in hounding to his ruin an unpopular minister. Precedent was the soul of their reasoning, and the precedent of Middlesex was glaring. And before Middlesex there had been the Lord Chancellor Bacon.

There was no good that the Crown could conceivably expect from this Parliament ; every day enhanced its possibilities for evil. Charles was touched on his most sensitive point, that of loyalty to his friend. If he could do nothing else, he could at least save Steenie. Parliament must be dissolved ; and at once.

It is to Buckingham's credit that he should have done his best to hold back the King from this step ; and here for once he was at one with the super-subtle Lord Keeper Williams. He was less sensible of his own peril—and to do him justice he was never one to shirk facing the music—than of the consequences to his

Sovereign of an open breach with his first Parliament. He actually went down on his knees to dissuade him.

But now Buckingham, for the first, and perhaps the only time, had come up against the quiet obstinacy that everybody who had to deal with Charles was bound to encounter sooner or later, and that, once aroused, not the strongest will could break. Where Steenie's safety was concerned, Charles was capable of withstanding even Steenie.

It had been Tuesday, of the second week of the Oxford session, that Buckingham had made his appeal. It was on Friday, the third day of the great debate, that it became known that the King was about to dissolve Parliament. A number of members, who feared, we are told, the evil consequence of such an abrupt parting, were for sending a humble petition imploring His Majesty to grant some further respite ; but the indomitable Phelips was on his feet to prevent them. A final, desperate attempt was made by a half-brother of Buckingham's to get the House to reconsider its determination to withhold supply ; it died stillborn. Black Rod was already knocking at the door, but was unable, for some time, to obtain admission, while within the House, amid a scene of tumultuous confusion, a protestation was being voted affirming, in terms of extravagant loyalty, the determination of the Commons to discover and reform the abuses of the State—or, in plain English, to impeach Buckingham—and to afford all necessary supply, when they were plainly determined to afford none whatever.

That afternoon the members were settling accounts for their insufficient accommodation, and doubtless by night-fall a goodly proportion of them were on homeward roads, thankful at least not to have discovered in themselves the first symptoms of plague.

8

DISGRACE AT SEA

"Ought" is a word of which historians are rightly chary, but there can be little doubt what course Charles and Buckingham ought to have taken, after the collapse of the Oxford Parliament had demonstrated the hopelessness of obtaining financial support for any warlike enterprise. It was still not too late to draw back ; there was no open breach with Spain, nor was there the least chance of the Spaniards attacking England unless they were goaded into it by intolerable aggression. Peace was to be had, not even for the asking, but merely for the sitting still.

What, under the circumstances, the King ought to have said to his Faithful Commons on—or even without—dismissing them, would surely have been something to the following effect :

"I am sorry, gentlemen, but with the best will in the world, I cannot oblige you both ways. I am perfectly ready to make war for you in any just cause you happen to fancy, but war is the most expensive of all businesses, and if you insist on my undertaking it, you must really provide me with the wherewithal to do so. Otherwise I am afraid that you and I will have to resign ourselves, with as good a grace as possible, to the success of our prayers for peace in our time."

Whether Charles would have seen the logic of this if left to himself, is a matter for speculation. But in policy he was wholly under the influence of Buckingham, and Buckingham had all the invincible obstinacy of the gambling maniac. He had not the least idea of cutting his losses and retiring from the table. The more desperate his situation, the more desperately he would plunge in the hope of retrieving his losses.

This great expedition to Cadiz, on which he had set his heart, was the throw that was going to bring back everything. What if the odds against it were doubled, quadrupled, by the lack of means for its equipment—it should go anyhow, and muddle through somehow. And then, when the loot of the Spanish ports and the silver of the Plate Fleet were brought in triumph to Plymouth Sound, there would be no more trouble with Parliament.

But if we suppose Buckingham to have been finally determined to stake his master's and his country's fortunes on the success of this expedition, the least he could reasonably have done would have been to concentrate all the resources that he had still, by any means, available, on its success. He ought to have abandoned, at any rate for the nonce, those grandiose European schemes that were wildly beyond his powers to realize ; to have brought home without delay the survivors of Mansfeld's force, and to have informed the King of Denmark that in future he must finance any crusade he liked to undertake out of the pockets of the Danish taxpayer. It might then have been possible, by heroic efforts and the windfall of Henriette's dowry, to have sent forth the expedition with some prospect of success. Above all, it would be the first thing needful that the fleet should sail under the orders of the most competent seamen that the country could produce, and with a clearly defined objective.

Nothing of this seems to have occurred to either Charles or Buckingham. They were possessed with a Micawber-like confidence that victory would somehow or another turn up with or without the means to finance it, and certainly without any extraordinary exertions on their part. They made not the slightest effort to cut down their European commitments, and went ahead for all the world as if the Parliament had just pressed on them a good dozen subsidies to go on with.

The story of the Spanish expeditionary force in Devon and Cornwall was a repetition of that of Mansfeld's army in Kent. The men, dragged from their homes, arrived in driblets from all over England. We find one of their officers reporting that he had never met with such unruly men, especially those from Northumberland, who, for the most part, had arrived naked save for their coats.* The Staff, at Plymouth, was in a state bordering on distraction. In August, pay was three weeks in arrears, "the soldiers complain, their diet is impaired, and they are of a dejected spirit."† By September, the farms and cottages were no longer able or willing to maintain these starving men who were billeted on them ; where they could, they thrust them out of doors, while the men had started robbing and marauding all over the countryside, slaughtering the sheep and cattle before their owners' faces, saying that they must have them rather than famish.‡ Desertion and disease were rife. It was scarcely the semblance of an army, but an undrilled, undisciplined, and imperfectly armed rabble of civilians, whose officers were, for the most part, as incompetent as themselves. The fleet that had been got together in Plymouth Sound was not much better ; it consisted mostly of merchantmen, disgracefully ill-found, with rotten planks, and tackling that in some instances had done duty against the Armada.

The commander was a scion of the great house of Cecil, who,

---

* Capt. W. Courteney to Sec. Conway. Undated—probably June.
† Commissioners at Plymouth to the Council. The 12th of August.
‡ *Ib.*, the 1st of September.

as an amateur infantry officer in the Dutch service, had acquitted himself with reasonable credit, but who knew nothing whatever about the sea. *Sitstill* was his nickname. His second in command was the Earl of Essex, that unfortunate but rather lumpish youth who had failed to consummate his brief marriage with Frances Howard ; who now, at the age of thirty-four, knew no more about the sea than his chief, and whose experience of land warfare was almost negligible. Add to these the Rear-Admiral, Lord Denbigh, whose only qualification for the post, as Gardiner dryly comments, lay in the accident that he was married to Buckingham's sister. Above all these was the Lord Admiral, Buckingham himself, who did not elect to accompany the fleet, but at least provided the sailors with some much needed merriment, by assuming the title of its Generalissimo. It would, perhaps, have been better if he had gone, as he was at least no more ignorant of seamanship than its trinity of land-admirals, and might have infused some energy into the proceedings.

On the 5th of October, the crazy armada, powerful in numbers if nothing else, managed somehow to get out of harbour. Not, however, for long, for the wind shifted to the south-west, and they were soon making for their lives back to port. When they got into the Sound they crowded in a *sauve qui peut* for the smooth anchorage of the Cattewater, bumping into each other indiscriminately, with the Admiral dodging about in a boat trying frantically to assert his authority.

On the 8th, the wind having shifted to a more favourable quarter, they again got to sea, the rear being brought up, on the following day, by fourteen vessels whose skippers had refused to weigh anchor until commanded from the shore to do so, under pain of death. They were now in company with a Dutch squadron, that probably formed the most efficient part of the fleet. This time they did actually leave England behind them, and had arrived in the neighbourhood of Cape St Vincent, when it occurred to the Admiral that it would be as well to decide upon an objective. It was finally decided to land in Cadiz Bay, and march to seize San Lucar, twelve miles off.

However, the sight of some Spanish vessels at the mouth of the harbour was too much for Essex, who dashed off on his own responsibility to attack them. Cecil did his best to support him, but his merchant captains had other views, and the Spaniards did not wait. Nevertheless, a great and double opportunity presented itself. The shipping in the harbour could have been followed up and captured ; and Cadiz itself, which was practically ungarrisoned, lay at the mercy of a prompt attack.

However, promptness of any sort was unthinkable under Cecil's auspices. It was not till after dark that a council of war was summoned, and decided to attack a fort that commanded the harbour entrance. For this service, five of the Dutchmen and twenty English merchant vessels were detailed ; but only the Dutch came into action, the English, through incompetent staff work, or sheer cowardice, or both, leaving them in the night to fight it out alone—two of them were destroyed. Come daylight, it was the turn of Essex, in the *Swiftsure*, to be left unsupported, or worse, since one of the merchantmen, blazing away her ammunition at a safe distance, succeeded in lodging a ball in his stern. Only in the evening did the fort capitulate to the overwhelming numbers of a landing force.

By this time Cadiz had been amply reinforced, and the ships had got safe away into the inner harbour. Cecil, however, with some hazy idea of a siege, landed his soldiers, called yet another council of war, and on news of the approach of Spanish forces, ordered an advance along a causeway towards the bridge that separates Cadiz from the mainland. Six miles they trudged, before Cecil became convinced that the alarm was false. "Since we are thus forwards on our way," he observed, "if you will, we will march on. It may be we may light on some enemy." At this point it was discovered that the unfortunate men had nothing in their knapsacks. Cecil, not at all put out, answered that it was no time to be thinking of provisions with the enemy in their front. But the men, famishing and exhausted, arrived at a village where there happened to be large stores of wine for the West India fleet. Soon the whole force was blind drunk; and the best that could be hoped for, was to get as many as could stand back to the ships, before the Spaniards arrived. As it was, about a hundred who were abandoned unconscious were pitilessly butchered.

After this, there was nothing for it but to give up the attack on Cadiz as hopeless, and get to sea in the hope of intercepting the Plate Fleet. With this object Cecil spread out his ships in what he thought the most probable direction, but two days after he had left Cadiz the galleons, which had made a detour to the south, sailed quietly into the harbour. It was perhaps a blessing in disguise that the encounter did not take place. Cecil, however, remained on the watch till the state of his fleet compelled him to make for home. The condition of the ships was on a par with everything else in the expedition. The hulls were leaking, the sails and tackling rotten, the provisions stank, and sickness was beginning to carry off the men like flies. On the flagship alone 130 died, 160 were ill. The ships limped home, lucky to get there before they fell to pieces, and with their surviving occupants, in the last extreme of misery, bringing and spreading disease.

Never before or since has there been so disgraceful a chapter of cowardice and mismanagement in the history of the British Navy. Though it would be an insult to any navy in the world to talk of such a floating rabble of pressed merchantmen as part of it. The trouble was that England had practically ceased to possess a navy. It was a lesson that, when he had had time to digest it, would not be lost on King Charles.

9

PATRIOTIC MELODRAMA

THE war policy, by which Charles and Buckingham had hoped to dominate the European situation, and which Parliament had first encouraged and then starved, might well seem to have touched the rock bottom of failure. In no single direction had it achieved the least of its objects. Sea war against Spain had been no more successful than land war in Germany : to the folly of the Mansfeld expedition had now been added the ignominy of the Cadiz armada ; thousands of Englishmen dragged from their homes to perish miserably, the national prestige shattered, allies deluded with vain promises, the royal coffers empty, the King seeking to pawn the Crown Jewels, war undertaken without the means of waging it, and—as the first-fruits of a Protestant crusade —H.M.S. *Vanguard* at the head of a British squadron, manned by French crews, engaged in quenching the last embers of independent Protestantism in France.

But the Duke of Buckingham had not exhausted his genius for making a bad situation worse. He was that type of vicarious gambler who, when he has parted with his master's shirt, will continue the game with his skin. The one hope left for his policy was in co-operation with France against the Hapsburg alliance. On the chance of this, the desperately unpopular French marriage had been concluded ; it was in order to keep that wire uncut that public opinion had been affronted by the employment of English ships against the Elect of Rochelle. It might seem almost incredible that he should now wantonly demolish the structure he had been at such pains to build, and as if it were not enough to have saddled the country with a war against Spain, to pile on the top of this an equally unnecessary war against France. And yet it was to this very end that his course was now beginning to shape itself.

Buckingham had by this time got fairly turned against France. He had not forgotten the snubbing of his attempt to make love to the Queen, and he could not forgive King Louis for having practically forbidden him the country. He had become more and more uneasily conscious that Cardinal Richelieu had been all along making a dupe of him, and most signally of all in that unlucky transaction of the hired ships, which no amount of eloquence could display in any other light than that of a humiliating blunder. And it was Buckingham's nature to go to all lengths, and shrink from no consequences, when it was a question of wiping out a personal humiliation.

Besides, his inexhaustibly fertile mind had conceived of another diplomatic masterstroke, this time, a triple Protestant alliance of England, Holland, and Denmark, which Buckingham himself went over to the Hague, in all his glory, to negotiate. The main condition of this scheme was that England should finance Denmark to the tune of £30,000 a month, out of a treasury that was scarcely able to meet the everyday expenses of the palace housekeeping. He seems to have been capable of imagining that a new Parliament would foot this, and any other Bill that His Majesty might see fit to charge to the taxpayer's account.

So, by the beginning of the new year, England had changed her attitude of friendship towards France for one of defiance and provocation, of which the end must inevitably be war, however much Richelieu might desire, as he certainly did, to remain on friendly terms. French ships were already being seized, on the flimsiest of pretexts, and their cargoes confiscated. Naturally France was minded to recoup the loss out of any English property that might be handy.

Such was the state and drift of affairs when, on the 6th of

February, the King opened a new Parliament. It says much for his own and Buckingham's optimism that he could have still ventured to hope for any support in that direction. The situation was far worse than it had been when, six months before, he had dissolved his first Parliament, lest, having denied him all help, it should turn and rend his chief minister. If Buckingham's cup had been full then, it was overflowing now.

That Charles should thus complacently have elected to gamble against a certainty, may be best accounted for by that peculiar reserved nature of his, that had so few contacts with the outer world. He felt so plainly the justice of his cause ; he, the King, waging the very war for which Parliament had clamoured—was it credible that his Faithful Commons should deny him the means ? That they should aid and comfort his enemies by engineering revolution at home ? And if disaster had attended his arms hitherto, what moral could he be expected, or expect anyone else, to draw, except that of the criminal folly of waging war without providing its sinews ?

What is really amazing is that he should have imagined, as he evidently did, that the reasonableness of this should have impressed itself upon the Commons, without any special effort of his to convince them. It is true that he had, this time, bethought him of Bishop Williams's advice—who had by this time gone the way of other ministers who had fallen foul of Buckingham—and done what he could to doctor the composition of the House. He had hit upon the plan of nominating some of his most intractable assailants as sheriffs for their respective counties, and by this means getting rid of the impossible Phelips and Seymour, not to speak of Coke and Wentworth. But the plan was wrecked, as is the way of such plans, by the fact that getting rid of the old leaders only served to clear the way for one more formidable than any of them. Charles had forgotten Eliot.

This is not surprising, when we consider that up to the very meeting of Parliament, the Vice-Admiral of Devon had evinced no signs of intransigent hostility to his Sovereign, or his old friend, Buckingham. On the last day of the year we find him writing, civilly enough, to the Secretary of State, Conway, whose son had passed the holidays at his house, begging him to put through a little job on behalf of his father-in-law, who had been charged, under a Privy Seal, with a larger contribution than he felt capable of paying. Perhaps encouraged by the success of this request, we find Eliot, barely a fortnight later, instructing his agent in London to solicit for him certain offices fallen vacant by the death of Sir Richard Edgecombe—and Conway would no doubt have obliged again, but for the trifling circumstance that Sir Richard turned out to be alive. The King might have been excused for failing to apprehend, in Eliot, the makings of a patriot revolutionary.

But Eliot's mind was capable of becoming as divorced from reality as that of Charles himself, though in a different way. For whereas it was Charles's weakness to be incapable of appreciating any standpoint but his own, so it was Eliot's to be hypnotized by his own imagination. Once let him see any image clearly in his mind's eye, and he would become convinced of its reality. Such a mind can only too easily dramatize, or melodramatize, any situation. And for all his fiery and pugnacious disposition, Eliot's imagination was fed at least as much by books as by life. He could hardly express himself on any subject whatever without drawing on that classical erudition of which his time was prolific. He seems to have visualized his spiritual form as wrapped in a perpetual toga.

Eliot's patriotic melodrama had already found its hero in Parliament itself, a body almost incapable of doing, or willing, wrong. Only a villain was needed, and here Buckingham was so obviously the man for the part that it was inevitable that sooner or later his villainy should flash on Eliot with all the certainty of inspiration. These two leading parts having been assigned, it was the logic of such a mind to fit every circumstance that was, or could be, known, into the plot. Moreover Eliot, being not only a visionary, but a great orator, had the power of making all men within reach of his eloquence simplify reality in precisely the same way.

The great, simplifying notion had been incubating ever since that bedroom interview in which Buckingham had accomplished the always disastrous feat of putting a friend in the wrong. Eliot had seen the breakdown of the Oxford Parliament ; in his capacity of Vice-Admiral of Devon he had witnessed the muddle and mismanagement of the Cadiz expedition ; he had seen the miserable plight of the survivors, and of the countryside of which they were both the burden and the terror. The fact that he himself had been adamant in repulsing Buckingham's urgent plea for the minimum necessary for equipping that ill-fated expedition, does not seem to have occurred to him. To recognize that would be to put the blame on Parliament or—even more blasphemously —on Eliot himself ; which was, by hypothesis, absurd. That it must, that it had got to be, the fault of the wicked Duke, was a subconsciously logical conclusion. At what precise moment it flashed into the light of Eliot's considered judgment we can only guess—but it must have been not far from the time when Charles's second Parliament opened.

Charles signally lacked Eliot's gift of making the world at large appreciate his point of view. The tongue-tied child was father to the man. At this time, when his only chance lay in an over-whelming appeal to the loyalty and patriotism of his Commons, he contented himself with briefly referring the Houses, for what he had to say, to the new Lord Keeper, Coventry, who, in his turn, spoke a few official and perfectly colourless platitudes, and with that, left them to their own devices. It was soon evident that the spirit and tactics of the new House in no way differed from those of the old. The ventilation of grievances, and not the support of the war, was to be the order of the day ; and Mr Pym, whom Charles had also forgotten for the honour of officiating as sheriff, was there to keep his fellow members up to the mark of persecuting zeal. Even the crusade for gagging goose-gagging Montague was resumed with a fervour impervious to boredom.

Above all, it was clear, from the first, that Parliament was determined on applying its now customary technique of grievance before supply. That meant that however dire his necessity, the King need not expect to be vouchsafed a penny for the service of the nation, until he had submitted to whatever permanent diminution of his constitutional prerogative, or other terms that his Faithful Commons liked to impose on him.

The first step would obviously be to inflate the alleged grievances by the breath of oratory. This was Eliot's opportunity. Only four days after the sitting had commenced, he was on his feet with a speech that easily outclassed the greatest performances of Phelips and Seymour. His sentences followed one another in what was almost a succession of gasps. "View the state we are in ; consider the loss we have received ; weigh the wrecked and ruined honour of our nation ! Oh the incomparable hopes of our most excellent Sovereign checked in their first design ! ... Our honour is ruined, our ships are sunk, our men perished ; not by the sword, not by the enemy, not by chance, but as the strongest predictions had concerned and made it apparent beforehand, by those we trust. Sir, I could lose myself in this complaint. The miseries, the calamities——" and so on, in this style of glorified tubthumping, in which the audience is not allowed to reflect but compelled to feel. Buckingham, the real object of attack, was, with consummate art, not mentioned by name—the suggestion, continuous and cumulative, of his arch guilt, was all the more powerful for that.

Eliot had captured the House, and henceforth it was through his eyes that it would see, and with the fire of his passion that it would burn. The gamble in which Charles had indulged when he had summoned a second Parliament had already proved a failure ; the leadership that he had neglected to give was now to be supplied by the most uncompromising of his assailants.

The drama at Westminster, Sir John Eliot's patriotic melodrama of Fair Parliament and the Wicked Duke, developed swiftly on the now inevitable lines. Nothing that even Divine Majesty could do, short of putting out the lights and closing the theatre, would arrest its swift development towards the climax in the downfall of the villain and the triumph of avenging virtue.

It was not only on the floor of St Stephen's Chapel that such a drama was billed. Avenging virtue had its equally formidable embodiment in the House of Lords, where the Earl of Bristol had appeared after his long open arrest on his estate at Sherborne. The bungling vindictiveness with which Charles and Buckingham had continued to persecute this maddeningly just man, who would not save their faces by owning himself in the wrong, was now to find its Nemesis. They had had every opportunity to dispose of his case on honourable terms. Only just before Parliament had met, the Earl had begged for permission to take his place, among his peers, at his Sovereign's coronation. With no less boorishness than injustice his Sovereign had denied him the privilege, and couched the denial in a libellously abusive letter. Charles probably, and certainly Buckingham, regarded Bristol in the light of a man who knew too much to be at large.

But now Bristol appealed, not to his King, but to his peers, in claiming the writ of summons that had been withheld from him during the last Parliament and was still not forthcoming. The Lords were naturally indignant at this royal presumption to tamper with the composition of their House, and there was nothing for it but to send the writ, accompanied with a ministerial intimation that it was not to be used. Used, however, it was, for, as Bristol explained with unimpeachable logic, his Sovereign's writ overrode every other command. He was coming as a man intolerably wronged, determined to vindicate his honour, and to launch a deadly counter-attack on the Duke, who had been instrumental in silencing him for so long.

In his desperate determination to prevent the ex-ambassador from disclosing Buckingham's part in the fiasco of the Madrid visit, the King, almost certainly at his friend's instigation, proceeded to put himself wholly and hopelessly in the wrong ; by launching at Bristol an accusation of High Treason, an accusation in which he himself did not believe, and in which he had previously, in the most explicit terms, avowed his disbelief. The expedient proved as futile as it was unkingly, and did not deflect Bristol from pursuing his indictment against Buckingham, the flimsiness of the one case only emphasizing the strength of the other.

IO

ELIOT *IN SEJANUM*

BY this time the Commons, headed by Eliot, had unmasked their batteries against the Duke. With an irony that was perhaps unconscious, they proceeded to vote the King three subsidies, with the condition that nothing was to be paid until all grievances had been redressed to the Commons' satisfaction. One of these grievances consisted in the payment of customs duties, whose cessation would have brought the whole machinery of government to a stop, and involved bankruptcy. But there were others, and it was only too evident that the Commons intended to employ the form of constitutional blackmail involved in the refusal of funds, in order to deprive the King of his hitherto unchallenged right to choose his own ministers, and to exercise their right of striking down the chief and most trusted of them all. It was time for Charles to face the bitter fact that the price—and that not the whole price—of even the smallest dole, was Buckingham's head upon a charger.

It was a price that some of his predecessors would have made

little enough difficulty about paying. Henry VIII had never had
the least hesitation in making popular scapegoats of his own, or
his father's, most loyal servants. But Charles was of different
mettle. It never crossed his mind that there could be the least
question of saving himself, or his throne, by casting Steenie to the
wolves. With his friend he would stand or fall.

It was a tragic conflict that had now developed between him
and Eliot. That emotional Cornishman was only capable of
seeing that under Buckingham's auspices the nation's affairs were
going from bad to worse,—it did not even strike him as disingenuous to make a grievance of the King's despairing efforts to
obtain the funds which Parliament had denied him, by pawning
his own jewels. Charles, on the other hand, was only able to see
the injustice of the attack upon his friend and—through his friend
—upon the time-honoured and constitutional prerogative of the
Kings of England. He, in his turn, was incapable of appreciating
that Buckingham, in spite of Parliament having done everything
it could to render his task impossible, might yet be a blunderer
whose continued presence at the helm was a danger to the State.

Under modern conditions the remedy would have been easy.
A hostile majority in the Commons would have proceeded to
pass a vote of no confidence in the Buckingham administration,
and the King would, as a matter of course, have called upon Eliot,
or whoever happened to be the leader of the opposition, to take
his place. But that, in 1626, was outside the range of practical
politics. Nothing would have surprised Eliot, or Parliament,
more than such a request. They had not yet got to the stage of
choosing the King's ministers for him—that, by general consent,
was his own business. Their claim was to knock them down like
ninepins as fast as he put them up—not, in fact, to govern, but,
at will, to make government impossible. Only a tact and genius
almost miraculous, such as enabled the Roman Republic to
function in spite of the tribunes and their veto, could have preserved so unstable an equilibrium. It was certainly far to seek in
such protagonists as Charles and Buckingham on the one hand,
and Eliot on the other.

One thing was certain ; that from the moment Eliot launched
his first philippic, the situation had passed utterly beyond the
King's control. The Commons were in a mood of revolutionary
ardour that, in spite of their continued protestations of loyalty,
would allow them to stick at nothing in pursuit of any end or

victim that their leader might mark down for them. But if there had been anyone capable of saving that situation, by a supreme effort of conciliatory genius, the last man capable of doing so would have been Charles himself. Secure in the consciousness of his own rectitude, equally certain of his duty as a King and as a friend, righteously indignant at the monstrous unfairness of the treatment meted out to him, he could only answer them with the honest but unappreciated resentment of the animal who, when attacked, defends himself.

Before the attack had focused itself on Buckingham, it had opened with the demand—outrageous even by modern standards —that the King's ministers should furnish their accusers with ammunition by disclosing to Parliament the advice that each of them had given in the privacy of the Council Chamber—or take the consequences. But Charles was not going to stand this :

"Let them do what they list," he had said to one of them, the Elizabethan veteran Lord Totnes, who had chivalrously offered to sacrifice himself on the altar of his Sovereign's necessities, "you shall not go to the Tower. It is not you that they aim at, but it is upon me that they make inquisition. And for subsidies, gold may be bought too dear, and I thank you for your offer."

Here, at least, he was on firm ground and even the Commons did not dare to press further this particular point. But their energies were only diverted from the inquisition into the proceedings of ministers in general, to the attack on the chief minister of all. And to this Charles did not react in the spirit of a prince faced with a difficult problem in statecraft, but of a plain, blunt man, who loves his friend, and is determined at all costs to shield him from injustice.

In consequence, he blurted out what he felt, with entire disregard of its probable effect on his audience. "I see," he protested, with passionate indignation, "you specially aim at the Duke of Buckingham ; I wonder what hath so altered your affections towards him." He went on to remind them how they all, only two years ago, had so much honoured and respected the Duke that no honour was thought too great for him, "what he hath done since to alter and change your minds I wot not." It was a cry from the heart all the more poignant from the fact of its being delivered to ears so entirely unsympathetic. But the note of pathos changed in the concluding sentence to one of challenge and menace :

"I would you would hasten for my supply, or else it will be the worse for yourselves ; for, if any ill happen, I think I shall be the last to feel it."

A more inept way of handling an excited crowd it would be hard to imagine. And this is only one of several similar specimens of Charles's language at this time—the nerve-racking tactlessness of the tongue-tied man to whom overmastering emotion has given a voice.

No wonder that Eliot, and the very astute politicians with whom he was associated, found the Commons like wax to their moulding.

Inexorably, in spite of the King's protests and the expressions of devoted loyalty that were now becoming almost consciously ironic, the attack on Buckingham, and through him on the Throne, developed. Committees of the House had been diligently raking up every scrap of colourable evidence ; Eliot himself, assisted, amongst others, by an immensely rich landowner called John Hampden, was busily engaged in working up these into the substance of an impeachment ; and it is not without significance that in a memorandum, drafted by Hampden, we find, conspicuous among the Duke's crimes, "Men of mean condition and estate raised to honour and greatness which otherwise they could not get."*

Charles and Buckingham had now bitter reason to remember that prophecy of King James, that they would have their bellyful of impeachments. The indictment, when in due course it was presented by the Commons' managers to the Upper House, was a terrific production, under thirteen headings, in which every malicious interpretation that could possibly be put on the Duke's many activities was not only set down but, in the language of the day, "enlarged and aggravated," clause by clause, by a team of the most expert orators the Commons could produce.

It took two days for these distinguished juniors to say each his appointed piece to the Peers who would be the Duke's judges. Then Eliot proceeded to sum up the case for the prosecution in one grand concluding oration. It was the supreme opportunity of his career, and as a burst of sustained invective is fit to rank with the fulminations of Burke and Sheridan, before the same tribunal, against a not less considerable defendant. Like these, it was more a masterpiece of soul-stirring propaganda than an appeal to reason.

* Forster's *Life of Sir John Eliot*, I, p. 494.

The most revealing sentence was that which commenced the peroration : "My Lords, I have done—you see the man !" That was exactly the case with Eliot. Having once seen, in his mind's eye, the figure of the wicked Duke, it became so real to him that he was incapable of seeing anything else, least of all the real and much more interesting Buckingham. And by his faith, at once blind and lucid, in this creature of his imagination, he was capable of making others see through his eyes.

A less acute intelligence than that of Charles might have perceived that an attack on the man whom the King delighted to honour was, by implication, an attack on the Throne itself. But the attack had not—in his opinion at least—stopped short at implication. Eliot, even in his moments of intensest emotion, had not been able to dispense with his classical tags, and nothing would serve him but to compare Buckingham with another monster of iniquity—according to the not wholly unbiased account of Tacitus—in the shape of Sejanus. Charles's logical Scottish mind at once saw, and credited Eliot with seeing, that if Buckingham was Sejanus, he, the King, must be Tiberius. That to an artist in emotional oratory the logical implication of his periods could be a matter of stylistic irrelevance, probably did not occur to him.

But this was not the worst shock he had received in the course of the two days' speechmaking. So great had been the eagerness of the prosecution to find any stick for the Duke's back, that they had not scrupled to bring up against him the scandal about his ill-starred efforts to doctor the dying James I, and though the charge of poisoning was not specifically brought, it was not obscurely insinuated. And a certain Sir Dudley Digges, a wealthy company promoter and a well-known opposition leader, who had been chosen to move the prologue of the impeachment, had let fall some words which Charles at least took to imply that he himself had had a hand in expediting his father's decease. It is to the last degree improbable that Digges would have dared, even if he had desired, to do anything so plainly suicidal. His fellow members had still enough respect for Royalty to be horrified at the very idea, and explicitly and severally to repudiate it, as, indeed, did Digges himself. The King himself eventually accepted the explanation, and Digges, who was more of a careerist than a revolutionary, was in after years received into favour and office. But at the moment Charles was naturally furious. Brought up as he was in the Romano-Scottish rather than the English tradition, he was unable to see why the Palace at Westminster should be a Liberty Hall in which the subject could slander his Sovereign with impunity. And he defended himself by having both Eliot and Digges sent to the Tower.

It was a human and natural retort, but to the last degree unwise. Charles had violated—what he did not yet understand—the great English taboo that was called Privilege. He had done the thing that was not done, and put into motion against himself forces against which he was powerless. The Commons refused to function while the outrage remained unredressed. There was nothing for it but for the King to surrender in public, and restore his victims to their seats, with enhanced prestige and capacity for mischief.

It could no longer be doubted that the second Parliamentary experiment of the reign had broken down even more hopelessly than the first. The King was at the end of his resources. Something of his distress of mind is revealed in what someone at this time overheard him say to Buckingham : "What can I do more ? I have engaged mine honour to mine uncle of Denmark, and other princes. I have, in a manner, lost the love of my subjects. What wouldst thou have me do ?"* What indeed !

The thing that he would not think of doing, under any pressure, was to save himself by abandoning Buckingham. So little question was there of this in his mind that he seized the opportunity of making a defiant gesture, when the Chancellorship of Cambridge University fell vacant, by openly using his influence to have the Duke elected, and thus add to the grievance of his favourite's many honours. The Commons were of course furious, and were for calling the dons who had voted to account, but the King—with the law on his side—would have none of it. The incident was again one that did more credit to his heart than his head.

The only question now was whether the impeachment should be allowed to go through to the end. As far as the merits of the case were concerned, there seemed every reason for allowing the Duke to stand his ground and fight it out. The Commons' charges against him were so monstrously exaggerated, and on many counts so absurd, that the Duke, in a singularly temperate and persuasive defence, had no difficulty in tearing most of them to shreds. To accuse him of criminal negligence in his conduct of

* *Court and Times of Charles I*, i, p. 104.

the Admiralty, or of corruption in conforming to the universal practice of compensating his predecessors in office, was not even plausible ; to tax him with compassing the death of his late Sovereign and benefactor was most appropriately answered in the words, that Buckingham himself quoted, of the dying James : "They are worse than devils that say it." The real case against him, that of being a reckless and feckless amateur in a task beyond his abilities, was allowed to go by default in this attempt to prove him a stage villain and a traitor.

Before any impartial tribunal, the impeachment would not have had a leg to stand upon. But was the House of Peers an impartial tribunal ? It is notorious that in political trials, a judicial frame of mind is as frequent as grapes on thistles. The Peers would have been more than human, if they had not harboured a bitter but suppressed resentment against this upstart who had been preferred before them all. And for many reasons, they were in a state of highly inflamed irritation against both King and the Duke. Nothing could have been more calculated to alienate their sympathies than the outrageous attempt to convict one of their most respected members of High Treason ; and it did not prejudice them in the Duke's favour that they had before them Bristol's entirely independent counter-charges against him —so much more convincing than the Commons' indictment, because so much more restrained and temperate. In various other ways, too, their nerves had been set on edge ; particularly by the arbitrary incarceration of the very important Earl of Arundel, on account of his son's having married a lady whose hand the King had intended to bestow elsewhere. The bickering over this incident resulted in their Lordships resolving to cut from a message asking for a "gracious answer" from His Majesty, the word "gracious." It was a straw, but it showed how stiff a breeze was blowing up against the Court even from these exalted regions.

But it was the attitude of the Commons that finally decided the King to end a situation that was not only hopeless but dangerous. Drunken with Eliot's eloquence and thoroughly disgruntled by the King's lack of tact and temper in handling them, they had now turned into the equivalent of a mob, howling at the Palace Gates for the Chief Minister to be thrown out to them—a mob who if they were once allowed to taste blood, would be less likely to go home than to storm the Palace itself.

They were clamouring for the Lords to incarcerate Buckingham in advance of his trial ; they were preparing a defiant remonstrance to the effect that whether he was found guilty or not, they were resolved to get rid of him, and that until that was done, not a penny of the promised dole should the King receive ; they denounced the payment of customs in such terms as to afford a patriotic excuse for anyone who wanted to import goods duty free. The King was in check, and his most valuable piece might at any moment be taken. After that, it would be mate after a few more moves. There was nothing for it, under the circumstances, but to sweep the board and return the pieces to the box.

The Lords, who much relished the dominating position that the Impeachment had conferred on them, were aghast at the news that the King was about to carry out his threat, in default of supply, to dissolve Parliament, and they sought to dissuade him. But Charles had made up his mind. In words almost precisely the same as those he was destined to use in a yet more desperate crisis, he answered—"Not for a minute."

I I

MASTER OF HIS HOUSE

As if it were not enough that, within little more than a year from his accession, the King had found himself faced with the choice between governing without Parliament and ceasing to govern at all, his married life, which had opened with such fair auspices, seemed to have arrived at an equally hopeless deadlock.

That fatal secret agreement with France, which had been the price of the marriage, had, in fact, created a situation with which a very Prince Charming might have found it beyond his power to cope. Even if they had been left to themselves, the pretty, high-spirited bride of fifteen, and the shy, self-conscious bridegroom, ten years her senior, would have found it difficult so to harmonize their temperaments as to consummate a marriage of minds. But it was wildly impossible when the girl had come attended by a little army of her countrymen and countrywomen, who were her playmates and confidants and spiritual advisers, and who, in their aversion from the ways and beliefs of her adopted countrymen, formed as much of a perpetual opposition to Charles as his own Parliament. The proverbial trials of the young husband saddled with the entertainment of a mother-in-law, were, in his case, multiplied a hundredfold, besides being perpetuated by international treaty.

Henriette had, from her first sight of him, been prepared to fall in love with her good-looking prince, and if left to herself might have settled down happily enough in her new environment —to judge at least from her answer, just after her arrival, to an English attendant who had asked whether she could endure a Huguenot :

"Why not ? Wasn't my father one ?"

But to accommodate herself to her father's excellent example of humouring the religious prejudices of his subjects, was just what Henriette's governesses, spiritual pastors, and companions were determined to prevent her from doing. And their task was the easier, because the girl very soon began to have grievances of her own, as annoying in their way as those of her husband. The position of a Catholic Queen in a fanatically Protestant environ-ment was bound to be difficult, and Charles was not the man to make it easier. Kind and affectionate as he was, nature had denied him that tactful urbanity by which difficult situations are made easy. After the easy gallantry to which she had been accustomed at the Louvre, she must have found him terribly heavy in the hand.

He was no doubt a model husband—a naughty word would start him blushing furiously—but was not the model a little too like a dummy ? Is it not possible that this extremely sprightly child, who had turned the head of young Soissons, and had had as great a crush for Charles's portrait as any modern schoolgirl for a film star's, would in her heart of hearts have preferred some-thing a little more spicy ?

But Henriette's arch and overshadowing grievance coincided, curiously enough, with that of the English Parliament—to wit, the Duke of Buckingham, plus Buckingham's relations. No young wife likes to find even a male friend given the place that she claims, by right, in her husband's confidence and affections. And when she finds herself saddled with the company and chaperonage of that friend's mother and relations, and expected to show them a proper deference, it is fairly safe to predict trouble.

Buckingham's conduct was not calculated to reconcile her to this state of things. Charles, with all his faults, was at least a gentleman ; but Buckingham, as his hosts at Madrid had discovered, had always some streak in him of the bounder—the word is the only one that will fit. Once let his will be crossed or his vanity touched, and the veneer of his magnificent manners would be broken through—he would become arrogantly outrageous. When Henriette became *difficile*, he flattered himself that he could break down her will by bullying—and it was not Buckingham's way to do things by halves. Towering over the unfortunate child, he would remind her how, in England, Queens had paid for their faults with their heads ; and he would threaten to make her the most unhappy woman alive. And Charles, King Charles, could put up with this treatment of his Queen by a subject ! It seemed that he was capable of putting up with anything from Steenie. Even if the daughter of Henri IV had not been capable of deducing unflattering conclusions about her husband's manhood, there was no lack of sympathizers at her ear to deduce them for her.

And yet—if we may presume to interpret her—at the bottom of her heart she remained faithful to her lover, whom, at first sight, she had grudged to the Infanta ; whose portrait she had worshipped in secret ; who had consoled her with such sweet gallantry at that first, agitating meeting. She had loved him then ; she wanted to love him now—if he would only come alive, instead of being the cold image of the lover she desired in him.

Such a conflict of hope and frustration in the mind of a high-spirited girl, with the hot blood of Italy in her veins, would exactly account for a course of behaviour that drove Charles to the verge of distraction. Until such time as he came up to her expectations, she was going to make herself as tiresome and intractable to him as she had it in her power to be.

Perhaps, without consciously realizing it, she wanted to goad him into asserting that real self of his that she divined beneath the surface, and to which, without dishonour, she could make her joyous surrender. It is surely not without its significance that, until this conflict was resolved, she could not—or at any rate did not—conceive a child by him.

This may be the explanation of the militant piety—so foreign, one would have thought, to her frivolous nature—that she soon began to flaunt in the face of her husband and her husband's countrymen. It was, after all, the most obvious way in which she could assert herself in this unsympathetic environment. Her priests, her austere and saintly confessor, and her almoner, the

young, fiery Bishop of Mende, were her staff in a war of perpetual
pinpricks. Very light-hearted, for so solemn an issue, was the
spirit in which it was conducted. When the royal couple went
down into the country for the first time, there was an unedifying
scene at dinner, during which, at grace, her confessor entered into
a shoving and shouting competition with the royal chaplain, until
His Majesty left the table in a passion, taking the Queen with
him. On this same visit, the King having gone on to inspect the
fleet, the Queen and her suite took the opportunity to invade a
service given by the local parson in the guard room, walking about
the room laughing, and making all the noise possible. Nor was
this the worst in store for the unhappy clergyman, for one of them
frightened him out of his wits by letting off a gun just behind him
as he sat on a bench.

It was more serious when the Queen not only refused to be
crowned—her Bishop had had the audacity to suggest doing this
himself—but even to look on at the coronation from the box that
had been prepared for her in Westminster Abbey. And though
she did watch the procession from a window outside, she allowed
her ladies to advertise their contempt of the whole proceedings
by romping and dancing about in the room. This, to put it mildly,
was not the way to win the hearts of the English people.

At the opening of Parliament, only four days later, the Queen
attempted to repeat this performance without even the excuse of
religion. Charles had provided her with a seat alongside old Lady
Buckingham. Henriette appeared to fall in with the unwelcome
arrangement, but when the time came, suddenly announced that
it was raining, a phenomenon not apparent to Charles, and that
as it was out of the question for her to wet her feet crossing the
street, her attendance must please be excused. Charles, thoroughly
nonplussed, went off to Steenie, who after telling him off soundly
for his failure to assert himself, proceeded to talk to Henriette in
the style of a sergeant-major. It was only, however, when the
French Ambassador came to the rescue, that Henriette consented
to oblige *him* by going ; whereupon Charles, who seems to have
thoroughly lost his head, and to have now determined to assert
himself at all costs, sent to order her out of her seat again. For
three whole days he sent her to Coventry. Then, when she ventured
to ask him what was the matter, he told her, with all appropriate firmness, to admit herself in the wrong. Henriette didn't
understand—would he kindly explain ? Charles was not good at

explanations, and could find no better retort than, "You said it rained when I said it did not rain." Henriette could still not see what there was to take offence at, but if that was all Charles wanted, she would make no difficulty about confirming his weather report. And with that he had to be content.

Another of these tiffs took place in bed. Henriette took the opportunity to present her husband with a list of the officers she wanted to administer the lands in her jointure. Charles said he would read it in the morning, but rashly reminded her—what she probably knew quite well already—that the treaty had left these particular appointments in his hands. But, wheedled Henriette, there were English as well as French in her list. Charles, no doubt remembering Steenie's rebuke, replied that though he would accept any Englishman he thought fit to serve her, there could be no question of any Frenchman. But, said Henriette, she and her mother had already commissioned these people. She and her mother, Charles intimated, had had no business to do anything of the sort. Very well then, he could take his lands back and make her an allowance instead.

"I bade her then," is Charles's account of the matter, in a letter to Steenie, "remember to whom she spoke, and told her she ought not to use me so. Then she fell into a passionate discourse, how miserable she was, in having no power to place servants, and that business succeeded the worse for her recommendation ; which, when I wanted to answer, she would not so much as hear me. Then she went on saying she was not of that base quality to be used so ill. Then I both made her hear me, and end that discourse."

At what time in the night or morning that peaceful consummation was attained, he does not record.

No man can put up with this sort of thing indefinitely. The child of sixteen, as she was now, was fully capable of holding her own against the man of twenty-six. With the reinforcement of her French suite the odds became overwhelming. If the King could not call his crown his own when Parliament was sitting, when he retired to his palace he could not call his soul his own, and he had not the resort, when the situation became desperate, of being able to get rid of his wife as he could of his Parliament.

But was this equally the case with that incubus of a suite ? It is true that he was saddled with it by treaty, but such scraps of paper were of even more perishable texture in the seventeenth

SIR JOHN ELIOT—*from a portrait in the collection of
the Earl of St Germans at Port Eliot*

APOTHEOSIS OF THE DUKE OF BUCKINGHAM—*from
a print of the painting by Rubens in the collection of the Earl of Jersey*

than in the twentieth century. So long as it was a question of a
French alliance, it might be necessary to maintain the letter of
the bond at almost any cost ; but now that the weathercock of
Buckingham's policy was veering in the direction not of alliance
but of war, there was less need for tenderness to Bourbon susceptibilities. And the situation, treaty or no treaty, was quite frankly
impossible.

No husband, who values his wife's affections, can endure to
have them stolen from him, as Charles complained, not without
reason, the "Monsers," or Monsieurs, were trying to do ; nor
can he, if also a King, be expected to put up with a colony of
licensed mischief makers about his path and about his bed,
spying out all his ways. It was even reported that the Queen's
confessor used to exact from her a strict account of the most
intimate secrets of the royal marriage chamber !

What probably galled Charles most of all, was the obvious fact
that the suite were teaching Henriette to make fun of him. This
was a form of attack against which he was peculiarly defenceless.
The armour of self-conscious dignity that his impediment of
speech had compelled him to assume, disqualified him from
mental agility : though no friend of Puritanism, he was at least
at one with the strictest of his Puritan subjects in his intolerance
of mere frivolity. Henriette's peals of laughter among her Parisian
cronies, and the more than suspicion of their being at his royal
expense, must have been, for his grave, Scottish mind, the most
exquisite form of annoyance.

More serious still, was the Catholic queen's steadily accumulating unpopularity. If Henriette had been an angel of tact, she
would have found it a hard enough task to overcome the inflamed
suspiciousness of her Protestant subjects. As it was, she, with the
aid of her French colony, was doing everything she possibly could
to rub them up the wrong way, and they, for their part, were
ready enough to make the worst even of her most innocent actions
—her love of amateur theatricals was counted against her for
sinfulness, and an innocent Christmas shopping expedition, that
she undertook incognito, was frowned upon, by the surly Lon-
doners, as another French trick.

The worst scandal of all was caused by an incident, to which
Henriette herself pleaded not guilty, but whose occurrence was
certainly believed in at the time. The story, at any rate, was, that
she and her suite, on one of their country walks, had crossed not

only St James's but also Hyde Park, and so came to what must have been one of the most popular sights of London, the gallows at Tyburn. Here, it was alleged, the Queen had fallen on her knees in homage to the noble army of Catholic martyrs who had suffered for their faith, or, as every good Protestant believed, the traitors who had got their deserts, at this spot. "This," was the comment of that indefatigable letter writer, the Rev. Joseph Mead, "can these damned priests make her do."

Charles's resentment, as is the way with reserved natures, had been gathering for a long time beneath the surface, and now it burst forth with volcanic fury. One midsummer afternoon His Majesty went across to the Queen's side of Whitehall Palace, where he discovered a number of the "monsers," "unreverently dancing and curvetting," as one account put it, "in her presence." This was the last straw. The King, still further roused by a pert answer of Henriette's, took her to his own apartments, locking the door behind him, and then sent to inform the suite that every French man and woman among them was dismissed to Somerset House, to await his pleasure, which was their departure, bag and baggage, to their own country at the earliest possible moment. There was naturally a fearful scene, the Bishop taking his stand on the treaty and flatly refusing to go, the women in a state of noisy hysterics, until the yeomen of the guard had to be called in to bundle the whole lot unceremoniously out of doors.

As for Henriette, she could never have believed her mild husband capable of such conduct. Like the spoilt child she was, she gave way to a paroxysm of unrestrained temper, finally rushing to the window, below which some of the suite were passing, and smashing the glass with her little fists—"Adieu ! Adieu !" He followed her ; he seized her wrists as she clung to the iron bars ; he dragged her by main force back into the room —he was, for the first time, master. She might—and oh, how she must at that moment, have hated him ! But she would never again laugh at him. It was the turning point of their married life.

Luckily the suite itself did its unintended best to assuage the bitterness of parting. They were no doubt loyal to their mistress, after their fashion, but they would not have been French if they had not had an extremely keen eye for the main chance. In spite of the fact that Charles showed a kingly generosity in his distri-bution of parting gifts, they proceeded to share out, among them-selves, every scrap of Henriette's property on which they could lay hands, as vails, or perquisites. The Master of the Horse put in a modest claim to her whole stud, not to speak of all the furniture under his charge. This was successfully resisted, but the rest of them did manage to get hold of Her Majesty's complete wardrobe, with the exception of a gown and two smocks, and even the Lords of the Council, who intervened on her behalf, could only get them to disgorge one old satin gown. It was reported, too, that they had left their apartments in so filthy a condition that it would be a long time before they could be cleaned up for the new suite.

So one imagines that Henriette may even have begun to feel a certain sympathy with her husband, when, tired out with the endless excuses by which, for more than a month, they contrived to postpone their departure, he wrote to Buckingham, commending him to send them all packing next day by force if necessary, "driving them away like so many wild beasts, until you have shipped them, and so the devil go with them !"

That settled it ; and next day they really were off. But that indomitable governess, Madame de St Georges, kept up her end to the last, gesticulating violently before the crowd that had collected in the Strand outside Somerset House, and giving them such a piece of her mind that one sturdy patriot tried to shut her mouth with a stone, whereupon a certain gentleman of their English escort very properly ran him through for his pains.

Charles had relented enough to allow Henriette to retain her nurse, and some half dozen more picked and inoffensive French attendants, but she was naturally miserable at the parting from her friends and—as the keen eyes of the Venetian Ambassador noted—seemed to be constantly on the verge of tears. But tears with her, like April showers, were as quickly succeeded by sunshine, and her nature was too mercurial to endure a settled gloom about anything. Early in October we find the Florentine representative writing home that the Queen seemed very happy and cheerful—thoroughly absorbed, in fact, in her new, splendidly fitted, residence of Denmark House, which had belonged to James's Queen Anne.

The most serious question was—what would Henriette's brother, Louis, do about this combined insult to his sister and breach of treaty stipulations ? Louis, as it happened, was the last person to be put out of his stride by his sister's matrimonial troubles. He was, though quite normal in every other way, so averse to everything connected with sex, that for many years he avoided the company of his own wife—and after all, Charles, in getting rid of his wife's foreign attendants, was only following his brother-in-law's example. So that Louis' attitude to his sister's troubles was that of a Gallio. He had enough trouble on his hands already, and it was against his and Richelieu's policy to aggravate the already strained situation with England.

Still, with one's family prestige at stake, one must do something, and Louis did the most sensible thing possible by sending over to England, as his special envoy to straighten out the tangle, the Marshal de Bassompierre, than whom a better man could not have been found for the post. Though now in advanced middle age, he was still one of the most attractive men in France, a famous lady-killer, with a collection of six thousand love-letters from different admirers. Twenty years before Henriette had been born, he had followed her father's white plume on the great day of Ivry, and it was in something of a fatherly, or avuncular spirit, that he now approached the difficulties of this slip of a girl, who must have reminded him at times poignantly, both in feature and disposition, of the gay and gallant Henry of Navarre.

It was not long before he had won the instinctive confidence of both parties to the dispute. They found in him no Machiavellian diplomat, but a wise and understanding friend, of an older generation, who had come with no other object than to be helpful. They were soon pouring out their grievances to him, like two impulsive children, and he, with sympathetic tact, contrived to play the part of impartial umpire. With the utmost patience, he set himself to elicit what had really happened—no easy task, since it proved almost impossible for them to discuss it in his presence without sparring at each other.

If Henriette had imagined that he had come to take up the cudgels for her in the spirit of blind partisanship to which she had been accustomed from members of her suite, she was soon undeceived. The Marshal had had too much experience in the ways of love to take seriously her pose of injured martyr. After he had seen one or two specimens of the tantrums with which Charles had had to cope, he did not hesitate to tell her, with the most unflattering candour, what he thought about it. One particularly hectic scene, that she created in front of him, ended in his threatening to go straight home to inform her mother and brother that it was all her fault. This was just the sort of thing that no one—except the egregious Buckingham—had ever dared to say to Henriette, and it was just what she needed to pull her up. Besides, her father's gallant old friend had such a way with him in saying it !

At the same time, the Marshal went to work with Charles, who, when handled in the right way, proved only too anxious to arrive at any reasonable compromise. De Bassompierre perfectly understood what his difficulties had been, and was able to fix up an arrangement by which, while retaining the predominantly English and English-controlled suite on which her husband had insisted, Henriette should have a sufficient number of her own countrymen about her to prevent her from feeling homesick.

De Bassompierre's mission would have been an unqualified success, had his own Government been prepared to endorse its results. But by the time he returned, just before Christmas, things had drifted too far in the direction of war to make any compromise acceptable in Paris. But for any failure as a diplomatist, the Marshal had more than compensated by his success as a friend. He had brought Charles and Henriette together ; he had made them see their common interest in adjusting differences that, compared with their underlying affection, were, after all, superficial.

The course of their love could never run perfectly smooth so long as the disturbing influence of Buckingham remained, and so long as Charles persisted in his infuriating habit of making his friend his confidant about his wife. But at least he was able to set down in a postscript to a letter sent to the Duke's headquarters at Rhé, almost exactly a year after the expulsion of her suite :

"I cannot omit to tell you that my wife and I were never better together ; she ... showing herself so loving to me, by her discretion upon all occasions, that it makes us all wonder and esteem her."

12

AMATEUR STRATEGY

The collapse of his second Parliament, without its having granted him a penny of relief, had rendered the King's financial position even more desperate than before. He was at war without the means of paying or munitioning his forces, let alone of keeping faith with his allies. The results were deplorable, and would have been catastrophic had the Spaniards been capable of a serious offensive. There was no army worthy the name, and in the navy desertion was rife and mutiny chronic. In the Autumn a fleet under Lord Willoughby did, after many delays, get to sea, but it never this time even reached Spanish waters—the rough weather in the Bay proved more than either ships or crews were capable of standing.

Meanwhile it had been demonstrated, in the face of all Europe, what fate was in store for those who put their trust in British promises. The King of Denmark had undertaken the championship of Protestant Germany on the strength of those promised subsidies that Charles had not the means to pay. Without them he was as incapable of waging effective war as Charles himself ; he was incapable, even, of getting away. His army—such as it was—was overtaken by Tilly and smashed to pieces, and the King himself driven off the mainland. Wallenstein meanwhile, at the head of another army, nominally imperial, but really a huge private concern with himself as director, had at last finally disposed of Mansfeld, who, having wandered to the confines of Bosnia, died, game to the last, bolt upright in his armour. The whole of Germany now lay at the feet of the Emperor, and the dearest wish of Charles's heart, the restoration of his sister and her husband to their Palatinate, was further off then ever.

There was no question but that if he was to make even the semblance of performing his kingly duty, he must put money in his purse. But how ? The experience of two Parliaments had shown it to be worse than useless to look for aid in that direction. A certain amount could be, and was, raised by disposing of the crown plate ; but this was only a drop in the ocean. A start was even made with debasing the coinage, but this all too modern expedient was not persisted in.

The King had a mind to throw himself upon the patriotism of his subjects, and passed round the hat for a voluntary loan. Practically the only contributors were the clergy, and office holders dependent upon Court favour. He was thus driven to his last resource of making the loan compulsory. It is of all the acts of his reign the one that comes nearest to justifying those accusations of lawlessness that at one time it was so fashionable to level against him. There have been few monarchs more habitually scrupulous about honouring the law, but on this occasion Charles can hardly be acquitted of violating at least its spirit, and perhaps its letter too.

For to what did his demand amount, but a plain declaration that if Parliament refused to provide subsidies for the Crown's, and the nation's, elementary needs, the King would make a virtue of necessity and help himself to the subsidies under another name ?—for no lender was simple enough to imagine that, having once parted with his money, he was ever likely to see it back.

If this could be done once, and allowed to become a precedent, there was no reason why a King of England should not repeat it as often and for any amount that he pleased, and it would be hard to dispute Hallam's conclusion that, in such a case, "our freeborn high-minded gentry would not long have brooked to give their attendance in such an ignominious assembly, and an English Parliament would have become as idle a mockery of national representation as the Cortes of Castile." But what the great Whig advocate omits to add is that no high-minded, conscientious Sovereign can long endure to watch the affairs of the nation going to wrack and ruin because he is denied the means of doing his kingly duty. The King may have been wrong in what he did, but short of resigning himself and his successors on the throne to the position of crowned puppets, he might have, and presumably did, ask himself what else he could have done.

There was one thing at least, which, as it was, does not seem to have occurred to him—and that was to have given himself the chance of balancing accounts, in a normal way, by denying himself the unnecessary luxury of war, and taking to himself, for the remainder of his reign, his father's wise motto, "Blessed are the peacemakers." But that was not the way with the man into whose hands he had with such blind trust committed his destinies, and who, having failed in the gamble of one war, was now preparing to double the stakes.

Buckingham was not the type of man to commit his thoughts to paper, but it is not difficult to follow the direction in which they were beginning to move. The events of the last Parliament must have shown even him how badly his credit had been damaged by the failure of the Cadiz expedition. He would not have been Buckingham if he had taken any part of the blame to himself. Cecil had pretty obviously muddled the whole business, and the expedition had put to sea under the fatal handicap caused by

Parliament's refusal of the money necessary for its proper equipment. What if another and greater expedition could be sent out, that should be both properly found and brilliantly led ? The thing could be done, if by hook or by crook enough money could be got together even for one or two months' vigorous war. And as for a leader, this time Buckingham was going to take no chances ; he would go himself.

But where was there the opportunity for such a coup ? The Lord Admiral's imagination must have travelled along the coastline of Western Europe. Cadiz would not do for a second attempt, and he does not seem to have thought of Gibraltar— though this had been considered as a possible alternative for Cecil's armada. It was only when he had arrived at the French seaboard that the great opportunity showed itself. For nothing had he been more bitterly nor, as he conceived, more unfairly attacked, than for that unlucky loan of ships to be used against Protestant Rochelle. It was evident that Richelieu would never rest till he had ended this nuisance of a practically independent seaport, which could only serve as a perpetual focus of resistance to that power of the French Crown that it was his life's work to build up. The maintenance of a royal fort at the harbour mouth in defiance—so the citizens alleged—of a solemn agreement, was plain evidence of the King's intention to be master in this, as in every other part of his realm.

This intention, so vital to the welfare of France, could, Buckingham believed, be paralyzed by the use of that British sea power which he himself had been at such pains to foster. The most obvious way would no doubt have been by garrisoning the town. This, however, was barred by the objection of the citizens, who, though Protestants, were also Frenchmen, and as such, not prepared to embark on open treason. But Buckingham was not thinking of anything so crude. Outside the harbour there were two large islands. By the occupation of both, or perhaps even one of these, such a situation might be created as to render impracticable any attempt to reduce the town by siege—and it was impregnable to storm. It was possible for a power possessing command of the sea to concentrate unexpectedly, and in overwhelming force, on its selected island—in this case, the smaller of the two, but the one more immediately adjacent to the harbour mouth. Once this Isle of Rhé was occupied, the communications of Rochelle with the outside world could be permanently safeguarded. Without any act of open rebellion, Rochelle would thus become virtually a free Protestant city under the English King's protection, with all the effect of a second Calais. Here would be the master-stroke, that in the eyes of Britain and all Europe would vindicate Buckingham's genius, and be such a resounding triumph for the royal policy as would enable the King, with full national support, to snap his fingers at Parliamentary opposition.

For the idea of an amateur strategist this was subtly, and even brilliantly, conceived. But as is the way with such conceptions, it suffered from the lack of adjustment of means to ends. It assumed too much. To make a neat job of the occupation required not necessarily a large but an efficient and disciplined regular force, instead of the mere rabble of forced levies, which was all Buckingham had to rely on. And then suppose—a very big supposition under the circumstances—that all went well, and Rhé were effectively occupied. What then ? England would be committed to maintaining, and garrisoning, an advanced base far away from her own shores. This, at the best, would cost a great deal of money, more, by a long chalk, than could possibly be supplied without breaking the back either of the Constitution or the royal finances.

And could it safely be taken for granted that the occupation of Rhé would solve the problem of Rochelle as neatly and automatically as might be hoped ? If one thing could be more certain than another, it was that the whole energies of the French monarchy, backed by the outraged patriotism of the French nation, would be concentrated on the removal of the open menace that an independent Rochelle would then constitute. At all costs, that diseased growth would have to be cut out of the national system. Had the English monarchy the resources, or anything like them, for maintaining indefinitely a life and death contest of this kind ? The mere presence of a garrison on Rhé would not prevent the bottling up of Rochelle by the means that were actually adopted in the siege, namely the building of a mole across the harbour mouth. It would be necessary to land and fight the royal army on the mainland, if that were to be countered. And such a possibility was much less on the cards than of a French landing on Rhé itself, for it was too much to expect the fleet to maintain a permanent guard on the narrows that separated the island from the mainland.

As for safeguarding the French Protestants, they little knew the French nature, or the nature of French patriotism, who counted on it. Such open alliance with the foreigner, whatever might have been the effect at fortified Rochelle, would, almost past a doubt, have caused a massacre of the Protestants shut up and left in the rest of France, that would have put St Bartholomew into the shade.

Buckingham's was, in fact, one of those bright amateur ideas that work out admirably on paper, and whose essential soundness is so easily demonstrated, even after the event, that no other explanation of their failure will pass current than that of sheer bad luck—they always ought to come off, if something wholly unpredictable did not go wrong with the working. And something always does.

One element of bad luck may, however, be conceded to the Duke's memory. He was pitting his talent against the genius of one of the few civilian strategists in history to whom nature had given that detailed capacity for proportioning means to ends, that normally is developed by a lifetime of professional experience. To say that Richelieu was a born soldier would be verbiage— what was extraordinary about him was that he should somehow have acquired the capacity of a trained soldier. Among other things, he had spotted the importance of this Isle of Rhé ; he had placed on it a small but highly trained garrison, under an excellent commander, the Comte de Toiras ; he had had the little town of St Martin fortified according to the most advanced notions of military engineering.

Having formed his scheme, Buckingham threw all his magnificent energy into its realization. The first and most essential thing was to raise the money. For this it was necessary to see that the forced loan should be as strictly exacted as if it had been a regular tax, even if this involved, as it did, the stretching of the powers of the Crown almost to breaking point. Everywhere, up and down the country, there was resistance ; citizens standing on their rights and having to be threatened, imprisoned, or punished by conscription into the levies that were being raised. What was worst of all was that the judges, the traditional "lions beneath the throne," found themselves unable to reconcile their consciences to endorsing the legality of the imposition, and that the Lord Chief Justice was actually dismissed in consequence. That things had come to such a pass shows how desperate was the course on which the Crown had embarked. It could only be hoped that the success of the great gamble would atone for everything, as at a later day the violence that Bismarck did to the Prussian Constitution was forgotten in the triumph of Sadowa.

But there was another and more popular way of raising funds for the expedition, which was by making the enemy himself contribute. It must be noted, though, that right up to the setting forth of Buckingham's armada, there was no French enemy, and no war, in the strict sense of the words. In spite of the diplomatic deadlock that followed Louis' repudiation of de Bassompierre's compromise about his sister's rights, that matter might have dragged on till doomsday before either Louis or Richelieu would have drawn the sword about it. What had caused a state of war to develop without the name, was the high-handed action, first of England, and then, after great provocation, of France, on the sea. For months, in spite of all protests, the English had been seizing French ships, and confiscating their cargoes, on suspicion of trading with the Spanish foe. At last the Governor of Bordeaux, a nobleman who had no love for Richelieu and wanted to force his hand, seized the whole English wine fleet, carefully waiting till the wine had been paid for. After this outrage the English navy, that was, at least, overwhelmingly superior to anything the French could muster, swept their commerce from the seas, and the resultant loot was so considerable that, along with the proceeds of his loan, Charles was able for the first and only time to send out an expedition that was not starved for funds.

But not even this modest and temporary windfall could improvise an army out of the pressed contingents that were brought together at the rendezvous, Portsmouth. It was the old, familiar story of mismanagement and indiscipline—"they are all absolutely broke," as we read in one dispatch, "both officers and men, and for the last week have been as near a mutiny as possible, for want of money."* It was an armed mob, rather than an army, that eventually, on the 27th of June, put to sea in the fleet of over a hundred ships—only ten of them, however, belonging to the Royal Navy—that Buckingham had got together.

They did, at least, make the voyage successfully, and arrived before Rhé in what ought to have been overwhelming strength, for they outnumbered the forces at Toiras's disposal by six to one. But from the first, things began to go wrong. The landing on the east end of the long island, was a scrambling and confused affair, and as the men were trying to form up on the shore, a handful

* Capt. T. Goring to Sir George Blundell, the 9th of May, 1626.

of French cavalry, that had been concealed behind some sand-hills, dashed down on the disorderly groups, and were only eventually driven off, by sheer weight of numbers, after inflicting grievous loss. What was the worst feature of the affair was the display not only of indiscipline, but of cowardice ; Buckingham, whose exertions and example at least averted a major disaster, had literally to cudgel his men ashore.

If energy and courage alone could command victory, history would record few greater commanders than Buckingham now, and throughout this whole campaign, proved himself to be. He was everywhere ; sharing the worst hardships of the trenches, sleeping in his cloak among his men, transforming himself, on due occasion, from general to admiral ; taking charge of everything, making his presence felt everywhere. But nothing could make up for his lack of apprenticeship to the soldier's trade, and conse-quent ignorance of those necessary details that spell the difference between success and failure. Moreover, his gallantry was quite untempered by that coolness of judgment that has been defined as the first quality of a soldier.

Either because the force had been too badly shaken on landing, or because it was impossible to make adequate staff arrangements, valuable days were lost before it moved on to the essential operation of shutting up Toiras and starving him out—for it was soon evident that there was no shorter way—in his fortress at St Martin. After his invariable practice of playing for the highest stakes, Buckingham altogether neglected a smaller fort, close to the original landing place, that itself would form an ideal landing place for the French forces that Richelieu was now beginning to rush to the opposite mainland.

From the first it was evident that things were not working according to plan. The Huguenot aid, without which, according to the strict letter of his instructions, nothing was to be attempted, materialized at first in less than a score of volunteers. But Bucking-ham was going through with it, come what might, and the busi-ness of starving out the garrison was entered on with such thoroughness as to include well-poisoning, and the driving of women and children from the surrounding country under the walls, where the soldiers fired into them until they were admitted to help consume the rations of the garrison. All this did not prevent the most gentlemanly interchange of courtesies between the two commanders.

The siege dragged on from the middle of July to the end of September, before the garrison had consumed everything that the human frame can be forced to assimilate. On the 27th, the indomitable Toiras had actually arranged to surrender on the following day. But during that night a flotilla of small craft that Richelieu, by almost incredible exertions, had collected for the purpose, crept through the thick darkness, close up to the British blockading squadron, before they were discovered, and then— their password being, *"Vive le roy, passer ou mourir"*—dashed against the chain of hawsers, stretched from ship to ship, by which the blockade was maintained. There was a wild fight, "The English," it was said, "raged more than the sea itself," and a score or more of the attacking vessels were destroyed ; but at one point the chain was broken, and enough of them got through to provision the fortress for another month.

It was the turning point, and it was the unanimous opinion of the officers on Buckingham's Council of War that the game was up, and that the only thing to do now was to get what was left of the besieging force out of Rhé while the going was good. It was by this time in a miserable condition. It spells just the difference between Richelieu's and Buckingham's staff methods that during the long siege of Rochelle that followed, the Cardinal succeeded in maintaining his army on the marshy mainland fit and healthy, whereas two months on Rhé was enough to knock up the Duke's, and every day the fighting strength was being depleted by dysentery and other diseases. And it was not only among the besieged that provisions were now beginning to run short.

But Buckingham had that faculty of never knowing when he was beaten, that, though it may be heroism when it occurs in the British soldier, merits a different name when it is possessed by the British general. He had already started to remove his siege train, when he changed his mind and resolved, as he so often had before, to recoup his losses by doubling the stakes. He had one last chance to gamble on, for the King was known to be preparing a new fleet and army whose arrival would double the forces at his disposal.

Since the departure of his friend, Charles had come out in a new light. While Buckingham had been at the helm, the King had almost ceased to function. He appeared but rarely at the Council Board, and then only to lend the weight of his authority to some decision of the Duke's. But now that Buckingham was at the post of danger, the loyalty of friendship that had kept Charles passive heretofore, now stimulated him to an activity positively feverish. He gathered up the reigns of government firmly into his hands, and commenced to hustle his ministers in a way of which no one would have thought him capable.

"If Buckingham should not now be supplied," we find him writing to his Lord Treasurer and Chancellor of the Exchequer, "not in show, but substantially, having so bravely and, I thank God, successfully, begun his expedition, it were an irrecoverable shame to me and all this nation ; and those that either hinders or, according to their several places, furthers not this action as much as they may, deserves to make their end at Tyburn or some such place ; but I hope better things of you."

That was no doubt the spirit, but unfortunately the means were lacking to implement it. The financial spurt that had sufficed for the equipment of the expedition was exhausted. French ships no longer put to sea to be captured, and the proceeds of the loan were almost swallowed up. The team of ministers whom the King was trying to drive, had had all energy and initiative taken out of them by their all-managing Duke.

The new expeditionary force was, if possible, more hopelessly muddled and inefficient than any of its predecessors. The best commander who could be found for it was that amiable fop who, from the Barony of Kensington, had now been promoted to the Earldom of Holland. His army was a scratched up rabble of ne'er-do-wells and malcontents, some of whom were beginning to dispute the legality of their impressment. The fleet was a collection of crocks mostly unfit to put to sea. Stores and equipment were utterly insufficient, and there was not the money to buy them.

Despite Buckingham's desperate appeals, and the King's frantic efforts to expedite matters, the start of the expedition kept on having to be postponed, and when at last—with everything still in the utmost degree of confusion and the men only partially armed—a start was attempted, a strong south-wester began to blow in the Channel, which not only drove the ships back to port, but knocked them about so badly as to necessitate at least a fortnight's repairs to render them seaworthy.

Meanwhile, the toils of Richelieu had begun to close upon the unhappy Duke. The French concentration was now sufficiently advanced for troops to be passed over the narrows each night to the fort that Buckingham had left unassailed. The flower of the

French regular army was mustering on the island ; famous regiments, those of Navarre and Piedmont, with the Royal guard, a force incomparably superior in quality, and soon to be superior in numbers, to the besiegers.

Even in this now hopeless situation, Buckingham could not resist one last desperate, and under the circumstances, wicked throw. He would launch his men to the assault on the still unbreached walls, and owing to his depleted siege train, without adequate artillery support. Typical of all his staff arrangements, he had provided scaling ladders too short for the purpose. With pathetic gallantry, the storming parties mounted to the assault, until they found themselves faced by sheer wall at the top of their ladders, and at the mercy of the defenders. A hundred perished by stones alone—and the butcher's bill had mounted to over 400 before the mad attempt was called off.

That was the end ; and it now only remained to perform that most difficult and delicate of all tactical manoeuvres, an embarkation in face of a superior force. The beach of the original landing was no longer available—the French army barred the way. The only point considered practicable was on a smaller island that was connected with Rhé by a causeway and a bridge. Orders had been given to build a defensive work to cover the retreat at this point, but by one of those blunders of staff work that would be incredible, had we not such frequent record of them, it was constructed on the wrong side of the bridge.

Even so, the Duke might perhaps have got away clear, had he done so at once after the failure of his assault. But he was unwilling to abandon his sick and wounded, and so, when he did start, it was too late. The French, declining the battle he offered, closely shadowed him until the causeway and bridge were packed with men—then they proceeded to overwhelm the miserably insufficient rear-guard of sixty horsemen, and a frightful massacre commenced of the helpless and panic-stricken crowd, ridden over by their own fleeing cavalry. Even that ill-sited entrenchment beyond the bridge was taken, but some stout fellows rallied and retook it by a counter attack, which enabled what was left of the force—less than half of its original strength—to get away to the ships without further molestation, the Duke being the last to leave.

Thirty-two colours had fallen into the hands of the enemy, whose losses were negligible. All told, including reinforcements, the Duke had had upwards of 7,000 men on the island, of whom less than 3,000, many sick and all wretched, returned with him to Portsmouth.

So far from having aided Rochelle, they had sealed its fate. The only possible reply to the English on Rhé was the subjugation, once and for all, of the Huguenot free city on the mainland. The royal army, that had driven out Buckingham, now commenced to dig itself in, under the Cardinal's supervision, round the walls, and the great engineering work was put in hand for the blocking up of the harbour. As long months dragged by, the one question that must have dominated all others in the beleaguered city was whether Protestant England could, after having gone so far, stand by, in shameful passivity, until the agony of starvation had done its work.

13

WENTWORTH'S EIRENICON

"This every man knows"—it is Denzil Holles, afterwards to become famous as one of the Five Members, writing to his kinsman, Sir Thomas Wentworth—"that since England was England, it received not so dishonourable a blow."

He was wrong to the extent that there were two, and perhaps only two, who were perfectly unconscious that anything of the sort had occurred—two not without importance, for they were the King himself, and the Commander-in-Chief of the ill-starred expedition.

The loyalty of Charles to his friend was never more touchingly displayed than in this hour of adversity :

"With whatsomever success you shall come to me," he wrote, "you shall be ever welcome, one of my greatest griefs being that I have not been with you in this time of suffering. ... You have gained as much reputation with wise and honest men in this action as if you had performed all your duties."

The consolation was hardly needed. It would have taken more than the loss of a mere island and 4,000 men to damp Buckingham's spirits. The fact that his luck had been out at Rhé only stimulated him to try it again at the first opportunity. The

CHARLES I—*from a print of the portrait by Daniel Mytens*
(1590?–1642) in the British Museum

CHARLES I—*from a bust by Bernini, presumed destroyed in the fire at Whitehall in 1698, and done from the three heads by Van Dyck sent to Bernini*

besiegers of Rochelle had not seen the last of him—not if he knew it.

It did not even depress him to be told, from more than one source, that a plot had been formed to murder him on his way from Portsmouth to London. He refused to take the least precaution, and when his nephew offered to muffle himself up in his uncle's hood so as to be indistinguishable from him, the Duke caught the boy in his arms and assured him that he would never accept such a sacrifice.

Very different was the effect of Rhé on the spirits of the nation. The Cadiz expedition may have caused a more noisy outburst of indignation—nobody believed that such a thing could happen twice—but this crowning ignominy produced, as Clarendon tells us, "such a general consternation as if all the armies of France and Spain had united together and had covered the land." It came as the climax of one unrelieved series of disasters ; England was not only beaten, but seemed to have become incapable of anything else. And all this, in a bare two and a half years of Charles's reign and Buckingham's power.

It is no wonder that the country was seething with discontent. In the fleet and army, underpaid as they were, mutiny had become chronic. The billeting of these disorderly levies on the peaceful countryfolk was a grievance bitterly resented ; and the very method of recruiting by impressment was meeting with more and more opposition, now that it had become apparent how little chance those dragged from their homes had of ever seeing them again. And on the top of all this came the grievance of the forced loan, with the spectacle of leading persons—Eliot, Hampden and Wentworth among them—standing for their rights on the letter of the law, and suffering imprisonment. The very right of the Crown to imprison, at its own discretion, was challenged by five knights—one of them a relative of Hampden's who died of the effect of his confinement ; and this right the King's Bench, while it allowed the Crown to carry its immediate point, significantly refused to affirm as a matter of principle.

"The discontent," in short, "was so universal, the least spark still meeting with enough combustible matter to make a flame, that all wise men looked upon it as the prediction of the destruction and dissolution that would follow. Nor was there a serenity in the countenance of any man, who had age and experience enough to consider things to come ; but only in those who wished the destruction of the Duke, and thought that it could not be purchased at too dear a price. ..."

And even with the loan, with the mortgage or sale of Crown lands, and anticipations of revenue to the utmost limit, the Crown was again at the end of its financial resources, and saddled with huge war expenses that it had no means of meeting.

And yet it is the amazing fact that, discredited and almost bankrupt as they were, neither Charles nor Buckingham seems to have been at all put out, still less to have recognized the necessity —that had become apparent, even to members of the King's Council—of ending the thoroughly unpopular war with France, not to speak of that with Spain. Nothing was further from either of their minds. Charles, as he put it in a remarkably frank interview with the Venetian Ambassador, had pledged his word to the relief of Rochelle, and meant to keep it—his simple solution of the problem being to send out another army, this time, of 20,000. How he proposed to raise and finance it, he did not explain.

Buckingham, however, was not at a loss even for this. With an optimism that almost passes belief, he, of all people, began to press the King to summon another Parliament. This was too much, at first, even for Charles, who saw only too plainly the danger that it portended for Steenie, and actually withstood him to his face. But what was he to do ? He cast his eyes frantically around, exploring every avenue to solvency, but all were closed. He thought of an excise, which the law courts would certainly rule illegal ; of repeating his experiment of the forced loan under a slightly different form, an act of palpable madness in the already inflamed state of public opinion. Even at the Court it was recognized that a Parliament was the only solution, and it would appear that certain influential persons were in a position to guarantee that the impeachment of Buckingham would be dropped. Under those circumstances, the King was prepared to make a virtue of necessity.

The elections were ominous ; the opposition swept the country. Everywhere those who had suffered from refusal to pay the loan were triumphantly elected. At Westminster, even then a key constituency, Buckingham's nominee, whose name was Pye, was fairly howled down with shouts of "A pudding ! A pudding !" and "A lie ! A lie !" His fate was typical. It was too late this time to nominate obnoxious members for sheriffdoms ; the sheriffs were already pricked, Phelips and Seymour, Coke and Wentworth, were back in their places. Back, too, was Eliot, his fiery temper super-heated by his spell of imprisonment for loan resistance. The House of Commons presented, in fact, one solid front of opposition to what would now be a Front Bench, of ministerial ciphers whose business it was to present the case for the Crown. There was one further characteristic of these Poor Commons that is worth noticing. They were, beyond all record, plutocratic. It was computed that they would have been capable of buying out the House of Lords, three times over.*

It was on the 17th of March that the King opened the first Session of this, his Third Parliament. In both his previous opening speeches, he had suffered from the natural incapacity of the tongue-tied man for self-expression, and had, to all intents and purposes, told them nothing at all. This time he was not going to repeat what had proved the fatal mistake of letting matters drift. He would provide them, from the start, with both guidance and inspiration. But unfortunately the tongue-tied man, when he does force himself into speech, is apt to come out with things that produce a very different impression on his audience from that which he had intended to convey.

"These times are for action," he began, typically enough, "wherefore ... I mean not to spend much time in words"—and he proceeded to make what he evidently intended for a rousing appeal to their patriotism—Parliament, he told them, was "the ancient, speediest and best way, in this time of common danger, to give such supply as to secure ourselves and to save our friends from imminent ruin."

If he had ended on this note, all might have been well. But he must needs go on to weight the appeal with a threat. If they would not (which God forbid) discharge their duties, His Majesty would be compelled to use other means which God had put into his hands—which plainly implied that if Parliament denied him the means of discharging his duty, discharge it he would, in despite of Parliament, and provide himself with the means.

Then follows that superb and famous sentence :

"Take not this as a threatening, for I scorn to threaten any but my equals."

Charles, when he spoke it, probably had no other intention

* *Court and Times of Charles I*, p. 331.

than that of softening his previous words. But there can have been few of his English audience who can have regarded it in any other light than that of a flaming challenge. The tongue-tied King had expressed himself, for once, only too well—and it was in the style of a Divine Caesar.

It is no wonder, that as soon as the first necessary formalities had been disposed of, the new House should have settled straight down, with a greater zest than any of its predecessors, to the inevitable business of inflating grievances. Seymour opened the attack, his form in no way impaired by his enforced absence from the previous Parliament ; and then, after two ministers had tried to strike a note of peace and conciliation, Sir John Eliot was on his feet with a terrific, inflammatory invective, designed not only to make any idea of peace unthinkable, but to enlarge the sum of grievances by piling heresy on tyranny, and declaring war not only on unparliamentary taxation, but on the High Anglican principles that were gaining ground in the Church.

But as yet Eliot was not destined to carry all before him in this new Parliament as he had in the last. He had already been overborne in his intention to renew the attack on Buckingham; and now his dominance of the House was to be challenged by a personality equally forceful, and an intelligence incomparably more statesmanlike, those of Sir Thomas Wentworth, the rich Yorkshire baronet, whose beetling brows and haughty reserve inspired more fear than affection among those who did not know him intimately, and whom the Court had considered a dangerous enough man to be shelved with a sheriffdom during the last Parliament. That was a profound mistake, for even at this early stage, Wentworth's—if the King had only known it—was the one intelligence comprehensive enough to provide any solution, short of absolute surrender, to the now almost insoluble problem with which the Crown was faced, that of maintaining its place in the Constitution with the goodwill of its subjects.

There was no hope in the other Parliamentary leaders, least of all in Eliot. So far as we can judge either by their words or actions, they were barren of any sort of constructive policy. Their one idea, or instinct, seems to have been to make it impossible for the King to govern, until he had surrendered the last vestiges of his power—when it would perhaps be time to think what to put into his place. Not so Wentworth. On his lips alone such expressions of loyalty as those with which even Eliot did not fail to season his eloquence, really meant what, in plain English, they implied. He wanted to give the Crown a fair deal within the limits of the Constitution. He wanted the Constitution to work ; and he was prepared with a plan for making it work.

Eliot's speech had been followed by another governmental appeal for conciliation, any will to which he had certainly killed, and then Wentworth rose to his feet. By the time he had sat down, the leadership of the House, which had been so indisputably Eliot's in the last Parliament, had passed—for the time at any rate—to him.

It was no wonder. This man possessed that rare gift, shared by Chatham and Parnell, of being able to command his audience. They yielded, hypnotized, to the sheer force of his personality. It was not only that he possessed the Ancient Mariner's secret of holding them with a glance that must have flashed like lightning beneath the thundercloud of his brow ; but that he knew so exactly what he wanted, and that he had gone so manifestly deeper into the heart of the question at issue.

They had felt Eliot like a storm ; and as a storm he had gone by, leaving nothing but destruction in his trail. Here was light as well as power, a constructive and comprehensive programme, calculated to reconcile the legitimate aspirations of both contending parties, the programme of an ardent royalist who was also a great Parliament man.

For what was it that the King might be presumed to want ? What else than a fair chance to carry on the government of the nation, and the necessary means for so doing ! And Parliament ? that, if its professions of loyalty meant anything, desired, not that the King's government should be starved or hamstrung, but that it should be carried on, with reasonable efficiency, within the letter and spirit of the law, both of which had been so notoriously strained within the last few months.

Very well then ! was the effect of Wentworth's speech—let the House approach the King with the most frank and cordial offer of assistance possible. But at the same time, let it get the law defined with such precision on the various points of recent dispute, that it would be impossible for the King to overstep its bounds in future, or to effect a repetition of any of the grievances that were agitating the nation.

"By one and the same thing," he said, "have King and people been hurt, and by the same must they be cured ; to vindicate what—new things ? No, our ancient and vital liberties, by re-inforcing the ancient laws made by our ancestors. ... No, our desires are just, I speak truly, both for the interest of King and people, if we enjoy not these, it will be impossible to relieve him."*

It was the sound old English way, the way of Magna Charta, not of inventing new law, but of re-stating—and in the process amplifying—the existing law.

But Wentworth was not content with this mere statement of principle. He defined exactly the grievances he meant to remedy, in four points—in brief :

(1) Arbitrary imprisonment.
(2) Unparliamentary taxation.
(3) Impressment for service abroad.
(4) Compulsory billeting of troops on civilians.

To which was subsequently added

(5) Martial law.

This programme of Wentworth's, which was eventually realized in the famous Petition of Right, has been the subject of a great deal of nebulous declamation, but nowhere—at least so far as the present author is aware—has any serious attempt been made to explain the precise nature of the sacrifice it demanded from the Crown.

Its effect was nothing less than to debar the King from exer-cising what had been always esteemed the first and most honour-able function of kingship, that of levying war. For offensive purposes, his hands would be tied. He would have no adequate means of raising an army ; nor, if he raised it, of housing or disciplining it. He was to the last degree unlikely to have the means of paying it. Even for keeping order at home, his powers would be seriously, and perhaps dangerously, curtailed. The option of keeping some suspected conspirator or potential rebel under lock and key, was one with which few of Charles's pre-decessors could have safely dispensed. And it is safe to say that if any kingdom with a land frontier, any State in fact, but England, had disarmed its Government to this extent, it would have been inviting disaster.

---

* I have followed Rushworth's version. The one quoted by Gardiner is slightly different.

But Wentworth's keen eye had detected the element in the situation, peculiar to England alone, that rendered the departure practicable. There was no reason, so far as could possibly be foreseen, why an English King should ever indulge in the luxury of war. For all that it mattered to England, the Electress Elizabeth might have remained in exile for ever, and the King of France have settled accounts with his Protestants in any way he preferred—Wentworth cared for none of these things. He was neither a crusader nor a knight-errant, but a patriot, and because a patriot, a pacifist. England, by grace of her encircling sea, had the possibility of keeping the peace, and everything to gain by doing so—why then should loyalty provide the Crown with the means, and the temptation, to break it ?

Viewed in this light, Wentworth's plan for reconciling Crown and Parliament is seen to be a masterpiece of the subtlest statecraft, and though its subtlety was not likely to be apparent to his fellow members, the completeness with which it safeguarded their cherished liberties could not fail to make it attractive enough, in itself, for their opposition to yield to the tempestuous energy of his will-power. This was rendered the more certain by the singleness of his concentration upon this one object. Though as devoutly religious a man as any of his fellow-members, Wentworth had not the faintest interest in the sectarian grievances that so exercised minds like those of Pym and Eliot—new gags might have been devised every day for old geese, and Communion tables shifted towards any point of the compass, without deflecting his political course. He drove straight on to his goal, looking neither to the right hand nor the left, and for the moment, at least, he had the House following him.

His leadership was a wonderful blend of firmness and conciliation. On the five essential points, he was as determined to make the Crown toe the line as Eliot himself could have been. No mere promises or assurances would avail ; these rights of the subject were to be embodied in a Bill, and to that Bill His Majesty's assent would be demanded. But Parliament, for its part, was to afford practical expression of its goodwill, in the shape of five subsidies, payable immediately the Bill had become law. The idea of such generosity was horrific to Eliot, and he was not ashamed to advance the ridiculous argument that the money could not be collected without military force—but even so he did not venture to challenge a division.

A tense struggle now developed between Wentworth's policy of conciliation, and the mere wrecking instincts that found their voice in Eliot. Provided he could carry his main points, Wentworth was anxious to meet the King in any way he could. No one realized better than himself, born administrator as he was, that government must at all costs be carried on, and that there comes a point beyond which it is unsafe to weaken the power of the executive. He was ready, therefore, to leave a loophole for a certain latitude, beyond the strict letter of the Bill, for the exercise of the prerogative in cases of extraordinary emergency. And in this he was in agreement with a majority of the Upper House, who themselves, in the rôle of mediators, were anxious to find a means of safeguarding the liberties of the subject without openly trenching on the Royal Prerogative.

It was essential to Wentworth's plan to avoid anything like a public humiliation of the Crown, or an open victory of Parliament over its Sovereign. It was a real peace at which he was aiming, one that should fairly eliminate the friction between these two partners in the Constitution. He therefore proposed to forget and forgive whatever grievances might have accumulated in the past, and to start on a new basis of loyal co-operation. With this end in view, he wished to make the Bill a simple statement of the law, without embittering it by any references to its alleged violation.

It is conceivable that if Wentworth had had to deal with Parliament alone, he might have carried through his scheme substantially intact, and that English history might have entered upon another course that would have led to no civil war and no regicide. But he was in the predicament of one who has successfully swum through perilous waters to the rescue of a drowning man, and finds himself helpless against his frantic struggles. It was part of Charles's tragedy that his mind moved at so deliberate a pace that he was seldom able to realize his opportunities until it was too late to snatch them. By failing now to close with Wentworth, he defeated the difficult game that Wentworth had been playing, and opened the floodgates of extremism that Wentworth had with such difficulty kept closed.

And yet we need not be too hard upon the King for the line he took. He had not come under the spell of Wentworth's personality, and to have seen the situation with his eyes would have required an answering genius equal to Wentworth's own. What he was capable of seeing was that a pistol was being held at his head, in order to force from him such a surrender of the powers of the Crown, as had never been dreamed of by any of the Kings his predecessors, a surrender calculated—in the journalese phrase— to reduce England to the level of a third-class Power, a Power, that is to say, with a minimum of influence on the course of European politics. That European politics can be left to run themselves well, or badly, enough without England's assistance, and that it is better to be prosperous and peaceful in the third class than war-ridden and impoverished in any other, is a discovery sufficiently rare to make the lack of it understandable in King Charles.

The acceptance of Wentworth's solution implied, as its logical consequence, the acceptance of peace. It meant abandoning Rochelle ; it meant abandoning Charles's sister to the consequences of her husband's folly. And Charles had summoned Parliament for the specific object of raising enough money to retrieve his own and his country's honour in arms. Neither he nor Buckingham had the least idea of accepting failure, or cutting their own and their friends' losses.

The result was that Charles strained every nerve to avoid the unheard of sacrifice that even Wentworth's plan would have exacted from him. He was ready to pledge his royal word to preserve the liberties of his people intact, and that was all, he felt, that could reasonably be demanded of him. His own royal prerogative was equally a part of the Constitution, and that also he was determined to preserve intact. He hedged ; he qualified ; and at last—most fatal of all—tried to bring the Commons to their senses by the angry assertion of his royal authority.

These tactics were effective in defeating not the Commons, but Wentworth. He might have prevailed against Eliot, but against Eliot and the King combined even he was powerless.

14

THE PETITION OF RIGHT

THERE was no longer any question of a statesmanlike compromise. Wentworth had shot his bolt, and the cries of "Well spoken, Sir John Eliot !" that greeted the Cornishman's perfervid denunciations, showed that once again the extremist faction was in control.

It was all or nothing now. Instead of the statement of the law that Wentworth's Bill would have contained, the irreducible minimum of the Commons' demand was now embodied in a Petition of Right, prepared under the auspices of that redoubtable old Common Lawyer, Sir Edward Coke, which was not only an Act, but an indictment, or, from the King's point of view, a confession of the way in which the law had been violated by his own proceedings. His assent to this formula would be calculated to weaken his prestige even more than his authority. Not since the time when the monks had scourged Henry Plantagenet, had such public penance been exacted from a king in the sight of his people.

It is no wonder that he should have struggled against the acceptance of such humiliation. Charles had dissolved two Parliaments already, and that last resource was still available to him. At one time, it would seem, he had almost decided to take the plunge.* But this would have meant the utter collapse and bankruptcy of his war policy, and what, in his eyes and Buckingham's, would have involved a shameful betrayal of friends who trusted him.

And at this time came the news of two further disasters, which emphasized the desperateness of his position. The unfortunate little army that had once followed the banners of Mansfeld, or what survived of it, had lingered on in the service of the King of Denmark, but in the pay of King Charles, which usually came to the same thing as no pay at all. Its new commander, a gallant veteran called Sir Charles Morgan, had the greatest difficulty in keeping the starving and mutinous men together. At last, in the general collapse of Danish power on the mainland, he had stood at bay in a fortress at the mouth of the Elbe, "forgotten by all the world," as he had expressed it in a desperate, but vain, appeal to Buckingham for relief. At last, reduced to less than half their original strength, they were allowed by Tilly to embark for home with the richly-deserved honours of war. Charles had no other idea than to send them out again to the Danish front, but, as old Morgan was soon to take the liberty of informing him, soldiers will not fight without pay, rations, or clothes to their backs. And what could Charles do, with his empty coffers ?

* If, that is to say, Gardiner is right in referring to this time a draft of the Attorney-General's, calendered in S.P. Dom. on the 7th of March of the ensuing year.

This was at least an episode of which England might be proud, but a far more important operation, that was undertaken at this time for the relief of Rochelle, though bloodless, touched a new depth of shame and humiliation. The fleet was this time under the feckless Denbigh ; the ships were if possible in worse condition, and the men on board a more hopeless rabble, than on any previous expedition. However, they did somehow manage to fetch up opposite Rochelle, and had a look at the vast works with which Richelieu had barred the harbour entrance. The more they looked, the less they liked the reception in store for them ; and then, after they had hung about helplessly for some days, it seems to have occurred to the Admiral that he was too close to the enemy for perfect safety, and his order to withdraw to a more secure anchorage had the effect of starting a *sauve qui peut* of the whole armada for the even greater safety of home waters. Arrived there, Denbigh expressed his willingness to try again, but by this time the ships had had as much as they could stand, provisions were running out, and Spanish privateers from Dunkirk were snapping up their corn ships ; so there was nothing for it but to get back to port, and prepare for an expedition on a grander scale, under the command of Buckingham himself. Even now that invincible optimist was convinced that he could bring victory out of defeat. But even he could not hope to succeed without the means that Parliament alone could provide.

If, therefore, Charles was to retrieve his own and the nation's honour, he could by no means forgo those five subsidies that Parliament had fixed as the price of his endorsement of their Petition. But even so, he clung to the hope of a compromise. On the 2nd of June he summoned them before him to give what purported to be his final answer. Let right be done according to the laws and customs of the realm, and the statutes put into due execution, that his subjects might have no cause to complain of any wrong and oppression contrary to their rights and liberties. This was gracious enough, as far as it went, but it was not the unconditional surrender demanded of him.

Sir John Eliot, with the genius of a born tactician, perceived that this answer had given the game into his hands. Next morning, when the Commons came to consider it, he launched straight out into an attack, on the King's Government, that surpassed all his previous efforts of invective. In quick, gasping sentences, grievance was piled on grievance—

"Witness the journey to Algiers ! Witness that with Mansfeld ! Witness that to Cadiz ! Witness the next ! Witness that to Rhé. Witness the last ! And I pray God we shall never more have such witnesses ! Witness likewise ..." this, that, and the other, in a catalogue whose effect must have been overwhelming. Having now at last completely re-established his ascendancy over the House, and worked it up into the desired state of emotional suggestibility, he came out with the proposal for which all this had been the preparation. Let the House prepare a Remonstrance —in other words, let it pass a vote of censure on the Crown.

The King, with all the viciousness of the animal who, when attacked, defends himself, made desperate and unskilful efforts to retrieve the situation. He launched what was practically an ultimatum—he had said his last word in concession, and if the subsidies were not at once forthcoming, he would dissolve the House. Next day, seeing that no notice whatever was taken of him, he sent a stronger and curter message, positively forbidding the House to lay any scandal or aspersion on state, government, or ministers.

Only the condition, bordering on hysteria, into which the House had been already worked up by Eliot's oratory, can account for what followed.

"There appeared," according to one contemporary account, "such a spectacle of passions as the like had seldom been seen in such an assembly ; some weeping, some expostulating, some prophesying the fatal ruin of the kingdom ; some playing the divines, in confessing their own and their country's sins, which drew these judgments upon us ; some finding, as it were, fault with those that wept, and expressing their bold and courageous resolutions against the enemies of the King and kingdom."*

Members were jumping to their feet, and then finding themselves unable to articulate a word. Phelips could only stammer some incoherent sentences about their all going home to pray God to avert His fearful and imminent judgments, and then Eliot, who had himself perfectly in command, rose to exploit the opportunity. Hitherto, with consummate tact, he had forborne to name the man whom, by insinuation, he had singled out as the villain of the piece. But now—

"I am confident," he was declaiming, "no minister, how dear soever, can——"

* *Court and Times of Charles I*, i, p. 360.

The Speaker, Finch, one of the few present on whose loyalty the King could count, saw what was coming. Weeping as copiously as any of them, he checked Eliot, pleading the King's command.

A less accomplished debater would have hurled back some flaming defiance. But Eliot—and one marvels at the man's self-control—quietly sat down. The gesture was more deadly than any words could have been.

Its effect was to heighten still more the fever heat of emotion. It was Digges who first spoke : "Let us sit in silence ; we are miserable, we know not what to do" ; and the House, keyed up to respond to any suggestion whatever, accordingly sat mum for what must have been a nerve-racking period.

At last another member came to the rescue with the counter-suggestion, "Let us now speak or for ever hold our peace !" This had the effect of loosening their tongues in a babel of conflicting proposals. The Speaker asked and obtained permission to leave the chair, and hurried off to acquaint the King with the situation. Wilder and wilder things were said, one Member actually going so far as to invoke God's assistance in cutting the throats of the enemies—among whom they all knew that he included the chief minister—of King and State.

Here Wentworth made his solitary attempt at intervention. We can picture him sitting apart, his dark brow darker still as the chorus of ululation swelled around him—it was Eliot's House now, and he knew better than to oppose himself directly to such a spate of unreason. But, doubtless seeing what was coming, he now proposed to go straight to the King with their Remonstrance, while it still remained a mere statement of grievances, and had not been sharpened into a weapon against any individual.

But no sooner had he finished than Sir Edward Coke rose—not for the first time, if we can find it in us to credit the story that the hard-bitten old judge was among those whose previous efforts to speak had been choked by their tears. If so, he had recovered pretty thoroughly by this time, for never—even in the days when he had been notorious at the bar for the brutality of his prosecutions—had he driven home his point with more deadly effect.

"I think," he said, "the Duke of Buckingham is the cause of all our miseries ... that man is the grievance of grievances. Let us set down the cause of all our disasters, and all will reflect on him."

The effect of his words was likened, by an eye-witness, to that of an old hound picking up the scent at a check, and drawing the rest of the pack after him in full cry. It only remained for John Selden, a legal genius hardly inferior to Coke himself, to break cover with the demand that they should proceed with that which had been so well begun by the last Parliament, and renew the charge against the Duke, that had been the immediate cause of its dissolution.

They were in such a mood, that if he had asked for the Duke's head they would have voted for it. In tumultuous haste they rushed through the various clauses of their Remonstrance, not forgetting to sandwich in the High Church grievance, and they were just proceeding to crown their work by citing Buckingham as "the chief and principal cause of all evils," when Mr Speaker, who had only been away for about half an hour, returned with a peremptory command from His Majesty that the House should adjourn forthwith till the following morning. It was the wisest course to take with men who would be fitter to control their own proceedings after a night's sleep.

Few of the Members can have doubted that the King's intention was forthwith to dissolve a Parliament that had got more hopelessly out of hand than any of its predecessors. But here they had reckoned without the extraordinary fixity of purpose that was one element of Charles's nature. The five subsidies, whose gift Parliament had only to confirm, were absolutely necessary if he was to carry on the war and keep faith with his friends. To this he was now ready to sacrifice every other consideration.

Besides, his mind, though it moved slowly, was capable, when its thought had ripened, of inspiring bold and even startling decisions. Perhaps a great act of conciliation might even now win him back these hearts that had never ceased to flaunt their loyalty. Accordingly, instead of the expected dissolution, the next day's sitting opened with a King's message of studied graciousness, breathing respect for their privileges, and pleading for a sweet parting between him and his people.

But no message, however gracious, was now capable of satisfying the Commons. They were determined on nothing less than the King's unconditional assent to the Petition of Right, and now at last the Lords, abandoning their rôle of mediators, joined with them in presenting a request for a full and satisfactory answer. The fact that this was conveyed to His Majesty by a deputation headed by Buckingham himself, shows that even the Duke was now convinced of the necessity for surrender.

Accordingly, at four in the afternoon, the Commons were summoned to the Bar of the Upper House, where the King was seated on his throne. They were in perfect ignorance of what line he meant to take, and when, after commanding them to read their Petition, he made it law with the traditional formula "*Soit droit fait comme il est desiré*," their shouts rent the air. They were shouts of triumph, like those of a besieging army when the white flag is run up on the citadel.

His Majesty had still a few words to say: his maxim, he assured them, was that the people's liberties strengthen the King's prerogative, and that the King's prerogative is to defend the people's liberties—words that might have become classic had they only been spoken by one of his opponents.

"You see," he pleaded, "how ready I have shown myself to satisfy your demands, so that I have done my part; wherefore, if this Parliament have not a happy conclusion, the sin is yours, I am free from it."

The cries redoubled ; they were taken up in the street; soon all of London's forest of steeples were clanging and booming together, and, as the long twilight faded, bonfires began to light up the sky—as many as had greeted Charles's return from Spain. But the mobs were rejoicing not so much for the signing of the Petition, as for a rumour that someone had put about, of Buckingham having been sent to the Tower. It was even reported that certain apprentices had made a bonfire of the scaffold on Tower Hill, on the ground that they would have a new one built for His Grace. Far out into the country the rumour spread, and everywhere the Favourite's imaginary downfall started the fires blazing.

15

TOWARDS REVOLUTION

IF the King had been simple enough to think that by a grand gesture of conciliation he would be able to win the hearts of his Commons, he was soon to be undeceived. The spirit in which Eliot and his fellow politicians regarded it, was that of a

commander who having effected a break-through at some vital
point, resolves not to give the enemy a moment to recover himself, but to follow up with blow upon blow, until he has been
completely destroyed.

It had been a Saturday on which the King had given his
assent to the Petition. No sooner had Parliament resumed
business on the following Monday, than that specialist in persecution, John Pym, who had all this time held himself in reserve,
widened the attack to include that sector of the royal defences
which the Petition had left intact. He carried up to the Lords an
impeachment against a clergyman called Manwaring, one of the
High Church group who had been injudicious enough to mingle
politics with his preaching, and to threaten loan-resisters with
being damned. His sermons had been published—ostensibly by
royal command—and duly licensed. But the King's command
was only calculated to aggravate, in the eyes of his Faithful
Commons, the crime of an indiscreet royalism, and the Peers had
no hesitation in backing them up. Manwaring, in spite of his
having made abject submission and retraction, received, before
the week was out, a savage sentence of fine, imprisonment, and
disqualification, that gave him a greater advertisement than he
could ever have hoped to receive otherwise, and proved the first
stepping-stone on the way to pardon and a Bishopric. For Charles,
though he had been so little in sympathy with Manwaring's
effusions as to have remarked of the sentence, "He that will
preach more than he can prove, let him suffer for it," was bound,
in self-defence no less than in honour, to make it clear to all
whom it might concern, that the path of loyalty to himself was
one of promotion rather than martyrdom.

This was not the only shock that Monday had in store for
Charles. The least he could have expected from his complete
surrender to the Commons' demands, was that they should have
dropped that extreme measure of a Remonstrance, or vote of
public censure on himself, on which they had been engaged. But
they went straight on with its preparation as if nothing had
happened, even though it had been enlarged to comprehend a
denunciation of Buckingham—the thing of all others that was
known to be most offensive to Charles. It was in vain that the
King did all he could, by various concessions on disputed points,
to conciliate their goodwill—the extremists who were driving
them on were determined not to allow him a moment's respite.

The Remonstrance was finally debated on Friday, and even the uncompromising Phelips was inclined to mitigate to some slight extent the severity of the attack on the Duke. But Eliot followed him with one of the most·violent of his inflammatory speeches, and as usual carried the House with him.

However little such a manifesto might be calculated to appeal to the King, there could be little doubt, after the bonfires on Saturday night, what would be its effect on the mob. "So," Eliot might have reflected, with no less cause than Mark Antony,

> "Let it work ! Mischief thou art afoot,
> Take thou what course thou wilt !"

That very evening there emerged among the rest of the audience, from the Fortune Playhouse, in Finsbury, a certain Dr Lambe, a fantastic creature who had been drawn by a sort of natural affinity into the orbit of the equally fantastic Duke. This man had for many years specialized in the occult arts, and was even credited with having raised something like a waterspout over the Thames. The mob found no difficulty in believing that his present employment was to supply the Duke with love philtres, to enable him to debauch any lady, however chaste, who happened to take his fancy.

On this unlucky evening, Dr Lambe was spotted by a party of apprentices, who, no doubt in a ragging spirit, followed him through the streets, calling him the Duke's devil and other choice names, until he paid some sailors to escort him to a tavern, where he had supper, in the company, it was said, of two pretty ladies. When he came out, he found his tormentors waiting for him, and very foolishly lost his temper and threatened to make them dance naked. Soon he was being followed by a large and threatening crowd which, when he had turned on them with his escort and driven them back, became murderous. He sought refuge in a second tavern, and yet a third, but the mob made each of them too hot to hold him, and at last, in spite of a new guard of four constables, they got him down, and did not leave him until they had beaten one eye out of its socket and injured him mortally.

Charles was furious about it, particularly when it appeared that the lynchers had declared that they would have done as much, and more, to Lambe's master, had he been present, and when it proved impossible, through default of witnesses, to bring a single one of them to justice. No help could be got from the Lord Mayor or city authorities, though the King threatened them with the loss of their charter and imposed an exemplary fine. On the night of the tragedy it was remarked that a portrait of the Duke, at Lambeth Palace, fell out of its frame.

It is no wonder that, on the following Tuesday, His Majesty should have given no very cordial reception to the Remonstrance, which proved to be a long-winded document in which not only Buckingham was pilloried, but also his mother "who, herself openly professing that (the Catholic) religion, is a known favourer and supporter of them that do the same," and Bishops Laud and Neile, "who are suspected to be unsound in their opinions." Having heard it out, he merely remarked to the assembled Commons that he had not expected such a Remonstrance from them after he had so graciously granted their petition, and added that he would consider their grievances as they deserved.

No sooner had he finished than Buckingham fell upon his knees, imploring to be allowed to answer for himself. But Charles, with quiet dignity and in front of them all, merely held out his hand for his friend to kiss. It was a gesture that, in after years, it may have given him some comfort to remember.

The Commons were properly indignant at what almost amounted to contempt. It was even suggested that they would have marked their displeasure by bilking the King of the five subsidies that they had bargained to give him on his grant of their Petition, but for the fact that they had incautiously honoured their word, and that the money was now legally his. But they had a deadlier attack in preparation, and one that, if pressed home, would prove decisive. The Petition of Right, by cutting off the King from all extraordinary resources of direct taxation, had left him more than ever dependent, even for the most economical peace expenditure, on the proceeds of the customs. Of this they now proposed to deprive him altogether, or at best to dole it out to him for such short periods as to hold him completely and permanently at their mercy.

The politicians who directed their manœuvres did so with admirable finesse. They did not start with an open and brutal refusal. On the contrary they professed their generous readiness to provide for His Majesty's necessities on as generous a scale as at present, and meanwhile, until the necessarily lengthy business of revising the tariff rates had been accomplished, they would allow the customs to be collected. All that they wished to secure was some formal recognition of their right to give or withhold the customs as they chose.

The effect of this innocent offer may be best stated in the words of Gardiner, an historian bitterly hostile to Charles :

"The more persistent they were in asserting their right, the more determined he was not to give way on a point where concession would make it impossible for him to govern the Kingdom except in accordance with their views. If the Commons saw fit at their next meeting to vote him less than the old tonnage and poundage and the new impositions put together, he would be landed in a perpetual deficit."*

And what would a perpetual deficit imply but the virtual abdication of monarchy ? The Commons would certainly put on the screw to secure the downfall and ruin of Buckingham and every other minister who allowed the King's will to prevail on any point against that of their own leaders; they would have destroyed the Anglican compromise in the Church, and made it a stronghold of persecuting Calvinism ; and in order to maintain their ascendancy they would have kept the government and services permanently starved—what else they would have done may be judged from what they did, when at last, as the Long Parliament, they got the King at their mercy.

Charles was at least wary enough to avoid putting his neck into the noose so obligingly held out for him. His recent experience had been enough to convince him that the more he gave, the more would be taken from him. He stood quietly firm for the treatment that had been accorded, as a matter of course, to his predecessors, and meanwhile had no intention of allowing the normal routine at the customs houses to be interfered with.

But the politicians were not to be baffled so easily. Without the least hesitation, they began to put into shape another Remonstrance, which this time did not stop short at being a vote of censure, but was a direct incitement to everyone with goods to import to take the law into his own hands, and defy the King's officers, and presumably the King's courts of law.

They had the audacity to claim that the King had already signed away his right to the customs duties in the Petition of Right, though nobody can have known better than such great

* Gardiner, VI, pp. 322-3.

lawyers as Coke and Selden that the words, "any gift, loan,
benevolence, tax, or such like charge," could under no conceivable
interpretation be stretched to include indirect taxation. That lie
had not even the merit of plausibility.

"And therefore they do most humbly beseech your Majesty to
forbear any further receiving of the same ; and not to take it in
ill part of those of Your Majesty's loving subjects who shall refuse
to make payment of any such charges, without warrant by law
demanded.

"And as by this forbearance, your most excellent Majesty shall
manifest unto the world your royal justice, in the execution of
your laws ..."

If Charles had been a humorist he might have derived a certain
amusement from this last touch. As it was, his one thought was to
be beforehand with this open incitement to anarchy. Immediately
after prayers on the morning of the 26th, when they were just
about to give the Remonstrance its final reading, the King,
without even waiting to put on his robes, summoned the Speaker
and the whole House into his presence, and proceeded to address
them in a strain so different from the haughty aloofness of his
opening speech, that one realizes how deeply he must have
profited by the bitter experience and frustration of the past three
months.

Thanks to his promptitude, it was now the King and not the
subjects who spoke the Remonstrance, and that with an admirable
blend of firmness and conciliation. Even the impudent claim to
include the customs duties in the Petition of Right, he did not
more than put gently aside :

"This is so prejudicial unto me," he said, "that I am forced to
end this Session some few hours before I meant, not being willing
to receive any more Remonstrances, to which I must give a
harsh answer ... But as to tonnage and poundage it is a thing I
cannot want, nor meant by me, I am sure, to grant."

Not a word, this time, in anger, though he must have been sorely
tempted after the provocation he had received. And so great was
his will to conciliation that, for the first time in his reign, he only
prorogued and not dissolved Parliament—a surprising decision,
since one would have thought that a fresh appeal to the constitu-
encies, though it might slightly have bettered matters, could by
no possibility have made them worse.

16

"THE DUKE SHALL DIE"

For the King, the prorogation afforded no respite. He had now to turn his attention to that desperate business of relieving Rochelle, where resistance was only being prolonged by the iron resolution of the Governor, and where grass and leather had already begun to be eaten. He had now the temporary relief of the five subsidies, though he had only the undisciplined men and unserviceable ships that had made English arms a byword for failure. But he had still Buckingham ; and his faith in Buckingham was only equalled by the Duke's own invincible confidence in himself and his star.

It was a confidence of which they had almost a monopoly. A very different feeling had begun to percolate the consciousness of that many-headed personage whom our own time has christened "the man in the street." The Commons had done their work only too well in focusing hatred upon Buckingham. If the King had put aside their Remonstrance, his subjects had not. Sir John Eliot had accomplished the orator's supreme feat of making not only Parliament, but the people themselves, in ever expanding circles, visualize their world in the form imposed upon it by his own imagination. They were the audience of Eliot's all too thrilling melodrama of Fair Parliament and the Wicked Duke, and were becoming worked up to that pitch of excitement in which audiences have been known, on the fall of the curtain, to storm the stage and wreak physical vengeance upon the villain.

Ex-Chief Justice Coke, when he had singled out Buckingham as the grievance of grievances, had—if he had only known it— been pronouncing the last of his many death sentences.

For that, and nothing less, was the feeling—sharpened to a dreadful purpose—that was now abroad : the Duke must go ; the Duke must die. It had first broken into consciousness on that night of the signing of the Petition, when the wish had fathered the thought of his downfall, and started bonfires blazing, and 'prentices rioting about the scaffold. That thought had translated itself into murderous activity with the lynching of Dr Lambe ; and the mob knew very well to what that was

intended to be the prelude. There was a rhyme on everyone's
lips in London :

> "Let Charles and George do what they can,
> The Duke shall die like Doctor Lambe !"

and, what was more, conviction was growing that the words
would come true.

Omens, that are born in the general subconsciousness, were
beginning to multiply—and all pointed to the same conclusion.
The Rev. Joseph Mead, in a letter dated the 29th of June,
mentions one of the Duke's pictures falling on the day that Lambe
died, and goes on to add : "Not long since, his nose bleeding, my
Lord Keeper's mace was clapped upon his neck to staunch the
blood. But these are toys, though my Lady Davis, the prophetess,
says his time is not till August."

Clarendon tells the story, "upon a better foundation of credit
than usually such discourses are founded upon," of an official of
the King's wardrobe who on three successive occasions was
visited in the night by the Duke's late father, who adjured him to
warn his son that "if he did not do something to ingratiate himself with the people, or at least to abate the extreme malice they
had against him, he would be suffered to live but a short time" ;
and how, when terror of the dead had at last overcome fear of
the living Villiers, and this most unwilling medium had not only
gained the Duke's ear, but supplied him with certain confirma-
tory details emanating from his informant, "the Duke's colour
changed, and he swore he could have come to that knowledge
only by the devil ; for that those particulars were only known to
himself, and to one person more, who, he was sure, would not
speak of it."*

It would, however, be wrong to talk as if such a grim purpose
as the murder of a chief minister could be born spontaneously in
the mind of the people. We have evidence of a widespread and
deliberate propaganda having been engineered, though from
what source we can only guess. The printing press, a weapon
whose powers were only just beginning to be realized, was hard
and secretly at work, amplifying the story of the wicked Duke

---

* It is true that Clarendon, writing so many years later, puts the first vision above
six months before the Duke's murder. But even if we are to accept this date, it must
be in the light of the now accumulating evidence of dreams anticipating the future.

and his misdeeds. Nothing was too crude or too improbable to be put into circulation and believed. Hardly any celebrated person, from King James downwards, had been able to die in the past few years without the assistance of the Duke's potions ; he had been in league with the Dunkirk privateers, in their raids on British shipping, taking 33 per cent of the profits ; he had deliberately engineered the defeat of Denbigh's expedition, in order to keep the war going ; he had shown abject cowardice at Rhé ; he was ripe for Hell—

> "Devils take your due : for if there be
> One you can claim in all the world, it's he."

Such seeds of murder, for they were nothing less, were sure to fall upon fruitful soil in some one of all the minds on which they were scattered. Wandering obscurely about London at this time was an army lieutenant, of the good Suffolk name of Felton. His nickname in the service had been "honest Jack," from which one deduces a bluff, likeable sort of fellow. He had, however, been unfortunate enough, on the Cadiz expedition, to come to blows, in some matter of a woman, with one of the Duke's many *protégés*, and to that cause he attributed his failure, in due course, to get his company. He had become an unemployed man with a grievance, aggravated by the fact of his pay being in arrear to the extent—so he claimed—of no less than £80. According to one account he had gone with this grievance to Buckingham, who had lost his temper and told him to go and hang himself. At a scrivener's office, where he had next gone to get his claim made out, he obtained a copy of Parliament's Remonstrance against the Duke, and his slender library included one particularly foul and detailed specimen of the many libels about the great man's enormities. Utterly at the end of his resources as he now was, he had nothing to do but to brood ; and as he sat poring over another book in his miserable lodging, his eye was caught by a sentence :

"That man is cowardly and base and deserveth not the name of a gentleman or soldier, that is not willing to sacrifice his life for his God, his King, and his country."

These words, which he copied out and sewed into his hat, caused a sudden, lurid light to break through the gloom that had now settled on the poor lieutenant's mind. His purse might be

empty, his prospects ruined, and he the most outcast and perse-
cuted of mortals, but he had still his great soul and his right arm
—the other had been disabled in action—and that was all he
needed to become the saviour of his country, and to make his
fame resound far beyond her shores. All, that is to say, except a
weapon, and that was easy, for a serviceable knife, at the nearest
cutler's, cost him no more than tenpence.

It was well on in August, and the "cause of all our miseries,"
as Coke had described him, had gone down to Portsmouth,
presumably to sacrifice English lives and English honour in a
repetition of the Rhé disaster. John Felton knew now what he
had to do. After having tried, in vain, to cadge some money out
of his mother, who was as hard up as himself, he started to foot-
slog along the Portsmouth Road, picking up a lift where he could.
At the start of his journey, he had gone into one of the Fleet
Street churches, and left a request that they should pray for him
as for "a man greatly discontented in mind."

Buckingham was indeed at Portsmouth, pushing forward with
feverish energy the preparations for this great enterprise, that was
going to wipe out the memory of Rhé, and put him far beyond
the machinations of his enemies. But even he might have despaired
at the chaos that he found, had it not been that he was now bank-
ing on the prospect of effecting an honourable settlement with
Richelieu, in which the Protestants would be included, on his
arrival at Rochelle. That deal was to be arranged through the
good offices of the Venetian Ambassadors to both courts. The
idea that Richelieu would have relaxed his grip upon his prey,
now that it was at its last gasp, or that a third appearance of the
English fleet was likely to make the slightest impression on him
was optimistic, even for Buckingham.

The King had also gone down to keep in touch with the expedition, and was lodged just on the other side of the Portsdown
Hills, in the Manor of Southwick ; though Henriette, who was
tremendously interested in the dances of a still merry countryside,
was away at Wellingborough. Only a few days before, when he
and Buckingham had gone to inspect some of the warships at
Deptford, Charles had been heard to remark, "There are some,
George, who wish that both these and thou mightest both perish.
But care not for them. We will both perish together, if thou
doest." Perhaps it was some share in the sense of impending
tragedy that urged him to keep within his friend's call.

There was reason enough for anxiety, for it was only too evident that the hatred that had been worked up against the Duke had preceded him to Portsmouth, and that his life was no longer safe even among his own men. His coach was surrounded by a mob of sailors clamouring for their pay, and one of them even made as if to pull him out of it, had not the Duke himself leapt out, collared the man, and run him into the house that he had made his headquarters, and which the sailors now threatened to pull down about his ears, unless their shipmate was restored to them.

The prisoner was nevertheless court martialled and duly sentenced to be hanged for mutiny. It was on the 22nd of August that the sentence was to be executed, though the good-natured Duke fully intended to let him off, at the last moment. However, the sailors were determined on a rescue, and fell in overwhelming numbers upon the execution party. This was a situation with which Buckingham could deal. At the head of a few horsemen, mostly officers, he charged into the mob, killing two and wounding several, and then, having cleared the street, himself rode with the prisoner to the gibbet—there could be no question of mercy now. Even so, the mutinous spirit was not quenched, and the Duke had to be brought back to headquarters guarded by a ring of officers.

That same day the King rode over to Portsmouth. He found the Duke in bed slightly indisposed—not improbably from the shock of what must have been a terrible experience. For a long time the two friends remained closeted together, in earnest conversation, and then, when the King took his departure, it was observed that Buckingham embraced him "in a very unusual and passionate manner".

That night the Duke slept badly. His wife, who adored him, was distraught with anxiety, and implored him to take precautions for his safety. He had lost his temper with her for a moment, but then, with that charm that he could make so irresistible, he told her that he took it all as a token of her love. The summer morning and the sea breeze brought back all his habitual exuberance of spirits—it was told afterwards how, on getting up, he had cut two or three capers. So glorious it was to be alive !

When, a little after his usual time, he came down for breakfast, they told him of a rumour that the Rochelle garrison had itself raised the siege. The Duke was as delighted as a schoolboy ; the Huguenot commanders attached to the fleet were afraid of his taking the yarn seriously enough to cancel the expedition—their violent gesticulations positively alarmed the phlegmatic English bystanders. The house was thronged with people coming and going about the business of a headquarters staff, engaged in rushing through the equipment of what was now, at best, an almost impossibly forlorn hope. Among the jostling throng, no one was likely to notice the arrival of a bedraggled and travel-stained person, who took an inconspicuous place near the entrance of the passage that led from the breakfast room to the great hall.

Buckingham was not the sort of commander to bother himself about the prosaic routine of staff work : he must hurry to Southwick, to push forward those negotiations of his with the Venetian Ambassador. As he strode from the breakfast room, the throng must have tended to bunch together after him through the passage. As he came out into the hall, little Sir Thomas Fryer, one of his colonels, saluting, claimed his attention for a moment. The Duke, in his affable way, bent down towards him, and at that moment some one in the press behind slipped round an arm in front of him on his blind side, and he heard the words—the strangest perhaps ever uttered by an assassin—"The Lord have mercy on thy soul !"

It was all so quick that nobody realized what had happened. The crowd in the hall saw the Duke clap his hand to his breast ; they saw him stagger forward ; those nearest heard a cry, though no two versions agree what it was ; and then the towering form, with blood gushing from its lips, went crashing to the floor, and lay still.

Nothing would have been easier than for John Felton to have walked quietly out of the house and got clean away. Half the houses in Portsmouth, or London, would have been proud to shelter him. But that would have been to miss the supreme moment of which he had been dreaming ; to forgo those laurels of immortal fame for which the bitterest death was worth dying. As he stood undecided, his poor, clouded brain convinced him that they were already crying his name : "Felton ! Felton !" Calmly—proudly—he stepped forward :

"I am the man !"

At Southwick King Charles was partaking of the daily comfort afforded by his beloved Anglican ritual. As he knelt in prayer, some one breathless and booted, disregarding all bonds of ceremonial, hurried to his side and whispered into his ear.

Charles gave no sign—except for Mattins to proceed. Many centuries ago, one of his predecessors, a King of Wessex, when the Viking host was at death grips with his own, had refused to leave the service of God for that of men. The restraint that King Ethelred had imposed upon himself then, must have been easy compared to that found by King Charles in this hour.

It was only when service was over that he retired to the solitude of his bedchamber. There he flung himself down and let his grief have way. Steenie was dead. . . . Steenie. . . .

And meanwhile, as the news flew from town to town, there were triumph and jubilation—everywhere healths were being drunk to, and blessings invoked upon, the hero of the hour, honest John Felton, little David who had slain Goliath !

V

King Charles

I

IN COMMAND

NO man still young, and least of all one so sensitive as King Charles, can sustain so frightful a shock as that news of his dear and only friend's murder must have been, without its making a profound difference, for better or worse, to his character. It may equally well poison or strengthen his inner man, and which it shall be—some of us at least are free to believe—he himself shall freely determine.

Even before the blow was struck, it would seem as if some very significant change had been in process of accomplishment. It was as if, in his twenty-eighth year, the King had at last come to spiritual maturity. We no longer find him yielding to those occasional crude and even ignoble impulses, which those who know him by the record of his later years find it so hard to reconcile with their idea of him. We have had to record the boorishness—to use no stronger word—of his conduct to his almost betrothed Infanta ; his unprincely ingratitude to Lord Bristol ; the feckless irresponsibility of his part in the impeachment of Lord Middlesex ; the tactless arrogance with which, more than once, he had aggravated the already strained relations between himself and the Commons. No doubt in every one of these lapses the influence of Buckingham had played its part, but the mere fact of his yielding to it so absolutely, shows how little confidence he had yet acquired in his ability to stand on his own feet.

But lately there had been signs of a change. Perhaps it had been germinating since the time when Buckingham's absence at Rhé had forced him to act as his own Prime Minister. But it first became definitely noticeable at the Parliamentary crisis, or series of crises, in June ; in which, after the breakdown of his ill-advised attempts at coercion, he proved capable, as never before, of blending firmness with concession, and of keeping his head and his temper under the most trying circumstances.

After the close of that session, we feel that the captain has come on the bridge, and the Ship of State begun to respond to the control of a helmsman who at least knows his own mind, and is capable of holding a determined course. That long persecution of Bristol is at last dropped, and the Earl is restored to some semblance of favour ; a reconciliation is effected with the powerful Earl of Arundel ; an excellent appointment is made to the key post of the Treasury, in Sir Richard Weston, afterwards Earl of Portland. The most important step of all is the attachment of Wentworth, lately classed among the most dangerous of the Parliamentary leaders, to the royal service by the grant of a Barony, with a view to high office in the near future. If Charles had understood, only a month or two earlier, what the enlistment of Wentworth's support would mean for the Crown, it is possible that the supreme tragedy of his reign might yet have been averted. But it was part of that tragedy so often to read the hour of his visitation on a losing clock.

And now he had come to one of those crises that compel a man to summon to his aid whatever spiritual resources may have hitherto lain dormant in his nature. During that ordeal of repressed grief in the prayer room at Southwick, one stark truth must have burnt itself into his consciousness—from henceforth he would have to stand alone, and in such strength as God might give him. The staff on which he had leaned had snapped in his hand. No longer would his natural diffidence find compensation in the splendid self-assurance of his friend ; no longer would his hesitations be resolved by Steenie's unfailing certainty.

Those who judged the son by the father, might have imagined that the removal of one favourite would merely mean the substitution of another ; perhaps Holland ; perhaps, eventually, Wentworth. But the trust of such reserved natures is not easily transferable, and his bereavement had come just at the moment when Charles was learning to trust himself. How long if, by some miracle, Buckingham had been spared, he would have retained his ascendancy over his King, is a matter of nicely balanced speculation. What we know for certain is that no man, at any time after Buckingham's death, could ever have been described, by the remotest stretch of imagination, as the King's Favourite, in the sense of possessing his whole confidence.

It was not only that Charles had acquired the capacity for standing alone, but that the affection he had lavished on Steenie, and which it was almost a necessity for him to lavish on somebody, found a natural and immediate object in his wife. Ever since that dramatic assertion of his mastery, in the matter of her French suite, they had been drawing together. It was only Buckingham now, who had stood in the way of their perfect union. It was symbolic, that immediately after the murder, they had gone north and south to meet each other. Henriette, whatever she may have suffered from Buckingham during his lifetime, knew how to rise to the occasion of his death. Her understanding sympathy was able to break down the last barriers of reserve between them. In the beginning of October, that very shrewd observer, Lady Carlisle, was able to assure her husband that "he cannot wish more affection nor happiness between the King and Queen than he will find."*

Of even greater significance is the evidence of dates. Buckingham was murdered on the 23rd of August. Charles's and Henriette's first child was born and died on the 13th of May in the following year, at least two months before its time. It was therefore some time during that autumn that their marriage, after more than three barren years, became fruitful. And fruitful it was destined to remain all through, and beyond, the ensuing decade.

A new reign has, in effect, begun. The Duke is dead—God save the King !

2

THUS FAR, NO FURTHER

ONE blessing in disguise for the bereaved monarch was that he had no time to abandon himself to grief. The whole machinery of government had been under Buckingham's control ; he had functioned not only as Prime Minister, but, to some extent, as a Super-Secretary of State for all departments. As Charles had no intention of replacing him, except by himself, he had once again, as at the time of the Rhé expedition, to gather all the threads of policy into his own hand. On that occasion he had merely been acting, in the Duke's absence, as his agent. Henceforth, for better

* S.P. Dom., cxviii, p. 15.

or worse, it was to be his own policy. Never again, not even as a prisoner, would he submit to be made the instrument of another's will.

One lesson—and that the most vital of all—experience had taught him. Buckingham's dashing foreign policy, which was to have enabled England to dominate by force of arms the European situation, was allowed to die with its author. Whether Charles had figured to himself consciously that, for a King of England, foreign war was constitutional suicide, he certainly acted henceforth as if he had inherited his father's passionate desire for peace.

There was, however, one commitment that it was too late to get out of. The great expedition was almost ready—or as ready as it was ever likely to be—to put forth for the relief of Rochelle ; and with Rochelle at its last gasp, looking for its arrival, it would have been impossible to countermand it. The Commander was the Earl of Lindsey, who, as Lord Willoughby, had commanded the expedition, two years ago, that had never got any further than the Bay of Biscay. It must have been an imposing sight, upwards of two hundred sail, or nearly twice the number that had gone with Buckingham to Rhé. They arrived in due course off Rochelle, and then the old story was repeated. The merchant captains, who commanded the bulk of the fleet, had no more stomach for fighting than their crews. Provided that themselves might save their skins, they were ready to let their heroic allies starve and rot. They played the safe and familiar game of bombarding the sea with the King's hard-bought ammunition, and though the Admiral threatened them with death for their cowardice, that was the one risk that they were capable of despising. When fireships were tried, they were turned adrift out of range, to run ashore or be towed out of harm's way by the French. And so there was nothing for it but for Lindsey to linger about as helplessly as Denbigh before him. Charles—what else could he do ?—sent him an encouraging message exhorting him to stick it out.

Meanwhile, what of that wonderful Venetian plan for a little arrangement with Richelieu, that should achieve all the objects of the expedition without the necessity of fighting ? An English envoy did indeed get received at the French headquarters. The Cardinal was charming, taking him round and letting him see everything, including his own impregnable harbour defences.

He was ostentatiously frank and reasonable—what interest could King Charles possibly have in promoting rebellion? Once let the Rochellese submit to their lawful Sovereign, and they could continue to worship their God as before, without let or hindrance, while the way would be cleared for the treaty of peace, or even alliance, that the Most Christian King would meet his Brother of England more than half way in concluding. It was a fair and genuine offer—but it was no solution of the Admiral's difficulties.

That was, however, soon to be furnished by the Rochellese themselves, or the minority of them that disease and starvation had left. It was only too evident that no hope was to be expected from that chicken-hearted armada in the offing. They accordingly surrendered, and the Cardinal, having celebrated Mass with all pomp in the bare Cathedral, proved as good as his word, and gave an example of tolerance wonderful in that age—doubly wonderful in a Prince of the Church—but inspired by a calculation of pure national self-interest. Not only did the French Protestants gain as much freedom of worship as an English victory could have secured them, but they gained it with the goodwill of the King and their fellow countrymen. And now, having ceased to be a house divided against itself, France was free to destroy the last chance of the Church recovering her lost provinces of the Reformation, by taking up the old feud of her Royal House against that of the Catholic Caesar.

With the homecoming of the fleet, it was possible to close one of the most ignominious chapters in British history. Never again would Charles be tempted to send forth one of these grandiose expeditions for which, under the terms of the Petition of Right, he was now more than ever debarred from providing either the men or the money. And at last, if he could keep his remaining revenue intact, he might have some chance of making ends meet.

That was to be the first pillar of the new policy—peace. The second was to preserve intact those rights of the Crown that the Petition had left. Charles had looked upon that surrender of his as the price of a constitutional settlement, and not as the first instalment of a revolution. He was prepared to carry out honourably his side of the bargain, but this much and no more was he minded to concede. If Parliament was determined to drive him further, it would find itself confronted with a purpose as firm as its own.

There was one part of his prerogative, especially, that he meant to preserve intact, and that was his governance of the national Church. This was not a matter of policy, as it had been with Elizabeth, but of a deep and abiding conviction that had no afterthought of self-interest. The man who could remain on his knees in that first agony of bereavement, was not the one to sacrifice principle to expediency in his trusteeship for the Church's welfare. Those who condemn Charles for refusing to recognize the signs of the times, or to trim his sails to the gale that was blowing up from the direction of Geneva, are looking at the matter as from the standpoint of one who is free to set his course in any direction that suits his convenience. With Charles it was different —he had his course marked out for him, and he would rather die than deviate from it.*

Here, then, there could be no question of compromise. On the religious issue, the King's last word was, and would remain, "Hands off the Church of England !" Had he felt less deeply on the subject, he might have made some show of tactful concession, or at least have refrained from anything calculated to offend Puritan susceptibilities. But as it was, no prudential considerations could restrain him from making it clear that he was no more going to take his orthodoxy from the Calvinist left, than from the Roman right, or to sacrifice the beauty and seemliness that were the inheritance of the old order, to a blind desire to consummate the Reformation.

No more defiant gesture could he have made than to single out for special honour the two men who, of all others, had been the quarry of the Parliamentary heresy hunt. Not only was the impeached Manwaring's terrific sentence cancelled within a few days of Parliament rising, but a fat living was found to compensate him for his few days' incarceration. As for Montague, whose shocking charity to his Catholic opponents had become a hardy annual in the way of grievance, he received the Bishopric of Chichester, while Laud, one of the two Bishops whom Parliament had gone out of its way to pillory in its Remonstrance, and whom Charles rightly regarded as the outstanding figure of his episcopal team, was promoted to London. These things had been done before Buckingham's death, but religion had sat lightly on the Duke, and they may be regarded as indicating Charles's settled policy. Though they beyond doubt invited trouble, the

* The same idea is very beautifully brought out in the play, *Charles the King*, by Mr Maurice Colbourne.

King may well have thought it necessary to show to anyone whom it might concern, that no Calvinist terror would be tolerated within the fold of the Church, and that no loyalty to Anglican principles would be allowed to prejudice any divine's career.

Parliament was to have met in October, but the sitting was postponed till January. The omens were anything but propitious. The deliberate incitement to anarchy that had been the final move in the Parliamentary offensive, had found only too willing a response among merchants with a conscientious objection to paying duty on their goods. One of these gentry, of the name of Chambers, being summoned before the Council on account of his refusing to pay duty on some silk consigned to him, chose to inform them that in no part of the world were the merchants so screwed and wrung as in England, and that they had more encouragement in Turkey. This open defiance not unnaturally led to his being committed for contempt to the Marshalsea, though an application to the King's Bench procured his release on bail, owing to some technical flaw in the indictment. If once it became apparent that this sort of thing could be practised with impunity, and the customs officers successfully defied, there was nothing to prevent England from becoming a smugglers' paradise, and the whole machinery of government from breaking down.

The Crown, however, had not done with Chambers, and the Attorney-General had lodged an indictment against him in the Court of Star Chamber, which had been expressly formed to vindicate the authority of the State against anarchy. But before this, which was only one of a crop of similar cases, could come up for final decision, Parliament would have returned to Westminster, either to put the whole matter of the customs on an agreed and permanent footing, or to bedevil the situation still further by lending support to the anarchy it had invoked.

If the customs question had stood alone, there might have been some faint hope of a settlement, but nobody knew better than Eliot, Pym, and the other opposition leaders, that it was only by depriving the King of his revenue that they could compel him to surrender his authority over the Church, and withdraw his protection from the incomplete Calvinists among his divines. And they had committed themselves too deeply to the utmost rigour of the skin game against their Sovereign, to make it likely that they would let him off now.

But what they perhaps did not realize, was that they had ceased to possess the winning advantage that had enabled them hitherto to put pressure on the Crown. Though England was still formally involved in not only one, but several wars, she had practically ceased to make war, and nobody had the least desire to make it on her. No expeditionary force was any longer in course of preparation, and consequently the Crown could now proceed to budget its expenses, more or less, on a peacetime footing. Which meant that at a pinch, and by pinching, the King might contrive to live of his own, and defy the politicians to do their worst.

But it had come to be such a near thing, financially, that it would be ruin, now, for him to be bullied or cozened into forgoing any one of his remaining sources of revenue. "Hands off the Church !" could only be made good by "Hands off the Customs !" And there is this at least that can be said for the skin game—it is a game that two can play.

3

SOUND AND FURY

THE second and concluding session of Charles's third Parliament, though to outward appearance more sensational than any that had gone before, was the one that can have afforded fewest surprises to any intelligent observer. The course of events was almost exactly determined in advance, unless some god from the machine or unexpected calamity intervened to deflect them.

It had been evident at the prorogation that all hope of amicable co-operation between the Crown and the Commons had broken down, and that the House had passed completely under the control of its extremists, who had committed themselves to a programme of revolution, and were prepared to stick at nothing in the attempt to force it through. Only on one point might a very innocent and sanguine person have been tempted to harbour doubt. In the recent attack on the Crown, "the grievance of grievances" had been ostensibly Buckingham. That grievance had now been removed, thanks in no small degree to the effect of the Commons' own indirect incitement to its removal. Now, surely, it might be argued, would be the time to give effect to

those protestations of loyalty to the Crown, of which even its
most intransigent opponents had never ceased to be prolific.

Unfortunately, to their legally trained minds, such verbiage
had as much literal significance as the kindred fictions that the
King could do no wrong, and the King could never die. There
were those sitting among them who would not scruple, when the
time came, to levy war on the King in the name of loyalty, and
to cut off his head for the crime of treason.

How much Buckingham's removal had made any difference
whatever to their intentions, was shown the moment they got
down to business. Without any of the usual beating about the
bush, the attack on the Crown was resumed, and with greater
fury than before. That His Majesty had dared to collect his
customs at all was grievance enough, but that he had actually
put the law into force against those individuals who had responded
to the Commons' appeal to take it into their own hands, was even
worse. Worst of all was the fact that one of those who had had his
goods distrained on in default of payment was a certain Rolle,
who happened to be a Member himself. This was to violate the
Ark of the Covenant ; it was Breach of Privilege, and a sufficient
occasion for summoning the King's officers to the Bar of the
House.

It had come to this, that even when the House was not sitting,
not only was the person of a Member to be free from arrest, but
his goods from distraint. It did not in the least matter whether
the duties were lawful or not—according to this new doctrine,
the fortunate owner, who might be in a large way of business,
would be in a position to have his crates or bales carried straight
from the landing stage to his own warehouse, without His
Majesty's officers daring to lift a finger or charge a penny. This
was not only revolution, but revolutionary anarchy.

This ominous beginning to the Commons' proceedings made
the King resolve on a supreme effort for conciliation. On the
fifth day of the Session he summoned both Houses to his presence
in Inigo Jones's Banqueting Hall. Here he made a speech of
which the conciliatory and even pleading tone showed how much
he had acquired of tact and temper since, a year before, he had
put up all their backs by his talk of scorning to threaten. Even on
the question of the customs, he was careful to avoid any provoca-
tive assertion of his rights or challenge of their claims, but merely
urged them to carry out their repeatedly professed intention of

regularizing the whole position by passing a Bill, "not doubting but ... you will be deaf to ill reports concerning me, till my words and actions speak for themselves ; so that this Session beginning with confidence towards one another, it may end with a perfect, good, understanding between us ; which God grant. Amen."

Fairer words he could not have used, and the applause with which they were greeted showed that the first impression at least was favourable. It may have been in some confidence of their effect, that on the House resuming business, Secretary Coke, on behalf of the Government, begged to introduce the required legislation. But his heart must have sunk when, as he sat down, Eliot rose to his feet with a more than usually exuberant profession of loyalty as a prelude to ruling the measure out of order on some technical point of procedure.

Then, after Selden had bent his unrivalled legal talents to the same effect of obstruction, the religious offensive was opened by one of the most uncompromising of the Puritan hotheads, Francis Rouse, an indefatigable controversialist, who had written a book called *Oil of Scorpions* and numerous works of similar tendency. The debate on the customs was switched off, in the name of the King of Kings, to the new paintings laid on the old face of the Whore of Babylon ; to the designs of the High Church-man to open the gates to Roman tyranny and Spanish monarchy ; "for," thundered Rouse, "an Arminian is the spawn of a Papist ; and if there come the warmth of favour upon him, you shall see him turn into one of those frogs that arise out of the bottomless pit." The distraint of goods at the customs houses was likened to Satan counselling God to lay His hand on all that Job had, but, counselled this eminently practical evangelist,

"Let us do what Job did, he held fast his religion, and then, his goods were restored to him with advantage."

They were fairly off now, and on the desired lines. It is improbable that the very shrewd organizers of the Parliamentary opposition took Rouse's fulminations much more seriously than the modern reader is likely to do. But no one could have played more effectively the part required of him, for by the time he had sat down all danger of the King's conciliatory words bearing fruit in a friendly settlement of the customs dispute, was now at an end. The religious grievance was to have precedence, and till the Church had been surrendered, not a penny of revenue would the House sanction. The revolution was to proceed.

Next day a champion of very different calibre struck in. Pym, as chairman of the committee on religion, sounded louder than ever before his now familiar call to the heresy hunt, reminding the House of the example set to it by previous Parliaments, which had enacted laws for the trial of heretics. "The Parliament," he added, "punished the Earl of Essex for countenancing of heretics ; and there is no court that can meet with this mischief but the Court of Parliament." This high Protestant appeal to the principles of Bishop Bonner and Bloody Mary was strengthened by invoking the memory of martyrs like Ridley, who had been burnt in fulfilment of these same laws to whose precedent Pym thus eloquently appealed.

It was in vain that the King, who saw only too plainly the way things were going, sent down a short message, couched in most conciliatory terms, requesting that they should get the business of the customs settled before embarking on the religious question. As well might some benighted traveller have requested the highwayman to put away his pistol before discussing business.

Any lingering hope that he may have had, must have been quenched, on the following day, by another of Eliot's terrific invectives, wherein, in what must have been one of the most moving perorations in Parliamentary history, he appealed to a ceremony used in the Eastern churches, of the congregation standing at the repetition of the Creed with swords drawn. This, if it meant anything, signified that Eliot was ready to go to all lengths, even of armed violence, in pursuit of his offensive against the Crown—and indeed it was destined to come to this, though he would not live to see it. For the moment, a more appropriate ceremony would have been that of sitting tight on a money box.

Four days later, after he had successfully burked a third almost despairing appeal from His Majesty for the settlement of the customs revenue, Eliot proceeded to a more extraordinary length than any yet dreamed of. He seriously proposed to the Commons that they should take to themselves the powers and functions of a Puritan inquisition.

"Let us," were his words, "look on them that have offended us in this our truth. ... Are there Arminians—for so they are properly called—look to those ; see to what degrees they creep ! Let us observe their books and sermons ! Let us strike at them, and make our charge at them and vindicate our truth that yet seems obscure ; and if any justify themselves in their new opinions, let us deal with them !''

After this, if the King was not to surrender unconditionally to the forces of revolution, it could only be a question of how long these reckless proceedings could be allowed to continue before he should resort to the last weapon in his armoury, that of dissolution. For now, even on a balance of accounts, he had much to gain and nothing to lose by its employment. The Crown, for the first time, was asking for no new gift from Parliament, no grant of special taxation to save it from disaster or bankruptcy. The *status quo* was the utmost of its demands, and it was this that the Commons were straining every nerve to upset. The last limit of possible concession had been reached. Once let the King surrender the Church or the customs, and the fate of monarchy in England was sealed. But let Parliament cease to function, and the *status quo* would continue to flourish under the sanction of the law, or, at least, of the law's recognized interpreters.

It was like a fairy story, in which the King's palace is besieged and at the point of capture by an army of metamorphosed toy soldiers, and in which he has only to speak the magic formula to restore them in the twinkling of an eye to their original condition, so that he can pick them all up and put them back into the box. In other words, Eliot, this time, was bluffing on a very weak hand.

But the King had no doubt a case for holding his own hand till the last possible moment, and giving Eliot and his supporters the chance of piling outrage upon outrage, until they had unmasked their real and revolutionary intentions beyond the shadow of a doubt. The only danger—and it was not to be despised—was lest the continuance, at Westminster, of this anti-monarchical propaganda, backed by the prestige and authority of Parliament, should result in the situation getting beyond control, and that what actually happened in France a century and a half later should have been anticipated by some tennis court oath in Westminster Hall—which, by the way, would have literally justified the name—or perhaps a storming of the Tower or march to Whitehall by the London mob. It was, as Wellington would have put it, a damned near run thing ; but the ingrained English respect for law had not yet broken down to quite that extent.

Meanwhile, all through the month of February, the King kept his patience and his temper, while Eliot continued to urge the Commons to wilder and wilder excesses. The threat of a lay inquisition was swift to materialize. Every unpopular High Churchman was singled out for destruction. The attack on Montague was of course resumed with special fury—an obscure bookbinder called Jones delighted the House by unearthing some technical flaw in his episcopal appointment, which gave them an excuse for doubting whether he was really a Bishop at all.

Every bit of gossip or tittle-tattle about a sermon or an altar was eagerly raked up, and magnified into a danger to State and Religion. Among the other contributors to this work was an uncouth and explosive gentleman, silent hitherto, who had heard from his old schoolmaster, Dr Beard, how he, Beard, having been appointed to recapitulate the sermon of a certain Dr Alablaster, had been forbidden, by the High Church Bishop Neile, to turn the occasion into one for controverting it ; and how when, in defiance of this, Beard had proceeded to denounce not only the doctrines but also the person of the devoted Alablaster, the Bishop had gone so far as to reprove him. Only in such a House could such a maiden speech have been taken seriously, though one is tempted to imagine that there was something in the man's forthright vehemence that may, even in those early days, have compelled attention. His name—he sat for Huntingdon—was Oliver Cromwell.

It was not only the High Churchmen who were thus marked down for persecution, but also, and of course, the Roman Catholics. That the King should have exercised his prerogative of mercy on behalf of condemned priests, including one who had been doomed to an agonising death and was reprieved the night before his execution, was a particularly shocking grievance :

"I hear," declaimed Sir John Eliot, "a priest was condemned, and Mr Recorder made a reprieval. No man could vent his malice more to the kingdom than in the preservation of these men."

The religious offensive culminated in a series of proposed resolutions in which, after every possible grievance had been recapitulated, the remedy was prescribed in a comprehensive and minute programme of persecution, including the merciless application of the existing code and its reinforcement by "stricter laws" ; "severe punishment" of anyone who by speech or writing should deviate a hair's breadth from the strictest Puritan orthodoxy ; "condign" punishment for "such as have been authors or

abettors of those Popish or Arminian innovations in doctrine" ;
the burning of certain High Church books and strict censorship
on all books in the future ; and finally what amounted to the
control by Parliament of every ecclesiastical appointment, down
to that of the humblest parish priest.

Meanwhile the persecution of the unfortunate customs officers,
who had distrained on Mr Rolle's goods, went merrily forward,
and it looked as if the judges themselves, who had refused to
admit the lawfulness of a claim for their restoration, might be the
next to feel the wrath of the House. It was in vain that the King
tried to shield his servants from punishment by declaring that
they had merely been carrying out his orders : this was rather
calculated to aggravate their offence, than otherwise, in such
eyes as Eliot's.

By this time the pace had proved too killing even for the more
cold-blooded Pym, who, conscious of the tactical error involved
in magnifying this very doubtful side issue of privilege, and,
perhaps scenting trouble ahead, now dropped discreetly out of
the running, and played no part in the final and culminating
scene on which the curtain was about to rise.

For the King, it was evident, had at last decided that the cup
was full. The only way of saving either his innocent officials or
the threatened churchmen, was to put the House out of action.
On the 25th, he adjourned it for a week, to try—it would seem—
whether it would be possible, by negotiation, to persuade the
leaders of the opposition to see reason. He must have soon had
cause to realise that there was no hope in that direction. And they,
in turn, can hardly fail to have foreseen that when, on the 2nd of
March, they assembled again, it would be for the last time.

Eliot, seeing that the revolution on which he had embarked
was in danger of being postponed indefinitely, resolved on a
course of extraordinary boldness. With such extremists as he
could enlist for the purpose—for there were lengths to which
even the hard-bitten older leaders shrank from following him—
he determined to carry the House with him in the most open and
sensational defiance of the Crown that could possibly be staged.

He had prepared a series of three resolutions, whose effect on
the country would be that of a revolutionary manifesto, calling
upon all and sundry to set at nought the King's authority in
certain specified matters, and endeavouring to create such a
reign of terror, for those who conformed to, or sheltered under it,

that even when Parliament was not sitting, the machinery of government would be thrown out of gear.

Stripped of their verbiage, the effect of these Resolutions was to proclaim the following classes of persons "capital enemies to this Kingdom and Commonwealth" :

(1)   Anglican divines and others found guilty of disagreement with "the true and orthodox [in other words Puritan] Church."
(2)   Any officer taking part in the collection of customs, or statesman advising that they should be collected.
(3)   Anyone even offering to pay duty on his goods.

When, on the 2nd of March, the House re-assembled, Speaker Finch did the expected thing by announcing the King's pleasure for a further adjournment. There had never, on any previous occasion, been the least question of such an intimation being disputed, but now there arose—and one strongly suspects by previous arrangement—shouts of "No !" that were soon taken up on all sides in that easily stampeded assembly. After a hubbub, great enough to drown even Eliot's voice, the Speaker, after again endeavouring to plead His Majesty's command, began to move away from the chair, but two of Eliot's confederates, Denzil Holles, and a Mr Valentine, who sat for Eliot's own borough of St Germans, rushed at him, and, each seizing an arm, started to haul him back again to the chair. There was a lively scuffle, the few Privy Councillors present joining in on the Speaker's side, but in the end the unfortunate gentleman was bundled, willy nilly, into his seat, with Holles swearing by God's wounds that there he should stop, till it pleased the House for him to rise.

It was one thing to get possession of the Speaker's body, but quite another to overcome his passive resistance. Eliot's purpose had been to rush through his Resolutions without delay, and he was already on his feet trying to get them put to the House ; but Finch, not for the first time in tears, and excusing himself with pathetic volubility, refused to be party to so unprecedented a defiance of the royal command. It was in vain that Eliot, in his most terrific vein, threatened him with the curse of the House. Mr Speaker wept but stood, or rather sat, firm. "I am not the less," he reminded them, "the King's servant for being yours."

This was a serious hitch in the programme, and one on which Eliot and his friends could not have reckoned. It seemed only too probable that the House would end by breaking up in confusion ; at least one Member had already resorted to fisticuffs ; others had only been prevented from leaving by Sir Miles Hobart— the Sergeant-at-Arms having hesitated to do so—locking the door and putting the key into his pocket.

Eliot, who seems by this time to have lost control both of himself and the situation, now launched out into a violent, diffuse tirade, in which, after fulminating against Arminians, Jesuits, and Bishop Neile, he started a new hare by denouncing the Lord Treasurer Weston, in unmeasured terms, as a second Buckingham, "in whose person, I fear, is contracted all the evil that we do suffer," and declaring his resolution to "fall upon his person"—in other words to have him impeached—at the first opportunity.

But at this point another unexpected hitch occurred. Weston had a son in the House, a fiery young fellow who rose to protest against the flagrant injustice of this attempt to pre-judge the case against his father, with such manly eloquence as to attract to himself considerable sympathy, and to extract from Eliot a rather sheepish qualification of his words.

All this was wandering far away from the original point, and fatally detracting from the impressiveness of this carefully planned scene. It was time to get the Resolutions put somehow, and there was even talk of putting Eliot in the chair to do it. But then it turned out that, in his excitement, he had thrown the paper containing them into the fire. And now Black Rod was knocking in vain at the door, with a message from the King. There was not a moment to lose, for Charles, now thoroughly roused, was about to have the door forced by the royal guard.

Holles came to the rescue with a copy of his own—a proof, if any were needed, of previous arrangement. Assuming the combined functions of proposer and Speaker, he shouted the Resolutions to the tumultuous mob who, whether they understood them or not, were in a mood to shout back "aye !" in sufficient numbers to warrant the assumption of a majority. And then the House was able to go through the formality of adjourning itself and dissolving into its component units.

Eliot's great revolutionary coup had, to a large extent, miscarried. Instead of the awful and deliberate pronouncement that had been intended, the affair had developed into an undignified brawl. That the Resolutions had ever been properly carried at all, was something more than doubtful. That they ever intimidated anyone, or were taken seriously by the country at large, there is no reason for believing. The lawless violence of extremists is the last thing to attract the sympathies even of biased Englishmen.

4

FAREWELL TO BRILLIANCE

IT was now just upon four years since King Charles had come to the throne, years of continued difficulty and frustration, that had brought him to a pass unprecedented in the history of English monarchy. For now one tremendous fact stared him in the face : Parliamentary government had broken down ; had become, for the time being impossible, from the standpoint of a monarch who aspired to govern as well as to reign.

That riot in the House had been enough to prove that under such leadership as Eliot's, there were no lengths to which the Commons could not be driven along the path to revolution. Not content with openly defying the King's authority, they were capable of inciting his subjects in general to set it at naught— nay more, of actually intimidating them into doing so. They were determined to take all before giving him anything ; to destroy everyone on whom he leaned, or on whose loyalty he could count, in Church or State ; to strip him of the barest minimum of necessary revenue ; and to leave him as abject a puppet as Richard II had been in the days of the Merciless Parliament, or Henry III when he was the crowned captive of Simon de Montfort.

It is therefore misleading to talk as if, after that memorable scene which closed the career of his third Parliament, Charles had formed some novel and sinister design of governing without Parliament. Humanly speaking, he had no choice in the matter. He had to do so if he was to govern at all and the only question was—how to do it ?

That he should have come to this had no doubt been partly

the fault of his own temperament and inexperience, and still more the result of his fatal loyalty to Buckingham. Whether his brother Henry, if he had lived, or any Sovereign whatever, could have perpetuated so unstable an equilibrium as that between Crown and Parliament, is at least doubtful ; but it is hardly conceivable that any other Sovereign could have caused it to collapse more completely, and in a shorter time, than the Charles-Buckingham combination had done. But now Buckingham was dead, and Charles had assumed the managing directorship of his own business, it remained to be seen whether he could profit enough from the effect of his fatally misplaced confidence to master his present accumulation of difficulties.

One thing he had learnt, and that was never to allow a repetition of the Buckingham experience ; never to resign his freedom of choice and judgment to the keeping of a favourite. He was the King ; and his ministers, even the ablest and most trusted, should be his servants in fact as well as name. But this was no bar to his availing himself to the full of the talents or advice of any one of them. No manager, royal or otherwise, however tight a hand he keeps upon his staff, can well avoid doing so, unless, like Buckingham himself in the days of his greatness, he is content to be served by human automata, incapable of functioning for themselves.

It will be remembered how one of Charles's appointments had been that of the newly-created Lord Weston, only a month before Buckingham's murder, to the Treasury ; and how, in that final tirade of Eliot's, Weston had been singled out and threatened with impeachment as a second Buckingham. That, in itself, was ridiculous—never could there have been any man whose character and career were less reminiscent of the Duke's, than this barrister of the Middle Temple, who had built up his position at Court by a long course of discreet and industrious service in various official posts. Indeed there is some reason for believing that only Buckingham's death saved him from being pitchforked out of the Treasury as suddenly as he had been put into it. Such a man may make his services indispensable, but he is the last in the world likely to become a King's, or anyone else's, favourite. Eliot had been right, all the same, in detecting in Weston the cornerstone of the post-Buckingham administration, the supremely dangerous man who possessed the secret of rendering the Crown independent of Parliamentary support.

That secret was so simple, and even commonplace, as to come more naturally to a pedestrian than to a soaring intelligence. It was of the kind that earns little thanks or praise for him who communicates it. The doctor who merely orders his patient to eat less, may well, if obeyed, be the means of saving his life, but such advice is not likely to make him popular. And Weston's secret might equally have been comprehended in the two words, "Spend less."

To this he was prepared to subordinate every other consideration ; it was his touchstone of policy. Did the King wish to assert England's authority and prestige in the affairs of Europe ? That would cost money—a great deal of money : let him keep it in his purse. Did he want to send aid to his uncle of Denmark, or restore his sister to her inheritance ? Either of these ventures, even if successful, would over-balance the debit side of the account— conclusive reason for dropping both. Peace was cheap, war dear : blessed therefore are the peacemakers.

Weston, though the least heroic of mortals, had at least the courage of his convictions. He was even able to dissuade the King from putting up the costly monument in the Abbey, by which he had intended to discharge the last tribute of his affection to Buckingham. And what was more damaging to himself, he had actually succeeded in inducing His Majesty to ration the incurably extravagant expenditure of his frivolous French wife ; a thing for which Henriette never forgave him, and which she did her best to avenge by making herself the focus of perpetual court intrigues against him, not unlike those of her mother against Richelieu.

And indeed, it required no ordinary strength of character in Charles to support such a minister, for Weston was desperately unpopular. To his other handicaps was added the known fact that his family was Catholic, and that he himself was suspected, and not unjustly, of a secret leaning to the older faith. But it was characteristic of him that, like the second Charles, he kept this attachment to himself till he was dying, and it could do him no harm. It is even more characteristic that under his auspices, the fines imposed on Catholics should have been more strictly exacted than ever. That was an item on the credit side of the account, which was all that mattered.

But it did not need the accidental circumstance of Weston's religion to account for the dislike that has pursued him beyond the grave. Few historians have a good word to say for him ;

to Clarendon he is "a man of big looks and mean and abject spirit" ; Gardiner who, with his usual desire to be fair, admits that he cared for England alone, hastens to add that it was with no exalted patriotism* ; to Pollard, he has no claim to be considered a great statesman, or even a great financier † ; to Fletcher, he is a mean creature whom history would do well to forget.‡

He belongs, in fact, to a class of unpopular statesmen ; Henry VII being one of them, Sir Robert Walpole another, Lionel Cranfield, the Earl of Middlesex at whose ruin Charles himself had so recklessly connived, a third. These men are of the world, worldly ; no despisers of the main chance, nor ashamed, while serving their country, to feather their own nests. They have no more romantic notions about honour than Falstaff, and are despisers of any glory that cannot be justified on a balance sheet. They are content to plod stolidly and cheaply along, avoiding trouble and never parting with an unnecessary penny.

For the biographer, avid for human interest, the only possible line to take with them is that which Virgil enjoined on Dante in the words,

"Speak not of them ; look only, and pass by !"

But there is this to be said for them ; that if material prosperity is the sole good to which they aspire, they do at least succeed in delivering it. If we survey the whole field of modern history, we shall find no periods during which the country has more thriven and prospered than during the reign of the close-fisted, first Tudor ; the two decades of Walpole's power ; the time when James I was keeping the peace and Cranfield keeping down his expenses ; and finally, this period of eleven years between the meeting of Charles I's third and fourth Parliaments, during which what we may call Weston's plan—though he himself survived less than half of the time to supervise it—was in operation.

Not that its author went to the length of formulating his principles ; such men are content to follow their instincts, and let the theory take care of itself. But if we can imagine him, in some moment of confidence, putting his secret into words, he might have said something to the following effect :

"The King's Government stands or falls with his ability to finance it. Now it is possible, but only just possible, for him to

* _History_, vi, p. 326.   † _D.N.B._   ‡ _Historical Portraits._

balance accounts with the resources still lawfully at his disposal. But in order to do this, he must lighten the strain by cutting down expenditure to the bone, and on no account whatever must he allow himself to be drawn into the supreme expense of war— a thing that will infallibly bring him face to face with bankruptcy, or Parliament. Even so, he will need to supplement his assets by the uttermost farthing that the courts will still uphold him in extracting from the well-to-do classes of his subjects. Above all. he must continue to assert his full rights to the customs revenue.

"By this means he will not only tide over his immediate necessities, but link the prosperity of the Crown to that of the nation, which only needs peace, along with the practical immunity from direct taxation secured to it in the absence of Parliament, to go on continually increasing in wealth and prosperity, thereby ensuring a solvent administration and, presumably, a contented people."

Whether or not Weston had thought out and Charles adopted this plan with conscious deliberation, the administration of the next decade was certainly conducted as if by its primary inspiration. And, as far at least as material well-being was concerned, the event justified the rosiest estimate that could have been formed. The nation did indeed bask in the sunshine of prosperity ; and that at a time when the continent of Europe was squandering its wealth and manhood in the most cruel and desolating war it had known since the Barbarian Invasions.

It is odd that even so prejudiced an historian as John Richard Green should have chosen to describe this period in a section of his famous *Short History* entitled *The Tyranny*. The idea of setting up a despotism on the Continental model had never entered Charles's mind. It was Parliament and not he that had been trying to upset the balance of the Constitution. There was nothing in the law or practice of that Constitution to compel him to summon Parliament before he needed its help. If he could carry on without it—so much the better for the Taxpayer !

Meanwhile the law, stiffened up as it had recently been against the Crown, remained supreme, and the King had not the power, even if he had the will, to set it at defiance. For unlike the real tyrants overseas, he had practically no armed force to back him. The handful of royal guards would not have been equal to defending his royal person against a really determined mob. Thus the King was compelled to govern with at least the passive acquiescence of a people, who certainly would not have endured any flagrant assertion of arbitrary power.

His position was not one of strength, but of weakness and perpetual peril. Weston's plan was only a guarantee against catastrophe as long as everything went smoothly. Once let the peace be broken, for any cause, and the game was up. The case of the Crown resembled that of a patient suffering from an extreme form of hæmophilia, who can go about with every appearance of health, until he happens to cut himself, when he bleeds to death.

Thus we find the English monarchy bound, at its mortal peril, to the strict observance of the Sermon on the Mount, translated into terms of foreign policy. It could not afford to resist evil, or be anything else than meek, merciful, and a peacemaker, in its dealings with its neighbours. And if the occasion should arise, it would need to turn the other cheek, lest a worse thing should befall it. We do not for a moment say that Charles was capable of adapting himself consciously to so unprecedented a reality ; but that did not make it any the less real.

And looking back on it now, across the gulf of three centuries, one is tempted to ask whether so humiliating a necessity laid on her government were really a bad thing for England. If ever there was a country for which non-aggression was practical wisdom, it was this England of Charles I. No one dreamed of attacking her. She had everything to lose and nothing to gain from taking a hand in the swindling and ruinous game of universal beggar-my-neighbour that was being played between the potentates of the Continent. Apart from the fact that her warlike adventures of the past four years had lost her more prestige than a century of peaceful abstention could possibly have done, was it not a fair exchange for any conceivable glory that it could be said of her, with truth,

"Thou shalt eat the labours of thy hands : O well is thee, and happy shalt thou be !"

As for Parliament, even if it was not sitting, it was never more alive, or, in a sense, more powerful. There was no question of its becoming superseded and practically extinct like the States General in France. It was there in effect all the time, holding down the King to the task of securing for his people the blessings of peace, prosperity, and freedom from "any gift, loan, benevolence, tax, or such like charge."

What more indeed could Parliament, had it been continuously in session and power, have done for the common man ? If these be the fruits of tyranny, it is to be feared that the cry would be almost universal of, "Now gods stand up for tyrants !"

5

UNBENDING : UNFORGIVING

BEFORE the new policy could be given a fair chance, there was need for cleaning up the effects of the old. At the beginning of March, 1629, the King had two major wars on his hands, and what might easily have been the beginnings of a revolution at home.

This latter danger called for immediate action. No sovereign could afford to pass over such outrageous provocation as that of Eliot and his confederates. And yet for two days the Royal Council was anxiously debating whether to take up the challenge ; timid official personages, with the threat of impeachment suspended over every one of their heads, being doubtful, even now, whether to grasp the nettle. Not so Weston, who knew what was to be his fate at the hands of this Parliament, and whose only and natural anxiety was to get it sent packing. But it is unlikely that there was any serious doubt in the King's own mind. The man who had been prepared to use his guard to break open the doors of the House, was not likely to shrink from so obvious a sequel to the Commons' riot as that of dissolution. But Charles's actions were seldom precipitate, nor was it his way to cut short discussion.

His proclamation, drawn up on that self-same day, but not published till two days later, leaves no doubt of the intensity of his resentment :

"We," it says, "and our Royal Authority and commandment, have been so highly condemned as our kingly office cannot bear, nor any former age can parallel. And therefore it is our full and absolute intention to dissolve the said Parliament; ..."

An intention duly carried out on the 10th, when His Majesty, without even condescending to send for the Commons, came down to the House of Lords and made a brief speech in which he attributed the whole trouble to the influence of "some few vipers," who, he said, "must look for their reward of punishment."

And indeed, by this time, Eliot and his fellow ringleaders in the disturbance had been arrested and lodged in the Tower.

But before dealing with them personally, it was the King's first care to counteract, as far as possible, the seditious propaganda for which that deliberately engineered scene in the House had afforded such magnificent publicity. With this object His Majesty addressed a Proclamation to his subjects, which might well have borne the title of the Royal Grand Remonstrance. It is, in fact, a moderately worded and closely reasoned statement of the case for the Crown : "that we may appear to the world in the truth and sincerity of our actions, and not in those colours in which we know some turbulent and ill-affected spirits (to mask and disguise their wicked intentions dangerous to the State) would represent us to the public view."

It is a document of the highest interest ; because only on one other occasion did the King so frankly unbosom himself, and his motives, to his people, and then the ranks of armed men, who were assisting at his murder, prevented his voice from carrying beyond. Whatever verdict we choose to pass on it, or him, it at least disposes finally of the common notion of Charles as a mere drifter, a weak, prejudiced person without any guiding principle or vision of a goal to his policy.

Nothing could be more lucid, or—one might add—more convincing, than his indictment of the extremists whose proceedings had compelled him to dissolve Parliament, and in particular the unheard-of extension of privilege, "by setting up general committees for religion, for courts of justice, for trade, and the like ... to the unsufferable scandal and disturbance of justice and government, which, having been tolerated for a while by our father and ourself, hath daily grown to more and more height ; insomuch that young lawyers sitting there take upon them to decry the opinions of judges ; and some have not doubted to maintain that the resolutions of the House must bind the judges, a thing never heard of in ages past. ..."

Thus does His Majesty proceed with the exposure of a revolutionary conspiracy, which has resulted in "the sincerer and better part of the House" being overborne. Particularly telling is his scornful reminder of the way in which the men, who had professed to regard Buckingham as the sole author of all the evils that had fallen upon the nation, had continued their agitation, with unabated venom, now that he was dead :

"So that now it is manifest, the Duke was not alone the mark these men shot at, but was only as a near minister of ours taken up, on the by, and in their passage to their more secret designs ; which were only to cast our affairs into a desperate condition to abate the powers of our Crown, and to bring our government into obloquy, that in the end all things may be overwhelmed with anarchy and confusion."

The King went on solemnly to guarantee the traditional and established liberties of his subjects, but he added, "as we well maintain our subjects in their just liberties, so we do and will expect that they yield as much submission and duty to our royal prerogatives." It was the theme to which he was to recur on the scaffold, the constant philosophy of his mature years—a Sovereign and a subject are clean contrary things, but the strength of the Sovereign's prerogative is the safeguard of the subject's liberties.

And as Sovereign, he intended to make it clear that under no circumstances would he allow his servants to be intimidated or his authority set at nought.

"And now," he concluded, in words that clearly set forth his intention and ideal during the years of his personal government, "... all wise and discreet men ... may discern, by examination of their own hearts, whether—in respect of the free passage of the Gospel, equal and indifferent administration of justice, freedom from oppression, and the great peace and quietness which every man enjoyeth under his own vine and fig-tree—the happiness of this nation can be paralleled by any of our neighbour countries ; and if not, then to acknowledge their own blessedness, and for the same, be thankful to God, the author of all goodness."

It was a proud and inspiriting claim—one that might have been repeated, and justified, at any time during the ensuing eleven years. What acknowledgment or thanks would be forthcoming, yet other years would reveal.

But Charles had something to do besides issuing proclamations. There were Eliot and his confederates to be disposed of. These men, whatever their motives, had thrown down the gage to their King in the sight of the whole nation, and he could not, if he was to remain a King, avoid taking it up. In any other country, the State would have taken a short way with such rebels. But Charles was determined to proceed by due process of law, and not only had the Petition of Right tied his hands to a dangerous extent, but he had also to take account of that comprehensive and sacred notion of Privilege, that was gradually being extended towards including everything, however seditious, that could be said or done within the walls of Parliament.

The task of bringing the offenders to book was therefore extremely ticklish, especially when they included so consummate a legal genius as Selden. A false step, that would have entailed the defeat of the Crown in its own courts, might have been as disastrous to Charles as the attempt to prosecute the Seven Bishops was to prove to his second son. And the judges were anything but the King's subservient creatures—less than ever since the terror of Parliament had fallen upon them. And so no less than eleven months were consumed in those complicated manœuvres so dear to lawyers, before the Court of King's Bench sentenced the defendants to various fines, and to imprisonment during the King's pleasure, with a proviso that none of them should be released until he had made submission and acknowledged his offence.

This was all the King wanted. Having gained his point he had no wish to press hard on the prisoners, and was only too glad to make retreat easy for them. As soon as it became apparent that an attitude of unbending defiance might entail detention till the Greek Calends, only two of them, with the exception of Eliot, proved stout enough to perpetuate a martyrdom that had ceased to have even the solace of publicity. Denzil Holles was soon persuaded by his family to give the required security for his good behaviour, and exchange the bread of affliction for the joys of a rich man's life on a country estate ; Selden, after a little more delay, found no difficulty in saving his face and returning to his lucrative practice. One or two of the rest were turned loose without any formality whatever.

But the case was different with Eliot. He, as no other man before or after him, had succeeded in arousing an element in Charles's nature strangely in contrast with its dominant gentleness. One might best describe it as one of frozen fury. Charles was never the man to express his feelings, but the accumulated provocation he had received from Eliot had pierced the shell of his innate reserve, and burnt into his very soul. It was not only that the man had waged unrelenting war against him, none the less deadly from being conducted with words instead of swords ; it was not only that he had wrecked every possibility of an understanding between King and Parliament, and that he had followed this by stirring up his subjects outside Parliament to resist him—these things might perhaps have been forgiven ; but there was one thing, with Charles, admitted of no forgiveness, and that was the leading part that Eliot had played in hounding to death his own former comrade and benefactor, Buckingham. The King must have felt that if it had been Felton's hand, it had been Eliot's brain that had driven home the dagger ; that Eliot's implacable vendetta, Eliot's ceaseless propaganda, had created such an atmosphere of hatred against his only friend, that his murder, by some hand or other, had been only a matter of time.

Something of the strength of Charles's feelings may be gauged by the fact that in a proclamation on the 27th of March, 1629, he actually went to the length of singling out Eliot individually as "an outlawed man, desperate in mind and fortune."

So that there could be no question of Eliot's far from severe sentence being relaxed by royal intervention ; until, at any rate, he had made submission to the authority he had defied. But this was the one thing of all others, that it was not in Eliot's nature to concede. Charles was confronted by a will equal, and a pride more than equal, to his own.

There is something tragically similar in the cases of these two men, so implacably opposed. However impossibly—not to say treasonably—Eliot might have behaved, he had not the least doubt in his own mind of the rightness of his cause. He now, as much as Charles a score of years later, felt that he was a martyr to the people ; he, too, refused to recognize the right of his judges to try him. And he, as much as Charles, could be steadfast unto death.

All that was noblest in his nature came out, now that he was cut off from the fever and turmoil of political agitation. He made no complaint, even against those less single-hearted colleagues who had forsaken him and made their peace with the enemy. He settled down quietly to make the best of prison, in the spirit of those classical philosophers from whom, much more than from the faith for which he was so uncompromising a zealot, he derived inspiration. His restless energy he diverted into the task of literary composition, whose effect is to leave us wondering how the eloquence that held the Commons spellbound, could run on paper to such diffuse unreadability.

After two years in which his fiery spirit had suffered what

must have been, for it, the most terrible of all deprivations, that of an outlet in action, it became apparent that the supreme sacrifice would be demanded of him. He developed tuberculosis—perhaps he had had the seeds of it in him all along, a thing that might account for that peculiar hectic energy of his. His one chance would have been to get back to the air and freedom of his native Cornwall. He had only to say the word—the word he would rather die than say—and that freedom was his. At last, when the first autumn mists were beginning to creep up the Thames, the dying man—for such he now was—did bend his soul to petition the King "to set me at liberty that for the recovery of my health I may take some fresh air."

His Majesty merely commented that the petition was not humble enough—he had had to deal with Eliot before, and he must have remembered how little Eliot's dutiful professions had signified in the past. This time he should be made to toe the line, as remorselessly as Charles himself had been forced by Eliot to do so in the matter of another Petition.

Then, out of the Tower came the following message—almost too heart-rending to record :

"I am heartily sorry I have displeased your Majesty, and, having so said, do humbly beseech you, once again, to set me at liberty, that, when I have recovered my health, I may return back to my prison, there to undergo such punishment as God has allotted unto me."

In vain ! This was not the submission that Charles had required, and Eliot's pathos was merely evasive. The gates of pity were barred ; the iron had entered too deeply into the King's soul on that dreadful morning when he had remained kneeling to the end of prayers at Southwick, while at Portsmouth Steenie. ... What pity had Eliot had for *him* ? He should make submission now or—undergo such punishment as God had allotted unto him.

The Lieutenant of the Tower, whose office it was to forward the petitions of his prisoners, could only urge on Eliot to try a third time, acknowledging his fault and craving pardon, when all would doubtless be well. But Eliot was by this time past even the capacity of defiance. "My spirits," he said, "are growen feeble and faint." When it should please God to restore him to full vigour he would take it into consideration. Meanwhile ...

The end came on the 27th of November. Not quite, however, the end of the King's long duel with Eliot. For there was another petition, this time by Eliot's young son—the father had been no more than forty-two—to be allowed to take the body to rest in that Cornish land, which the closed eyes had longed in vain to see. His Majesty minuted the request :

"Let Sir John Eliot's body be buried in the church of the parish where he died."

It was not like a gentleman and a Christian, which is as much as to say, not like King Charles, to have penned these words. Perhaps he may have remembered how his friend's murdered body had had to be brought secretly, by night, to the Abbey, for fear of the London mob. That might partly explain what only God, in His infinite understanding, could condone.

Meanwhile the very serious situation created by Eliot's agitation, and those three Resolutions that had been its final and culminating manifesto, had gradually quieted down. But for a time it had been extremely alarming, and it had almost been a question of whether the King might not have found himself checkmated after all. For a large number of merchants, some of them no doubt from genuine conviction, but others admittedly from terror of Parliamentary wrath to come, refused to pay duty, or indeed to import goods at all, and the financial margin of the Government was so extremely narrow that the drying up of one of its principal sources of revenue might, in a quite short time, have reduced it to bankruptcy.

But London merchants are seldom of the stern stuff of which successful strikers are made, particularly when it is a case of downing not tools but profits. It soon became apparent that the authorities did not mean to be trifled with, and that the prospect of a Parliament materializing was quite indefinitely remote. The most redoubtable of all the resisters, Richard Chambers, he who had got himself committed for contempt by informing the King's Council that merchants were more screwed and wrung in England than in Turkey, and who subsequently wrote on a form of submission tendered to him the most uncompromising defiance he could think of, was, after a great deal of legal difficulty, sentenced to a swingeing fine and imprisoned for what eventually lengthened to a term of six years. The example made of this indomitable litigant was enough to discourage imitation. Gradually the merchants tired of mixing politics with business, and trade resumed its normal course. The King's victory on the home front was for the time complete.

6

BLESSED NECESSITY

THE first item in the new peace programme to which the King, under the advice of Weston and pressure of necessity, was now committed, was that of liquidating the wars bequeathed by Buckingham's policy. This was a matter of no great difficulty, for it suited Richelieu's book to be friends with England, and as for poor, exhausted Spain, she might defend herself when attacked, but was perfectly incapable of hitting back.

The French peace was concluded in the spring of 1629 ; the Venetian ambassadors, who had already employed their good offices during the siege of Rochelle, continued them till they were rewarded with success. The peace may almost be said to have made itself, for there was nothing left to quarrel about. Charles quietly abandoned his championship in arms of the French Protestants, and Richelieu did as much for the English Catholics—even the question of the Queen's suite could be dropped now that Henriette had fallen too much in love with her husband to harbour any sense of grievance. And thus that fatal marriage treaty was at last put out of the way, and one major peril removed.

The English, if they had realized it, had in their grasp a conquest far more valuable than that of Rochelle, for before the news of peace had had time to cross the Atlantic, a certain Captain Kirke had sailed up the St Lawrence River and taken Quebec. But the treaty provided for a mutual restitution of conquests, and nobody knew or cared enough about Quebec to make any particular difficulty about handing it back.

Richelieu would have liked to follow up the peace by some sort of Anglo-French alliance against the Hapsburgs, the eternal bait of the Palatinate being dangled before Charles's eyes. But however much Charles may have been tempted by his loyalty to his sister, Weston was determined to follow up the peace with France by one with Spain, and made it clear to Charles that the only alternative to this would be to summon Parliament. The negotiations pursued the leisurely course that any dealings with Spaniards must needs do, and peace was only signed in the following year, on terms that, like those with France, practically restored the *status quo ante*.

There was only one other commitment to liquidate, which was to that now very forlorn and shattered hope of German Protestantism, the King of Denmark. But here, too, Weston was able to convince the King that he would really not be able to afford his uncle anything except a nephew's heartfelt sympathy, a commodity that proved so little in demand that King Christian had serious thoughts of distraining for arrears of a more material sort, by seizing British shipping in the Sound.

Thus under the guidance of Weston did King Charles succeed in reversing the Buckingham policy of active intervention in European conflicts, and in bringing back England to a state of peace with her neighbours. Five years of bitter experience had showed how wise had been King James's policy of seeking peace before all other blessings. His son's self-willed departure from this path, that had brought down the father's prematurely grey hairs with sorrow to the grave, had led, through dissension at home and disaster abroad, to the verge of ruin. For the rest of his reign, so long as he retained the power to decide, it was in the spirit of his father that Charles acted in his dealings with foreign Powers. His diplomacy had no element of brilliance, and was notoriously without force to back it ; it had every appearance of being tortuous, undecided, and ineffective, but it did achieve the end of keeping England at peace, at the time, of all others, when peace was what she most needed. For the supreme danger that threatened her, during the sixteen-thirties, was that of being sucked into the bloody maelstrom of the Thirty Years' War. And that danger was fearfully imminent.

For the war was now entering on its most dramatic and intense phase. If Charles and Buckingham had had the least insight into the conditions of the German problem, or the character of that very typical Hapsburg, the Emperor Ferdinand II, they might have known that a too complete success of the imperial cause would merely have the effect of giving the victor enough rope to hang himself. The fact that with the exception of the fortress of Stralsund, nothing between the Alps and the Baltic had been able to stand up against the armies of Wallenstein and Tilly, emboldened Ferdinand to order the return to the Church of such of its lands, all over Germany, as had, since a certain date, been looted in the course of the Reformation. This was to touch the hitherto lukewarm Protestant princes in a tenderer spot than their consciences. Next Ferdinand proceeded to knock away one of his two military props, by depriving of his command the formidable and sinister Wallenstein.

And now at last Richelieu, still keeping the strength of France in hand, was able to launch a deadly bolt against the House of Austria, in the shape of a new Protestant champion, Gustavus Adolphus of Sweden, who, being as shrewd a business man as any old Viking, would not bring his military genius into play until he had secured the requisite backing in the shape of five tubs full of French gold. The result exceeded the Cardinal's expectations, and probably his desires. The drooping spirits of every Protestant community were revived by the tremendous news of Tilly's invincible army having been smashed to pieces in the neighbourhood of Leipzig ; of the hosts of the Lord sweeping on, through the heart of Catholic Bavaria ; of the Emperor, as a last desperate resource, recalling to his service the dismissed Wallenstein.

The inevitable effect of such tidings on the dominant Puritanism of England was to stimulate a mood of bellicose exaltation. Why was England out of these glorious proceedings ? Was she to incur the curse of Meroz, by refusing to come to the help of the Lord against the mighty ? And most especially when the Lord's side appeared to be winning.

Even before Gustavus had appeared on the scene, the new peace policy had been regarded with no small amount of suspicion. Though Parliament had paralyzed the war against Spain by refusing to finance it, the idea of making peace was regarded, in extreme Protestant circles, as veritable treason to the cause ; and Weston, who was known to be in favour of a Spanish entente, and who was doubly suspect from his Catholic associations, became more hated than ever. Lampoons appeared about him ; a play was got uncensored on to the boards by no less an author than Massinger, one of the last inheritors of the grand Elizabethan tradition, pillorying the Treasurer under a transparent classical disguise. This was uncomfortably like what had preceded Buckingham's murder, and Weston, in spite of a blustering manner, was really an extremely nervous man, and began to be troubled with fears of assassination.

Nevertheless he stuck to his pursuit of peace and economy with an obstinacy that not even his fears could bend, and the King, in spite of all inducements to the contrary, continued to give him

his support. Not that Charles saw eye to eye with his minister ;
for Weston would have accepted the logical consequence of his
attitude, and had Britain cease to interest herself, even verbally,
in the affairs of Europe. But Charles was not prepared for so
uncompromising a programme of isolation, which would have
involved, amongst other things, the open and brutal repudiation
of his sister's cause. Against that his whole loyal soul would have
revolted. He would continue to do all for her that he could by
negotiation ; but he had now come to realize that, with the best
will in the world, he had neither arms nor money with which to
back it. And thus his diplomacy was at best one of bluff on a weak
hand, a fact likely to be realized by the hard-bitten experts against
whom he was pitted.

It was, in fact, precisely the same game as his father had played
for so many years, of spinning out time by negotiation. It is easy
to pour scorn on what even so great an authority as Gardiner
brands as "futile diplomacy", but the problem before Charles
was anything but simple, and it is by no means certain that his
solution was worse, in practice, than the more logical course
favoured by Weston.

For we must remember that he was not in the position of a
player calmly thinking out the ideal move on the diplomatic
chess-board ; but it was as if he were playing in front of excited
partisans who, if they thoroughly disapproved of the lines on
which the game was developing, might quite easily drag their
champion from the table and lynch him. Charles—that is to say
—had to reckon with an alert and suspicious public opinion, that
he dared not affront, even by the wisest policy.

How great that danger was may be realized from a dispatch
of the Venetian Ambassador, dated the 25th of May, 1629, just
after poor Henriette, who had been frightened by a fight between
two big dogs, had been delivered prematurely of a child who
only lived long enough for a hasty baptism.

"The catastrophe," he says, "is most unfortunate at the present
crisis, during the strained relations between the King and the
people, whose eyes are only too firmly fixed on the Countess
Palatine and her progeny. Many believe that, owing to this event,
the road of Parliament will be resumed, as the increase of discontent would endanger the King's very life."

It is the first hint that we have from any source that the King's
life might not be safe at the hands of his subjects.

The danger was all the greater, because the fact of the King's Catholic marriage, not to speak of Weston's Catholic connections, rendered suspect any failure to take the most aggressive Protestant line. Some colourable show of zeal was therefore a necessity of practical statesmanship, and if it produced no very tangible results abroad, it may have prevented the nerves of the King's subjects at home from being stretched beyond breaking point.

This might easily have occurred when Gustavus was holding his court at Mainz, like a Protestant Emperor of Germany, and when the unfortunate Elector Frederick, who had only a few more months to live, was following him about like a self-adopted poor relation, in the now reviving hope of getting back his Palatinate. Charles, all this time, was giving a masterly display of the art of doing nothing in particular, and doing it well. He negotiated hard, in the true spirit of his father, with all parties. He even offered his alliance to Gustavus, but that canny Swede knew well enough what an English alliance had meant to Denmark, and was going to see the colour of Charles's money before doing business with him.

All the same, Charles did his bit for the Protestant cause, by allowing the young Scottish Marquis of Hamilton to raise a force of volunteers for service in Germany. He even managed to scrape up eleven thousand pounds out of his attenuated finances to give it a start, with further driblets amounting to fifteen, and a little army of 7,000 Englishmen and Scots did eventually embark for Germany, where they were employed in safeguarding Gustavus's communications. But Hamilton was one of those persons who seem to be born with a genius for failing in everything they undertake, and Gustavus, who did not trust his loyalty, was not prepared to give him proper support. Before long sickness and starvation, those chronic enemies of Charles's expeditionary forces, had caused the army to melt away to a beggarly 500.

None the less, these volunteers had justified their existence, if they had provided a safety valve for the nation's bellicose passion during the time of the Swedish ascendancy. For in 1632 the pendulum had begun to swing back. Wallenstein returned to the front, with his great private army, now reconstituted, and dug himself in hard by Gustavus at Nuremberg, fairly starving him out of the city. Then, after some further manœuvring, followed, in a November fog, a great pitched battle, only a few miles from the site of Tilly's defeat in the previous year, in which the armies fought each other to a standstill, but in which, also, the great Protestant hero chanced to ride, through the murk, into a detachment of enemy cavalry, who made an end of him, and of the last hope of a clean cut issue to the struggle of the faiths in Germany. Little more than a year afterwards, Wallenstein, who might at least have ended the war by a reasonable compromise, was assassinated at the Emperor's instigation by his own officers.

Even now, it was barely half time in the war, which had ceased to be one of faith or principle, and become a dreadful parasitism of professional armies upon the civilization of Central Europe. Swedish, French, German, or cosmopolitan hordes moved about from one fertile district to another, leaving depopulated wildernesses in their trail, destroying each other at intervals, but destroying the helpless civilian populations all the time. All question of a Protestant or a Catholic victory had long ago disappeared— every warring potentate was playing frankly and brutally for his own hand in this game of beggar-my-neighbour all round.

It behoves every historian to be diffident in passing moral judgment, but nothing was ever certain if it be not that the expenditure of English blood and English treasure in this atrocious struggle, would have been in the highest and equal degree a crime and a blunder. The only conceivable business that England had with the Thirty Years' War was to keep out of it. And if, after the petering out of Hamilton's effort, Charles's diplomacy had the effect of accomplishing this, with at any rate the passive acquiescence of the people at home, throughout the rest of the decade, it would seem hard to conceive of any alternative method by which he might have deserved better of his country, or of mankind at large.

7

THE CHURCH, THE PURITANS, AND
THE PLUTOPURITANS

HOWEVER bitterly Catholic and Puritan and High Church Anglican may have contended among themselves, one thing on which they were all agreed was the supreme importance of a people's inner life, and its outward expression in religion. The idea that a man's faith is his own private affair, and that constituted authority is only concerned with his conduct to his neighbour, would have struck them as manifestly absurd, since conduct is the effect of which faith is the cause. Before you can do right to man, you have to get right with God.

This standpoint is far from being out of date, even to-day. It is that of the Totalitarian State, except that it is no longer fashionable to talk of God. Every dictator knows that not only half, but nine-tenths of his battle, consists in capturing and controlling the mind of the people, or—in more technical phrase—of conditioning its reactions. And it was for the right to exercise this control that the Parliamentary opposition had contended most fiercely with King Charles.

Here the position which the King found himself committed to defending, was a startling and to some extent anomalous one. For he was an entirely different sort of monarch in his spiritual, from what he was in his temporal aspect. As head of the State he was amenable to the Common Law, and he could scarcely undertake any important action without finding himself entangled in the undergrowth of its rights and precedents. But as Supreme Governor of the Church he was something more like a Divine Caesar, or local lay Pope.

Now the Church of England had come to have a unique and very startling significance, in a Europe in which the religious issue for the last time formally dominated all others. To any one who looked at the map, it might have seemed as if the clock had been put back for a millennium and a half, and the old Western Empire of Rome, standing on very much its old frontiers except for flanks flung precariously forward in Poland and Ireland, were engaged in the old death grapple with a combination of barbarian hordes from beyond the Rhine and the Danube. Only this time the frontiers delimited the spheres of contrasting ideologies, Catholic and Protestant. Outside a solid and static phalanx of Lutheran autocracies in the heart of Germany, the ideological choice presented itself, as one between two Orders—a new Geneva International, and the old Roman Supernational—of Christian civilization.

But the ancient Roman province of Britain, always the most superficial in its allegiance both to the temporal and the spiritual Caesars, had, under the guidance of its royal house, on declaring formal and final independence of the old order, come to what, before she actually made it, would have constituted the incredibly audacious decision to abjure membership of any communion but her own, and giving all ideologies the go by, to set up spiritual house for herself and call that house the Church of England.

That, at any rate, was the effect of it ; though assuredly no one had the remotest consciousness, at the time, what, in the long run, such a claim portended. For only on one sane ground could it be advanced, and only on one condition could there be the least hope of making it good, namely that England herself was pregnant with a new world order of civilization, as catholic as that of Rome, and offering an acceptable alternative of salvation to peoples bowed to the ground beneath the rods and axes of Caesarism.

And yet to those who voiced their patriotism through the saga of King Arthur, it might not have seemed so fantastically incredible had they been told that the walls and arches of Rome would one day echo to the tramp of emancipating armies, drawn from the uttermost ends of the earth, and flying the banners of a British-born civilization ; nor that the same banners would be victoriously unfurled over those barbarian outlands between the Rhine and the Elbe, that had been the grave of the legions.

But at the time with which we are concerned, the spiritual independence of England, or even of the Church of England, was far from being an accomplished fact ; it might rather have been described as an increasingly forlorn hope, to which King Charles had clung with what bade fair to prove suicidal consistency. For both within and without the Church the Geneva ideology had been rising like an irresistible flood. And just because the Crown had committed its faith and fortunes to the task of making spiritual independence a living reality, the revolutionary leaders had played the out and out Protestant card for all it was worth, and sought to rope the country into fighting membership of the Geneva ideology.

We, living in an age in which the Church has long ceased to express the spiritual independence of the country, and when the very idea is calculated to raise a faint smile, need to re-orient our minds if we are to grasp the tremendous significance of the fight that King Charles never ceased to make for the Church, as he had received and conceived of it ; the Church that rightly, from her standpoint, canonized him as her Royal Martyr. For it would have been open to him, almost up to the end, to have saved himself by abandoning her.

For good or ill, it is by their Church policy that the first two Stuarts have left the most distinctive mark on history. For under Elizabeth the Church had indeed stood greatly for national independence ; but rather by by-passing than asserting religion. It had formed a great, tolerant umbrella, under which all the Queen's loyal subjects of any faith, or absence of it, could shelter together on a common ground of patriotism. To its greatest divine, the Judicious Hooker, it stood for the supreme embodiment of the reign of law.

That was good enough to tide the country over the struggle to preserve her new-won independence against the overwhelming menace of a Catholic crusade for the reconquest of Britain. But when that menace was blown away on the winds that scattered the Armada, it became manifest that it would be impossible for the Church to maintain a merely negative or legalistic attitude towards that better half of the nation's activities which from time immemorial had been the province of the spiritual power. If it might now be regarded as settled that a re-establishment of the Roman Church was finally ruled out, the needs formally catered for by Rome had got to be satisfied in spirit and truth by whatever national Church was set up in its place. The nature of the seventeenth century Englishman abhorred a spiritual vacuum. One of two things had got to happen : either the Church *in* England, having cut herself loose from one Continental ideology, must go to the opposite extreme, and accept membership of the other and become hundred-per-cent Protestant ; or else the Church *of* England had got to make her independence positive, and work out her own solution of the spiritual problem, a solution which, in so far as she must needs adopt the familiar labels, was a compound of Catholic and Protestant, with the prefix Anglo attached to each—in effect, Anglican.

Now the policy favoured by the upper-class revolutionaries of whom Pym had come to be the leader, had tended more and more as time went on towards the extreme Protestant or—to take the word that was coming more and more into fashion—Puritan solution. For the enormous *nouveau riche* interest that had sprung up as the result of the share out of Church property at the Reformation, could not fail to perceive that its bread was thickly buttered on the Protestant side. Russells, Sidneys, Devereux,

Rich's, Dudleys, Cromwells—who more zealous than they in pushing the Reformation logic to its Puritan conclusion ? Though their zeal did admit of certain qualifications in practice ; and few of them, however austere their principles, were markedly disposed to cramp their own style of living. And indeed it would have been plainly ridiculous to have allowed the very Prostant-ism, that had endowed them with all the good things of life, to turn these into gifts of Tantalus.

No, the real Protestant fanaticism that produced the austerities and crudities with which we are apt to associate the name of Puritan, was of altogether humbler origin, and the result of an ideological ferment that was rising among the populace where it was most thickly congregated, and which the upper-class Pluto-puritans were engaged in playing up for all it was worth, because it provided them with the mob violence that was the winning card in their game against the Crown. But it was a dangerous game to themselves, and a time might come when these owners of great possessions might find themselves more concerned to depress the spirit of the people than ever they had been to cut the claws of the monarchy. And then would come the time when another King Charles would be able to fire off his cynical epigram that nonconformity was no religion for a gentleman.

We must draw a clear distinction, then, between the out-and-out Puritan fanatics of the sects and conventicles, and the Pluto-puritans, to whom their religion, even when they held it most sincerely, was essentially a means to a political, or economic end. These men, who now followed the lead of Pym, were no more committed to the overthrow of the national Church than they were to the abolition of the monarchy. They would have found it more convenient to have retained both, and run them in their own interests. It was more or less what, after the Glorious Revolu-tion, they actually did manage to bring off. But the Church of which Charles I was the Supreme Governor, was no longer what it had been under Elizabeth, a spiritual blank sheet on which the power in control of the State could write anything it chose. It had begun to acquire a life and purpose of its own, that were invincibly opposed to those which Pym and his Plutopuritans sought to impose on it. As with the Crown, so with the Church ; it stood right across their path, blocking the way, and leaving them no choice but, in the long run, to attempt its complete demolition.

For it is impossible to understand the great conflict that was to come to a head in the Civil War, without realizing that the Church of England was no whit inferior in zeal or vitality to either of the great rival ideologies whose militant fanaticism was sweeping the Continent with the lethal virulence of a second Black Death. She offered to Englishmen a way—a *Via Media* as Newman was afterwards to characterize it—to walk with God, and fashion the order of her own society, which was that neither of Rome nor of Geneva, but sought to infuse the uncompromising inwardness of the Protestant spirit into the ordered magnificence of the Catholic form, and to add thereto a sweetness and kindliness proper to the English temperament at its best ; which was what Archbishop Laud intended to comprehend in his favourite phrase, "the beauty of holiness". It was a merry and a kindly England that the Church strove to keep in being, and to crown with that beauty. Even when she was on the defensive against malignant aggression, her yoke was easy and her burden light beyond all comparison with the crushing imperialism of Rome and the sombre totalitarianism of Geneva.

8

THE BEAUTY OF HOLINESS

IT was implicit in the doctrine of sovereignty that had come to dominate political thought even in Catholic countries, and had received its most striking expression in the German religious compromise, that the Sovereign of every territory should have the right to determine its religion.

But the case of an English King was not quite on the same footing as that of the average Continental Sovereign. For abroad, when a monarch assumed religious control, it meant that he was bringing his spiritual into line with his temporal functions ; every petty Caesar was all the more Caesar from ruling in both his temporal and spiritual capacities by the same principles of Roman Law. But the status of a spiritual Caesar is fundamentally different

from that of an English Constitutional Sovereign, and it is hard to
see how the two can ever be harmoniously combined in the same
individual.

Charles was honestly determined to govern according to law,
even if it were the English Common Law, but there can be no
denying that he was more naturally inclined to the Roman than
the English view of a King's functions. And here, on the spiritual
side, he was outside the spirit of the Common Law, a monarch by
divine right in the fullest sense of the words, surrounded by a
staff of Bishops, nominated by the Crown, and as obedient as the
chiefs of an army to its generalissimo. Through them, he had at
his disposal all the immense resources of propaganda that had at
one time been at the disposal of Rome ; the continuous suggestion
of architecture and ornament, of music and ritual, and above all
of preaching. As governor of his Church he was able to act as
the true father of his people, exercising a benevolent control
over their daily lives as well as their minds.

Parliament had tried to snatch that control from his hands,
and establish one of its own, far more severe and inquisitorial ;
but Parliament was now in a state of suspended animation, and
Charles was free to take the utmost advantage of what fell not far
short of a spiritual autocracy, if we can apply that term to a
power that he was only able to exercise over the Church from
outside and as an outsider. For the Pope had been not only
Supreme Head of the Church, but also supreme churchman,
whereas Charles was not a churchman at all, nor capable of
exercising the functions of the humblest priest. He could be his
own Prime Minister, but never his own Archbishop of Canterbury ; never, like a Roman Caesar, his own Pontifex Maximus.

But he could exert a decisive influence, as well as constant
supervision in detail—his minutes of Church documents show
that he insisted on being kept in touch with everything that went
on, and getting what he wanted done. But at the same time, he
had nothing like his father's *flair* for theological controversy. It
was not that he was less firmly grounded in the theory of this
most abstruse subject—time would prove him capable, on due
occasion, of more than holding his own with the doughtiest of
Calvinist disputants—but that his natural disposition inclined
him more readily to a practical than a theoretical Christianity.
With the possible exception of Henry VI, we should have to go
back to Alfred to find an English King who can be said to the

same extent to have *lived* his religion. Not even the strictest of the
Puritans, with whatever political crimes they may have taxed
him, were able to charge his private life with a sin more heinous
than that of reading Shakespeare.

We shall never understand Charles unless we realize that his
Church, with him, was not, as it was to most kings, first and
foremost a matter of political convenience, a vehicle for the
exertion of his power. He loved her as passionately as a man is
capable of loving a woman, and as constantly as few men are
capable of loving any woman. He loved her—as he was to prove
in the hour of trial—more than power and more than life. It was
a love strong enough to over-ride all considerations of policy or
even of prudence.

But it was as simple, and as little concerned with theory, as all
great love should be. We have talked of Charles as encouraging
the High Church section of his ecclesiastics, but to talk of him as
a High Churchman in the modern sense would be as misleading
as it would be to label him Low or Evangelical. It would be more
to the point to say that he accepted the Church, in the spirit of a
lover, as he found her ; but that his constant desire was to enrich
her beauty by every adornment that love was capable of providing.

There is a phrase of Scripture especially dear to that great
Churchman, William Laud, to whom Charles confided the
direction of his spiritual policy. It is this—"the beauty of holiness".
Charles, with his love of Shakespeare, may perhaps have associated this with another :

A daily beauty in his life.

For it is just such a daily beauty, such an ordered and dynamic
peace, that they both sought and found in the life of the Church.
And whether we choose to regard it as a sign of strength or weakness, it is certain that no Churchmanship was ever less dogmatic
in its spirit than the High Anglicanism of the Laudian ascendency.

There was nothing so fateful in Charles's whole career, as his
choice of Laud as the chief instrument of his spiritual, and
indeed of a good deal of his temporal, policy. And yet that choice
was one that he could hardly have avoided, for—to use a modern
expression that exactly hits off the case—the little man was so
obviously the live wire among his ecclesiastics. At a time of such

crisis as that through which the Church of England was passing, one in which her very existence was threatened, she had need of the most energetic and resourceful leadership—and where else was this to be found in the upper ranks of the clergy ? There were learned and devout men in abundance, but they were none of them conspicuous for that quality of forcefulness, that capacity for getting things done, that was Laud's especial characteristic. There are times when the only way of saving a situation is to put the best fighting man in command, regardless of any other consideration, and in this sense it may be said that the choice of Laud was forced upon the King.

He was already, for those days, well advanced in life when Charles came to the throne—he had been just on fifteen at the time of the Armada, an Oxford don six years later, and President of his College, St John's, at the age of thirty-seven. Ten years later still he had become a Bishop, and Charles promoted him in quick succession from his see of St David's to those of Bath and Wells, and London. Here he was in the forefront of the battle against encroaching Puritanism. He was already the most powerful person in the Church, since Archbishop Abbot was not only under a cloud, but too manifestly breaking up to be capable of making himself felt. It was therefore hardly more than a confirmation of Laud's primacy, when, on Abbot's death in 1633, he changed his quarters from Fulham to Lambeth Palace, and entered upon the full powers of the metropolitan see.

There is no one, except Buckingham, who played a more decisive part in the tragedy of King Charles, and no one whose personality has been more grotesquely misunderstood. To the Whig historians of the nineteenth century he was an impossibly odious personage—the most merciful version of him being Macaulay's "ridiculous old bigot". On the other hand, when the Oxford Movement started a High Church revival, Laud was the obvious, and in fact the only possible candidate for the post of its proto-martyr, and was run for all he was worth in the assumption that his Churchmanship was high in the modern sense.

We shall have to clear our minds of both these conceptions— too wide of the mark to merit even the name of caricatures—if we want to become acquainted with the very human little don who rose from his President's stall to the Chair of St Augustine, and whose last pulpit was the scaffold on Tower Hill. We shall, I think, best visualize him, as all his contemporaries seem to have done, as "little Laud." That physical insignificance was the most significant thing about him. I remember that great inventor, Louis Brennan, propounding the theory that human beings are like bridges, the purely physical strain on them being increased in proportion to the square of their length, with the result that a long man has to expend a much greater proportion of his energy than a short one on the mere business of keeping himself standing. That would certainly explain why the average little man possesses so conspicuously greater an overplus of energy than the average big one. And it would go a long way towards explaining Laud.

He was as highly charged with energy as an atom. In his portraits, there is something birdlike about his appearance, and I cannot help thinking the impression would have been reinforced by his manner—one imagines something of the bird's quick, darting movements, its perpetual restlessness. He was enormously observant and interested in everything that went on around him, however trivial or seemingly irrelevant. His diary, or rather the book of occasional jottings that he noted down from time to time, is full of instances of this trait. He was a keen observer of nature, long before such observation had become fashionable—he notes in one place how the leaves on the elms have lasted into December; in another how two robins have flown into his room, seeming to chase each other. His High Church admirers have tried to read a mystical significance into these entries, but it is fairly obvious that Laud sets down such things—just as Virginia Woolf did in her novels—not because they signify anything, but because everything that catches one's attention does happen to be so very interesting.

This perpetual curiosity extended as far as that fantastic and elusive world of dreams. Even after he had become an Archbishop, Laud was in the habit of noting down any particularly vivid dream in his diary ; not because he attached any ulterior significance to such things—he more than once expressly denies this—but because even dreams were not too trivial to interest him. And this, from the standpoint of the modern psychologist, makes the diary of unique interest. For it is the one instance in which an historical character of any note has presented us with this key to the hidden places of his mind.

It does not need any great subtlety of interpretation to perceive that nearly all Laud's dreams are different variations of the same type, that of the anxiety dream. He is always having that mild form of nightmare in which everything goes wrong ; sometimes it is the crude physical form in which the teeth fall out, at others it is that people he has come to see are riding away or disappearing ; that he cannot find the book with which he is to officiate at service ; that the King is mysteriously displeased with him ; that the King rebukes him for serving him wine in a silver instead of a glass cup ; that he finds to his dismay that he has been reconciled to Rome, and that when he goes to seek pardon from the Church of England, a priest intercepts him. You can see that not even in sleep does he cease to bother about this, that, or the other thing ; and that all his deep and sincere devotion has never brought him that crowning solace of the religious mind, the blessing of peace.

Such a temperament is the reverse of mystical. Its excess of energy is always feverishly seeking an outlet, even the smallest, in action. It is fortunate indeed that Laud was never married, for he must have been one of those maddeningly tidy people to whom it is agony to see the least thing out of place or time, and who cannot rest till they have put it to rights. He could never have appreciated the element of worldly wisdom in Lord Melbourne's constant query—that might equally have been Weston's —"why can't they leave it alone ?" For this fussy, anxious little man, with his great heart and overflowing energy, could never endure to leave anything alone.

Those who attribute to Laud some deeply thought out system of Anglican doctrine, are using the looking-glass in the light of a window. There was never a man whose mind less ran to theory, or whose temperament was more furiously practical. His motto for all occasions might well have been, "cut the cackle and get to business". His sermons, except perhaps his last, when he had the business of dying to perform, must—if we are to judge by the few that have been preserved—have been pretty heavy going even for a Caroline congregation. His most considerable excursion in theology was his controversy with the Jesuit Fisher—good, straightforward, slogging work, addressed to the very practical purpose of demolishing his opponent's points, great and small, one after the other, in order to keep Rome from capturing so important a convert as old Lady Buckingham. The most attractive of all his writings is the little manual of practical devotion that he kept for his own private use.

To talk of Laud as a bigot is not so much uncharitable as inept. He dealt with the Church as he would have dealt with any other concern entrusted to his charge, and as, indeed, he did deal with the many matters of purely temporal policy that fell within the scope of his activities. As a military commander he would have been equally a stickler for exact staff work, and for the most meticulous parade-ground smartness ; as a Churchman he was the same. The beauty of holiness that he sought was before all things an orderly beauty, with the edifice cleansed and spotless from floor to roof, and the organization working with the smoothness of perfectly adjusted machinery. As long as there was one clank or loose joint anywhere, he could not rest till he had put it right. It was not a matter of dogma but of temperament. And it was because his opponents were in very truth dogmatists, and cared for dogma more than order, and more than beauty, that it proved so tragically impossible for Laud to understand them, or they him.

For the Puritans there was but one thing that mattered, and that was to push their main idea to its logical conclusion—or perhaps we should say the complex of ideas that underlay the Reformation. Rome, to them, represented a vast organization interposed between the individual Christian and the salvation that is in Christ. To be saved by the blood and grace of Christ without any human agency, not even that of the believer's own works or will—that was the supreme and only end, to which everything else was well sacrificed. But its uncompromising pursuit was already opening up new and alarming vistas. It seemed that the freedom of the sons of God was incompatible with that of the human will ; as if the crucifixion of the old Adam would involve that of all the adornments and joys with which his life had been enriched ; and, most obviously of all, the scrapping of the last vestige of the old ecclesiastical organization inherited from Rome, and of all the appertaining forms and aids of worship —everything, in short, that to Laud, constituted the beauty of holiness.

The logical "all or nothing" of the Reformation idea might, if pursued to the end, involve still more startling conclusions— perhaps the scrapping of the Bible, perhaps that of the Saviour Himself, and even of God. The men were already alive who would advance to the most extreme of these conclusions—but that time was not yet.

It would be interesting if some historian could give a precise answer to the question why, at this particular period of its history, the English people, or the most powerful section of it, should so far have departed from its otherwise habitually compromising mentality, as to lust after pushing the Reformation or any other idea to its logical extreme ; why it should have been possessed by this sudden passion for consistency, regardless of humour, commonsense, or any other of its usually dominant considerations. It is enough for our present purpose to record that, most unfortunately for Charles and Laud, this unprecedented and never-to-be-repeated phenomenon did occur in their time.

Laud's reaction to it was at any rate typically English, and he had the thorough sympathy of the King. These interminable arguments and doctrinal speculations struck him in no other light than of an unmitigated nuisance. They led nowhere ; their only effect was to breed anarchy, and to hold up all fruitful labour in Christ's vineyard. One of Laud's correspondents, a certain Dr Brooke, hit it off when he wrote,

"Predestination is the root of Puritanism, and Puritanism the root of all rebellion and disobedient intractableness, and all schism and sauciness in the country, nay, in the Church itself."*

The action that Laud urged upon the King, and to which the King needed no urging, was exactly the opposite of that which would have occurred either to a doctrinal bigot or a High Church father. It was simply to closure the debate. One of the first results of his influence as Bishop of London, was the issue, in 1628, of a Royal Proclamation enjoining "that all further curious search be laid aside, and these disputes shut up in God's promises, as they be generally set forth to us in the holy Scriptures, and the general meaning of the Articles of the Church of England according to them." This, which was merely an amplification of another Proclamation issued by Charles two years previously, laid down the line of policy that he and Laud were to pursue as long as they retained power. It was to muzzle all parties to the Calvinist-Arminian dog fight, and to get on with the really urgent business of reforming not the doctrine, but the practice of the Church.

* The 15th of December, 1630. Quoted by Rev. W. H. Hutton in *The English Church* (1645-1714), p. 34.

9

A CHURCH IN ORDER

THOSE who visualize the King and Laud as overbearing bullies, imposing a more than half-Romish tyranny over a simple Protestant folk with no other desire than to worship in peace, are seeing things upside down. Laud, as I have tried to show, was a fighting man put in command in order to save a situation already well-nigh desperate. The terrific aggressive strength of Puritanism already plainly threatened to overwhelm the Church of England, and extinguish for ever that beauty of holiness that it was its special mission to foster. The position had not yet been actually pierced, but its strongest points were undermined, and there was disloyalty among the defenders.

Laud's task was twofold. The first was to repulse attack ; the second, and more exacting, was to make the Anglican system impervious to attack. He was pitting the beauty of holiness against the logic of Calvinism—a contest that too much resembled that of a china vase and a steel bar. But he would at least make that beauty as beautiful as he knew how ; he would render the Church that he and his King loved so dearly, too manifestly lovable for any man to have the heart to destroy her.

It does not fall within our province to follow in detail the work that this indefatigably energetic little man undertook in pursuit of his ideal. It might, perhaps, best be described as a tremendous tidying up. For Laud found a state of things existing that was not only incredibly shocking to his orderly mind, but that would be calculated to horrify even the plainest and sternest Evangelical of our own day. All over the country there was a lack of reverence and seemliness, an ecclesiastical slackness and anarchy, that would seem hard to justify on any sane theory of Church government.

No use seemed too base or too sacrilegious for God's House or its furniture. The visitations that Laud had made in every diocese under his control, disclosed a shocking state of affairs. The parson at Stratford-on-Avon had to be suspended for letting his poultry roost and his hogs lodge in the chancel where Shakespeare lay buried. In Staffordshire, it was reported, churches were turned into barns, "or worse." In all parts of the country Communion tables were put un-railed in the middle of churches, and were used for any purpose that happened to suit human, or canine, convenience. There is even one instance on record in which the consecrated loaf was snatched off the table by a dog, and presently retrieved by the congregation—though the parson, one is happy to add, drew the line at celebrating with it.

The case of London's Cathedral, the old Gothic St Paul's—one that particularly moved Laud's indignation—is only typical of the sort of thing with which he had to cope. As if no one had ever read of Christ's proceedings in the Temple, not only the precincts but the interior of the consecrated edifice served, in the most literal sense, both as a house of merchandise and a den of thieves. The magnificent Norman nave was converted into a bazaar or forum, to which the whole city resorted for the trans-action of business or gossip. The arcade contained shops or booths. The worst characters in town haunted it, and fixed up their nefarious designs there. Children used it for a playground. So great was the noise that it made the services inaudible. It was part of Laud's and Charles's tyranny that they insisted on putting a stop to this freedom. It is true that they did not resort to the whip of small cords, and that they went to a good deal of expense in restoring the West front so as to provide alternative accommo-dation. It was not their fault that the greatest architect of the day, Inigo Jones, to whom the work was entrusted, disfigured the building with so grotesquely incongruous a sham classical façade, that the pictures we have of it make one almost thankful for the Great Fire.

It was not only neglect that needed to be combated. Any beauty of ornament or seemliness of ritual was branded with the stigma of idolatry, was pointed at as the thin end of the Roman wedge. "This," said Laud, "is the misery. 'Tis superstition nowadays for any man to come with more reverence into a church, than a tinker and his bitch into an ale-house." Even to bow at the name of Jesus was denounced as un-Christian. The fact that Laud had used some harmless ceremonial at the dedication of the new Church of St Catherine Cree, was treasured up against him as one of the offences for which he was to be adjudged worthy of death. From this it was no far cry to active vandalism. There were zealots who objected to the use of any sort of church music ; organs were an abomination before the Lord—one Puritanical judge described their music as "whistling at service". As for vestments—these went without saying !

There was an increasing type of Puritan mentality, or perhaps we should say Puritan logic, that would never be satisfied till it had stripped its places of worship as bare as barns, and the worship itself to the purity of a skeleton. There can be no disputing the sincerity of those who took this standpoint, nor the fact that, if their premises were once granted, their conclusions could hardly be resisted. But these premises, and this standpoint, were unintelligible to Charles and Laud. They lived in a different world, a world in which beauty and joy were desirable things in themselves, and where the service of God was worthy of an outward and visible adornment expressive of its inward and spiritual beauty.

If they lost, or seemed to lose, the fight they were making for their ideal, no one can deny the energy and the ability with which, during the sixteen-thirties, that fight—against steadily mounting odds—was conducted. Some of the results of it are before us to-day, and are available for such as care to study those most priceless of all historical records, constituted by the parish churches of England. What the Middle Ages are for church architecture, it may fairly be said that the Laudian decade is for church furniture. In spite of the reckless destruction wreaked by the saints, in the hour of their triumph, upon the external adornments that to them were sinful idolatry, there is enough surviving to this day in the shape of beautifully enriched pulpits, pews, lecterns, organs, Communion tables, to show how loyal and generous a response some, at least, of the parishioners must have made to the episcopal lead.

But it was not only, or even principally, in the matter of external adornments that Laud made his influence felt. There seems to be no doubt that a far higher standard was set among the clergy as the result of the parochial visitation that he caused to be made in every see of his Province of Canterbury ; and the same was done for York by Archbishop Neile. As Laud's biographer, Heylin, puts it—and there seems no reason for disputing his estimate,

"We shall find the prelates generally more intent upon the work committed to them ... the clergy more obedient to the commands of their ordinaries, joining together to advance the work of uniformity recommended to them, the liturgy more punctually rendered in all the parts and offices of it ; the Word more diligently preached, the sacraments more reverently administered than in scores of years before. ..."*

* Heylin's *Life of William Laud*, p. 217.

JOHN HAMPDEN—*from a portrait in the collection of the Earl of St Germans at Port Eliot*

THE THREE HEADS OF CHARLES I—*from a print of the painting by Van Dyck at Windsor, by kind permission of His Majesty the King*

How then, with the Church so flourishing and so ably administered as it was under Laud's auspices, are we to account for the fact that neither he, nor his fellow Bishops, were able to count on enough popular support to save them from being overwhelmed, when the dykes were at last broken, and the Puritan revolution came flooding in ?

Most of all, no doubt, because a revolutionary ideology, working itself to its logical conclusion, is the most powerful of all those spiritual forces of which history is the product. It is like a fever, that is bound to rise to a climax of heat and delirium before it can work itself out of the system. Charles and Laud, standing as they did for a compromise, equally unwilling to go back to Rome or on to Geneva, had as difficult a task as Canute, commanding the tide to stop. High water mark would be reached, and the waves cover them ; but it might be, when these had receded, that the throne and archiepiscopal chair would again be left high and dry, without substantial injury.

On this reading of the situation, it would seem inconceivable that the utmost tact or wisdom could have saved such a Church as Laud wished to preserve. But it must also be admitted that Laud was more the sort of man to provoke than to conciliate opposition. Tact was a quality that did not enter into his composition. He had all the nervous irritability of a little, bustling man who can never find sufficient outlet for his energy—and there is nothing in the world so irritating as irritability.

Old King James, who had possessed a practical shrewdness in judging men that his son lacked, had seen the danger in Laud :

"The plain truth is," he had told the then Lord Keeper Williams, "I keep Laud back from all place of rule and authority because I find he hath a restless spirit, and cannot see when matters are well, but loves to toss and change, and to bring things to a pitch of reformation floating in his own brain, which may endanger the steadfastness of that which, God be praised, is at a good pass."

It was just what Charles's more simple nature could never be got to see ; that ability and reforming zeal may become a positive danger when they are applied in and out of season, regardless of every other consideration. Men have a tempo of their own out of which it is impossible to hustle them. Laud, like Charles, possessed that dangerous single-heartedness which, when it sees a thing to be right, drives straight ahead, regardless of every other consideration. And, unlike Charles, he did so in a manner that was always brusque and sometimes bordered on the offensive.

The peppery little Archbishop, who was really one of the kindest and humblest of men, was certainly innocent of the wish to offend, and pathetically unconscious of doing so. But he was always something of a fish out of water in the aristocratic society of the Court—he was the son of a Reading clothier and had been a pupil at the free school there, before going with a scholarship to Oxford—and it was the most penetrating thing said about him that the greatest want he had was that of a true friend.

This was the opinion of the profoundest of all contemporary students of character, known to us as Clarendon, but then Edward Hyde, a rising young barrister in whom His Grace of Canterbury took the same sort of benevolent interest that he must formerly have done in many a promising undergraduate of his college. It says a great deal for both men, that one evening the younger ventured to approach the elder, when he was walking in his garden at Lambeth, and to tell him, with what must have been heroic frankness, how unpopular he was making himself in the country at large, and how he contrived to aggravate this by the way in which he was constantly wounding the amour propre of people who came to see him—a case in point being a snub he was recently supposed to have administered to a couple of gentlemen who had come up from Wiltshire on some business or other.

Instead of exploding, the Archbishop listened to this recital with the most patient attention, and discussed it point by point.

"I am very unfortunate," he said, "to be so ill understood. I meant very well."

He did indeed remember that when the two gentlemen in question had interrupted him in the middle of some important State business, he had cut short a ceremonious preamble by telling them that he had no time for compliments—and how every busy man must sympathize with him ! Finally when young Hyde stuck to his point, Laud answered, smiling, that "he could only undertake for his heart ... that he could not undertake that sometimes he would not speak more hastily and sharply than he should do (which oftentimes he was sorry for and reprehended himself for) and in a tune that might be liable to misinterpretation with them who were not very well acquainted with him, and so knew that it was an infirmity, which his nature and education had so rooted in him that it was vain to contend with it."

This is not the language of a ridiculous old bigot or of an austere fanatic, but of a singularly lovable nature whose faults are on the surface. If Laud had continued all his life at the head of his college, his little eccentricities would have earned him no more than a tolerant affection. But now that he was in a position of the highest power and responsibility, championing a losing cause against bitter and rising opposition, he was certain of having the worst possible interpretation put on every failure of his in patience or courtesy, by the real bigots whose most formidable adversary he was. And these men had resources of propaganda at their disposal that enabled them to work up a legitimate irritation into a complex of hatred and calumny, that even to this day has not been wholly dissipated.

IO

STAR CHAMBER

THERE were more serious counts in the indictment that was being worked up against both Charles and Laud. We must never lose sight of the fact that during these years of personal government, they were faced with the constant threat of revolution, a threat that had become open and undisguised with those three resolutions of Eliot's. It was practically certain that any fresh Parliament that came together would soon be committed by its leaders to the overthrow of the existing order in Church and State ; and even while Parliament remained in suspense, the revolutionary forces were actively at work beneath the surface.

There was a ceaseless battle going on of propaganda and counter-propaganda. Officially the supreme control of propaganda was vested in the Church. Her very buildings, her ornament and music and ritual, had from time immemorial served as what, in the latest psychological jargon, might have been described as a vast organized means of conditioning the habitual reactions of worshippers ; and that these should be universally applied, was provided for by the law enforcing attendance at Church, under pain of a fine, upon all the King's subjects. What, under Protestant auspices, had provided the most fruitful of all such opportunities, was the pulpit, for there was no surer accompaniment of the Protestant mentality than a susceptibility to sermonizing.

That is the reason that one of Laud's first moves was to tighten up the episcopal control of the pulpit, by supressing the so called lectureships, or delivery of sermons by laymen appointed and financed by well-to-do individuals, or even corporations. Not a few of these preachers openly rejected the Church's doctrine and discipline, and used her pulpits, more or less openly, as platforms for counter-propaganda against her. Charles, it need hardly be said, gave his hearty support to his Archbishop in the suppression of this nuisance—as ·it not unnaturally appeared to him. "I cannot," he minuted, "hold fit that any lay person or corporation whatsoever should have the power that these men would have to themselves."

But there was developing a new means of propaganda more powerful even than the pulpit. It was now some 180 years since Gutenberg had set up the first printing press, but it was only gradually that the application of this discovery to the art of mass suggestion had been developed. It was necessary, for really effective work, that tendencious matter should be produced cheaply and in sufficient quantities, and the way had already been indicated in Elizabeth's reign by that famous series of tracts, attacking the Bishops, over the signature of Martin Marprelate. During Charles's reign the output of pamphlets reached unprecedented dimensions, and it was a form of insidious attack extremely difficult to combat with the rudimentary machinery of coercion at the disposal of Church and State.

With the heavier artillery of books it was easier to deal. A decree of Star Chamber had committed the licensing of these to the two Archbishops and the Bishop of London, just as in our own day that of plays is entrusted to a court official. The idea of uncontrolled printing was no more entertained in the England of Charles I, than it is in most parts of the Continent to-day, or than the freedom of stage or screen is even in modern England. And neither in England nor anywhere else has toleration yet been accorded to the printing of open sedition.

The attempts of constituted authority to defend itself against the dissemination of revolutionary propaganda, led to certain notorious offenders being tried and sentenced by the Court of Star Chamber—which in modern terms would be roughly equivalent to a trial by the Cabinet.

The very name of this tribunal has become such a byword for arbitrary tyranny that it is seldom nowadays that any alleged abuse of official power fails to be denounced as "Star Chamber methods". So that it may not be out of place to indicate what Star Chamber actually signified to Englishmen of the sixteenth and early seventeenth centuries.

Its origins are lost in antiquity, but it had been formally constituted by an Act of Parliament in the 3rd year of Henry VII. When that Monarch had picked up the crown out of a bush on Bosworth Field, the memories of all but the oldest people were filled by a time of miserable chaos, in which the law of the land could be defied and overridden with impunity by the petty tyrants who, while they kept the country in a state of chronic civil war, were at least agreed among themselves in an open conspiracy to oppress and exploit those weaker and poorer members of the community whom the King's peace was no longer able to protect. For that chaos it was the object and achievement of the House of Tudor to substitute the reign of law, and the Star Chamber provided them with the necessary means for making the law respected, and no respecter of persons.

It was no constitutional innovation, but simply amounted to drawing on the reserves of judicial power that had always been inherent in the office of the Crown ; and the setting up, beside those already in existence, of a court of law of such strength and authority as—in the words of the great Tudor exponent of the Constitution, Sir Thomas Smith—

"To bridle such stout nobleman or gentleman who would offer wrong by force to any manner of men and cannot be content to demand and defend the right by order of the law."

At a time when judges on circuit could not, even if they would, put the fear of the law into magnates against whom no juryman dared, for the life of him, bring an adverse verdict, the one tribunal that could do the business had to consist of a picked body of the King's ministers, or—to take the nearest modern equivalent —a committee of the Cabinet, armed with summary powers, and capable of bringing the King's justice direct from the source, to bear without fear or favour on the greatest subject in the land. For in the ideal of monarchy upheld by the Tudors, and which the Stuarts had inherited from them, the King, or Kin Man, was in the fullest sense representative of his great family, the people ; and it was his business to see that the humblest subject in his realm could, in the people's English, have the law on the greatest.

This service Star Chamber had performed faithfully, and on

the whole, successfully ; and its work had been supplemented by district cabinets, as we might call them, for the Northern counties and Wales, those parts of the country where civilization was most backward,* and consequently the law was most easily set at defiance by great and powerful subjects like that very typical specimen, Lord Savile, who had once been bound over on account of his having compelled, by holding a naked dagger to his breast, the trustee for some land that he coveted, to sign a deed making it away. Such Patriots were never weary of denouncing the tyranny of these courts, and with what good reason, from their own standpoint, will best be realized if we take the trouble to dive into the records and see one or two everyday instances of Star Chamber methods in action.

The case, for instance, of one Best, a pauper, from whose cottage, wherein he dwelt with his wife, children, and mother, a certain Mr Neale, acting in concert with one Winter, a knight, and others, desired to evict him ; and—so runs the record :

"Knowing of no other way to get the possession but by starving them out, did to that end take away a woman's horse, as she was going with food to them, and turned her back again on foot, and threatened her with what violence he would use her, if she ever came to bring them any more food or sustenance ; and by this means the plaintiff's mother being fourscore years old, was starved for want of food, the neighbours not daring to come and relieve them for fear of Neale ; and Neale with others in his company came to the house and with an axe or hatchet did riotously cut down the doors of the house, the plaintiff's wife and children being therein, carried away the doors, and reviled his wife and children ; and another time, with others in his company, did riotously, being armed with a bill, throw and beat off part of the tiles of the house ..."

For which proceedings the pauper, Best, applied for redress to His Majesty's court of Star Chamber, which, with its accustomed high-handedness, not only proceeded to commit the energetic Mr Neale, but also to fine him to the tune of £500.

Or—if I may be pardoned for holding up the narrative to show the sort of thing that King Charles's tyranny was really up against—take the case of Susan Boyes and Grace Tubby, whom

---

* It is significant that these very districts that had been subjected to the "Tyranny" of the prerogative courts were those in which the King, during the Civil War, had the most devoted support of the common people.

two Justices of the Peace, Sir Thomas Jenkinson and Sir John Rouse, caused to be brought before them on a faked up charge of making faces at Mr Guthery, a preacher, at sermon time ; and on this bare information, without oath, caused them to be sent to the house of correction and so cruelly whipped that both were sick and Grace Tubby in danger of death : nor had the amiable Sir Thomas done with them even then, for in order to stop their complaint from being considered at the next quarter sessions, he "falsely and maliciously informed the Justices that the said Susan and Grace continued in their bold courses and after their whipping drank a health to him and Sir John Rouse ... and by this means got the Justice not only to forbear to examine the witnesses, but to make an order to commit them again to the house of correction."

Which would doubtless have ended the matter, had not Star Chamber methods been applied to Sir Thomas and Sir John, who were committed and fined 200 marks apiece, with an additional £20 from Sir Thomas for misleading his fellow-Justices, and £50 damages apiece to Susan and Grace, which one of them—and I am afraid it must have been poor Grace Tubby—died before she could receive.

It is this sort of case that was the routine work of these so-called prerogative courts, whose function might have truly been described to "keep the simple folk in their right, defend the children of the poor, and punish the wrong doer". Any one who cares to test this statement for himself has only to go to the London Library, or some similar institution, and turn up the third volume of Rushworth's Historical Collections, where he will find a long appendix of Star Chamber records, from almost any one of whose 75 folio pages he will be able to extract one or more similar examples of Star Chamber tyranny : a singularly mild tyranny when one considers, perhaps with some slight regret, that the like of My Lord Savile and Sir Thomas Jenkinson were seldom touched in any more sensitive spot than their already bulging pockets.

It is only fair to say that there is a sprinkling of other cases. There is the martyrdom, for instance, of a certain Sir Henry Sherfield, a Puritan lawyer of Salisbury, who, being "troubled in conscience and grieved with the sight of the pictures which were in St Edmond's Church", one of which pictures, "to his understanding", represented God creating the world, contrived to lock himself into the church, climb on a pew, and with his stick set about the window in such fashion that by the time he had done it presented the spectacle of creation in ruins, though he himself, in the violence of his zeal, toppled off the pew backwards. And for this feat, an unsympathetic Star Chamber, instead of canonizing him, required him to stump up the substantial fine of £500. It is even held up against Archbishop Laud that he had so little charity for these methods of Church reform as to have been party to running up the bill—a bill, however, that at Sherfield's death, a year later, was still unpaid.

But what is remembered against Star Chamber to-day, when its intervention on behalf of the innumerable pauper Bests, Grace Tubbys, and their like, has long been forgotten, are two or three sensational cases in which it had to deal with prosperous middle class and professional people who were engaged in openly seditious propaganda, and even incitement to rebellion and murder in a time of extreme public tension. That such cases were dealt with by Star Chamber at all, a court that had no power to inflict the death penalty, is proof of the extraordinary unwillingness of King Charles's government to push matters to extremities that on the Continent would probably not have stopped short of the wheel, or at home with the Tudors, of the quartering block. That the sentences included physical mutilations rightly shocking to our modern notions, is the fault of the tough nerves and rough justice of the time. Whippings and ear-croppings shocked no one when they were inflicted on poor delinquents all over the country for offences incomparably less heinous.

The victims whose sentences aroused so much indignation could have been counted, during a period of eleven years, literally on the fingers of one hand. Their offences were so deliberate and aggravated as to amount to a declaration of war on the existing order of society.

Take the first of them, Alexander Leighton, a Scottish doctor. He had written and circulated a book, which he had printed in Holland to evade the censorship, and of which the two Lords Chief Justices present in Star Chamber remarked that they would, without scruple, have proceeded against the author on a charge of treason. It set out to be an attack on the bishops, scurrilous and violent even for that age of unmeasured abuse, and exhorting all and sundry to "smite them under the fifth rib". But it went beyond even this. It glorified the murder of Buckingham—and that just after it had been committed. It railed at the Queen, calling her a daughter of Heth. Finally, it contained an unmistakable incitement to the anti-episcopal faction to rise and mutiny, sword in hand.

Even to-day, and in tolerant England, such a book would earn for its author a stiff sentence of imprisonment—on the greater part of the Continent it would cost him his life. Had the authorities chosen to make it a case of treason, Leighton would probably have died very painfully. Severe as it was, his sentence of fine, imprisonment, and two separate ear-croppings, nose-slittings, whippings and brandings, was the least that under the circumstances he could have expected, especially as it seems possible that he might have been let off the whole—instead of, as he actually was, half—of the physical part, had he not made a sensational escape from prison.

The second martyr was a lawyer of immense erudition, called Prynne, the state of whose mind would form an interesting study for a psycho-analyst. This man had published an enormous treatise called *Histrio-Mastix, The Players' Scourge or Actor's Tragedy*, which must surely rank among the world's masterpieces of unconscious humour, though contemporaries took it seriously enough. It is an almost interminable frothing denunciation, in which vast armies of fathers, divines, philosophers, historians, poets, emperors, princes and magistrates, not to speak of councils, codes, and constitutions, are cited to prove "that popular stage plays (the very pomps of the Devil that we renounce in baptism ...) are sinful, heathenish, lewd, ungodly spectacles, and most pernicious corruptions, condemned in all ages", and so on in the same strain, in smaller and smaller type, as the unfortunate printer strives to jam it all on to one title page.

Something of the state of Mr Prynne's mind may be gleaned from the entry, *Women*, in the index (which I have here somewhat abridged) :

"Skill in dancing no good sign of their honesty ; ought not to learn nor to train up their children to dance ; ought not to frizzle or cut their hair, to wear false hair, to paint their faces or to wear garish, lascivious attire ; ought to be stayers at home, not gadders abroad ; ought not to resort to plays or play-houses, which either find or quickly make them whores ; see *Whores*."

Prynne's book was less openly and obviously seditious than Leighton's, but it may well be that it was part of an even deadlier offensive. For Leighton was only attacking the outward and visible forms of government, while Prynne, and other fanatical kill-joys of that kidney, were aiming at all the colour and joy and zest of life that are comprehended in the term *Merrie England,* all that we associate with the world of Shakespeare and Chaucer, of Jack-in-the-Green and Robin Hood. Hunting, Christmas-keeping, bonfires, maypoles, almost every sort of innocent enjoyment, was sinful ; but not the major sins of spiritual pride, of implacable vindictiveness and conscientious denial of charity. Even laughter was not spared—under that index heading we read :

"This life no time of laughter but of tears."

And, he might have added, of godly, righteous and sober toil, for most of its livers, to the maximum profit of those energetic organizers of commerce and industry who were the backbone of the Puritan cause.

What brought Prynne within the reach of the law and cost him his ears was the insinuation—obvious to every one of his readers—that the King, who was known to take a delight in the stage, was Nero, and poor Henriette, who loved acting in masques, and was actually preparing to do so when the book was published, fell in the category of "women actors—notorious whores".

But the docking of Prynne's ears did not stop his pen. This was due to the fact that the kind-hearted Archbishop intervened against the proposal of the Attorney-General to deprive a scholar of the use of pen, ink, and paper, as well as the privilege of Church attendance.

"He hath undergone a heavy punishment," he said, "I am heartily sorry for him. ... I confess I do not know what it is to be close prisoner, and to want pens, books, ink and company."

He would know soon enough, poor old man !

And Mr Prynne, who in the hour of his own power was to take a fiendish revenge by rifling and garbling the Archbishop's most intimate papers, is reported to have said, "with a low voice, 'I humbly thank your Grace'."

So that Prynne was enabled to devote his enforced leisure in the Tower to seditious pamphleteering, driving his pen from morning to night, wearing a long, quilted cap like an umbrella to shade his eyes, and kept going by constant draughts of ale, a form of indulgence that for some reason he does not appear to have thought sinful. It is no wonder that four years after his first sentence, he was again before Star Chamber, this time in company with two other less erudite but equally violent and even more scurrilous pamphleteers, called Bastwick and Burton. The result was another ear-cropping exhibition, followed by imprisonment that the Government at last tried to make an effective silencer, by isolating the culprits in different island strongholds.

We may add that Prynne himself lived to have enough experience of triumphant Puritanism to turn him into one of the most uncompromising and—as might have been guessed—sternly intolerant royalists of the Restoration. If, he volunteered in his old age, "the King had cut off my head when he only cropped my ears, he had done no more than justice, and had done God and the nation good service."

The last of this group of victims, the so-called "free-born" John Lilburne, who started a career of life-long opposition to every sort of constituted authority, by the circulation of unlicensed literature and the defiance of Star Chamber, and who was consequently sentenced to whipping and imprisonment, also lived to testify, in the year of the King's execution, that "I had rather choose to live seven years under old King Charles's Government (notwithstanding their beheading him as a tyrant for it) when it was at its worst before this Parliament, than live one year under the Government that now rule."

The idea that either the King or Laud—who is sometimes treated as if he and not Star Chamber had been responsible for the sentences—were acting the part of brutal tyrants, is manifestly absurd. No Government can afford to remain passive in face of openly seditious propaganda, and one is less struck by the harshness than the helplessness of an administration that could allow a man like Prynne to use his cell in the Tower as an office for the continued output of the very propaganda for which he was imprisoned.

But what does strike one about these attempts to make a public example of the leading offenders, is their extreme unwisdom. They were merely conferring on the victims a publicity of which they knew well how to take advantage. For these men were one and all perfectly fearless, and as far as anybody can be said to enjoy so unpleasant a physical experience as that of playing the leading part in a martyrdom before sympathetic crowds—they rejoiced greatly in so ideal an advertisement. Leighton improved the occasion with the aid of his wife, by turning his sufferings into a passion play, applying to himself the prophecies usually appropriated to Christ, and informing the people that he was suffering for their sins. Prynne continued to display his inexhaustible erudition by spouting precedents from the pillory. Bastwick who, amongst other activities of a rolling stone, had included doctoring, added a human touch to the proceedings by supervising the operation on his own ears. As for the irrepressible Lilburne, flogging only stimulated him, and not only did he continue to insult and denounce the Star Chamber in the pillory, but he actually managed to produce from somewhere on his person a sheaf of Bastwick's condemned pamphlets, which he presented to the crowd. Even when the scandalized tribunal sent orders to have him gagged, he continued to demonstrate to his no doubt delighted audience by vigorous and defiant stamping.

No real tyranny would ever have displayed such helpless amateurishness in his own defence. They know better how to do those things nowadays, when tyranny has become scientific, and anyone who is even suspected of disaffection to the reigning authority is quietly spirited off to be beaten up in the decent privacy of a concentration camp, or worked to death in an Arctic timber forest, without the least chance of getting either sympathy or a hearing.

The Puritans themselves, when their time came, had a more workmanlike way of countering opposition. Time and again, in dealing with anyone likely to be dangerous to them, they acted—with or without the law—on the motto, "Stone dead hath no fellow", though the "tyrant" to whom this principle was at last applied, never once had anyone put to death for a political offence.

As for torture, it may be worth while to compare any one of these sentences of Star Chamber on really dangerous agitators, with that passed by one of Cromwell's Houses of Commons, and executed in full, on the Quaker James Nayler, whom nobody imagined to be in any way dangerous, but who had, like Leighton, allowed himself to play the part of Christ in a rather hysterical pantomime. The programme was to start with his being pilloried for two hours in New Palace Yard and then flogged at the cart's tail the whole way, that can hardly have taken much less than an hour, to the Exchange. Two days later (extended in the event to nine) he was again to stand in the pillory for two hours, and then have his tongue bored through and his forehead seared with red hot iron. The entertainment was next to be transferred to Bristol, where, after being ridden through the city with his face to the horse's tail, he was to be whipped through it. After that he was to be kept in solitary confinement, without pen or ink, and only allowed such food as he could earn by the labour of his own hands under such conditions. He went through it all—and survived.

Or we may perhaps remember that the Commons of the Long Parliament were only with difficulty and at the last moment persuaded to allow the aged Archbishop to be done to death mercifully, instead of being half choked, castrated, disembowelled alive, and quartered, according to the original, and illegal, sentence.

We can then afford to rate at its proper value the sob stuff that even to this day is turned out about the victims of royal and archiepiscopal tyranny. But the fact that even to this day it should continue to flow, is one of the utmost historical significance. For there could be no surer measure of the failure of Charles's Government to deal with the forces that were undermining it. Instead of suppressing revolutionary propaganda, it had provided it free. It had allowed two or three fanatical demagogues, on the borderline of sanity, to invest themselves with all the dignity of martyrdom. It had provided them with a platform on which they could perform their parts in the sight of the whole nation. It had managed matters so that even when they were sent in custody to their distant places of imprisonment, their progress through the country had been marked by scenes of wild enthusiasm, such as would never have greeted that of the King.

If it were indeed true that nothing is either good or bad but thinking makes it so, then indeed there would be a case for writing down Charles a tyrant and Laud a persecuting, and Romanizing, bigot. For this was the suggestion that was beginning to be stamped on the mass consciousness of the nation, so deeply that a dozen generations have not sufficed to obliterate it.

A competent tyrant, brought up in the school of Machiavelli's *Prince*, would have understood better the art of suppressing propaganda, and would never have made the mistake of giving his victims the chance either to express or advertise themselves. To cut off ink in a dungeon would have been more effective than cutting off ears on a platform.

But it may be added that if Laud's character had been, what Newman calls it, "of a stature akin to the elder days of the

Church", he might have combated the opposition by applying the principles of pure Christianity, meeting hatred with gentleness and calumny with charity. It might not have been practical politics, but it might have succeeded in a time, and in a way, of which Laud could not have conceived. For he was not a saint of the Church, but a little bustling man, as busy as Martha about the many aspects of a practical man's job.

I I

THOROUGH

So long as the Lord Treasurer Weston lived, so long did his policy of masterly—or, as some of his critics would have it, shameless—inactivity, continue dominant not only in the foreign but also in the domestic sphere. So long as the Government could carry on from one year's end to another, that was all he cared about. He did not even bother, overmuch, if the royal finances showed a modest deficit ; things would no doubt straighten themselves out in time, and meanwhile, sufficient for the day. ...

It can be imagined how maddening such a state of mind would be to men like Laud and Wentworth, who set no limits to the possibilities of administrative action, and who could never rest as long as a single abuse remained to be purged or any possible reform to be undertaken. It is no wonder that Portland— to which earldom in 1633 Weston had been promoted—became to these restlessly earnest men the very symbol of obstruction, and that they should have equated him in their correspondence with the Lady Mora—literally, delay—in whom we may perhaps see the ancestress of a modern cartoonist's "Dilly" and "Dally".

Now Wentworth, in his posts of duty, first at York, and then at Dublin, was not near enough the centre of things to put any very effective spoke in Portland's wheel ; but Laud, particularly after he had become Archbishop, was not the man to wink at slackness, and worse than slackness, even in so purely temporal a sphere as that of State finance. His instinct for having everything in ship-shape order combined with his perfect disinterestedness to give him a rare talent for what one might call the spade-work of

administration—in any department to which he was appointed
he would have functioned, with ruthless efficiency, as a new broom.
This he proved not only in the Church, but as Chancellor of his
own University of Oxford, where he reformed the whole system
from top to bottom, and where his work outlasted him into the
nineteenth century.

Such a man was frankly incapable of sitting still and tolerating
the spectacle of Lord Portland's easy-going ways, especially as he
had poked his sharp little nose far enough into the Treasurer's
proceedings, to suspect that his standards of financial probity
were as easy as his statesmanship. The one form of financial
leakage to which there appeared to be no objection whatever,
was that into his Lordship's own coffers. There was no such thing
in those days as a united Cabinet, and Laud's vigorous personality provided a spearhead for the opposition that was growing
up against Portland among his colleagues on the Council. They
managed to insist upon his furnishing exact accounts of some of
his past transactions, and the results had at least a fishy appearance. Portland was a very rich man, and a very unpopular one.
He was also a sick man, and this may have had its part in making
his manners even worse and more overbearing than before.
Nothing would have been easier than for Charles to have quietly
dropped him, or even squeezed him for that mysteriously gotten
fortune.

But that was just what Charles was incapable of doing. Except
for the one lapse of his ingratitude to Bristol—and in that he had
allowed himself to be hypnotized by his devotion to Buckingham
—he was loyal to a fault ; loyal as few Princes, who rather
expect than give loyalty, have ever been. He had given a striking
proof of this at the time when Hamilton was engaged in raising
his volunteer force for service in Germany. At that time some of
the Marquis's ill-wishers, including Portland himself, came to the
King with an alarming story about the whole thing being a
diabolical plot of Hamilton's, who was next in succession after
the House of Stuart, to seize the throne of Scotland ; nay, more,
that if the King gave him half a chance, Hamilton would not
stick at regicide. The King's only reply was to embrace Hamilton
as soon as he came into the Presence, and to insist—despite all
protests—on his passing the night in his own bedchamber.

And now he was just the same with Hamilton's chief accuser.
Nothing would induce him to throw over Portland, the man

whom no one liked, and whom his chosen Archbishop and his beloved wife each, for different reasons, wanted out of their path. But there was one enemy against whom not even the King could shield his servant. At the beginning of March, 1635, it was noticed that Portland's eupeptic appearance had undergone a terrible change ; he could only crouch shivering over a huge fire, and his clothes flapped loosely about his wasted figure. Within a few days' time, a terrible swelling in his throat almost prevented him from swallowing, and it was evident that the end could not be far off. The King came to his dying minister's bedside, where he lay gasping stertorously for breath—the spectacle was so terrible that Charles, whose sensibility to pain was that of an artist and quite abnormal for that tough-gutted age, could not endure it, and had to make his escape from the room.

Archbishop Laud would now fain have hurried to the bedside. A Greater than he would presently have the overseeing of Portland's accounts ; and the little man's only concern was to bring the last consolations of the Church to his stricken colleague. But Portland, at last convinced that he had nothing to lose in this world, was only concerned to insure his prospects, as far as possible, in the next, by being reconciled to that larger Church in which he had secretly believed, even while he had fleeced it. With courteous thanks he declined Laud's offer ; and it would appear that those Catholic offices, which by law it was death to administer, soothed the last of his many terrors. And then, at the time that he himself had predicted, after rolling and tossing for an hour in atrocious torments, "he fetched three great groans and died".

The great obstructionist, the Lady Mora in breeches, was out of the way, and Laud was free to overhaul the machinery of government with something like the thoroughness which he had displayed in his clean up of the Church. Many people expected to see him appointed to succeed Portland at the Treasury, but to combine this with his Archbishopric, not to speak of his Chancellorship of Oxford, would have been expecting a little too much even from his Gargantuan appetite for work. So the King put the office into temporary commission, with Laud as chief commissioner. It was only a year later that Laud persuaded the King to make the surprising appointment of another St John's don, his close friend, William Juxon, who, thanks to his influence with

Mr TOHN PYM, Burges
for Tavistock in Devonshire.

JOHN PYM—*from a print in the British Museum:*

THOMAS WENTWORTH, FIRST EARL OF
STRAFFORD—*from a print in the British Museum*

the King, had already succeeded him in the Bishopric of London. It was an appointment that caused a good deal of heartburning, because, as Laud himself noted in his diary, no Churchman had held the post since the days of Henry VII ; but the plain fact of the matter was that a better man could not have been found for it. For not only was Juxon, who, by the way, hunted the best pack of hounds in England, as honest and capable a manager as Laud himself, but, unlike Laud, he had a tact and sweetness of disposition that even in that time of ferocious hatreds, kept him from having a single enemy. "That good man," Charles called him, and acknowledged that he had never got his opinion on any subject without being the better for it.

This more than ever confirmed Laud's position as the most influential personage among the King's ministers, the one of them who came nearest of all to meriting the name of Prime Minister. And yet that would have been grossly over-stating his position, for there was nothing under Charles's personal rule to correspond to the modern team of Cabinet ministers, captained by what in fact, if not in form, is the President Elect of a Parliamentary majority. Charles's Council were anything but a united team, and so far as there was any equivalent of a Prime Minister, it was the King himself.

An extremely mixed team it was. When we try to place ourselves in the King's position, and see his difficulties through his eyes, we come to realize that perhaps the chief of them was that of finding competent and honest heads for the State departments. The aristocracy were of little use to him, few of them being inclined for the daily routine work of administration—the hopeless amateurishness of Holland was only too typical of his class. And that supreme amateur, Buckingham, had added to the immense sum of mischief he had done, by destroying whatever was left of ministerial independence and initiative, and preventing any chance of a revival of the great Cecil tradition.

Charles was accordingly driven to rely, for most of his appointments, on the sons of respectable but not great families, who, usually after an apprenticeship in one of the Inns of Court, had taken up the King's service as a career. The best of these men developed into competent head clerks of their respective offices, though hardly into statesmen. But there were others, and perhaps the majority, who were careerists in the worst sense of the word, playing merely for their own—and those not particularly clean—

hands. One of the greatest handicaps under which Charles laboured was the atmosphere of venality and petty intrigue that pervaded the Court, and seemed to emanate from the very spirit of the time.

Under such circumstances, unless the King intended merely to let matters drift, it was necessary for him to look for his chief counsellors outside the ordinary sources of recruitment. His reliance on Laud, and his fellow churchman, Juxon, was, on this showing, boldly and soundly conceived. The Church had been a nursery of statesmen up to the time of the Reformation, and even now incomparably the greatest figure in European politics wore a Cardinal's hat. And in Laud, Charles had discovered a little Hercules whose special talent was the cleansing of Augean stables, and whose chosen motto was Thorough, or Through, in the sense of the text.

"Whose fan is in his hand and he will throughly purge his floor, and will gather the wheat into his garner ; but the chaff he will burn with fire unquenchable."

12

WENTWORTH IN THE NORTH

THE Church was not the only source from which the King contrived to introduce fresh blood into the higher branches of his service. Certainly the happiest inspiration he ever had—though equal credit is due to Portland's advice in the matter—was his capturing the services of Wentworth. No man could have been more out of the ordinary run of administrative servants. He, in fact, represented the very type from which Charles had most to fear, that which was the backbone of the House of Commons, those propertied magnates who were already aspiring to substitute an oligarchy of their own class for the monarchy of a national Sovereign.

Even to-day, there is no county of England where the influence of a few great and exclusive families persists to a greater extent than in rural Yorkshire. The still imperfectly civilized and feudal conditions reigning in these Northern counties of England, were implicitly recognized in Tudor and early Stuart times by the existence of a special administrative Council of the North, under a president, who was practically a viceroy, and whose special function it was to enforce the reign of law on local dignitaries who would otherwise have become a law unto themselves. Even as it was, few normal Lord Presidents were inclined to ask for trouble by making enemies against whom not even the King might be able to protect his servants. And as for the Council, it had come to be manned by the very class it was intended to hold in check.

And here at last was one of the richest of these Yorkshire gentlemen, just such a man as John Hampden was in Buckinghamshire, and a leader of the Parliamentary opposition, come down to make the King's authority effective over men like himself, the great ones of his native shire. There is no more detested a person than the poacher turned gamekeeper, among his fellow-poachers, especially if it be seen that he really means to put down poaching.

It was at the beginning of 1629 that Wentworth took up his post at York, and for the four following years it was seen how the King's government could be carried on by a man whom neither fear nor favour could deflect from his purpose of Thorough, a man who could visit the slightest open contempt of the King's authority, vested in himself, with punishment swift and drastic, were the offender never so powerful ; one who, when a peer of the realm shut himself up in his ancestral mansion and defied a sheriff's warrant, brought up artillery from Scarborough, and shelled him into his senses.

This beetle-browed tyrant with his imperious will and his haughty manner to his equals ! What must have made it even more galling was the undeniable fact that the common people idolized their Lord President, and found his manner as gracious to them as it was intolerable to their betters. They had good reason for the love they bore him. At last the spectacle was seen of the King's Government functioning as a national Government in the fullest sense of the words, and of fair play being secured for all alike without respect of persons. The great Elizabethan statutes for the relief of the poor, and for the regulation of the wages and conditions of labour, which the rich man had been accustomed to treat as dead letters when they affected his own interests, were revived and put into full force—or Lord Wentworth would know the reason why. The capitalist organizers of the growing Yorkshire cloth industry found, to their astonished indignation, that they were no longer free to exploit their

employees under a regime of *laissez faire*. Wealthy squires were
outraged when they were required to put their hands in their
pockets, not only for the relief but also for the employment of the
poor. The highly capitalized company that had been formed for
the drainage and enclosure of the vast, waterlogged expanse of
Hatfield Chase, found that it would not be allowed to ride roughshod over the rights of the poor folk already in scattered occupation. Lord Wentworth came down himself to investigate, and
see that all parties, even the humblest, got a fair settlement. That
was his principle throughout, the grand old Hebrew ideal of
kingly power :

"He shall keep the simple folk in their right, defend the
children of the poor, and punish the wrong doer."

Or, as his friend and biographer, Radcliffe, writes of him,

"He loved justice, for justice itself, taking great delight to free a
poor man from a powerful oppressor, or to punish bold wickedness."

Or to quote a recent biographer, "The county throve under
his firm and just administration, the poor were relieved, the
unemployed set on work, and justice brought within the reach
of all."*

And in so doing he had sharpened an axe for his own neck.
The great men whose tyranny he had bridled ; the rich men of
whose profits he had taken toll ; the sluggards and obstructionists
he had warmed ; all those, in short, whom the histories of the
last generation include under the designation of "the Patriots",
had been offended by this terrible Lord President in a way that
brooked no forgiveness. The day might yet come in which the
King's authority would no longer be able to protect his servants,
and in that day—let Lord Wentworth look to it !

13

WENTWORTH IN IRELAND

By the beginning of 1632, it had become apparent to the King
that even the North was a field too narrow for the administrative
capacity of this man whom he had enlisted in his service. But
what was to be done with Wentworth ? There could be no

* *Strafford*, by C. V. Wedgwood, p. 112.

question of turning Weston (as he still was) out of the Treasurer-ship to make room for him, and in the routine of any other department he would have been simply thrown away. But there was a post that plainly called for—or at any rate challenged—his genius. But it was one that had been a grave to the reputation of almost everyone who had filled it. For even in those days, experience seemed to prove that the one task beyond the capacity of even the greatest Englishman was that of governing Ireland.

Here all the difficulties that had faced the King's representative in the North were reproduced in a monstrously exaggerated form, with the addition of others even more formidable. For in Yorkshire the rich magnate and the poor weaver, the great land-owner and the little man whose landmark he moved, were at least of the same English stock and Protestant religion. But in Ireland it was a case of naked conquest and explcitation of an ancient civilization by men of alien blood and hostile faith, who regarded their victims in the light of savages, whom they could plunder and exterminate with a clear conscience.

And it was not even a plain and honest tyranny of one nation over another. Ireland had come to be regarded as a field of exploitation for wealthy and usually titled adventurers who were out to fill their own pockets by any possible means, and most of all by that of land-grabbing. The King had no means of enforcing his authority over these men, and his Lord Deputy was more likely than not to be in the racket. A dreadful and typical scandal had ended the rule of Wentworth's predecessor, Lord Falkland.* Marked down for the next share-out had been the land, in the Wicklow mountains, of a tribe called Byrne. That the Home Government set its face against this iniquity, only stimulated the gang to more heroic activity. First Falkland clapped the chief and his six sons into jail, on a wholly imaginary charge of conspiracy. The next step was to obtain evidence from members of the tribe, by such means as putting one of them naked on a red hot grid. Luckily the King was not to be bluffed so easily, and to Falkland's great indignation insisted on the matter being sifted by an independent tribunal, whose investigations had resulted in the liberation of the Byrnes and the resignation of the Deputy. For more than two years after that, Ireland had to be governed without a Lord Deputy—it was not easy to find candidates for the post.

* Father of him who fell at Newbury.

There are even some of Charles's critics who would have it that his eventual appointment of Wentworth was with the deliberate object of compassing his downfall. So uncharitable an assumption is neither necessary nor plausible. As we have already seen, not only was Wentworth the only man for the post, but it would be little short of the truth to say that the post was the only one for Wentworth. To entrust him with Ireland was a compliment to his genius that turned out to be thoroughly deserved. Charles had for once put the right man in the right place, and he deserves every credit for it.

At the same time there was undoubtedly—up to the final crisis—a certain reserve in his attitude to Wentworth. He gave him nothing but trust, but never quite his whole trust. Not until Wentworth's support was seen to be the last hope of a tottering throne, did he receive the Earldom for which he had begged for the purpose of enhancing his prestige as Lord Deputy. Charles had had no real opportunity of making contact with this saturnine, imperious personality, this man whom he had so recently regarded as being tarred with the same brush as Phelips and Eliot. How if he were to develop into as powerful and dangerous a servant as Wallenstein, whom in some ways he so strikingly resembled? What Charles needed, and ultimately obtained, experience to realize, was the quality that put Wentworth on a moral level high above that of such magnificent adventurers ; the passionate loyalty that no ambition could deflect, and not even death could chill. As it was, since the experience of Buckingham, the King had been determined—perhaps a shade over-anxiously—that his servants should be his servants, and neither his masters nor his favourites.

It does not fall within our sphere to record in detail the history of that amazing viceroyalty. Nobody to-day, except a totalitarian, would maintain that Wentworth's solution of the Irish problem went to the heart of it ; and we might add that such a solution would not have been practicable even for a statesman of his calibre. The tragedy of England and Ireland consisted in the fact that the smaller island was small enough and near enough to render its conquest by the larger inevitable ; but just too large and too far to allow that conquest to become, like that of Wales, complete. England was perpetually straining at a task that, like that of Sisyphus, always seemed on the verge of being accomplished, and then had to be begun all over again. The ancient civilization of Ireland, the soul of her, survived defeat, and occupation, and enslavement—proved again and again strong enough to conquer and absorb even its conquerors. And at last, as century after century was added to the struggle for domination, bitter hatreds were engendered and all scruples and restraints thrown aside—England would make an end of this intractable civilization, even if she had to possess herself of the whole land and exterminate all its inhabitants.

Things arrived at a still more hopeless pass when Ireland, in spite of the Reformation, continued to cling, with heroic constancy, to her old Catholic faith. As England got more and more fiercely anti-papal, religious bigotry was enlisted in support of national antagonism. An Irishman came to be regarded as something outside the pale of Christian charity, several degrees worse than an ordinary savage.

When such prejudice was in the ascendant, it would have been out of the question for Wentworth, or any other English Lord Deputy, to have stood up for the cause of Irish civilization, or done anything calculated to promote Home Rule, or Catholic Emancipation. He had, as a matter of fact, no other thought than to impose, by force, the rule of the superior civilization. But where he differed from the other Englishmen on the spot was in his determination to take that civilizing mission seriously, to govern Ireland not only by the strong, but by the clean hand, and by sheer administrative efficiency to drive her into the way of prosperity. He would have agreed with Lord Salisbury's dictum, that what Ireland needed was twenty years of firm government. Only he would have been more likely to call it "Thorough".

And thorough it was, with a vengeance. The King's representative had a short way with the anarchs who were competing for the loot of this province of his. The worst of them all, a self-made lawyer adventurer called Boyle, who by divers shady means had accumulated for himself a vast fortune, and was now Earl of Cork—the great Earl, as he was called—was at last brought to book, and made to disgorge some of his ill-gotten gains, and— what perhaps annoyed him even more—to take down the pretentious tomb he had put up for the deceased Lady Cork on the site of the High Altar in St Patrick's Cathedral. Soon the Court at Whitehall was humming with scandal about the way in which the Lord Deputy was treating the greatest nobles in his island. It was unheard of that those who had thoughtlessly taken to themselves the property of the Crown should have it taken again, as if they had been common swindlers. And it was showing intolerable lack of respect to the Commander-in-chief, who, having assessed the country for the pay of some of his soldiers, collected it again and pocketed it himself, that the Lord Deputy should have been, in his own words, "so bold as to stop his entertainments, till his Majesty be satisfied for the double payment, as in all justice he ought.

But the cup of Wentworth's insolencies was filled by his treatment of Lord Mountnorris, who, as Sir Francis Annesley, had laid the foundations of his fortune by various lootings of Irish land, and to the usual repertoire of corrupt practices at the disposal of Anglo-Irish magnates, had added those of spying on successive Lord Deputies, and of relieving wealthy young gamblers of their cash by methods resembling those of Ah Sin. This great personage, with the assistance of a whole tribe of lesser Annesleys, determined to make things even hotter for this interfering Deputy than for his predecessors. A younger brother, an officer in the Irish army, started the game by being deliberately insubordinate on a review, and Wentworth's cane descended gently, but with humiliating publicity, on his shoulder. Another relative followed this up by dropping a heavy stool on the Deputy's gouty foot, and Mountnorris, at a dinner shortly afterwards, hinted at worse things to follow. He had forgotten that, holding, as he did, His Majesty's commission, this was the language of mutiny. Not so Wentworth ; having bided his time and first obtained the King's permission, he had the astonished Mountnorris up before a Court Martial, which, sitting under the Lord Deputy's dreadful eye, passed sentence of death. Perhaps unfortunately, Wentworth had not the remotest intention of putting this sentence into effect, but what it did mean was the downfall of Mountnorris, and the suspension of his opportunities for mischief.

The fate of this not altogether stainless martyr may have been a blessed thing for Ireland, but it was among the heaviest counts in the indictment that was accumulating against Wentworth. Tyranny of this sort over victims who, though they may have been sharpers and spies, had at least become gentlemen, was enough to make any Patriot's blood boil. There would be a heavy reckoning if Parliament were to come back to Westminster.

Heaviest of all in that reckoning would be the blow that Wentworth inflicted on the pockets of the rich London merchants and speculators. For the City had itself taken part in the recent share-out of Ulster, and had neglected even to fulfil the conditions of its own charter. That charter was accordingly forfeited and a huge fine demanded—of which all but a nominal sum was eventually remitted. But such shearing of the golden fleece was an offence not to be forgiven.

Meanwhile, the administration had been galvanized into sudden and prolific activity, and the not too common spectacle was witnessed of an efficiently governed Ireland. Whether Wentworth's methods would, in course of time, have turned a distressful into a smiling land, may be open to dispute, but there can be no question of his having worked miracles in every department that had felt the touch of his master hand. Such had been the helplessness of his predecessors that pirates had plied their trade all round the Irish coasts without let or hindrance, and Eliot's old friend, Nutt, had relieved Wentworth himself of a good part of his luggage, when he had first crossed the sea to take up his duties. It was not long before the tables were turned ; soon the Lord Deputy was policing the seas with ships of his own raising, and the hunters had become the quarry.

An even greater feat was his having laid the foundations of a small, but thoroughly efficient army. This would have appeared highly necessary in a country that was being held in unwilling subjection by a minority of aliens. But the only use that the leaders of this minority had been able to find for the King's army was as a pipe to direct the public funds into their private purses. Wentworth, having put the fear of God into some of these gentlemen, proceeded to create a properly paid, equipped and disciplined force. In spite of his lack of military experience and his chronic invalidism, he had all the instincts of a born commander, and one is inclined to suspect that if he had not been done to a timely death, he might have proved the one man capable of standing up to that other civilian captain, Oliver Cromwell. His way with insubordinate officers at least would have delighted Noll. This Irish army, small in numbers as it was, was yet the only regular force worth speaking of at the King's disposal. But an army of any sort at the King's disposal was, in the eyes of those who were working for the King's overthrow, the abomination of desolation standing where it ought not, and the man who created it beyond the pale of mercy.

Wentworth did not confine his attention to defence. He put

his administrative machine to work in order to force the growth
of Ireland's commercial prosperity ; and with what success is
shown in the figures of the customs returns, which rose from
£22,553 in his first year of office, to £57,387 in his sixth.*

One great and permanent result of his activities was that, in
the words of Welsford, "he imported flax seed, and not only
founded the linen industry of Ulster, but was one of the founders
of the Lancashire cotton industry."† For the linen yarn of Ulster
was worked up in Lancashire with cotton thread of the Levant
into fustians, vermilions, dimities, and so forth, for the London
export trade. Wentworth not only imported seed from Holland,
but also skilled weavers to give the industry a start.

It would have been better still, had he been capable of taking
a whole-heartedly Irish standpoint. But he was an English
patriot, devoted heart and soul to the policy of a British monarch,
and in the interests of this policy he discouraged the export of
Irish wool. This had much to do with perpetuating the cleavage
between the thriving colony in the north-east, and the chronic
poverty of the rest of the country.

To finance his policy Wentworth did not shrink from invoking
the aid of a Parliament. This to Charles, with his experience of
Parliaments, seemed a highly dangerous experiment ; "as for
that Hydra," he warned his Deputy, "take good heed, for you
know that here I have found it cunning as well as malicious."
But what Wentworth did not know about Parliaments was not
worth knowing. With the utmost skill he played off the English
and the native parties against each other, and drove them forward
by the sheer compulsion of his will-power, until they had voted
as large a sum of money as even he could have wished for.

As the result of all this, Ireland, instead of being a drain on the
resources of the Crown, was actually able to make a useful
contribution towards its ever-pressing necessities. Charles could
at least congratulate himself on one brilliantly successful phase of
his policy, and on having enlisted in his service a statesman not
unfit to be compared with any of his time, even in this age of
Richelieu.

There was another side to this policy of Wentworth's. It was
better fitted to emanate from an ancient, or not quite so ancient,
Roman, than a gentleman brought up in the English tradition of
rights and liberties. Wentworth was more qualified for a Carlylese

* Wedgwood, op. cit., App. v.   † *Strength of England*, p. 323.

hero than Cromwell himself, and it must have been only the
indurated prejudice of a Radical environment that prevented
Carlyle from effecting his transfiguration in heaven knows how
many volumes. There was a little too much confusion of right and
might in Wentworth's mind, a little too great a tendency to drive
or hack through to his chosen end, regardless of every other
consideration.

The intimidation of people like Mountnorris nothing but cant
could deplore, but the intimidation of juries has an ugly sound,
even though juries, in Ireland, were more often instruments of
corrupt oppression than of justice. And the fact that Ireland at
last enjoyed the blessings of good government and good trade
does not justify the fact that Wentworth pursued in Connaught,
which had hitherto suffered less than any other Irish province at
the hands of the conquerors, the now familiar English policy of
plantation, or the settlement of colonists on land filched from its
rightful owners.

But when we consider against what odds Wentworth was
contending, and with what single-minded devotion he conquered
his task, we shall be inclined to judge him leniently. Cleansing
Augean stables is rough work at the best, and the practice of
Thorough, or Through, may be hard to dissociate, at a pinch,
from that of hacking through. But there are at least none of the
men who felt the weight of Wentworth's hand, or of those who at
last pulled him down and made an end of him, above whom he
does not tower so high in moral as well as intellectual grandeur as
to defy comparison.

"This noble Earl," as one of his destroyers, Bulstrode White-
locke, had the generosity to write of him, "who for his natural
parts and abilities, and for improvement of knowledge by experience, in the greatest affairs, for wisdom, faithfulness and gallantry
of mind, hath left few behind him that may be ranked with him."

And even in the hearts of Irishmen, Wentworth's memory may
claim a warm place. Failing the free development of Irish
civilization on its own lines—and of this there was no question
in the mind of any contemporary Englishman—it was better that
the island should be governed honestly, and with stern efficiency
as a province of a budding empire, than to have her prostrate
body devoured piecemeal by innumerable vultures.

Dark days in Ireland had preceded the coming of Lord Wentworth ; darker were to follow his downfall.

14

KING CHARLES CREATES A NAVY

IT cannot be too clearly emphasized that the personal government of King Charles stood or fell by its success in compassing
one simple end, that of paying its way out of its own lawful
resources, without the necessity of applying to Parliament for
taxation ; and that this was only possible if no extraordinary
expenses were incurred, and even then by straining the legal
powers of the Crown to their utmost limits.

Now Charles, than whom a more scrupulously honourable man
never lived, never swerved from his determination to abide by
rules of the game between himself and his subjects, according to
their last very drastic revision in the Petition of Right. And these
rules were in no way to be modified by any arbitrary interpretation of his, for in every disputed case there were recognized
umpires, in the shape of the judges, whose decision would be
binding on Sovereign and subject alike. No doubt the judges
were appointed by the King and held office at his pleasure, but
that they were his pliable instruments is disproved by their own
record of intractability. The great lawyers' guild had its traditions
centuries old, and a loyalty to the law itself that in all but a few
time-servers kept its members true to its spirit. It was only when
Parliament reigned supreme that that loyalty was to be tried by
systematic and naked intimidation.

Charles, then, was prepared to abide by the law as defined by
its recognized interpreters, but his desperate need for money to
carry on his ordinary expenses practically compelled him to play
the game, within these limits, with its utmost rigour. For some
years, and particularly under Portland's easy-going auspices, the
unsoundness of his position might well have horrified any orthodox
economist. The Buckingham regime had saddled him with a
heavy load of debt, that he had to pay off as best he could ; and
even if he had had a clean sheet to start with, his yearly income
would have failed, by an appreciable margin, to cover his expenses.
He had not yet the resource of shifting his own burdens on to the
shoulders of future generations by means of a national debt,
though he had begun to feel in this direction by paying current
debts out of anticipations of revenue. But such crude expedients

could not be expected indefinitely to stave off the bankruptcy that sooner or later follows on a conjunction of unpaid debts and chronic deficits.

The King, then, was driven by stark necessity to be constantly putting on the screw in order to squeeze out the last farthing legally due to him, and this in spite of the fact that no form of activity is less popular in a monarch ; though we must remember that his subjects were in the happy position of being barred by law from any sort of direct taxation, except for such occasional and usually trivial contributions as the relics of feudal custom allowed the King to demand from well-to-do individuals. One source that proved extremely fruitful consisted in making every eligible person assume, and pay for, the dignity of knighthood.

Another sprang from a strict inquisition into the encroachments upon Crown lands, technically known as forests, that in past times had been committed by greedy magnates with whom the Sovereign had been powerless to deal. In the majority of cases, all that was exacted was that a legally valid title should be obtained—for a fee. But since these encroachments were anything up to three centuries old, the existing owners were not unnaturally annoyed at what must have appeared to them the legal sharp practice of raising the matter at all.

So by one means or another, the Crown managed to keep the wolf of bankruptcy from the door, and so long as Portland lasted, without any too drastic stretching of its powers. For to such a mind as his, a certain sacrifice of financial, or any other kind of purity, was well worth while if it was the means of avoiding trouble. A crash that could be postponed indefinitely need disturb no one's slumbers. And if the King were to avoid spending more than he was doing at present, it did not seem as if any crash was in sight.

But could he ? For there was one flaw in this otherwise admirable programme. We have seen how its very foundation consisted in the withdrawal of England from any sort of active interference in European affairs—while Continental nations were tearing each other to pieces, she was pursuing her peaceful avocations behind the shelter of her encircling sea. Yes—but would that sea be any shelter if she failed to command it, or if she had no means of protecting those of her citizens who made it their highway or fishing ground ?

The sea had conferred on England the unique blessing of

enabling her to dispense with a regular army, a circumstance that more than any other had prevented her Sovereigns from becoming despots. But this blessing was conditional upon her possession of a navy strong enough to keep her shores inviolate. And there was this advantage in a navy, that it was an eminently constitutional arm. No King was ever likely to hold his subjects in awe with a force of sailors—there is something in life on shipboard, where men are isolated for long periods of time in closed communities, with frequent opportunities for discussion, that has rendered sailors apter for starting than for quelling revolutions.

Charles, like his brother before him, keenly appreciated England's need for a strong navy ; and Buckingham, with all his faults, had done the best that in him lay for the assertion of British sea power. But the navy of which Buckingham was admiral had failed so ignominiously as to have earned the contempt of allies and enemies alike. This was no doubt due in the first place to the refusal of the Patriots in the House of Commons to vote adequate, or indeed any funds, for its equipment and maintenance. But it was due also to the fact that the fleets that put to sea for Cadiz and Rhé, though imposing in numbers, contained only a small stiffening of King's ships, and, for the rest, were composed of conscripted merchantmen, the cowardice or insubordination of whose skippers and crews rendered them a great deal worse than useless.

It must have been evident to everybody, after the series of disgraceful exhibitions culminating in the final abandonment of the heroic Rochellese, that nothing less would serve to maintain the King's power upon the seas, than a royal navy, constantly in commission, and manned by trained, professional, naval seamen.

But then, it might have been said, if the King's policy was one of peace and non-interference, why should he want to plunge into this new luxury of an expensive navy ? Why could he not allow matters to go on comfortably as they had in his father's reign, and as they were doing now, since he had ceased to make war ? Why not leave the policing of the seas to look after itself, and refrain from irritating his subjects by demands on their purses ?

This is far from being a rhetorical question. To such a mind, for instance, as that of Portland, as that of the late King James, or, we might almost dare to add, of the great Elizabeth, the answer that would most naturally have suggested itself, might have been,

"Why indeed?" And if Charles had been a tyrant or a cynic, playing for his own hand, it would have been the obvious answer for him too. He might well have decided to keep on in the old way, and bank on the improbability of any other Power having its hands free enough to take on so considerable an enterprise as an attack upon England. It would, in fact, have needed much less than the intelligence of King Charles to perceive that so far from having any personal interest in committing himself to a policy of naval expansion, he was plunging into a sea of troubles, and, in fact, upsetting that delicate financial equilibrium on which the whole prerogative and safety of his Throne depended.

But the tragedy of King Charles was not that of a tyrant, nor yet of a cynic, but of a man of abnormally sensitive conscience, who, when he believed a thing to be right, could be restrained by no prudential considerations from putting it into effect.

And the defencelessness of England at sea was not a state of affairs that any patriotic King could regard with indifference. For one thing, the scandal of piracy had now risen to an intolerable height. The Barbary corsairs had discovered that they could, with comparative impunity, use English waters as their happy hunting ground, and even indulge in slave raids on coastal villages. The horrors to which men and women, snatched away from the midst of their daily life, were thus exposed, baffle description. All that could be done, in default of an efficient navy, was to traffic with the Moors for any exorbitant ransom they liked to charge for the release of what was, at best, but a trifling minority of these unfortunates. This—especially as the Moors frequently stipulated for payment in guns—was simply an invitation to a return visit. It could hardly be a matter of indifference for the King, that conditions had come to prevail in his own Duchy of Cornwall, and along his western and southern shores, resembling those on the Slave Coast of Guinea.

But it was not only against these infidels that the protection of a navy was required. A new and formidable naval power had grown up on Britain's flank, in the shape of the United Provinces, by whose fleet the few ships flying the King's standard were hopelessly outnumbered and outclassed. The Puritan opposition had hitherto turned a blind eye on the Dutch, in the faith that being devout Protestants, they were England's natural allies, and would behave as such. They little knew the Dutch burghers if they imagined that these stolid realists had, for their part, an eye to anything but the main chance, or the least scruple in their choice of means. A dreadful massacre at Amboyna, in the East Indies, in which the Dutch had secured their monopoly of these valuable islands by wiping out a budding British colony, had been conveniently passed over.

But the Dutch were a very present menace nearer home. Their monopoly of the East Indies was a less serious thing than that of the immensely valuable herring fishery in the North Sea, and this they were in a fair way to secure. Now if there was one thing on which all patriotic Englishmen were agreed, it was their right to the sovereignty of what were known as His Majesty's seas ; which roughly comprised the Channel, and the part of the North Sea between England and the Low Countries. The King was as strong for this as anyone, and, in 1635, expressly arranged for the publication of a book, hitherto suppressed, by his sometime opponent, the lawyer Selden, in which this claim was asserted in the most uncompromising form.

Charles might assert as much as he pleased, but without power to enforce his demands he might as well have talked to the seas themselves. The Dutch treated his claims with contempt. Not only did they refuse to pay the fishing licences demanded by his representatives, but their fleets were strong enough to drive away anything English from their fishing grounds. They took even greater liberties—there is at least one instance on record of their landing on the East Coast to dry their fish, and driving off the local opposition with musketry.

The situation was more serious, because, ever since the taking of Rochelle, it had been part of Richelieu's policy to build up a strong French navy, and now that he had resolved to throw in the weight of his country on the Protestant side in Germany, he had formed an alliance with the Dutch against Spain, that gave the combined fleets an overwhelming superiority, and allowed them to cut the sea communication between Spain and her province of what is now Belgium.

As for England, her sovereignty not only of her seas, but even of her land, was ignored by this all-powerful combination. There was one occasion when the Dutch pursued a Spaniard from Dunkirk into a tidal creek at Blythe, in Northumberland, commandeered any local fishing boats that happened to be handy, took the ship, pursued her crew two miles inland and plundered them. And the Dover-Dunkirk mail boat was not once, but repeatedly, intercepted and rifled by French ships from Calais.

Now I repeat that it would have been quite possible for Charles to have shut his eyes to what was going on upon the seas, and to have continued in the old way without too great personal inconvenience. It would no doubt have suited his book to do so. The sufferings of a few Christian slaves would not have shaken his throne, nor is it probable that the abandonment of the North Sea fishing trade would have brought him into more odium than a demand for money to protect it. But it was not in him to act on such calculations, nor, if it had been, would he have been a figure of tragedy.

How then was he to find the money for this new and serious addition to a peace time expenditure that as it was, and with the utmost economy, still exceeded his income ? It might be, and in fact perpetually has been, said, that he could have summoned a Parliament. One sufficient answer to this is that he might as well have summoned Neptune himself, for all the chance he had of getting his naval estimates passed. Parliament had shown, even in time of war, its complete indifference to the most urgent requirements of the fleet. Nothing could be more certain than that if Charles, in time of peace, had come to Parliament with a request for special taxation for the navy, it would have been treated with contempt, or, at best, the doubtful prospect of some insignificant dole would have been held out, in return for the sacrifice of his Church, his most trusted servants, and his royal prerogative.

It might well have seemed to him that for so necessary a part of his duties as that of maintaining a fleet, he was entitled to some reasonable provision, instead of being exposed to blackmail. It was a time-honoured principle in England that the King had the right to call upon the ports and counties by the sea to furnish him with ships, or their equivalent in money. This principle had been asserted by James I, in 1619, and the money paid so much as a matter of course that even so careful an historian as Hallam never seems to have heard about it. Charles had made an attempt to do the same thing in 1628, and to break for the first time with the preposterous theory that only the maritime counties had any interest in the navy. But the opposition he encountered on this occasion induced him to draw back.

The idea of financing the now urgently needed ship-building

programme by this same expedient of levying ship-money, as it was called, seems to have been pressed upon Charles by a lawyer called Noy, who had figured in the Parliamentary opposition as long as Parliament had lasted, but had since then transferred his considerable abilities to the King's service, and accepted—though only after a businesslike enquiry about salary—the office of Attorney-General. It is probable that he regarded the King in no other light than that of an important client in whose interests he had been briefed, and in whose cause it was his professional duty to explore every possible avenue. But he had no need to search in musty records for an expedient that had never fallen into obsolescence. The right to levy money for the fleet, on occasions of emergency, was among the undoubted prerogatives of the kings of an island people.

The only question that arose was whether, in 1634, when the King made a demand for ship-money from the ports and maritime counties, the emergency was genuine. In the appeal that he sent forth he dwelt eloquently on the depredations of the Barbary pirates—and those who sneer at the inadequacy of the excuse might have taken a different view, had they had the experience of being chained stark naked for months to the same galley bench, and lashed into rowing at a racing spurt for anything up to twenty hours on end ; had they been flogged up and down the market to show off their paces ; had they seen their womenfolk ... Charles has been accused of calculated deceit in not disclosing his full objects, as if it would have been exactly wise to announce, in a public proclamation, that he was building also against his Dutch and French neighbours. But no one with the remotest appreciation of the facts can deny that a state of very grave emergency existed, and so far as the Moors were concerned, a state of war.

The first levy from the maritime districts went through without any excessive opposition. English folk are usually fairly reasonable about what they can understand, and the coastwise dwellers knew well enough that they were getting their money's worth in protection against Moors and Dutchmen. It was when the demand came to be made on the inland districts, that the real trouble started. The soundness of the King's assumption that sea-power was equally the concern of all his subjects, was not likely to be appreciated by midland squires and burgesses, who had perhaps never travelled as far as the coast ; who regarded a Dutchman as a Protestant and brother, and concerned themselves no more with Moors than with the man in the moon. It was human nature that they should resent an impost that was entirely new, as far as they were concerned ; and it would be only too easy to convince them that the King had started to levy taxes at his arbitrary will, and had set up as a tyrant, naked and unashamed.

The first levy was followed, in the two succeeding years, by two others, this time assessed on the principle that all parts of the country alike were equally concerned in its naval defence. The money was applied with scrupulous honesty to the purpose for which it was asked, and, in spite of Clarendon's statement to the contrary, there was never the faintest question of its being used "for a spring and magazine that should have no bottom, and for an everlasting supply of all occasions". His Majesty's finances were not a penny the better than they would have been if he had chosen to go on in the old way and let who would take over the sovereignty of his seas. On the legality of the operation the King was careful to take the opinion of his judges, ten out of twelve of whom assured him that he was perfectly within his rights.

The effects of the new policy were soon seen. Shipbuilding was a quick matter in those days, and by the summer of 1635, a grand fleet of over forty finely appointed King's ships, the like of which had never before been seen in Stuart times, put to sea to assert the King's sovereignty of the Channel, and to compel Frenchmen, and all others whom it might concern, to accord his flag the homage of a salute. The object was achieved without the slightest challenge. The last thing that Richelieu wanted was to fall foul of the British navy, and he very wisely instructed the French squadrons to keep out of its path.

The subsequent levies still further strengthened the fleet, and enabled the tables at last to be turned on the Moorish sea-wolves. In 1637 a squadron of eight ships under a capable seaman, Captain Rainborow, paid a visit to their Atlantic base at Sallee, and procured the release of no less than 339 English slaves. If Rainborow could have had his way, this harrying of their ports would have been repeated every year, till piracy had ceased to pay. But domestic trouble and civil war intervened, and it was not till eighteen years later that Admiral Blake was able to complete the programme by knocking the fortifications of Tunis about the pirates' ears.

Ship-money had, in fact, created the royal navy in the sense that we to-day use the term, of a regular, trained force, large enough to meet the requirements of an island Power whose command of her home waters is a matter of vital necessity. That navy of Charles I remained in being, without breach of continuity, to the days of Nelson, of Jellicoe, of Cunningham, and beyond.

Far from being too big for its requirements, it was still not strong enough to challenge successfully the sea power of the United Netherlands, and such attempts as were made to assert the King's authority over the North Sea fishing grounds, only led to his ships being warned off without ceremony by the Dutch naval escort. Sea-power capable of challenging those who have built up its tradition by decades of continuous effort and experience, is not to be improvised in a year or two of peace time service.

Charles might, all the same, have had some excuse for believing that in the creation of the fleet—if in nothing else—he had earned the gratitude of all Englishmen of good will, instead of having created a new grievance more bitterly resented than any that had hitherto been raised against him. But in this he had reckoned without the existence of an opposition that was ceaselessly watching for any action of his or his ministers that could be worked up into a colourable grievance.

15

PATRIOTS IN SYNDICATE

OUR knowledge does not permit us to say, though it might form a fruitful field for research, to what extent the opposition to the Crown, during the first three decades of the century, was the result of organized planning. Its leaders in successive Parliaments seem to arise by a sort of spontaneous generation, and to last for a comparatively short time—two of them, Wentworth and the company promoter, Dudley Digges, ended up in the service of the King, and a third, Phelips, became reconciled to the court.

But during the 'thirties there is plain evidence that an extremely powerful and highly organized group was at work, hatching revolutionary conspiracy against the Crown ; and that its

members supplied practically the entire leadership of the renewed
and triumphant Parliamentary offensive, at the beginning of the
next decade.

These men were anything but the patriot *ingénus* of the current
myth. They included some of the wealthiest in the country,
heads of houses whose fortunes had either been made or enormously swollen by the great share-out of church property at the
Reformation, and it is only natural that they should have
constituted themselves champions of an aggressive Protestantism.

Typical of these men was William Fiennes, formerly Baron
but now—thanks to a political deal with Buckingham—Viscount
Saye and Sele, who is described by Clarendon as "the oracle of
those who were called Puritans in the worst sense", and as having
"steered all their counsels and designs". "Ill natured, choleric,
severe and rigid, and withal, highly conceited of his own worth",
is the description given of him by the Oxford biographer, Anthony
Wood, who adds that being disappointed with his expectations
at court, he came to be looked upon as godfather of the Puritan
party, in which capacity he took all occasions to promote
rebellion.

From the same authority we learn that Lord Saye's castle at
Broughton, near Banbury, was used as the secret rendezvous of
the leaders of this faction ; that there was a special room appointed
for their meetings with a passage leading to it, into which not
even the servants were permitted to come ; that even the identity
of the visitors was kept carefully secret ; and that meetings of
the same group, and with the same conspiratorial precautions,
were held at other houses.

For indeed this wealthy, capitalist ring had every reason for
enmity to the King's Government. Their business interests, in the
words of a modern historian, "were so widely spread that the
King could scarcely make any kind of move without reper-
cussions through the whole group."* The royal policy of granting
patents or monopolies to particular corporations, affected their
profits—Warwick's speculations in the Bermudas, for instance,
were hit by the tobacco monopoly, while his income from his
English estates was being affected by the revival of the Forest
Laws. It was no wonder that such men as Warwick should have
intrigued for a regime more sympathetic to the claims of big
business, or that—without in any way restricting the freedom of

* F. C. Dietz, *Political and Social History of England*, p. 283.

their private lives—they should have sought alliance with the holy and business-like zeal of Puritanism.

But the activities of these men were by no means exclusively, or perhaps even mainly, political. For, as Wood goes on to inform us :

"What embryos were conceived in the country were shaped in Gray's Inn Lane, near London, where the undertakers for the Isle of Providence did meet, brought them to pass, and put them out to nurse in London."*

You will look in vain for Providence Island in the scriptures of Whig mythology. So vague have the notions of even recent writers been on the subject, that it has been described—evidently in confusion with New Providence—as a member of the Bahama group. It lies, as a matter of fact, in the Caribbean Sea, some 125 miles off that Central American coast which was then known as the Spanish Main.

Attention was originally directed to this and a neighbouring island by another Puritan magnate, Robert Rich, Earl of Warwick, whose speciality had for long been in the promotion of activities that are sometimes described as of a privateering nature, but of which a less polite name, beginning with the same letter, is at least equally descriptive. "He appears", to quote a recent authority,† "to have maintained constantly a fleet of his own for carrying on the illicit traffic in waters claimed by Spain, with ships that did not always think it necessary to fly the English flag." He had previously been concerned with all sorts of colonial speculations, including one for the exploitation of the Bermudas, the promoters of which had come into conflict with the Crown over the customs on tobacco, and had had their grievances, significantly enough, ventilated for them in Parliament by John Pym.

Providence Island was only one of a number of similar undertakings in the New World by which wealthy landowners in England had hoped to fructify the diminished proceeds of estates hard hit by the slump in the value of money, and by the shrinkage resulting from the war in the demand for English cloth, and consequently for English wool. But this particular speculation has features that distinguish it from the promotion of colonial enterprise on the American mainland, in which the profit motive had at least some veneer of political or sectarian justification. As Saye, who, like Warwick, had speculated in development of New

* *Athenæ Oxonienses*, II, p. 273.
† *The Maritime and Colonial Expansion of England under the Stuarts*, by A. D. Innes, p. 169.

England, remarked in switching over to this more congenial form of enterprise :

"No wise man would be so foolish as to live where every man is a master, and masters must not correct their servants, where wise men propose and fools deliberate."*

There was thus to be no nonsense about free democracy at Providence, which was not only to be developed by slave labour, but where the directors proposed to keep a tight hand on the colonists themselves.

But there was an even more sinister feature appertaining to this venture, that no one was better capable of appreciating than that inveterate buccaneer, Warwick. The island lay off the Spanish coast, and its occupation was certain to be regarded by the Spaniards in the light of a deliberate challenge, and resisted by all means in their power. It might therefore have been—as it no doubt was—foreseen that hostile action against the company's shipping would provide an excuse for reprisals, and that the ostensible business of tobacco planting would soon be supplemented, if not eventually superseded, by one for which the situation of the island on the flank of the shipping route from these wealthy settlements to the mother country rendered it ideally suited.

The company was incorporated on the 4th of December, 1630. The list of shareholder directors includes most of the names that have gone down to history on the Patriot roll of honour. There were Warwick, and his brother, the ineffable Earl of Holland (formerly Lord Kensington), the first Governor, whose dandyism must have imparted a certain tone to the proceedings, but who had as keen an instinct as any man for feathering his own nest ; Lord Brooke, the idol of the stern, unbending Plutopuritans ; Lord Saye, Benjamin Rudyerd, Oliver St John, and—most important of all—the Treasurer, John Pym, whose immense energy and capacity for business soon made him the life and soul of the whole venture. As of most of Pym's activities, the records are fragmentary—we can feel rather than follow him. The fact that he twice offered and withdrew his resignation suggests that he was determined to run the whole affair in his own way, and knew himself indispensable enough to get it. And not only with his fellow directors. It is characteristic of the strong religious tenor that he could always impart to his most practical proceedings, that the colonists should have been compared by him to the

* Quoted in his life in the *D.N.B.*

murmuring Israelites, for grudging a bare fifty per cent of the fruits of their own, and their slaves' labour, for distribution in dividends to the capitalist promoters at home.

But what is most valuable of all in the discovery of this long almost forgotten episode, is the light that it throws on the strength and limitations of Pym's genius. It is quite evident that he was a man of phenomenal drive and resourcefulness, the sort who, once he has committed himself to an enterprise, will carry it through to the utmost bounds of possibility.

But hardly less remarkable is the utter lack of statesmanlike judgment displayed by Pym in his choice of an objective. I am not referring to the moral aspect of association with piracy—the Spaniards were Catholics, and Pym would doubtless have seen no more harm in gutting a galleon than in disembowelling a priest. But it ought to have been obvious from the first that this whole Providence scheme was doomed to failure. It is doubtful indeed whether even if it had been left perfectly unmolested, the settlement, in its remote situation, could have been turned into a dividend-paying proposition except in a very remote future ; but that it could possibly be maintained against the concentration of force that the Spanish Empire, once it had been roused to end the nuisance, could bring to bear upon it, was wildly unthinkable.

It was just over ten years from the formation of the company that a Spanish combined military and naval expedition from the mainland cleared the island of the last miserable survivors of what was now little better than a nest of pirates. Pym and his fellow directors had by this time ceased to take much interest in their fate. They could well afford to cut their own losses, now that a richer island than Providence, and one nearer to Europe, offered itself as the field for their next adventure.

16

JOHN HAMPDEN AND HIS POSTHUMOUS EVOLUTION

In the current mythology the activities of Pym during the period of the "Tyranny" are so little regarded that we might imagine him to have been hibernating between Parliaments. It is only recently that his connection with the Providence Island bubble came to light at all, and in any case it would never have done to have displayed the austere Parliamentarian in the capacity of a rather shady financier. And without this clue it is easy to miss the significance of the work that was being done behind closed doors at Broughton and elsewhere, in forming the nucleus of a revolutionary organization, capable of striking with deadly effect when the time came.

It is not to the account of Pym that the downfall of the Tyranny is credited in the accepted version, but to that of the pattern Englishman, John Hampden, the compendium of all the virtues and father of all the liberties. This Stainless Patriot—the style under which he is canonized—is said to have opposed himself "with dauntless breast", single-handed to the levy of an arbitrary and perfidious tax called ship-money, and by that forlorn hope saved his own, and all subsequent generations, literally, from slavery. A reverential anthology might be compiled from the enlargements of standard authors on this theme during the last couple of centuries.

This phenomenon will seem the more remarkable when we come to discover, by reference to the sources, that the Hampden of the accepted version has about as much, and as little, connection with anybody who actually lived, as the King Arthur of Tennyson and Malory with the Roman-British commander of that name. There certainly was a John Hampden, who sat in several Parliaments, and fought an action about ship-money, and was one of the leading spirits in promoting rebellion against the King, and was killed in the course of it. But for the assertion that he ever was, or professed to be, a patriot in any intelligible sense of the word, there is not a shadow of evidence—or even that he was more stainless than any other man who is so immensely wealthy that he has no temptation to put his hand in the till. But that he was one of those aggressively virtuous persons of whom the saying goes that butter will not melt in their mouths, is certainly not suggested by the accounts we have from those who were actually in contact with him. That he was a politician of extraordinary address and skill in the management of men was universally conceded by his contemporaries, but it was almost equally agreed that this was a mask for the most calculating cunning, an impression that is certainly not belied by the shifty glance of his best known portrait.

Clarendon, in one of the outstanding masterpieces of even his character drawing, in which he has obviously taken the utmost pains to be fair to his subject, sums him up in unqualified terms as a plausible rogue, with "a head to contrive, and a tongue to persuade, and a hand to execute any mischief." One whose death "seemed to be a great deliverance to the nation."

"No man," he says in an earlier estimate, "ever had a greater power over himself, or was less the man he seemed to be, which shortly appeared to everybody when he cared less to keep on the mask."

But Clarendon, it will be said, was loyal to his King, and therefore biased against Hampden. But his account is substantially confirmed by that of the Parliamentary diarist, Sir Simonds D'Ewes, a Puritan and a rebel, who portrays Hampden as a fox, remarks on his "serpentine subtlety", and describes him as "a man of much greater cunning, and it may be of the greatest address and insinuation to bring anything to pass which he desired of any man of that time, and who laid the design deepest."

Another fellow member, Sir Philip Warwick, concentrating on the narrower field of Hampden's debating style, adds his testimony:

"He was . . . the mildest, yet subtlest, speaker of any man in the House ; and had a dexterity, when a question was going to be put, which agreed not with his sense, to draw over to it, by adding some equivocal or sly word, which would enervate the meaning of it, as first put."

This remarkably concurrent testimony suggests a character to which the plain man would be rather inclined to apply the adjective "slippery" (to put it at the mildest) than "stainless." The South African Boers have a word for it—"*slim*".

And it is from these accounts that the most substantial part of our knowledge of the real Hampden is derived. For it would never be believed, by those to whom his name is a household word, how little about him we actually do know. We have not the record of a single one of his speeches ; and in fact he seems, apart from such sly interjections as Warwick describes, to have taken very little part in open debate, most of his work being done behind the scenes. Of all the noble sentiments that are attributed to him, it would be hard indeed to quote a sample from his own tongue or pen that can claim to be authentic. The most famous tag of all, about fearing to incur the curse in Magna Charta, is also attributed to Pym, Saye, and a number of others ;* so unless we are to assume that they all intoned it in chorus, it is long odds against it having been said by any particular one of them.

* D.N.B. Hampden, John

One saying of Hampden's, however, which does appear to be authentic, is to the effect that if it were not for the reiterated cry about religion they—Hampden, that is to say, and his associates— could never be certain of keeping the people on their side. To the plain man it will appear as cynical an utterance as any that might be culled from the writings of Machiavelli or Hitler. One wonders what would be the verdict on King Charles, or Laud, or Strafford, if any such saying had been recorded of one of them !

The legendary John Hampden, a person of far greater historic importance than the actual rather obscure political intriguer of that name, awaits his biographer, and the theme is one of fascinating possibilities. His existence was hardly suspected until the real Hampden had been dead and his very tomb forgotten for more than a century. Its first definite notification was in 1751, when Gray, in his *Elegy*, created the figure of the "village Hampden"—at a time when the real village Hampdens were just getting into their stride enclosing the fields of the villagers. The next landmark is in 1775, when Edmund Burke worked up his idea of the ship-money case into one of his most Tyrian patches of Whig rhetoric. The culminating point is in 1831, when Macaulay produced his famous essay—some of it sheer fiction, and all of it extravagant special pleading such as even he could hardly have got away with, except amid the frenzy of partisan agitation that preceded the Reform Bill, in the promotion of which Hampden societies had played no small part. For the legend had already become an integral part of the Whig gospel, and where romantic imagination had failed to provide sufficient factual basis, the hand of the forger supplied the deficiency. The products of both were enthusiastically received by Macaulay, and by the chief priests and scribes of the cult, who throughout the Victorian epoch went on adding a touch here, and an ornament there, to an idol that had become so much an accepted part of the national heritage, that to criticize it in any way became as the crime of treason—and it would have been unthinkable for even the boldest iconoclast to have applied to the Stainless Patriot the verdict passed on another equally legendary figure :

"There ain't no such person."

It is in vain that our own debunking century has given the lie at one time or another to practically every item of the vast body of Acts and Logia compiled by the Forsters, the Nugents, the

Sandons, the Greens—those famous inventors of an age when

> "The blindest bluffs held good, dear lass,
> And the wildest tales were true."

—at any rate, in support of the reigning political dogma. Now that the authors in question (except, for other reasons, the silver-tongued Green) have been relegated to the honourable sinecure of adding weight to bibliographies, their inventions continue to be accepted for gospel without reference to, and perhaps without knowledge of, their source or their exposure ; and the soul of John Hampden goes marching on in greater glory than ever. Not even the latest world war could prevent the third centenary of his death being made the occasion for an orgy of hagiographical ballyhoo worthy of the purest Victorian tradition of the cult.

17

PROPAGANDA BY LITIGATION

ALL that it is essential to know about the affair of ship-money, and Hampden's part in it, can be briefly set down.

Let us remember that the object of King Charles's government was to tide over a situation in which it was only too plain that to summon a Parliament would be to open the flood gates of revolution. The policy of which Wentworth and Laud were to become the two leading exponents, was to observe the strictest bounds of constitutional propriety, narrowed as these were by the Petition of Right ; to scrape along on the peace-time income of the Crown without resort to taxation ; to withdraw from any attempt to interfere in the politics of the Continent ; and to devote all the energy and resources available to building up such a Utopia of ordered prosperity as would in time cause the revolutionary fires to die from lack of fuel, and enable the normal course of Parliamentary government to be resumed in an atmosphere of loyal co-operation between King, Church, Parliament, and people.

Now Hampden, who was an enormously wealthy multiple estate owner, was among those who were determined at all costs to upset this programme. It is true that he was not on the original board of the Providence Island directorate, his speculations being rather more closely concerned with the New England mainland, and in particular the exploitation of lands on the border of Connecticut. But he was certainly one of the innermost ring of the conspiratorial clique whose headquarters was Broughton Castle, and indeed one of the other mansions at which, with such elaborate precautions, they were wont to foregather, belonged to a son-in-law of his.

If we regard their strategic problem, as we can imagine Mr Pym presenting it to his fellow Patriots at their confabulations, we shall see that in the King they were attacking an opponent who was hoping to organize his resources behind a very thin covering line, that he was just—but only just—able to maintain by manning it with his last reserves, but a penetration of which, at any point, would spell his inevitable collapse. In other words, the King was just able to carry on his government by making do with the last penny of his lawful income, provided no extra call was made on it. That meant not only that the biggest call of all, that of war, would—under whatever circumstances or provocation—be certainly fatal ; but that any other extra burden that could be put on the royal exchequer would be the last straw. The King would be bound to come with his hat in his hands to a new Parliament. And then ... we can imagine Mr Pym rubbing his own hands as he got to this point in the exposition.

But nobody was better capable of realizing than Pym, that this position of advantage would not last for ever. Sooner or later the Thorough plan, if it were allowed to go through smoothly, would revolutionize the situation the wrong way. You could not go on indefinitely playing propaganda against prosperity. Sooner or later the people would discover that they were well off, and that life under King Charles, without war, without taxes, and without want, was the sort of life that the common Englishman would like to prolong indefinitely. And even the 160,000 or so who constituted the entire electorate, might come round sufficiently to this point of view to return a majority willing to carry on with the existing Constitution.

But that time had not come yet, and the King's position was one of the utmost precariousness. For one thing, the necessity of realizing the last farthing of an income that largely consisted of petty and antiquated calls on the resources of the wealthy, made the government extremely unpopular with just that class which alone could have been said, in any intelligible sense of the word,

to be represented in Parliament. And again, the King's isola-
tionist and pacifist foreign policy, though in the long run it might
come to be reckoned as the most priceless boon ever conferred by
any English Sovereign on his people and their posterity, was not
of the sort to appeal to a public opinion inflamed with ideologist
propaganda, and demanding a firm line and decisive intervention
on behalf of God's, and the Prince Palatine's cause, without
counting the cost. And there was a third factor of weakness, in the
personnel of the government itself. The King and his ministers
were weakest just where Pym and his friends were strongest, in
the now indispensable art of propaganda. They could confer
benefits much more easily than advertise them. Neither King
Charles, with his tongue-tied dignity, nor Wentworth, with his
thunder-charged brow and explosive temper, nor the little, bustling, rather old-maidish Archbishop Laud, could be described as
competent advertisers of their own goods. No doubt, in course of
time, the goods might be trusted to advertise themselves ; but he
who waits for that time, as any slick salesman will tell you, will
be in danger of missing his market.

To bring down the King, then, it was necessary to act with the
least possible delay, in order to catch him at a disadvantage that
would grow steadily less the longer time he had for his policy to
develop. The best thing of all would be for him to get involved in
war—but to count on this would be wishful thinking. But what if
he could be compelled, with his resources already strained to
breaking point, to foot some extra item of expenditure that his
income would not cover ? That—in his extremely delicate position
of the moment—would be just enough to do the trick.

It was only to be expected that Charles's difficulties with the
navy should have presented themselves, to the conspirators, as a
golden opportunity for upsetting that precarious equilibrium
between income and expenditure, that alone enabled him, from
year to year, to stave off the revolution that they were engineering.
That they were in the least affected by urgency of the need for
ships, or sympathetic with His Majesty's efforts to meet it, there
is no reason to believe. If he wanted to police the seas, let him
come to Parliament with his crown in his hand, and hear what
conditions Parliament was going to exact for his privilege of
performing the most elementary duty to his subjects. Verily he
should not come out thence till he had parted with its uttermost
jewel ! That he should find means, legal or otherwise, of escaping

from this dilemma, was sheer tyranny ; it was not to be borne !

All that was needed was for some champion to come forward and bring this new grievance into the light of fullest publicity, by challenging the legality of ship-money in the courts. The hour brought forth the man, or it would be more accurate to say that the Broughton camarilla brought him forth.

Hampden had served in five Parliaments, and during all that time we hear nothing of him in debate. His forte was in committee work, of which his tact and skill in management rendered him a master. From the first he had attached himself to the opposition, though he preferred to work behind the scenes, organizing the attacks that other men put through. We have seen how he had assisted Eliot in working up the charges against Buckingham. Among the inner circle of extremists who forgathered at Broughton, he carried a weight second to none, but he was better known to his own county of Buckingham than to the world at large. He was now destined to emerge into a blaze of publicity that has lit up his figure ever since.

It lay between Hampden and Saye, both of whom were owners of great possessions in districts far inland. The first choice appears to have been Saye, but on second thoughts Hampden was selected, possibly because he was known to be excellently versed in the law ; and he chose to resist an assessment of twenty shillings on one of his many estates. As money was no object to him, he was able to brief the most eloquent counsel at the Bar,* including one of his own group, Oliver St John, who, though of a saturnine and jaundiced disposition, rose magnificently to the occasion. And Hampden displayed his strategic insight in fighting the case, not on the obvious legal ground of the difference between maritime and inland districts, but on the King's right to make the levy at all, except with Parliamentary sanction. In view of the fact that the judges had already certified, by an overwhelming majority, the legality of ship-money, he could hardly have hoped to win. But he could obtain such nation-wide publicity for the opposition propaganda as had not been possible since the doors at Westminster had been locked.

He succeeded probably beyond his expectations. The case

---

* If we are to assume that he did this out of his own and not—as in the case of the nobbling dinners that he and Pym subsequently gave to M.P.s at their Westminster lodgings—out of the common purse of the ring.

came on early in November, 1637, and was argued by counsel till within a week of Christmas. So well had St John, and his colleague, Holborn, done their work, that even the Barons of the Exchequer were sufficiently impressed with the importance of the issue at stake to insist on referring its decision to the entire body of judges. It was not until the following June that all their opinions were collected, and this time the majority for the Crown was no longer 10 to 2, but a bare 7 to 5. Hampden had had a rare piece of luck, in the fact that two of their Lordships had decided the matter for him on technical grounds that had nothing to do with the main contention. The fact that legal technicalities could be strained in this way against the Crown, at least shows how fair, according to their lights, the judges endeavoured to be. To put it mildly, this is not the sort of thing one expects during a tyranny.

What was the revenge eventually wreaked by Hampden and his friends on the judges who had dared decide against them, and even those who had not decided emphatically enough for them, will appear later.

Charles had thus got the decision he wanted, and got it fairly enough. But it was one of those victories whose fruits are reaped by the vanquished. The King's zeal for the navy was likely to prove his undoing. Ship-money might be legal, but it had now been advertised throughout the length and breadth of the country as another grievance of grievances.

It was the most fatal time such a thing could have happened. For now clouds of war and rebellion had begun to darken the Northern sky, and the King would have need of all his prestige, and all the loyalty of his subjects, if he were not to be swept off his feet by the plainly impending storm.

As for Hampden, if ever man got his money's worth for twenty shillings and costs, it was he. He had not only achieved the publicity that he had been put up to secure for the opposition propaganda, but he had succeeded in getting himself accepted for three centuries—and for heaven knows how many more—as the very symbol and embodiment of heroic patriotism. Some years previously he had actually suffered the genteel martyrdom of imprisonment for resisting a forced loan ; that real though minor sacrifice* was no more remembered than that of any other of his

---

* It would seem that the stories about his having permanently impaired his health arise from a confusion between him and the other Hampden of the Five Knights' case. See *D.N.B.* Hampden.

fellow resisters. This time he had incurred no risk, had spent no more than he could easily afford ; it is doubtful whether even the idea of the action was his own ; it had been fought for him by his counsel ; we have no record of any memorable speech or grand gesture of his—his utmost contribution, beyond footing whatever he did foot of the bill, would seem to have been his idea, if it really was his idea, of fighting the case with a steady eye not to its legal, but to its propagandist aspect.

The fact is that the creation of the Hampden legend was an even more daring and successful piece of opposition propaganda than the case itself. And it may be said that the legendary figure of the great champion of liberty, with his steadfast mien and dauntless breast, standing, like Horatius, in the path of over-whelming tyranny, has become more a part of English history, and acquired a vastly greater significance than the reality of the hard-bitten political intriguer, the cunning extremist, whose eyes shoot back to us from the canvas of his best known portrait a glance of eternal suspiciousness.

"Would twenty shillings," thundered the greatest of all Whig orators, "would twenty shillings have ruined Mr Hampden's fortune ? No, but the payment of half twenty shillings, on the principle it was demanded, would have made him a slave."

We cannot help wondering whether those 339 of the King's subjects, whom Captain Rainborow brought home in the ship-money fleet from Sallee, realized that they had returned to a worse slavery than ever, in an island for the protection of whose shores even millionaires might be required to stump up twenty shillings once in a way ; or whether they found as many tears as Mr Burke, to shed over the spectacle of John Hampden, Esquire, in his invisible bondage.

18

HONESTY AS POLICY

UNTIL there appeared, in an utterly unexpected quarter, the first signs of impending catastrophe, it would have taken an inspired prophet indeed to have foreboded the collapse of King Charles's experiment in personal rule. By every conceivable test, that experiment had succeeded beyond hope or expectation ;

the financial position strengthened every year, and the country throve and prospered to such an extent, both in comparison with previous times, and the state of contemporary peoples, that it must have been hard for any ordinary mortal to imagine how there could exist, except in the minds of the few irreconcilable malcontents, the desire for change.

This impression might well have been strengthened had our imaginary prophet grasped, to a greater extent than anyone of his, or even of our time, how essentially the King's problem was one of everyday finance. Under the easy Portland regime, the solution had been postponed rather than found. But when Laud, assisted by the capable and honest Juxon, got a grip on affairs, it was unthinkable that his orderly mind would tolerate a succession of deficits. The royal accounts, like everything else with which the Archbishop's restless mind concerned itself, must be in ship-shape order.

Such was the end to which all others had to yield ; not, as with Portland, that of carrying on somehow with as little trouble as possible. To such a mind as Laud's there could be no distinction between unsoundness and wickedness in finance ; the obligation to be true and just in all one's dealings was plainly inconsistent with living beyond income, still less with an easy tolerance of corrupt practices. And if to tread the path of sound finance and sound morals involved also treading on a number of important toes, that was all one to Laud.

Among the first steps taken under his auspices, while the Treasury was in commission, was a thorough investigation both of assets and liabilities, and an endeavour to bridge the gap by a revision of the Tariff. That the Tariff could be so revised had been established in the courts during the reign of James I, and the result of the new book of rates was to add an invaluable £70,000, with a tendency to rise during subsequent years, to the exchequer receipts. At the same time a greater effort than ever was made to exploit every available resource, and above all, to stop all of the many leakages and wastages that had been tolerated, for the sake of a quiet or a prosperous life, even by the economical Portland. The new broom at the Treasury was applied with greater vigour than ever when grasped in the capable hands of Juxon. The gentle prelate turned out to be a first class man of business, who not only set his face unflinchingly against the long-tolerated jobbery and corruption in high places, but by sheer hard work in the checking and auditing of accounts, did really succeed in enforcing a new standard of honesty in the King's service.*

Such was the policy of Thorough translated into terms of finance, and Laud's untiring energy was the driving force behind it, as it was behind Church and University reform.

Now Thorough is the policy that critics, in all ages, have united in urging on the controllers of public finance. Absolute purity, rigid economy, these everybody supports in theory ; but the men who put them into practice seldom fail to incur an unpopularity as uncompromising as themselves. The new methods and standard of honesty were raising up for the Government, and through the Government, for the King, a host of enemies among those rich and powerful people whose purses were most affected, and to whom the King's very success in living of his own was the greatest grievance of all.

And it must be remembered that Laud, even when reinforced by Juxon at the Treasury, was never in the position of a modern Prime Minister. That was filled by the King himself, and the King was anything but an uncompromising supporter of Thorough. His naturally cautious and balancing temperament disinclined him from extreme courses of any kind, and it is doubtful whether, until the crash came, he had any clear realization of how precarious was his tenure of power, and how rigorous the conditions to be fulfilled if the delicate equilibrium of his Government was to be maintained.

Charles had counsellors at his elbow of a very different calibre from Laud, Juxon, and Wentworth. His temperamental aloofness denied him an insight into character—never was a man more frequently deceived in his estimate of others—and he would only too frequently lend his ear to mere flatterers and time-servers, with their private axes to grind. And though honest to the core, honest far above the kingly average, his honesty had not quite the austere and logical intransigeance that would have justified the epithet "Thorough", in the sense that Laud and Wentworth used, and practised it.

One sees this in quite little things. It will be remembered how Wentworth had got the City of London deprived of its Ulster charter, and cast in a huge fine in addition. Charles had intended to remit the whole of this fine, but finding at the last moment that the Queen was in need of £12,000, not much more than a sixth

* F. C. Dietz, *English Public Finance*, 1558-1641, p. 277.

of the total sum, he decided to make the City pay up to that extent. Assuming that the fine itself was just, there was nothing on which one could put one's finger as actually wrong in this expedient, but it does surely reveal a certain failing in delicacy.

A more serious lapse, and one that shows with what difficulties Laud, or any other honest statesman, had to contend, is that connected with the enclosure of Richmond Park. This was a scheme upon which the King had set his heart, as he was a keen sportsman, and it would give him a hunting ground ideally placed between Richmond and Hampton Court. Much of the land was already his own, and he was prepared to buy out the other owners at above the market rates. A majority of these allowed themselves to be squared, but there were a few who refused to part with their land at any price, and the King, rather than have the scheme wrecked for the sake of these impracticable Naboths, took the high-handed line of starting to enclose the whole area, with their consent or without it, by the perimeter of a brick wall.

This was one of the very few acts of his reign to which the epithet tyrannous could, with the least plausibility, be applied, and it was particularly bad because—largely under Laud's inspiration—there was nothing against which the Government had set its face more firmly than the attempts of rich men to enclose the land of their poorer neighbours. And there was the further consideration, that the cost of putting up this extent of high wall was going to be a serious addition to those expenses that Laud and Juxon were straining every nerve to keep down.

But Laud had one particularly dangerous opponent on the Council in the shape of Lord Cottington, now Master of the Court of Wards, whom Wentworth, in his correspondence with Laud, had nicknamed, not without reason, Lady Mora's hand-maid. He was, in fact, almost a caricature of the original Lady Mora, or Lord Portland, and had so much the instinct of making the best of both worlds, that, whenever he was at all seriously ill, he would be converted to Rome, and then, on convalescence, recapture the light of Protestant faith. He had a rich store of worldly wisdom, and was capable of giving excellent advice when it suited his book, but he coveted the Treasurership, and that alone would have made him welcome any opportunity of tripping up the Archbishop, whose methods and morals must, in any case have irritated him beyond bearing.

Cottington had perceived just as clearly as Laud the folly of the King's action, and in fact, kept on advising him against it, till His Majesty, who was not easily turned aside from anything on which he had set his heart, lost his temper ; whereupon Cottington, who was the last person in the world to obtrude good advice where it was not wanted, tactfully yielded the point. Shortly afterwards Laud, who was more than ever appalled by the scandal that this unhappy wall, so close to London, was beginning to create among its citizens, and whose honest mind had not conceived the least suspicion of Cottington's *volte face*, buttonholed him, in his usual vehement, excited way, and implored him to use his influence to stop the King from proceeding with this folly. Imagine his surprise when Cottington gravely began to argue in favour of the project, so convenient in all sorts of ways for the King ! The solemn cynicism of this was too much for the quick-tempered little prelate, who told Cottington that it was he and his like who were ruining their master and alienating the affection of his subjects. Cottington, delighted at having drawn Laud to this extent, went on to imply that anybody who opposed the King's known wishes was guilty of something not far short of High Treason. This had the desired effect of sending off Laud in a towering rage, and of causing him to denounce this evil counsellor, at the first opportunity, to the King. Charles, who had got over his annoyance with Cottington for voicing very different sentiments, was even more annoyed with Laud for his discovery of this mare's nest, and proceeded to administer a thorough snub, which was, of course, precisely what Cottington had intended. Against such difficulties, and in such an atmosphere, did the champions of pure and efficient government have to contend, even at the height of their influence. Lady Mora had a fearful strength, and she was as intangible as Proteus.

19

WORK AND PLAY FOR ALL

But it was not only a question of rooting out the malpractices of individuals. The strength of Lady Mora was that of a class, and that the richest and most powerful class in the Kingdom. Or perhaps it would be more accurate to use the plural, and talk of this intangible enemy as of the monied, or propertied, or capitalist, classes, though none of these words constitutes an exact or satisfactory definition. It comes to this ; that King Charles's Government, if, and in so far as, it was to justify its existence, must be that of a national Sovereign, lifted high above the least bias of class or respect of persons, and representative of his people in a more comprehensive sense than a House of Commons, consisting entirely of wealthy landowners in the shires, or the captains of industry and finance in the towns.

That was the true soul, the philosophic basis, of the policy Thorough. And the more we study the proceedings of its two great champions, Laud and Wentworth, the more clearly shall we realize the thoroughness of their devotion to this ideal. King Charles himself was treading the same path, but with a more hesitating and occasionally errant footstep. It was only at the end of his life that he came to see what the ideal of a national sovereignty implied, in all its height and depth and comprehensiveness, and to express that creed in language that not Laud, or even Wentworth, could command.

We must remember that Thorough was not only a State, but a Church policy. Those who think they have understood Laud by labelling him a High Church Anglican, seldom realize that the Church of England of Laud's ideal was utterly different to the sort of Church that rose from its own ashes after the Restoration. For that later Church was one that hastened to make and keep the peace with rank and property, and to show a becoming deference to the squire and his relations. But the clothier's son of Reading was scarcely more class conscious, in this sense, than the carpenter's Son of Nazareth. He did really intend to put the squire, like every other layman, into his proper station, which was that of an obedient child of Mother Church. And if the squire or any of his relations, male or female, notoriously transgressed the code of morals that it was the Church's mission to uphold, they were liable to her rebuke, or even her correction, as much as the humblest peasant or beggar.

Laud, says Clarendon—and with the substitution of State for Church, the same might have been said of Wentworth—"did court persons too little. ... If the faults and vices were fit to be looked into and discovered let the persons be who they would that were guilty of them, they were sure to find no favour or

connivance from him. He intended that the discipline of the
Church should be felt as well as spoken of, and that it should be
applied to the greatest and most splendid transgressors, as well
as to the punishment of smaller offences and meaner offenders ;
and thereupon called for or cherished the discovery of those who
were not careful to cover up their own iniquities, thinking they
were above the reach of other men's, or their power or will to
chastise. Persons of honour or great quality, of the court, and of
the country, were every day cited into the High-commission
Court, upon the fame of their incontinence, or other scandal in
their lives, and were there prosecuted to their shame and punishment : and ... the shame (which they called an insolent triumph
over their degree and quality, and levelling them with the
common people) was never forgotten, but watched for revenge."

Levelling them with the common people ! That was the feature
of the "tyranny" that could neither be forgotten nor forgiven ;
it was for that, more than any other cause, that the tyrant and
his two great abettors had to be put out of the world.

No one will deny that things were done under their auspices
that, to say the least of it, were ill-advised, but it was not these
things that were the cause of their ruin half as much as those that
nowadays most people would enter to their credit. For nothing
can be more false than the notion of Charles's policy during the
sixteen-thirties, as one of mere stagnation and repression. For, in
spite of the limited resources at its disposal, and the fact that the
abeyance of Parliament cut it off from the possibility of fresh
legislation, his Government displayed an active concern for the
betterment of the nation, of which Parliament had given not the
least sign, and compared with which the policy of rulers and
Parliaments, for generations after its downfall, can only be
described as one of oligarchic reaction.

This was most conspicuously of all the case in its efforts to
alleviate the condition of the poor. It is the opinion of Miss E. M.
Leonard, whose researches have thrown such a flood of light on
this aspect of seventeenth century history, that "during the
personal government of Charles I we have not only the first
thorough execution of the poor law, but a more complete organization for the help of the weaker classes than at any other period
of our history".*

And this was accomplished not by some one sensational piece

* E. M. Leonard, *Early History of the English Poor Relief*, p. x.

of legislation, a resource that Charles's Government had not at
its disposal, but by hard, and enthusiastic, and continuous,
administrative effort. For the difficulty was not to get good laws
passed, but to get those that there were, put into proper effect.
Already the uniquely English system had developed, by which
the threads of local administration, as well as of petty justice,
were gathered up into the hands of the principal local gentry, or
Justices of the Peace. It was a system with many obvious advan-
tages, but with the equally obvious defect of allowing the rich
man's possibly benevolent, but certainly interested, notions, to
have unrestricted sway in all matters affecting the interests of his
poorer neighbours. Human nature being what it is, it would be
fairly safe to predict that their Worships, if left to themselves,
would leave unadministered such parts of the law as involved
their own class in manifest expense or inconvenience.

The essential thing, then, was to keep the Justices up to the
mark, and this could only be done by the central authority of the
King's Council, continuously and actively exerted, as it was, in
fact, during the time of the personal government. It would seem
as if the spirit that Wentworth had imparted to his administration
of the North, and Laud to his reform of the Church, had communicated itself to the ministry. In 1631, a new book of orders was
issued for the guidance of the Justices, and thenceforth there was
a continuous output of royal proclamations, or administrative
instructions, for the speeding up of slack or obstructive local
authorities.

These instructions went far beyond mere poor relief. They
included the greatest effort ever made in England to provide
work at a fair wage for all able-bodied men. Each parish was
expected to provide a fund, out of which materials and wages
could be drawn for the employment of its surplus manhood, and
it was no infrequent thing for this store to be increased by private
munificence. The efficiency of the system depended more than
anything else on the drive imparted by the central authority—
otherwise it was pretty certain that the local squires would
consult their own interests by sabotaging it. And under
Charles's Council, that drive was applied with the honest will to
see that the poor man did at least obtain the elementary human
right of earning his bread by the sweat of his brow, and that his
better-off neighbour should, to this extent at least, act as his
brother's keeper.

Very different was the state of things after the overthrow of King Charles's "tyranny." The possessing classes got firmly into the saddle, and proceeded not only to scrap the whole attempt to intervene on the poor man's behalf to secure him a job of work and a fair deal with his employer, but also, two years after the Restoration, to pass one of the most shameless acts of class tyranny ever devised, that chained him like a serf to his parish, but made not the least attempt to provide him with a serf's certainty of employment, thus providing local employers with a stagnant surplus of labour that could be used, *ad libitum*, to force down the general level of wages and working conditions.

Another way in which the Government, under Laud's influence, endeavoured to hold even the scales of social justice, may be best described by the statesman under whose auspices this same Act of 1662 was passed :

"The revenue of too many of the court consisted principally in enclosures, and improvements of that nature, which he [Laud] still opposed passionately, except they were founded upon law ; and then, if it would bring profit to the King, how old and obsolete soever the law was, he thought he might justly advise the prosecution. And so he did a little too much to countenance the commission for depopulation, which brought much charge and trouble upon the people. ..."

The minority of rich people, that is to say, who were actively engaged in depopulating the countryside by laying house to house and field to field.

"Which," concludes Lord Clarendon, "was likewise cast upon his account."

It was not only with the work and wages of the people—the real people—that Charles and his Council were concerned. Recreation was almost equally important, and this was being threatened by the cult of austere gloom that was the most unlovely feature of Puritanism ; the tendency, almost certainly diseased, of detecting the taint of sin in everything that happened to please the eye or delight the sense. The habit of taking for gospel everything in the Old Testament, had prompted the most conspicuous of all manifestations of this cult in the identification of the Christian first day of the week with the Jewish seventh, and the transformation of the Sunday festival into the Sabbath taboo of the Mosaic Law, in spite of the fact that not even Calvin and Knox ever got quite so far as tacking on to the Fourth

Commandment the additional clause, "in it thou shalt do no manner of play".

King James had stoutly stood between his people and the growing threat of a Puritan Sabbath, and had ordered a declaration to be read from all pulpits confirming the freedom of Christian worshippers to enjoy themselves, innocently, after service time. His son, than whom no Puritan maintained, or expected, a more undeviating strictness of personal morality, could yet be virtuous without seeking to put the sun out of Sunday. In this he had the whole-hearted support of Laud, who, however hardly he may have borne on the rich and powerful, had always a warm place in his heart for the common man, and to whom the beauty of holiness was incompatible with gloom.

And in this both Charles and Laud stood for England, the merry and essential England that men like Prynne were so fiercely eager to destroy. We know what these men did as soon as the breakdown of the "Tyranny" gave them a free hand—how they stamped out every form of Sunday recreation, including even "vain and profane walking" ; how they proscribed the celebration of Christmas ; how they made a crime of the drama ; and how every sort of local or traditional festivity fell under their persecuting ban. And it was these very zealots who made it a mortal grievance against Laud, that he allowed the Church to deal with the moral delinquencies of ladies and gentlemen, as if they had been ordinary men and women.

One typical instance of the sort of thing that was counted against Laud for tyranny, was when a Puritan judge took it upon himself, with very doubtful legality, to suppress, under severe pains and penalties, the annual wakes with which the good folk of Somerset had been accustomed, from time immemorial, to celebrate, on the nearest Sunday, the anniversaries of their local saints ; and on which days, the Bishop of Bath and Wells reported, "the service of God was more solemnly performed and the church was better frequented both in the forenoon and the afternoon than on any Sunday in the year ... the people very much desired the continuance of them."

Naturally Laud was up in arms about this usurpation of what, if it had been anyone's business, would have been that of the Church, and complained to the King, who, after due enquiry, instructed the judge to revoke his order at the next assizes. But he, secure of backers among the local magnates, not only refused to

withdraw, but actually repeated it. This was too much ; he was
summoned before a committee of the Council, where Laud
treated him to such a wigging as judges are more accustomed to
give than to receive. "I have," complained his Lordship on
emerging, "been almost choked with a pair of lawn sleeves."
And the Western Circuit, no doubt to the relief of the local
farmers and their men, saw him no more.

No one, not openly biased, would try to make out that King
Charles's government, during these eleven years between his
third and fourth Parliaments, was without its share of human
mistakes and shortcomings. It would be absurd to pretend that
the King himself, in escaping from the leading strings of Buckingham, had become such a statesman as Richelieu, or hero as
Gustavus. He was always, as is the way with shy men, a little
uncertain of himself and niggardly of his confidence, and he had
a curious way of hiding from himself his real and sound intuitions
—he sought and ensued peace without ever quite facing the fact
that to break it would be suicide, and there was one time, in 1636,
when Wentworth was writing frantically to Laud to stop His
Majesty's latest idea of using his new fleet for another war with
Spain. A statesman's touch needs to be firm as well as sensitive,
and firmness is born of more assurance than Charles had, as yet,
acquired.

Charles was therefore not the man to impose his will on a team
of ministers, and drive them along the line of his chosen policy.
Nor was he, after Buckingham's death, going to allow anybody
else's will to supersede his own, and become, like Richelieu's,
that of the State. Let Laud and Wentworth chafe as they would,
they would never get the fair field they wanted for the policy they
called Thorough. Charles's thoroughness would always be
subject to some qualification or delay. There was too much of the
Hamlet, and too little of the Fortinbras in his composition, for
perfectly successful kingcraft.

But when every plea has been put in that the devil's advocate
could advance, we can reasonably claim, on behalf of this personal
government or "tyranny" of his, that it was enlightened and
progressive beyond the standards of its time, and that it gave
England such a period of peace and prosperity as she was not to
see return during that century. More than any Government for
two centuries to come, it was national, in the sense that it did at
least, according to its lights, try to secure a fair deal for all classes

alike, and not merely the supremacy of one. The complaints against it boil down to those of the rich and powerful ; of the great landowners who found a fraction of their rent rolls requisitioned for the navy or cut off in fines, who were bothered by the officious way in which they were kept up to the performance of their duty to their neighbour as by law prescribed, or outraged at the spectacle of people of their class being visited for their delinquencies or peccadilloes as if they were just anybody. But those without land or capital, who, after all, constituted the great majority of the population, had more reason to bless than to complain of King Charles's rule. The bitter cry of the unwilling knight paying for his spurs, or of the millionaire landlord dropped upon for depopulating his estates, can hardly have evoked a sympathetic response in the village alehouse ; but there must have been many, in the years to come, who looked back with regret upon the time when the Council was actively at work trying to see that there should be work and a fair wage for all, and after work was over, freedom for sport and play, in a still merry England.

20

FAITHFUL STEWARDSHIP

WE have only touched upon a small part of the multifarious business with which Charles and his ministers had to deal. It would, indeed, correct a good many false notions of history, could its students subject themselves to the discipline of sometimes reading through any month, taken at random, of the State documents that form the record of the day to day activities of government. That would be the best antidote to the popular idea of a fairy-tale King luxuriating in splendid ease, or a tyrant gloomily clinging to the sweets of assured power. We might then visualize King Charles as the manager of a vast and intricate business, and consuming laborious days, at the head of a very mixed staff, in the prosaic grind of office work—not only King in the modern sense of a ceremonial specialist or quasi-divine figurehead, but also and most of all a crowned Prime Minister.

Regarding him thus, without the least tincture of royalist

idolatry, and taking into account the limiting conditions of his task, and the very imperfect human material through which he had to work, I believe that the closer we get down to that every-day record, the more reason· we shall find for a verdict, on behalf of his country and people, of "Well done, thou good and faithful servant !"

To sum up the main grounds of this verdict, not all of which I have had the space to substantiate in detail, I would submit :

(1) The supreme blessing of peace in a Europe torn asunder by the most diabolical of all its wars.

(2) A prosperity so conspicuous that it could elicit from one of the Queen's Capuchin fathers the odd complaint, "England is an abundant country *and has no taxes ;* the inhabitants lead a luxurious life, far removed from the poverty of other places, for which reason austerities touch them deeply."

(3) A social policy in comparison with which that of the next two centuries is one of oligarchic reaction.

(4) An ecclesiastical policy that played its part in making this the golden and culminating age of the Church of England.

(5) A commercial policy that aimed with vigour and success at the encouragement of home industry, and particularly of the growing cloth trade that, largely thanks to the excellent relations maintained with wool-growing Spain, was beginning more and more to penetrate the markets of Central Europe.

(6) A naval policy that laid the foundations of a fleet perman-ently in being, and capable of safeguarding the shores and commerce of an island Power against Continental rivals.

(7) The most hopeful attempt yet made at creating a well-governed and prosperous Ireland.

(8) The sympathetic encouragement which King Charles, like his sons after him, never failed to accord to the beginnings of British expansion overseas.

We might add that this was accomplished within the limits of the law, as interpreted by the judges, and of the Constitution, as it was then, and had been in Tudor and early Stuart times. There was nothing to prevent Charles, any more than his father before him, from living of his own as long as he could lawfully do so. What would have been the decisive step to tyranny, the attempt to back royal authority by military force—the universal practice of despots abroad—was never taken, nor was there any thought of taking it. As events proved, there was no time when the Crown was not absolutely dependent upon—at any rate—the passive goodwill of its subjects. When the time came that it had to fight for its existence, it had to depend on whatever proportion of civilians it could induce to take arms freely in its support.

But when we have said all this, we must not forget that the Crown did conspicuously fail in securing more than the passive acquiescence of its subjects, or at any rate those of them who were most politically conscious. However many claims to applause it may have earned, it was strangely unsuccessful in getting them across the footlights. Even in traditionally loyal Oxford, the King could ride in state without eliciting one spontaneous cheer. The defeat on the propaganda front was hopeless ; its effects are with us to-day.

To what cause are we to attribute this strange and, it would seem, paradoxical denial of public appreciation where it would seem to have been so richly earned ? Not, I would suggest, to any one cause, but to a complication of causes. Some of these were no doubt personal. Charles was never a King that Englishmen were likely to understand. The shell of icy dignity with which he protected that fatal impediment in his speech, might have commanded reverence in lands habituated to the tradition of a divine Caesar ; but the English nature warms to a certain bluffness, the sort of quality in a Sovereign that made it natural to speak of Harry the Fifth and bluff King Hal and good Queen Bess. Imagine any Englishman talking of Charles I as Jolly King Charlie!* If that had been possible, there would have been no King Charles the Martyr.

Nor was there anyone round him to attract the popularity that he missed. His charming Queen was an object of hatred and suspicion on account of her religion, and because of the Catholic priests and agents of her entourage. Laud was one of those men who seemed fated, with the best intentions in the world, to put other men's backs up by everything they do, or rather, by their manner of doing it. Wentworth, even if he had been on the spot, was hardly cut out, with his sombre, imperious nature, for a popular rôle that he would certainly have disdained. And as for the other ministers, none of them, not even the excellent

---

* Though in one Scots ballad we do read of King Charlie.

Juxon, were much more than names to the ordinary Englishman.

Moreover, Charles had the misfortune to be pitted against invisible forces that neither he, nor the greatest man alive, could have withstood permanently. The great, blind impulse to consummate the Reformation, to go to the opposite extreme from Rome, was bound to work itself to a climax. Not till ritual and ornament, not till the hierarchy had gone under, would the time be ripe for the pendulum to swing the other way.

There was a parallel movement in the State. Ever since the sack of the monasteries had raised up an aristocracy of *nouveaux riches*, the power of the monied interest, and its ambition to control the machinery of government for its own ends, had been growing. At present the rich men and the zealots were in alliance —Dives gave himself out for the greatest zealot of all, and the King found himself confronted by a solid front of Puritans and Plutopuritans

There may—let us admit it frankly—have been something else that the protagonists themselves were incapable of understanding ; some deep, uncomprehended urge of English historical development that rendered it necessary that the Crown should fall, and Parliamentary supremacy be made absolute, no matter by what means or for what ends. It may be that not only the noblest individuals, but whole generations, are well sacrificed to a distant future. It is not necessarily the most attractive patriarch from whose loins springs the chosen seed.

But, when we have allowed for all these blind, or subconscious forces, let us not forget that there was much at work beneath the surface that was neither blind nor subconscious, but deliberately and cunningly organized. It is impossible to doubt that during all the time that Parliament was in abeyance, a ceaseless propaganda was being engineered for the undermining of the King's authority, and that the counter-measures of the Government were ludicrously inadequate. The inflation of Hampden, the almost canonization of martyrs like Bastwick and Prynne, did not just happen— they were triumphs of art. Floods of pamphlets are not the result of spontaneous generation. The Broughton conclave must have been only one of many foci or generating cells of disaffection, the full results of whose work would become evident in the ripeness of time.

21

CHARLES AND HENRIETTE

THIS time of the personal government was for King Charles not
only one of hard and constructive work, but also of a personal
happiness almost unclouded. If his life was a tragedy, it was at
least relieved by that one decade of continuous sunshine, a sunshine itself pregnant with tragedy, as on one of those almost
impossibly brilliant afternoons, when scarcely a leaf stirs or a
wave murmurs, and yet the whole air is electric with the fore-
boding of thunder.

His marriage, which had started with such misunderstanding
and dissension, had miraculously righted itself, since the removal
from her side of the French suite, and from his, of the all-dominat-
ing Favourite. They had blossomed into a pair of lovers, romantic-
ally devoted and ideally suited to one another. Henriette's
Southern vivacity was just what the tongue-tied son of Denmark
and Scotland needed to bring him out of his shell. Henriette, too,
had all the typical Frenchwoman's maternal instincts. After that
first unfortunate miscarriage, she settled down to the business of
producing and rearing the largest family possible. In 1630 an
heir to the Throne was safely brought into the world, a healthy,
though not, at first, very prepossessing looking baby. "He is so
ugly," his mother wrote to Madame St Georges, "that I am
ashamed of him, but his size and fatness supply the want of
beauty." A daughter followed in the next year, and two years
later a second son, James, Duke of York, whom his father,
preoccupied as he was with the creation of a navy, destined from
infancy to be a sailor prince, and invested with the title of
Lord High Admiral—one that he was destined gloriously to
adorn.

Henriette had found her true vocation in the fulfilment of her
maternal and marital duty. She had a temperament almost
exaggeratedly feminine, and no serious ambition for playing a
part in affairs of state. Her politics, such as they were, were more
concerned with persons than principles. She could never stand
Portland, but that was because he encouraged her husband to be
close with her about money. She never, until it was too late,
learnt to appreciate Wentworth ; but then, how many women

can have taken readily to that brooding thundercloud of a man ? She even, in a rather Platonic way, flirted with the aristocratic party in France that was ill-advised enough to work for the downfall of Richelieu, but this was because the Cardinal was making himself so extremely horrid to her mother.

She was certainly as earnest as she had it in her to be about her religion, but even here, she was far from being the determined and ruthless intriguer that her Protestant subjects imagined her to be. The austere Capuchin fathers, whom her husband allowed her to include in her household, were rather inclined to shake their heads regretfully over the light-hearted little queen, who seemed to live only for the moment. It was not until the iron had entered into her soul that she was to become, as she did in her widowhood, really hard and bigoted about her religion.

No doubt it was largely owing to her that, during the "tyranny," the ferocious persecution of Catholics, for which Parliament and Mr Pym had clamoured so persistently, had its edge blunted. But it was not difficult to persuade such a husband as Charles to refrain from persecution ; to his refined and intellectual nature the mere idea of such a thing would have been inexpressibly painful. The fact that Charles never dreamed of wavering in his attachment to his own Church, and was as likely to become a Confucian as a Catholic, did not imply an intolerant hatred of the older faith or its adherents. He was capable of realizing that however grave a menace to the State the Catholics may have constituted during the lifetime of his grandmother, Mary, Queen of Scots, they were now without the power, even if they had had the will, to be a serious menace. And the result of his willingness to live and let live was that when the hour of trial came, he found no more devoted loyalty than among his Catholic subjects.

It is true that the nerves of good Protestants were continually kept on the stretch by the dreadful plots and conspiracies of which, to minds obsessed with the dread of Popery, the Court seemed to be the hotbed. The Queen's Catholic chapel, to which the devout and curious were free to resort, her Capuchins, with their quaint garb and conspicuous self-denial, were the thin end of who knew what sinister wedge! Still worse was the presence at court of an accredited agent of the Vatican, an eminently sensible arrangement, one would have thought, considering that the Pope was one of the most important of Charles's fellow Sovereigns.

But to the full-blooded Protestant, it was as if His Satanic Majesty had appointed a resident fiend, with a fiend's intents.

As a matter of fact, very little of importance was, or could be, accomplished by the successive holders of this office. Charles was always ready to display the utmost respect and sympathy for the Catholic point of view, which was at any rate less antipathetic to him than that of the Puritans, but it was no more than the detached sympathy of an observer ; while as for Laud, such was his annoyance at the tendency of certain important personages, and particularly ladies, at Court, to succumb to the arguments so persuasively advanced by urbane ecclesiastics, that he lost his temper altogether, and at one time declined to be barely civil to His Holiness's representative. There were, as there have been in later times, one or two ultra-High-Church Anglicans in high places, who dreamed dreams of a reunion with the See of Peter on the Church of England's own terms, and had not discovered that with Rome it is not a question of bargaining, but of all or nothing.

But the effect of the Vatican diplomacy was only considerable in the impression it kept alive that the King and Archbishop were liable, at any moment, to sell the pass to Rome, and that the Queen was a public enemy of the utmost power and malignancy. All this was destined to count heavily against the Crown when the revolutionary forces were at length unchained.

It was hard on Charles and Henriette that the scales should have been so loaded against them, as if ever a royal pair were capable of making their Court a pride and example to the nation, it was they. It may with truth be said that never, in the history of the English monarchy, has the Court shown to such advantage as it did during the sixteen-thirties. The King maintained a standard of culture certainly not inferior to those set by Elizabeth and his own eldest son, and joined to it one of moral purity that would have satisfied Victoria and Albert. Virtue and art were met together ; beauty and innocence had kissed each other.

For certainly, if we may be allowed to talk of married innocence, never would the words be more exactly fitted than to the union of this so strangely contrasted, yet harmonious, pair. No writer of fiction who had to deal with so hot-blooded a Parisian beauty, joined to a husband so impeccably correct, could have resisted the temptation to make her flash her dark eyes on some more responsive lover. But truth is proof against the most urgent requirements of fiction. Henriette, the gay, the frivolous, was as conspicuous a model of wifely virtue as the most patriarchally minded Puritan could have desired to see, or to possess. One of the Pope's representatives, the Scotsman, George Con, who knew her intimately, describes her as "so full of incredible innocence, that in the presence of strangers she is as modest as a girl," and goes on to quote the testimony of her confessor, that she is never so much as tempted to sins of the flesh. "She has little care," he adds, "for the future, trusting altogether to the King."*

Their love never seems to have lost the freshness and wonder of that day of their first meeting, when Charles had snatched her up in his arms and kissed the tears from her cheeks. One little incident, preserved by Dean Swift, speaks eloquently of the sort of relationship there was between them. Charles "thought one day to surprise her with the present of a diamond brooch ; and fastening it to her bosom with his own hand, he awkwardly wounded her with the prong so deeply, that she snatched the jewel from her bosom and flung it to the ground. The King looked alarmed and confounded, and turned pale, which he was never seen to do in his worst misfortunes." In which the lover of the ill-starred Stella can only see proof of criminal uxoriousness. Such as he—would !

And yet, during these years of calm, it is impossible to say that the King allowed uxoriousness to sway his political action to any undue extent. He was fully capable of standing up to her on occasion—he would, for instance, have nothing to do with any intrigue against Richelieu. But she was too dependent upon him, and too much bored with the whole subject of politics, to wish to constitute herself a power behind the throne. Woman-like, she did try to use her influence on behalf of people at Court who knew how to gain her favour, which was one reason for her not being able to hit it off with so uncompromising a purist as Wentworth. And she did her generous best to shield her fellow Catholics from the great and petty persecutions to which, under the existing law, they were liable. But her real interest was in her private and not her political life ; in her children, her masques, the never-ending pageantry of Court life, and most of all in the love of her husband.

* Con to Barberini, the 23rd of August, 1636. Quoted in *The Dictionary of National Biography*, Henrietta Maria.

22

THE ARTIST AS KING

VERY different was King Charles's court from that of old King James, with its Rabelaisian and rather vulgar exuberances. The road of excess was now cut off by an impassable barrier from the Palace of Whitehall. He had as great a love of an ordered beauty at Court as he had in Church ; he required from every one about him an observance of the prescribed forms as punctual and undeviating as his own.

There is no need to point out the danger of such a regime engendering sheer pompousness, or the frozen formality of a Court like that of Madrid. But it was a danger that never materialized at the Court of Charles. For in spite of the ceremonious gravity that was natural to him, he was one of the least pompous men that ever existed. There was nothing in him of the magnificent self-assurance that was to earn for Louis XIV the name of the Sun King. In Charles the Christian virtue of humility was exaggerated to a fault. He was too scrupulously diffident about trusting his own opinion ; it was characteristic of him that in spite of his swiftness to suppress any deliberate liberty, he never, in conversation or argument, took advantage of his position to lay down the law, or even to express dissent without some such mild preface as "By your favour, sir, I think otherwise on this or that ground." It is a quality in him which reminds us of another intellectual Scot, Arthur Balfour.

There was thus no heaviness in his touch, and though he kept his Court as dignified as any in Europe, that dignity was mingled with a sweetness and intellectual beauty that were equally his own. He had all the temperament of an artist, and had he been born in a humbler station of life, it is by no means improbable that he would have become famous in some mode or other of artistic creation. As it was, it is probable that he felt less shy, and more in his true element, in the society of those engaged, or interested, in art, than any other.

For he was something more than a mere patron of the arts, as that term is usually applied to princes who, however intelligently, make use of art and artists for the enhancement of their princely dignity. Charles was less of a patron than a lover of the muses :

art, to him, was worshipful for its own sake ; just as his attachment to his Church was not that of a politician, but of a devotee.

It was Aristotle who defined the end of organized human society as that of living well. He might have added, had he been able to study the nation states of a later age, that one essential function of a monarch is to make his court into a working and public model of well living, according to the highest attainable standards. It is as when some champion athlete gives an exhibition of how the thing *can* be done, and thereby enables every beholder to improve his own form to some appreciable extent. It is thus that a modern royal family is supposed to realize every average family's wish dream of domestic bliss founded on virtue. If Charles could have done something of the same sort, had he stooped to sublimate the sober respectability of the well-to-do Puritan household, he might have achieved a much greater appreciation. But he was aiming at something higher and more dangerous, in giving the nation a lead for which it was not calling, and in setting before it a way of life that was less flattering than antagonistic to the self-esteem of the average Philistine. What were the canvases of the Italian masters, or the latest masque of Ben Johnson, compared with the delights of reading Mr Prynne, or of listening by the hour to sermons of long-faced evangelists ? The bulk of the nation was not, in fact, educated to the point of appreciating an artistic Court, and the standard of culture set by King Charles was more likely to render him an object of suspicion than of popularity. "Nonesuch Charles", as one pamphleteer described him, "squandering away millions of pounds on braveries and vanities, on old rotten pictures and broken nosed marbles."

But it was his nature and he must needs fulfil it. He was never more happy than when surrounded by beautiful things, and there was no society in which he took more delight than that of their creators. In an amateur way, he was an artist himself, keenly fond of music, and a skilled performer on the viol de gamba ; while he never lost his youthful skill in "limning", and is even said to have persuaded the great Rubens to take the brush from his hands and touch up some of his own royal studies.

In the society of artists that tongue-tied reserve, which was the bane of his whole career, and was like a wall of ice between him and his human environment, seems to have thawed. They found him a lovable and delightful companion, one of those elect spirits of whom Whistler might have remarked, "Ha ! ha ! This man *knows !*" Though a King, he was able to consort with even the greatest of them on a footing of equality, in that kingdom of the muses of which so few monarchs have the freedom. It is told of him that, in the company of several painters, he was once inspecting a portrait head that had just arrived from Italy. None of them were able to identify the painter, until at last the King said,

"This is of such a man's hand, I know it as well as if I had seen him draw it."

But then a doubt struck him ;

"Is there," he queried, "but one man's hand in the picture ?"

This notion of a second painter was one that had not occurred to the assembled critics, and after some discussion, most of them agreed in rejecting it. But His Majesty stuck to his point.

"I am sure," he said, "there are two hands that have worked on it, for I know the hand that drew the heads, and the hand that did the rest I never saw before."

And, as it turned out, the King was perfectly right ; for the painter in question had died with the picture incomplete, and his widow had got it finished off by another hand.*

The artist who is born to a throne is debarred from specializing in any of the creative arts except that of kingship itself. It was Carlyle who applied to Oliver Cromwell the term "hero as King." With at least equal plausibility might we cite Charles I as an instance of that even rarer phenomenon, the artist as King.

His passion for beauty, guided, as it was, by a rare sureness of taste, might, if his work had not been cut short, have made Whitehall as fruitful a centre of European culture as Versailles itself was to become under Louis XIV. It is marvellous how much, with resources incomparably less than those at the disposal of that magnificent autocrat, he actually accomplished. The pamphleteer's talk about his squandering away millions is the veriest moonshine. A few odd thousands were the utmost of which his limited resources permitted his disposing on works of creative beauty, and there was never any question of his allowing his æsthetic enthusiasm to unbalance his accounts. He had to trust to his connoisseurship to secure him the utmost possible value for every penny he laid out, and, in fact, to make him the most expert buyer in Europe. The results were astonishing ; before the final troubles fell upon him he had amassed a collection of

* *Lord Orford's Works*, III, p. 181.

pictures and works of art, whose break up and dispersal is a national loss the effects of which we have still reason to deplore. Nor can we fail to regret that the palace beautiful that he would, if time had been granted him, have made of Whitehall, was never allowed to materialize except as a mere fragment or torso of what it might and ought to have been.

It may be thought that Charles's devotion to art resulted in nothing but loss to him, without any compensating gain. But art repays her debts in her own coin, and Charles she repaid in a way that he at least would have appreciated. For, through the brush of his favourite artist, it succeeded in penetrating that icy reserve of his, and discovering the real man, who had hardly, as yet, discovered himself.

Of all the many artists who thronged the Court of Whitehall, there was none who enjoyed the King's favour to such an extent as Anthony, or, as Charles soon saw that he became after his arrival in England, Sir Anthony Vandyck. The King was quick to recognize a genius, whose distinctive quality of aristocratic refinement he was so well capable of appreciating, and he strove to bind that genius to the service, and quickening, of English art. Nothing pleased him better, after long hours of wrestling with the routine of State business, than to take the royal barge and drop in upon the studio at Blackfriars. Vandyck's was one of the three self portraits—the other two being those of Mytens and Rubens—that he had hung up in his royal breakfast chamber.

If Charles was attracted to Vandyck, to an even greater extent would Vandyck appear to have been fascinated and stimulated by Charles's personality, and he devoted all his matured powers to its elucidation. He succeeded so well, that he has impressed his own vision of it for ever on the imagination of posterity. Whatever our judgment on him may be, the Charles we see in our mind's eye will inevitably be that noble, melancholy figure, that appears on so many canvases of Vandyck's.

It seems the merest matter of course to us that he should appear thus, and yet at the time it was a new and startling, almost a magical discovery. We may look at the features of Charles as they are recorded before the advent of Vandyck, and particularly by that lucid and painstaking artist, Mytens, without finding the least trace of that serenity and that sadness which Vandyck knew so well how to impart to the royal image. We see a young man of handsome and princely appearance, it is true, but uncertain and ill at ease, inclining less to calm than to a nervous self assertiveness. Only when transfigured by the brush of Vandyck, do these all too human features become invested with a beauty godlike through suffering. It was only Vandyck who could make every portrait a canonization of King Charles the Martyr.

And in those days of the King's personal government, when Vandyck was immortalizing this interpretation of his in portrait after portrait, he was, we are convinced, recording what he had only, as yet, beheld with the third eye of Siva, which is that not of the sense, but of the creative imagination. For the Charles that he saw and painted was one who, even at the time of Vandyck's death in 1641, can hardly be said to have existed, except as the butterfly exists in the chrysalis. Not only had the world failed to discover such a King Charles beneath that diffident and enigmatic mask he presented to it, but it is more than doubtful whether Charles himself had as yet found in his own soul what Vandyck had divined in him. It was only in that last week of his life, in which he won back all and more than all he had lost through years of unbroken failure, that the portrait stepped forth from the canvas into the light of history, and the dead seer was justified of his vision.

Appendix

A BRIEF NOTE ON SOURCES AND COMMENT ON COMMENTARIES

I HAVE not the space, even if I had the ability, to catalogue all the printed and unprinted evidence bearing directly or indirectly on the life of Charles I. A complete bibliography would comprise most of the literature of and about the time. I shall attempt no more here than to indicate a few of the outstanding items.

Of contemporary documents the most important are the State Papers, of which the Domestic, Treasury, and Venetian series have been calendared. The Venetian series are especially valuable, as they represent the confidential impressions of a very well-informed diplomatic expert on current political events. Hardly less illuminating are the news letters of the Florentine representative, Amerigo Salvetti, which, up to the end of 1628, are printed in the Historical Manuscripts Commission Report XI, app. 1.

There are the Clarendon and Hardwicke collections of State Papers, and (for the reign of James I) the Winwood Papers, also the collection of state letters known as *Cabala, or Scrinia Sacra*.

Indispensable to any student of the period are the Historical Collections of Rushworth, in seven volumes, with an additional volume devoted to Strafford's trial. The similar collection of Nalson, though it only starts in 1639, contains a number of documents not printed in Rushworth.

The *Somers Tracts* and the *Harleian Miscellany* are all too scanty selections from a vast body of miscellaneous documents, once in private collections, and now preserved in the British Museum. There are also the numerous privately or corporately owned collections that are being made accessible by the reports of the Historical Manuscripts Commission.

The pamphlet literature of the time is almost unbelievably voluminous, the Thomasson Collection in the British Museum comprising some 21,000 of these historically valuable, but now, for the most part, hardly readable, propaganda missiles—though only a small proportion of these fall within our present scope.

For Parliament there are the official dry bones of the Lords' and Commons' Journals, but, as the reporting of debates was Breach of Privilege, these have to be pieced together, for the most part, from any private notes or diaries that individual members happened to keep. This has been admirably done for the Parliament of 1621 by Messrs. Notestein, Relf and Simpson. Among the Camden Society's publications are Gardiner's *Debates in the House of Commons for* 1625 and Elsing's *Notes on the Debates of the House of Lords in* 1624 *and* 1626.

Cobbett's *Parliamentary History* is a standard but woefully insufficient authority.

Among contemporary memoirs, are autobiographies of Sir Symonds D'Ewes, Archbishop Laud, Lord Clarendon, Sir John Bramston, and Sir Robert Carey ; Sir John Eliot's *Negotium Posteriorum ;* the Memoirs of Sir P. Warwick ; the Letters and Journals of the Covenanter Baillie ; the two great episcopal biographies of Laud, by Heylin, and of Williams, by Hacket ; the miniature biography of Buckingham (printed in the *Harleian Miscellany*) by Sir H. Wotton ; and the Memoir of the Embassy of de Bassompierre. Henrietta Maria communicated her own brief version of her part on the political stage to Mme. de Motteville, in whose memoirs it is printed. This same lady supplied Bossuet with some biographical notes for his funeral oration on the Queen, printed by the Camden Society.

The three great volumes of Anthony Wood's *Athenae* and *Fasti Oxonienses* come not far short of being a contemporary dictionary of national biography, so ingeniously does he contrive to rope nearly every celebrated character of his time—not to speak of multitudes otherwise forgotten—into the Oxford pale. The jottings compiled for Wood's benefit by John Aubrey are among the gems of biographical literature.

Among collections of Letters we have that of Birch, entitled the *Court and Times of Charles I*, with its predecessor for James I's reign, the *Original Letters Illustrative of English History*, by Sir H. Ellis, the second volume of Goodman's *Court of James I*, Halliwell Phillips' *Letters of the Kings of England* and Sir Charles Petrie's recent *Letters of King Charles I*.

Some curious scraps of information may be gleaned from the astrologer Lilly's *True History of King James I and King Charles I*, and Sanderson's *Complete History of the Life and Reign of Charles I* may be mentioned.

Among other works that call for special mention is the only

adequate account of Charles's youth in Mr Beresford Chancellor's *Life of Charles I,* 1600-1625.

There are lives, that I do not propose to cite, of James I, whose great but grotesque personality presents, I would suggest, a golden opportunity for some Scottish biographer. The amazing career of Buckingham likewise awaits elucidation, though there is a discursive Victorian biography by Mrs Thomson and a recent one by H. R. Williamson, and the Percy Society has published a collection of contemporary ballads about him.

For Henrietta Maria there is Mrs Strickland's life, whose homely good sense more than atones for a good deal of incidental carelessness. Of more recent lives the best is by Carola Oman.

For Strafford there is the collection of his letters by Knowler, containing an excellent summary of his life by his friend, Sir George Radcliffe, whose own *Life and Letters,* by T. B. Whitaker, form a necessary supplement. The most recent biographies are by Lady Burghclere, C. V. Wedgwood and Lord Birkenhead.

F. C. Dietz, in his *Political and Social History of England* and *English Public Finance* 1558-1641, and Miss E. Leonard's *Early History of Poor Relief* reveal aspects of Charles I's government unsuspected by the older historians.

It is right, though hardly necessary to refer to that vast mine of information, *The Dictionary of National Biography.*

The great history of Clarendon, with such reinforcement as it gets from his autobiography, stands without a rival among contemporary authorities. It has been the fashion to write down Clarendon both as a statesman and a historian. This is no place to defend him in the former capacity, except to say that not even his bitterest detractors have questioned his lifelong integrity in word, deed and thought—nor was there ever a writer who was at such pains to do justice to the parts and dispositions even of those to whom he was most bitterly opposed. And few will deny him a genius for divining and portraying character hardly inferior, in its proper medium, to that of his contemporary, Rembrandt. It is true that writing without documents and in exile, his memory was liable to play him false on points of detail, though the part of his history that covers the period with which we are concerned was written during Charles I's lifetime, and not, like the latter stages, in his stricken old age after his fall from power ; and such inaccuracies as there are make little substantial difference.

The main need for caution in our use of Clarendon lies in

another direction. It is only too common to treat him in the light
of a hundred-per-cent Royalist and Cavalier special pleader. But
Clarendon started his Parliamentary career as an uncompromising
opponent of King Charles and his "Thorough" administration.
It was only when he realized that Pym and his associates were out
not to maintain but to wreck the Constitution, that he put his
services at the disposal of his lawful—*qua* law-abiding—Sovereign.
Personal contact did indeed inspire him with unqualified love
and admiration for that Sovereign as a man and a Christian, but
he remained as critical in office as he had been in opposition, of
what appeared to him to be his political shortcomings. Whether
this was because Edward Hyde understood Charles Stuart too
much or too little need not concern us here. The point is that the
King's case does not stand by the advocacy, nor fall by the
admissions of his minister. And when Clarendon goes out of his
way to whitewash the proceedings of the Short Parliament, or
later on, to depreciate the military capacity of his chronic
opponent, Prince Rupert, he is pleading his own brief.

The treatment of Charles I by historians after his time would
form a history in itself. The bias during the eighteenth century
was distinctly Royalist or, at any rate, anti-Roundhead, partly
because the rule of the Saints was a horror seared deep into the
national consciousness, and partly because any sort of enthusiasm
was out of fashion, and the Puritans had been notorious enthusiasts. But this operated almost as hardly against Charles as against
his opponents. Such an historian as Hume, who tried to combine
the unblendable ideas of Toryism and rationalism, was debarred
from appreciating the characters and ideals of Charles and Laud,
no less than of Cromwell.

In the nineteenth century, enthusiasm for Liberal and Parliamentary institutions resulted in the building up of a veritable
gospel about the Parliamentary chiefs of the seventeenth. The
first impetus was given in 1827 by Hallam's classic and still
valuable *Constitutional History of England*, whose very appearance
and intention of judiciousness enhanced the effect of its essential
Whig advocacy. He was followed by Macaulay, who in an essay
on this very book, and on Hampden,* swept away all Hallam's
qualifications and produced a masterpiece of eloquent and
unscrupulous special pleading. It was in vain that Isaac Disraeli,

---

* It would, perhaps, not be fair to cite against him the purple rhetoric of his
youthful effort on Milton.

father of the statesman, stated the case for the other side with unsurpassed erudition—it was not what people wanted to be told, and his *Commentaries on the Life and Reign of Charles I* had the sole, but not unimportant effect, of helping to form the Tory philosophy of his son.

The triumph of the new Gospel was decisive, and for the rest of the century hardly any serious attempt was made to challenge it. It was capable of producing such books of pious devotion as Forster's Lives of Eliot and Pym ; it reached its culminating point in Green's famous *Short History*, where Charles's Government is the "Tyranny" and his opponents the "Patriots"—an odd description of the men who did not scruple to achieve their political ends in league with an invading army on English soil.

But I should be ungrateful were I to belittle the achievement of Victorian and post-Victorian research workers in unearthing every scrap of evidence that has not physically perished. If he can only compass the task of separating the nuggets of fact from the alloy of inference, the writer of today starts with incomparably richer material to hand than his predecessor of a century ago. But a talent for research by no means implies a commensurate genius for combining and interpreting the results, failing which every new fact is liable as soon as it is quarried, to be fitted into an edifice of preconceived fiction.

It is by this touchstone that I would ask leave to appraise the history, or series of histories, of Dr Samuel Rawson Gardiner, which was designed to cover the fifty-seven years from the accession to the restoration of the House of Stuart, but of which eighteen ponderous tomes were all that the unremitting labour of four decades enabled its author to complete by the time of his death at the age of nearly seventy-three. And these needed another four to complete the scheme.*

It is now more and more on the authority of Gardiner that the Whig-Liberal myth has come to repose, even now that its Whig foundations have crumbled to dust, and the name of Liberal has, unhappily, passed under a cloud.

A weightier authority than Gardiner, in every sense of the word, it would be difficult to conceive. Judged by almost every formal test he would qualify for the title of *Doctor Invincibilis*, the irrefutable historian. One needs to have worked the period oneself to realize the vastness, and the minuteness, of the

* Amassed eventually to scale and style by his faithful disciple, Firth.

research that must have gone to the making of his every chapter and almost every paragraph. He deciphered innumerable manuscripts, and toured the Continent to comb out foreign archives for documents bearing on the English domestic situation ; he let nothing escape him. And he was as scrupulous in the weighing and sifting of his material as he was in its accumulation.

Indeed what most contributes to the almost undisputed authority that is conceded to his judgment on any issue or person falling within his scope, is the appearance of judicial impartiality with which he balances the evidence for and against—so different from the naked partisanship with which Macaulay and his successors had gone about their work of transmuting history to legend. To speak of this attitude as a pose would be to wrong Dr Gardiner, who would rather have died than knowingly colour or doctor his facts, and would have been the last person to envisage the possibility that he was writing propaganda without knowing it, and all the more convincingly for not knowing it.

But he had been brought up in the strictest Puritan tradition ; steeped in the consciousness of his direct descent from Cromwell and Ireton, and associated in youth with that Irvingite sect, then in its first glow of millenial enthusiasm, which was the nearest thing the Victorian age could produce to the Fifth Monarchy movement. He had dedicated himself from boyhood to his life's work of becoming the historian of the great struggle in which these mighty ancestors of his had played the decisive part, and which all the contemporary writers by whom his historical consciousness had been formed were unanimous in presenting, in the crudest form, as one of light against darkness and freedom against tyranny. What else could have been expected than that the earnest young student's inherited faith should have hardened into a lifelong fixation ?

A man thus assured of the essential righteousness of his cause, can afford to be magnanimous to its opponents, and to make all possible allowance for them up to a point. It is only the main assumptions, on which the whole edifice is supported, that have to be preserved intact at all costs. That is a truth known to every good advocate—the greater the candour about unessentials, the more persuasive the plea. Most persuasive of all when the advocate is first able to persuade himself of his own almost superhuman impartiality.

Thus Gardiner can do justice to the nobility and good intentions even of Strafford, that Parliamentary Lucifer, whose destruction by his former chorus-mates in the Patriot heaven he can regard, and credit them with regarding, in the light of a piteous though stern necessity.

Such strengthening of the Patriot case by purging it of its crudities, Gardiner is prepared to undertake. But with the hidden dogmas on which that case reposes he is not prepared to tamper in the slightest degree. As a good Puritan he cannot help ranging himself on the side of God's elect against God's enemies, between whom, however critical he tries to be of the one, and however fair to the other, he draws a rigid moral distinction, and to whom he applies radically different standards of judgment.

Contrast his treatment of the "Patriots" with his treatment of King Charles. With the former, he does not attempt to argue or establish, but simply assumes their perfect integrity of purpose. Such explanations as they chose to publish of their own conduct he unhesitatingly accepts, and where they vouchsafed none, he is fully capable of supplying the omission. That such political Galahads should have found it in their consciences to proceed to all necessary lengths of treasonable conspiracy and collaboration with the invader, in order to compass the downfall of the Sovereign to whom they continued to profess their loyal devotion, merely shows what sort of a King Charles must have been, and how little these simple souls can have trusted him ! And thus by what, granted its initial assumptions, is irrefutable Calvinist logic, even the most outrageous proceedings of the elect can be brought up in evidence on their behalf against their enemies, and victims.

Except when Gardiner's conscious desire to be fair may betray him into some momentary admission at variance with his main thesis, the Charles he puts on his canvas is throughout the necessary counterpart and foil of his Patriot heroes. His character has got to be such as to justify their darkest suspicions. As *they* are assumed to be perfectly straight and sincere, so *he* has got to be incurably false and crooked, and every word and action of his is to be interpreted on that assumption. Even when he goes to all lengths of concession and conciliation, it is because he has some deep ulterior design—though not deep enough to escape the penetrating and shocked scrutiny of *ingénus* like Hampden and Pym. I have, in the course of the text,* tried to show how on every possible occasion Gardiner applies to the interpretation of the

* Particularly in the next volume of this series.

King's proceedings methods more worthy of the Holy Office or a Soviet treason trial than of an impartial historian. And when later on Cromwell comes to dominate the stage, and events begin to move towards the mock trial at Westminster and the scaffold at Whitehall, Gardiner's denigration of the King becomes more and more desperately tendentious, until at last—in the words of his devoted panegyrist, Mr C. P. Gooch—"so penetrated is he with the impossibility of Charles, that he has no words of blame for his execution".*

For failing the King's complete and proven impossibility, what must needs be the judgment of so austere a moralist as Gardiner on his own two honoured ancestors for what on any other hypothesis must rank as the cold-blooded murder of an innocent victim, in defiance of all laws human and divine, and to the horror of the vast but disarmed majority of the people of England ? Dr Gardiner, like his Great-Grandsire Oliver, reconciled his conscience in the name of their common Lord to taking the necessary action against the Lord's Anointed ; and so well was that work performed that the legend of the Crooked King strikes as deep roots beneath the consciousness of every educated Englishman as that of the Stainless Patriot.†

I have had no choice, even in so cursory a survey of authorities, but to define my attitude to Dr Gardiner : because it is *his* authority that overshadows everything that is written on the period and *his* implied veto that stands in the way of any substantial modification of the current myth to which he himself has imparted so specious an air of plausibility. And this is all the more necessary because Gardiner, like Bradshaw, is an authority that every serious inquirer is bound to consult, but no one, without the digestion of an academic ostrich, could consummate the labour of *reading*. But that would equally apply to such literally epoch-making modern masterpieces as those of Marx, Freud, Joyce and Einstein, which are numbered in the catalogue of "books which are no books, *biblia abiblia*", and for that very reason, defy refutation.

Having had his relevant volumes at my elbow for many months past, I have the best reason to know how indispensable he is on any question of fact, and how faithfully he has laboured

---

* *History and Historians in the Nineteenth Century*, p. 363.
† Though Gardiner is capable of out-maudlin even this by canonizing Eliot—of all people—as the Stainless Martyr !

to discover, and indicate, every existing source. But being—as his style of writing reveals with deadly insistency—abnormally deficient in imagination, the moment he would rise above the spade work of research to the historian's art of bringing together the dry bones of fact and infusing them with the spirit of life, he can do nothing but wrap them up in the mummy cases of inherited prejudice, which he will display to the world stacked in interminable corridors beneath a pyramid of verbiage, and scored all over with venerable pronouncements which the world accepts for the verdict of the most up-to-date history.

But there is this to be said for Gardiner. The facts are there, so far as any one human being is capable of amassing them—for he neither selects for himself nor lets his reader off anything—and you have only to empty them out of their sarcophagi to form your own conclusions, which need bear no relation whatever to what appears over the initials "S.R.G." The best antidote to Gardiner is thus—to his honour—Gardiner himself.

The historians and biographers who have dealt with the period during the present century have added little to his work, except in the one extremely significant direction I have already indicated. So impregnable, however, has proved the dominance of the Tyrant-Patriot myth, that even the Providence Island episode has proved capable of being worked up into it as a jolly adventure in empire building, and/or the product of a holy zeal for propagating the Protestant faith in distant lands !

The unadulterated Whig Liberal gospel has still its honoured evangelist in Macaulay's great-nephew and namesake, Dr Trevelyan ; and though evangelistic faith has gone out of fashion, and Liberalism has long yielded place to creeds less nobly inspired, the orthodox version of the Charles myth continues to be reproduced in the biographies that periodically come out on one or other of its *dramatis personae*, spiced and humanized according to the desired prescription. I have particularly in mind two biographies of Hampden that have appeared during recent years, and might have received the *imprimatur* of Forster and the *nihil obstat* of Macaulay.

These, however, are extreme instances—and, indeed, at this time of the day a certain defiant imperviousness to evidence is needed in those whose task it is to keep the idol of Hampden on its pedestal. But on others the effect of the light that modern research has thrown on the purposes and proceedings of the King and his enemies, respectively, may account for a certain tendency to develop still further Gardiner's tactics of abandoning all that is not essential to the main thesis. After all, it is argued, one can make allowances or some sort of an apology, even for Charles, without seeking to impugn the motives or question the integrity of those Parliamentary heroes who, in their fight for democratic liberty, may sometimes have been a little lacking in tolerance, or —must we put it—scruple. They were after all men, and as such liable to error—but they were good men, striving with simple piety and selfless patriotism for what they believed, and what we now know, to be the good cause of their country's liberty.

Nothing could be more plausible, if it only happened to be true. But does it ?

Index